MARILYN MONROE – A CREATION OF THE ICE-BLUE FLASHBULBS THAT POWERED HER

Marilyn Monroe had a love-affair which alienated her three husbands and finally destroyed her. She committed adultery with the camera.

A fragmented and emotionally insecure childhood had robbed little Norma Jean Baker of a sense of identity, and the seductive camera became a magical friend which helped her create one – the superlative Marilyn Monroe. But although this cold lens was to split her in two, it also helped her achieve her final ambition – to ensure that Marilyn Monroe would live forever and only Norma Jean would be buried that day in 1962.

Norma Jean Baker was the frightened insomniac whose barbiturates had finally worked. And Marilyn Monroe was the ghost-goddess who rose from the little girl's ashes.

'*Help Help*
Help I feel life coming closer
When all I want is to die'
A poem by Marilyn Monroe which formed part of a hugely successful exhibition of retrospective Monromania photographs.

FRED LAWRENCE GUILES

Norma Jean

The Life of Marilyn Monroe

PANTHER
Granada Publishing

Panther Books
Granada Publishing Ltd
8 Grafton Street, London W1X 3LA

Published by Panther Books 1971
Reprinted 1973 (twice), 1974, 1975, 1977, 1979,
1980, 1982, 1984, 1985

First published in Great Britain by
W. H. Allen & Co. Ltd 1969

Copyright © Fred Lawrence Guiles 1969

ISBN 0-583-11834-8

Printed and bound in Great Britain by
Collins, Glasgow

Set in Intertype Times

Norma Jean

Work on this biography – recognized as the
most complete and thoughtful – was begun in
1962, before Marilyn's death. Much material
for it was obtained from her close friend and
press agent, from two of her husbands, from
four of her most important directors and from
others associated with her from her childhood
to her death. An accurate portrait is drawn of her
childhood – her father and family situation –
and of her adulthood – her struggles with
husbands, film directors and drugs.

"This frank, sincere and honest book makes
compelling reading . . . Author Guiles has done
a brilliant job . . . A first-class book.
Don't miss it."
Photoplay

For
Dorothy Brewster
Lelia Guiles and
Ruby Hanson

Contents

ACKNOWLEDGEMENTS

This work is a close collaboration between the author and a number of persons close to Marilyn Monroe at various critical points in her lifetime. Among those who volunteered to go beyond the initial interview and review phases of the book itself out of a deep interest in the subject and on behalf of accuracy were: James Dougherty, Arthur Miller, Ralph Roberts, Allan Snyder, and Frank and Nan Taylor.

Additionally, I am indebted to Lee Strasberg for giving over several hours of his time to tape recording his observations of Marilyn at work in the Actors Studio; to Marilyn's directors: John Huston, Joshua Logan, Otto Preminger, and Billy Wilder for reviewing with the author their working relationships with her; to Mr. and Mrs. Albert Wayne Bolender, Erwin Goddard, Margaret Ingram, and Dick Rodgers for going over Norma Jean's childhood years; to Samuel Berke, Mrs. Michael Chekhov, John Conley, Mrs. Dona Holloway, James Hyde, Mrs. Anne Karger, Fred Karger, Tom Kelley, Mrs. Murray Randolph, Lucille Ryman, Emmeline Snively, and Earl Theisen for reviewing Marilyn's early career; to Marilyn's publicists, Rupert Allan, Patricia Newcomb, and John Springer, for their personal help and for opening many doors; to the publicity department at Twentieth-Century Fox; to Lauren Bacall and Lotte Goslar for their observations of Marilyn at work in the film studio and in class; to Marilyn's attorneys, Aaron Frosch and Elliott Lefkowitz, for answering legal questions; to attorney Bob Montgomery and accountant Joseph Carr for discussing Marilyn Monroe Productions at both early and late phases; to business manager Inez Melson for background on Marilyn's affairs; to Angela Allen, Elizabeth Hannum, Edith Palmer, and Edward Parone for important background material regarding *The Misfits*; to Milton and Amy Greene, Joseph Curtis, Mrs. Joshua Logan, and Mark and Curtice Taylor for rendering significant help in clarifying Marilyn's transitional period; to James Haspiel, Margaret Parton, Margie Plecher, Michael Selsman, Lawrence Schiller, Florence Thomas, and Mrs. Charles Vidor for giving the author valuable background on Marilyn's final years; to C. Robert Jennings and William V. Canale for their material on Marilyn's trip to Korea; and to Anita Loos for discussing Joseph Schenck with the author.

Beyond these persons are those who wish to remain anonymous and the librarians of the New York Public Library System and the *New York Times* and *Los Angeles Times* library staffs – a debt is owed for their courtesy and assistance.

The author is grateful, too, for the critical help of Lawrence Grow, Dr. Dorothy Brewster, Miss Vicki Cummings, Nadine and Lawrence Jackson, and Carlos MacMaster, as well as the editorial encouragement of Jean Todd Freeman and Shirley Horowitz, with special thanks to Mrs. Florence Edwards in whose hospitable inn in Virginia City this all began.

New York   FRED LAWRENCE GUILES
September 1, 1968

PART ONE

In the Time of Cal and Aimée

CHAPTER ONE

In late October 1925, Calvin Coolidge, aroused by the lawlessness sweeping the country, declared to a body of clergymen convened in Washington that religion was the only remedy.

Piety and Gangsterism were two extremes of existence in the America of the mid-twenties. In Los Angeles, Aimée Semple McPherson had opened her million-dollar Angelus Temple and already had over 10,000 converts enrolled. Known as "Sister" to her fanatical followers as well as to a grateful press, she brought a bizarre sort of glamour to the old-fashioned business of evangelism. Like Al Capone, she was a star, and among her ardent fans was one Della Monroe Grainger.

Southwest of Los Angeles in a middle-class community of verandahed bungalows known as Hawthorne, Mrs. Grainger lived in a stucco house set among trees and shrubs. She was alone much of the time and did not make new friends easily. Except for the trips to the Angelus Temple or brief excursions to the store, she was rarely seen on the street. Although there was little socializing with the neighbours, Della was regarded with respect, perhaps because they believed she had once known wealth. But this had more to do with her manner than with reality.

By 1925, she had spent twenty-one of her forty-nine years in California. Born Della Hogan, she had come from lower-middle-class stock in Missouri. The family moved to the West when she was in her teens and Della met her first husband, a man with the last name of Monroe, in the Northwest. Their marriage was terminated by divorce soon before he was committed to a state asylum. Della married again, a man only remembered as Grainger, and around 1919 they moved to Hawthorne.

During the Fall of 1925, Della was unable to give generously to a drive to collect funds for Sister Aimée's Twentieth-Century Crusade to the Holy Land. Her enthusiasm had not flagged; she was saving for an even longer journey of her own. Grainger had been transferred to India in September by the oil company that employed him. She planned to join him as quickly as money for a one-way, first-class ticket could be saved. What Grainger thought of her plan is not known, although it is clear that he sent her no money for the trip. Some of her neighbours believed he had plotted his transfer in order to put considerable distance between himself and his wife.

At the time a deep-seated melancholia seemed to take hold of Della, an indication of the manic-depressive psychosis that was to destroy her ability to function within two years. She may have had some premonition of how her journey to Grainger's side would end – in disaster. But in him she would, at any rate, have a handy target for her mercurial moods; she would no longer have to take her frustrations out on delivery boys and sundry neighbours who crossed her path on the wrong day. Grainger was soon to discover that his wife was genuinely ill, for she was to return from India crippled by wild emotional swings that terrified her and others. There is no evidence, however, that he was moved to return with her or even to see that she was properly looked after.

These upheavals in Della's life destroyed anything that she had built with Grainger and she was left with what she had before their marriage – a life lived almost entirely in solitude. She was stubbornly determined to gloss over her illness and dismiss her sudden rages by rationalizing them as best she could. Perhaps this is what kept her from being institutionalized earlier than she was. She would conveniently forget her wrath and be considerate and gentle with its target as soon as her emotion was drained.

Nearly fifty, her coppery hair unstreaked by any grey, Della was a woman of considerable beauty. The years had not touched her skin, and her eyes were an unusual mixture of blue and green with a moist sweetness about them. When some fury would possess her, a rage whose origins she could not explain, her eyes would cloud over and the sweetness would disappear in a flash.

In October Della was visited by her daughter, Gladys.

Mother and daughter were not particularly close, and during the past year Gladys's visits were infrequent and made out of a sense of duty. On a Wednesday evening, she came down by trolley-bus from her furnished room in Hollywood and waited until her mother returned from the mid-week prayer service at the Temple.

Gladys Baker was Della's second child by her marriage to Monroe. Her first-born, a boy named Marion, was now married and lived nearby with his wife and three children. Marion showed to a lesser degree some of his mother's irrational bad temper and this jeopardized his marriage more than once.

At twenty-five, Gladys was the mother of two. A boy, Jack, was followed by a daughter, Berneice. The children's father, whose name Gladys still used, had left her before Berneice was born in 1923. For reasons unexplained, relatives of Mr. Baker took the children from Gladys, apparently with her consent, and they were brought up in a rural section of Kentucky. Gladys who, after the separation, had lived with the children at her mother's, then moved to Hollywood.

Baker was followed in Gladys's affection by Edward Mortensen, a man of Norwegian extraction. Sometime late in 1924, soon after he began seeing Gladys, he suggested a quiet wedding. After the civil ceremony, they moved into a cottage in a new development along Santa Barbara Avenue in Hollywood.

Mortensen had no steady employment. For a time he was a mechanic, then a builder's helper. It was Gladys who paid the rent more often than not. Although Mortensen sought the stability of a home and family, either something in his relationship with Gladys or in his own restless spirit militated against it. While he worked at a garage, he sank a week's wages into a motor-cycle, and after repairing it, would disappear on it for as long as three days at a time.

When Mortensen moved to San Francisco, sending his regrets, Gladys broke her lease and moved into a furnished room.

Outwardly she appeared calm. Only close friends and her mother were aware of the turmoil below the surface. Frugal with words, she saved them for important occasions. She was difficult to befriend, seemingly cold or disinterested. But underneath this reserve she was warm and considerate. She had few friends, and on those few she depended greatly. Gladys worked steadily and was not known to break her routine of working five nights a week at the processing laboratories of Consolidated Film Industries.

Her sudden appearance on a Wednesday evening at her mother's house could only mean that something unusual was afoot. She had come to tell her mother that she was pregnant and to ask if she could stay with her for a while after the birth of the baby. Apparently she had no intention of keeping the infant in her furnished room. For one thing, she was tight-lipped about her private life and didn't want the pity of her fellow tenants.

Della told her that because of her trip to join Grainger in India, the house had been rented. She must have pointed out that Gladys could not manage by herself and, as a solution, Della suggested that they talk to Ida Bolender, a neighbour who had been taking care of small children for several years. Gladys and her baby might stay there for a few weeks after the delivery.

There have been several surmises regarding the father of Gladys's third child, Norma Jean, most of them focussing on Mortensen or Baker. Years later, Norma Jean, then known as Marilyn, said that Mortensen had been killed in a motor-cycle accident long before she was born, and that Baker had come and gone before the appearance of Mortensen in Gladys's life.

Marilyn told her first husband, Jim Dougherty, that some-one had seen her father at Paramount Studios. On rare occasions as a child, she had heard his name discussed, but it was not until she was nearly a grown woman that she learned that he had been more than a boy-friend to her mother. Her father, Marilyn came to believe, was another employee of Consolidated Film Industries, C. Stanley Gifford.

Gladys's co-workers at Consolidated are mostly agreed that the infant was born of a serious love affair lasting several months between Gladys and Gifford. He was known as some-thing of a Lothario, but word of his numerous attachments had probably not reached Gladys's ears prior to her liaison with him. Not being gregarious, she was unlikely to hear gos-sip. If she had heard rumours, most likely they were rejected. Some of Della's tolerance for human frailty had rubbed off on Gladys, as it would on her third child.

Gifford was a man who took good care of himself. In his early thirties, he was nearly six feet tall with broad shoulders and a trim moustache above a wide, rather sensual mouth. Except for the time during which he was briefly involved in the technical side of the business, he and Gladys worked in different departments. She was a negative assembler in charge of a group of five women whose job it was to splice together processed negatives for such major studios as Metro-Goldwyn-Mayer or Paramount.

Gladys wasn't a very popular section head. The girls who worked under her considered her a compulsive worker who would drive them to slavery if they didn't resist. But the men found her attractive and desirable. She had delicately-carved features, a hesitant and flickering smile, eyes surprisingly bold and challenging. And she *was* something of a challenge. She was never easily compliant, as were so many of the single girls and divorcees working for Consolidated. Even Gifford had approached her with respect.

Gifford had been transferred to the sales department. He spent most of his time out of the office making the rounds of the major studios. Because he kept his own house, he was free to pick up Gladys after her shift and take her to the apartment he shared with a cameraman. Gifford had been married and divorced.

In 1950, Marilyn Monroe told her drama coach and friend, Natasha Lytess, that her father was running a dairy near Palm Springs and that she was thinking of going to see him. After World War II, Gifford had settled in Hemet, California, where he bought the Red Rock Dairy. There can be no doubt about Marilyn's belief that Gifford was her father and, despite all of the published inaccuracies, little mystery about it.

CHAPTER TWO

In December of 1925, Della Grainger departed for India, her house rented to an insurance salesman and his new bride. On May 31, 1926, Gladys went into labour and was rushed to Los Angeles General Hospital. If she supplied incorrect data to the admissions officer, she did it for a good cause. She was admitted as Gladys Pearl Mortensen, and her child was given the departed Norwegian's name. Gladys had not gone to the trouble of divorcing him; moreover, as Marilyn asserted in later years, he may have died, a traffic victim, long before Gladys entered the hospital. Gladys also told the officer that her other children were both dead. She may have persuaded herself that they were.

Gladys could afford proper care; Consolidated Film Industries had been especially helpful. One of the executives, Dick Rodgers, had taken up a collection "for the baby", and when it was converted into larger bills, the sum amounted to one hundred and forty dollars. She asked Rodgers if Gifford had contributed. Unable to lie, he declined to answer. Gladys must have wondered how her judgment could have been so poor, a question which would return to her in other situations as life moved on. It would eventually drive her into a withdrawal from which return would be difficult.

Norma Jean Mortensen was born at 9.30 A.M. on June 1, 1926. Gladys had already chosen the name, taking the Norma from one of the Talmadge sisters then at the peak of their careers. It was not a difficult birth, in fact the easiest of the three Gladys had undergone, and the child was healthy, bright-eyed and normal in every way. Gladys nursed her and seemed determined never to be separated from her baby. And that was how it turned out to be for over two months.

On the twelfth day, Gladys climbed into a taxi at General Hospital and went to Hawthorne to Ida Bolender's house.

The Hollywood into which Norma Jean was born was on the brink of dramatic change. Near bankruptcy, the Brothers Warner, gambling on a new discovery, were equipping their studio for sound; and *The Jazz Singer*, while still running on Broadway, was being filmed in Hollywood with Al Jolson in the lead. He had been persuaded to accept shares in the faltering company in lieu of salary.

Clara Bow had just completed *Kid Boots* and Joan Crawford had a silent release entitled *Paris*. The films of Greta Garbo, Nórma Shearer, Colleen Moore, and Alice White were nearly as popular as Clara's. Among the leading men, Richard Dix and Richard Barthelmess, John Barrymore, the elegant Adolphe Menjou, and the classically handsome John Gilbert dominated the screen. Valentino was to die late that August at thirty-one, leaving the Arab world to Ramon Navarro. All of these stars were to be seriously affected by the sound revolution, which also altered the future fortunes of such comic giants as Charlie Chaplin, Buster Keaton, and Harold Lloyd.

While the industry watched the progress of the Warner venture in sound-on-film, there had been no pause in film-making. Silent features were being made in great numbers with larger budgets than ever.

Hawthorne was very nearly as remote from the film industry as Omaha, and Gladys must have found the open fields and wooded acres of the small community a restorative. The Bolenders were rural people. Ida Bolender had come from a small farm near Buffalo, New York. Albert Wayne Bolender came from an eighty-acre farm in Brown County, Ohio. Because many farmers were exempt from service, he was never drafted during World War I. It was during the war that he found his future bride "in a blackberry patch" on one of his meadows where she had gone on an outing with a cousin of his.

Ida had visited California, and she convinced her husband to move West. They sold their farm in Ohio and, in 1919, Albert and Ida settled on the two acres of land where they would remain for the next half century.

Both Albert Wayne – Ida preferred to use his middle name – and his wife were devoutly religious. When he was not busy working as a letter carrier in Los Angeles, Albert Wayne could be found cranking out tracts about salvation on a printing press that he kept in a shed attached to the house. Ida, on the other hand, busied herself around the house and with the pet rabbits and baby chicks she kept in the back-yard.

Gladys and her baby were given a rear bedroom whose walls were a cheerful pink; the bed was large and comfortable. It was the best possible arrangement Gladys could have made, under the circumstances. She was back in a town that was both easy and familiar and her mother was half a world away. She could put Aimée Semple McPherson out of her mind and when she regained her strength, could enjoy a Sunday sermon with the Bolenders at the nearby Community Church, although there is no evidence that she was a regular churchgoer.

As soon as she was back on her feet again, Gladys returned to work at the lab, leaving the baby in Ida's care. "I'll come every Saturday and stay over whenever I can, if that's all right." Gladys probably made a serious effort to believe she

loved Norma Jean and that she wanted to be with her. Apparently she had already decided she could never entrust
Norma Jean to her mother's care.

Gladys must have sensed for some time that there was something wrong with her mother, who was soon to return from
India. Gladys's childhood had been blighted by violent behaviour between her mother and father that spoiled nearly
every day. She could still recall Monroe snatching a pet kit-
ten from her hands and hurling it against the brick fireplace.
Monroe's violence had unleashed Della's own turbulent
nature, so much so that very few people could feel at ease with
her, especially in her later years.

Throughout her life, Gladys suffered from a terrible frustration when stronger persons did her some hurt. To even the
score she wanted to strike out at the innocent, the available,
the vulnerable. She was given to weeping for no reason and
would laugh unaccountably. Everything became badly mixed
up and desperately needed sorting out. It has since occurred
to those who were close to her that there was some, possibly
unconscious, reluctance to take on personal responsibility for
any of her children. Gladys was afraid of feeling, of over-
reacting, of being hurt. This hard-won aloofness permitted her
to think dispassionately much of the time. Yet in spite of her
efforts to protect herself, she could not help suffering from
loneliness, isolation, and rejection.

So Norma Jean began her life with the Bolenders. Gladys
would come nearly every Saturday around noon to spend the
day with her baby. Occasionally, she would stay overnight
and attend the Community Church with them, carrying
Norma Jean in her arms. The infant girl almost never cried
and was singularly well-behaved on such excursions.

But more often than not, Gladys had a date on Saturday
evening and would have to hurry back to Hollywood immediately after an early supper. In the back of her mind, judging
from her future actions, was the hope of finding a decent man
who would provide a home for her baby and herself.

Life with the Bolenders was easy, although austere. A
chromotint Christ stared down from the living-room wall and
was so frequently referred to that Norma Jean, as she became
more aware of her surroundings, accepted him as one might a
kindly uncle at sea who could never quite make it home.

In Hawthorne there were numerous vacant lots overgrown

with wild flowers and thickets. Even the street paving was of a temporary sort easily rutted by a cloudburst. The Bolenders were not poor though Norma Jean's first home has been described as a slum by journalists more often than not. This is one of the many fabrications to be dealt with in the life of Norma Jean. But as pleasantly bucolic as were the surroundings of the Bolender bungalow, it was still a home where carpets faded and became worn. Caring for Norma Jean and often as many as four other children provided the Bolenders with the few extras they all enjoyed. An old model-A Ford kept running for infrequent trips to the beach, nickels for Sunday school, a tricycle Norma Jean shared with the others, and trinkets at Christmas time.

In late October, nearly a year to the day from Gladys's announcement of her pregnancy, Della returned to Hawthorne after ten months in India. Her stay there with Mr. Grainger had turned out disastrously.

Somehow she was able to get the tenants to break their lease, and she sued Grainger for divorce, charging desertion.

There were still some good days ahead for Della, but not many. She appeared to be enchanted with Norma Jean. She often crossed the street to visit her grandchild, always careful not to make too much fuss over her because of the other children. These included a boy named Lester, two months younger than Norma Jean, whom the Bolenders later adopted.

Once Della saw Ida Bolender spanking Norma Jean for throwing a bowl of food on the floor. "Don't ever let me catch you doing that again!" she reprimanded Ida in a voice unduly harsh and threatening. After that episode, she would take Norma Jean across to her house for long afternoons once or twice a week. Ida was concerned, but felt that she could not interfere. Gladys, finding her savings were accumulating much too slowly, sought a father for Norma Jean ever more frantically. But her desperation drove a number of good prospects away.

During Della's stay in India, Aimée Semple McPherson had gone for an afternoon dip in the Pacific Ocean (or so her mother claimed at the time), and disappeared. One report followed another; she had been drowned, kidnapped, and finally newspapers published a report, later verified, that she had run away with the lean and handsome operator of her Angelus Temple radio station. Della's eccentricities did not include religious fanaticism. She rang no doorbells, attempted no conversions. But for Sister Aimée to fall into disgrace was as shameful in Della's eyes as Christ being accused of a lustful affair with Mary Magdalen. Della's world had been shaken, and she gave up all but Sunday morning attendance at Angelus Temple. None the less, she insisted that her grandchild be baptized in the Foursquare Gospel Church. Sister had officiated, thereby redeeming herself only slightly in Della's eyes.

The six-month-old baby was baptized Norma Jeane Baker. The "e" on the Jeane would come and go when the child learned to write her name. Although the Bolenders had small use for Aimée McPherson, they felt there was more than one road to salvation, and Norma Jean could now be counted among the saved.

At thirteen months, Norma Jean was learning to talk. Mimicking Lester, who was now able to say "Mama" to Ida Bolender, she attempted to call the woman by the same name while being bathed. Ida picked up the dripping child and looked sternly at her. "I'm not *Mama*. I'm Aunt Ida. *Aunt Ida*. The lady with the red hair is your mama." Quick in other ways and already far ahead of Lester in her vocabulary, Norma Jean was slow in getting this message and always looked a little hurt and bewildered, especially since Lester could get away with using the same word. Even as a baby, she loved to dramatize her situation, and one of her first complete sentences was "there goes a mama", upon seeing a woman leading a child by the hand.

There was a holiday air to Gladys's visits. Discipline was non-existent at such times. Perhaps for this reason and because she was affectionate by nature, Norma Jean adored her and hoped that each day would turn out to be Saturday when the pretty woman with red hair would come to hold her and wheel her in the carriage as far as Washington Street and back. Gladys's red hair especially attracted Norma Jean and she liked to touch it.

Gladys waited for the day when Norma Jean would be old enough to realize that she was more than just a fascinating visitor, that she was her "Mama". She hoped the child would then understand why they couldn't be together. Hopefully, they then would be. Gladys's drive towards that goal was a stabilizing factor in her life.

An incident involving Norma Jean and her grandmother occurred during the summer of 1927, probably in early July, for later that month Della was committed to the Metropolitan State Hospital at Norwalk in Los Angeles County. Ida Bolender disclaimed any knowledge of its occurrence, but Norma Jean was never to forget it, and many years later she would recount the near fatal account to her third husband, Arthur Miller.

Della had taken the baby for the afternoon. What provoked the assault that followed is something of a mystery. In Marilyn's words, "I remember waking up from my nap fighting for my life. Something was pressed against my face. It could have been a pillow. I fought with all my strength."

Although this was one of the few happenings Marilyn could recall from her infancy, she couldn't remember the details of how or why this attempt on her life failed. It would seem that just as suddenly as the murderous impulse had come over her, it died in Della. She must have stood by the child's bed appalled and this may have been the turning point in her illness that was soon to lead to her commitment.

There are some who heard this story later – for it was to enter the Marilyn canon of deprivation and horror – who discounted it, insisting that it was impossible for an infant of slightly more than a year to remember anything. Its authenticity, however, is well vouched for.

CHAPTER THREE

Because Lester and Norma Jean were so close in age and so much alike in temperament and colouring, the Bolenders began referring to them as "the twins". Ida would often place them in the same carriage for sunning on the front verandah.

Neighbours who did not know the Bolenders very well often mistook the babies for actual twins and commented on how much the "brother" resembled his "sister". And then Lester's adoption went through.

Norma Jean had a sixth sense, quick to detect the slightest change in a voice or a glance. A sense she would retain and which would sometimes provoke her unwarranted mistrust.

Essentially, the Bolenders made no distinction between Norma
Jean and Lester, and there were two or three other children
in the home whose feelings had to be considered. But Marilyn
thought she could remember when Lester was adopted. It
made her, she recalled, more alert to any preference shown
the boy. To her credit, Ida continued to parcel out the same
amount of love and attention to each of the children. She considered their health first and then their souls. As they grew
older, this consideration would be reversed, although she
would never fail to feel a suspiciously warm brow or to ask
one of them to stick out a tongue.

Della's condition was worsening rapidly. Her church attendance ceased altogether. During her Saturday visits, Gladys
noticed with alarm her mother's inability to hold a conversation without a sudden transition to anger provoked by some
imagined slight. And Della rarely came to fetch Norma Jean
for an afternoon alone with her any more, perhaps out of fear
of herself.

Della's last day in Hawthorne was a Saturday. She had not
seen Norma Jean in over a week; Gladys had been socially
involved and had skipped her weekly visit – unusual for her –
but having to spend a part of her day with Norma Jean in
Della's house was something of a strain, and she had eagerly
accepted an invitation to an outing with friends.

A few neighbours had noted the hostility Della projected
on any chance encounters, but they considered her harmless.
A news boy asked the distribution company to send Mrs.
Monroe (she had given up the name Grainger altogether) her
weekly bill by mail. He was afraid to knock on her door.

Early that critical Saturday, Albert Wayne Bolender heard
a commotion in his front yard. (He could remember the details vividly even forty years later.) Della, in a rage, was hurry-
ing up the walk towards their porch. Seeing her approach he
slammed the front door and bolted it.

No one could make out a word she was saying. It was
clear, however, that the subject was Norma Jean, she had no
other reason to be there. Ida came into the living-room from
the kitchen and peered out at the woman, who was now
pounding on their door. "Call the police, Wayne," she said.
"Hurry!"

Within minutes, a black patrol car pulled up in front of the
Bolender home. By this time, Della had succeeded in breaking

a panel of the door, injuring her hand. Two policemen subdued her and dragged her to the car. Her head was thrown back as though seeking God's help.

A few weeks after her entrance into the asylum at Norwalk, mercifully Della died of a heart attack during her last seizure on August 23, 1927.

Norma Jean was an attractive and intelligent small child, whose vocabulary was fairly original. When the Bolenders went to Manhattan Beach over what she called the "roller coaster road" in their model-A Ford, Norma Jean clapped her hands joyously at her first glimpse of the ocean. "It's a big wet!" she cried. The world outside excited her and she would often run the risk of a scolding by opening the front door and running into the street long before she was three years old.

Two things ruled against the Bolenders adopting Norma Jean, assuming they wanted to. Forty years after Norma Jean's birth and four years after her death, Ida Bolender stated with conviction that she had loved Norma Jean "just like my own". Gladys had no intention of giving up her child and she was regular in her payments of twenty-five dollars a month for Norma Jean's care; the money was important to the Bolenders. Soon after her third birthday, the country was plunged into the Great Depression. But its effects were not apparent in Hawthorne, nor in the Bolender home; soup lines were something shocking seen on visits to Los Angeles. Wayne Bolender's work as a letter carrier continued, and he would never experience unemployment.

Misfortune continued to hound Gladys Baker. Her brother, Marion, proved himself unable to cope with their mother's burial arrangements, so that Gladys was obliged to choose the grave site and secure a pastor from Angelus Temple for the services.

Ida recalls that it was about this time that Gladys began to act peculiarly. The impact of the deaths of both of her parents in mental hospitals and her brother's retreat from reality began to undermine her foothold on normality. Not long after the funeral, Gladys appeared in Hawthorne for an afternoon with Norma Jean wearing dark glasses. Ida caught a view of her as she removed the glasses briefly before a bedroom mirror. One eye was bruised and half-closed.

When she asked Gladys if everything was all right, Gladys

nodded affirmatively, but immediately thereafter she betrayed her nervousness by taking out a cigarette and lighting it. Then as if remembering where she was, she inquired if Ida minded. She had never been seen to light a cigarette before.

Ida *did* mind, not so much the smoking which Gladys had taken up so suddenly, but the combination of the two oddities, the black eye and then a cigarette. Still she remembers telling Gladys, "It's not a thing I would do, but this is your house when you are here."

Two or three years passed in this fashion. Marion Monroe was hospitalized, and his children came for a few weeks to Ida's until the family could make more permanent arrangements for them.

In 1929, Gladys suffered a less personal calamity. The huge film lab on Melrose Avenue caught fire. When the alarm began to ring, Gladys was on the second floor in the negative room, surrounded by combustible film. Panic spread among the girls, but Gladys remained calm and herded her group out into the hall and down the stairs. That night the Melrose plant of Consolidated Film Industries was levelled to the ground.

Within a few days, C.F.I. moved their operations to what had been a subsidiary of theirs, Bennett Film Labs, and Gladys was asked to return to work. She made the journey far out on Santa Monica Boulevard for a short time, but she was unhappy with the change and resigned. She may have been out of work for a month or two, yet Ida Bolender cannot remember her ever falling behind in Norma Jean's board bill. Apparently, Gladys had put aside some money for just such contingencies, some of it possibly coming from a small inheritance from Della.

Since Norma Jean and Lester almost never cried or had tantrums, as soon as they were able to walk the Bolenders sent them to Sunday School. Norma Jean's first song was learned there: "Jesus Loves Me, Yes I know." This was her favourite and she would sing it as other children might have sung "Barney Google" (a hit song of the twenties she never had occasion to hear). Once in a crowded cafeteria she sang the hymn wholly unprompted, and she would often run through a bar or two in the Bolender Ford while they were on their way to the beach.

The children shared a tricycle bought by "Uncle Wayne" and discovered under a Christmas tree with no name tag. Communal property. Sometimes there were bitter fights over whose turn it was to ride; during one of these, Norma Jean pushed over the vehicle with Lester on it, bumping his head and earning her a whipping with a razor strap.

There is some disagreement over how sternly the Bolenders disciplined the children in their care. Norma Jean was not specially picked on; she was livelier than the others. Marilyn once said in the presence of Rupert Allan (her Hollywood press agent for many years) that the Bolenders were well-intentioned people, but that they had put emphasis upon "salvation and the strap". When asked if she got more whippings than the others, she freely admitted that she did and added, "I got into more trouble than the other kids."

But Norma Jean had no martyr complex nor did she show any signs of being "the natural victim" so many analysts of her life have claimed. She was never resigned to punishment and was never a child to keep any hurt, real or imagined, to herself. On the Saturday following Lester's minor head injury, Gladys was greeted by Norma Jean whom she barely recognized behind a screwed-up old Chinaman's face, which she at once buried in her mother's skirts as she began wailing and crying out bitter complaints. When Ida explained why Norma Jean had been punished, Gladys could only concur in its necessity.

Lester paid Norma Jean back, quite innocently, by giving her his whooping cough. The evening after she came down with it the Bolenders phoned Gladys, who wanted to come to Hawthorne immediately but was persuaded to wait until daylight. Recently, she had become a film cutter at Columbia Pictures on Gower Street, not far from her old job at C.F.I. She had been befriended at Columbia by a woman named Grace McKee, who was then an assistant in the studio film library. Grace was highly regarded by her employers and soon moved ahead in her job. She was useful to Gladys as her spokesman at the studio where it was explained that Mrs. Baker might be away for a week or more because of the serious illness of her child.

Gladys stayed for three weeks in the guest bedroom at the Bolenders. She brought Norma Jean into the room with her and nursed her back to health. With the exception of another period of a month or so when Gladys took the child up to her Hollywood room, it was the longest time they spent together during Norma Jean's early childhood.

Both Ida and Albert Wayne Bolender were much moved by this devotion. As is often the case during the serious illness of a child, the parents became more indulgent.

One night Albert Wayne was followed from the trolley line by a black and white dog. By now, Norma Jean was allowed out of bed part of the time and she spent nearly all of it playing with the dog. It gradually became accepted that the dog, named Tippy by Norma Jean for no discernible reason, belonged to her.

In all likelihood, this time of closeness with her daughter was a significant factor in Gladys's decision to find a home in Hollywood they could share. In a little over two years she would achieve this, however abortive it turned out to be, and she may have begun saving for that day right after leaving Hawthorne to return to Hollywood and her work.

That Fall, Lester and Norma Jean were enrolled in the Washington School kindergarten. The walk was only four blocks, and Ida would take the children over the first few times until an older child down the block was pressed into service. Usually, Tippy would follow Norma Jean and hang around the school-yard, waiting for recess.

Norma Jean was much like any other girl at school. She wore a huge bow in her hair and she grimaced quite a bit, her wide mouth a tight line and turned up slightly at the ends. Her cotton dresses, many of which Ida made for her, were starched and changed every day, and in cooler rainy weather she wore a sweater under a yellow raincoat. She was seldom in any sort of trouble and her grades were average. Somehow, at about the time she began her schooling, she had learned to put a brake on her ebullience.

Life was suddenly brighter for Norma Jean. She had a dog, new playmates, and the prospect of a home where she could live with her mother. On her Saturday excursions with Gladys to El Segundo beach or to the movies, her mother must have told her that she was saving to buy a house.

As winter turned the corner in 1932 and the rainy season stopped, Norma Jean and Lester were given roller skates. They would race along the pavement with Tippy following.

There were also nights during that spring when Tippy would

scratch to get out and it must have been distressing to the child to see the dog run out into the darkness. And then one night she was suddenly awakened by a blasting sound. The milkman found Tippy's body shortly after dawn that morning. One of their neighbours had sat up for Tippy, a shotgun in his hand. He complained to the Bolenders that the dog had rolled in his garden for three nights running. There were no laws to protect pet-owners then from uncivilized neighbours, or to protect Norma Jean from real hurt.

CHAPTER FOUR

In October 1933, Gladys finally made good her promise to Norma Jean. She had been saving as much of her salary at Columbia as she could afford and after more than a year found she had enough for a down payment on a white bungalow in North Hollywood near the Hollywood Bowl.

Today the house is gone, bulldozed away to make room for the extensive Bowl parking area; then it was one of the most attractive homes in a community of bungalows just off Highland Avenue. Gladys set about furnishing it with pieces bought at auction, among them a white piano that would become Norma Jean's particular pride. At Ida's she had already spent a year studying piano with a Miss Marion Miller. The piano had once stood in the Hollywood home of actor Fredric March and his wife and would one day, after being lost for years, be found again by Marilyn when she was furnishing her large Doheny Drive apartment.

Norma Jean was livelier than Lester, more imaginative and thus more troublesome, but when the taxi pulled away with Gladys and her daughter, the Bolenders knew they loved this half-orphan child. And they remember being a little afraid of her.

What happens when the world you have known is suddenly turned topsy-turvy? When grown-ups spend their evenings and weekends playing rummy and poker, drinking scotch, brandy, and bourbon; when you sing "Jesus Loves Me", make everyone uncomfortable, and you resolve not to sing it again?

More than a score of years later, Marilyn could still remember vividly the incredible changes that occurred during the Fall of 1933. She remembered wondering if her mother, and the English couple in their early sixties who had been invited to share the new house, might not have abandoned all hope of heaven. She was sure at the time they were all prey of the devil. She was to feel Ida Bolender's presence for a long time.

Gladys rented the entire house to the English couple and leased two rooms from them, one for Norma Jean and one for herself. The wife was a registered "dress" extra, often used as a walk-on in drawing-room comedies, sometimes in films starring Ina Claire or Joan Crawford. Her husband had steady employment as the stand-in for George Arliss. Their handsome daughter, in her early twenties, lived with them and in a few years she would move up from Central Casting to stand-in for Madeleine Carroll. No one recalls their names.

The Britishers were not particularly skilful at handling young children, nor were they terribly interested in them. But they were decent people and so long as Norma Jean did not make a nuisance of herself there was a pleasant rapport. There was never any tomfoolery, and she was expected to behave, an attitude which Ida had already ingrained in her.

On Saturdays, when everyone was home, Norma Jean would be given a dime and escorted to Grauman's Egyptian Theatre where she would watch the monkeys outside on the wide patio until the box office opened. Once he had deposited her there, the Englishman would leave her and go about his own business, which ritually included buying a copy of *Hollywood Variety* and sitting on Gladys's new front porch reading every item, a glass of bourbon in his hand. Sometimes it was at Grauman's Chinese, where Norma Jean would idle away the pre-opening minutes by fitting her feet into the cement prints of Gloria Swanson, Janet Gaynor, and Clara Bow, only to discover that her feet were already larger than theirs.

The movie would begin, often a C. B. DeMille or Metro spectacular or sometimes a musical, and she would sit through the film at least three times, lost in the splendour, adoring Claudette Colbert's milk-white complexion (apparently made that way by bathing in asses' milk), memorizing the songs as she first heard them sung by Rogers and Astaire. She was under orders to be home before dark – where Gladys would often join them for dinner unless she had a date – but how was Norma Jean to know when it got dark outside? Sometimes a film like *The Crusades* would run for over two hours and she would have to make her way along the darkened streets to the house just off Highland Avenue.

Gladys's relief and sense of achievement at finally getting Norma Jean into a home of their own was brief. She soon felt a malaise, an unhappiness she could not explain. Possibly she felt uneasy with her daughter in a day-in-day-out situation. Used to living alone and to giving free expression to her moods, she found the effort of "putting a face on things" for the child's sake too great. The more uncomfortable she became, the more she stayed away from the house. Her work took her out of the house on weekday evenings, and on the weekends she had a succession of beaux who would attempt to cheer her, fail, and fade from view.

It was a time of deepening uncertainty for Norma Jean. She began to miss Lester back in Hawthorne. At this point she had made few friends in Hollywood, probably because she was something of a tom-boy and the sort of character who needs time to win acceptance in a new environment.

But if she was becoming a loner, she was also learning something invaluable in that household. George Arliss spoke impeccable English and he expected his stand-in to do the same. The very first "hardly never" that came from Norma Jean's lips was pounced upon and done to death. So conscious of *how* she should say things did she become, she would hesitate in the midst of delivery. Marilyn herself was to date her stammer from her entrance into the orphanage, which occurred eighteen months later, but those who remember her as a child in Hollywood also recall her stuttering then. It would never leave her altogether, but she could parse most sentences before she was in her ninth year, and she would find her superior grades in English at school would balance out her failure in other subjects.

With little warning, the interlude ended. One morning while Norma Jean was off at the Hollywood Grammar School, her mother called in ill to the studio. Her depression had reached a point where she had lost all control. By mid-morning, she was in such a pitch of hysteria that the English couple phoned Grace McKee, who advised that an ambulance be called.

January is an extraordinarily bleak month in Hollywood, with rains nearly every day. Los Angeles needs sunshine to make it tolerable nearly as much as Las Vegas needs darkness and neon. That January in 1934 was no exception, and Gladys must have found her increasing malaise, combined with the gloom out-of-doors, unbearable.

There was a scuffle when the attendants came into the house. Apparently the elderly couple were too frightened to make any effort to calm Gladys, and it is likely that nothing short of heavy sedation would have done it. It is difficult to understand why one of the attendants did not administer some sedation, but perhaps they had not anticipated violence and had come unprepared. She was taken, tightly strapped to a stretcher, first to the General Hospital where she had given birth to Norma Jean and then, after diagnostic study, to the state asylum at Norwalk where her mother had died. Her illness – paranoid schizophrenia. It had destroyed both of her parents and her brother, and now it had finally caught up with her as she had feared.

Marilyn remembered her return home from school that day. The Englishman gently took her by the hand and said, "Your mother was taken ill today. She's gone to the hospital for a while."

Marilyn couldn't recall that she made any comment. Out of habit, she must have accepted this collapse of the promising new life with stoicism. Her mother's absence was something she unwittingly had been getting adjusted to for a long time. And she was not to discover what was really wrong with Gladys, beyond her having suffered "a nervous breakdown", until she was a woman.

For another month or two, almost until the onset of spring, the English couple stayed on with Norma Jean in the house, selling some of Gladys's furnishings on Grace's advice in order to pay the instalments on the house and for the gas and light. Grace gave them occasional tens and twenties, whatever she could afford, for Norma Jean's care, and the county may have been approached to ensure that the child had everything she needed, although there is no evidence that she became a "county child" until some time later in the middle of her ninth year.

With the exception of a singular year over a decade later, Gladys and her daughter were permanently parted. Gladys would make extended visits into the world outside the hospital walls in the future and would even remarry during one of them, but she never again made any effort to assume the responsibilities of a parent. For this reason more than any other, Marilyn felt considerable bitterness towards her mother. There would be a sense of strain between them whenever they would meet and Marilyn would say, "I never really knew my mother."

The studio on Gower Street, run by the paternalistic Harry Cohn, continued to pay Gladys's salary for a few weeks and that was turned over to Grace to dole out as needed.

But finally the elderly English couple felt obliged to find a furnished flat and allow the bank to take the house. Norma Jean went with them when they moved. When the money from Columbia Pictures ran out, the county took over completely in subsidizing Norma Jean, with Grace McKee named as her guardian.

All told, the child was with the English family for nearly a year until Mr. Arliss completed his current contract and returned to England where an aristocratic friend was always employed as his stand-in. Then, facing lean times in the heart of a great depression, they elected to leave films and go home.

Some neighbours, the Harvey Giffens, took Norma Jean into their home. Mr. Giffen worked for the Radio Corporation of America as a sound engineer. He and his wife were southerners from western Mississippi and had three other children, one a girl close to Norma Jean's age.

All of the Giffens became fond of Norma Jean. But circumstance was soon to separate them. At the time she came into their spacious ranch home in the North Hollywood hills, Harvey Giffen was planning to leave picture work and return to Mississippi. After a family conference, they contacted Gladys to see if an adoption could be arranged. As an alternative to this, an old friend of Gladys at C.F.I. — Reginald Carroll and his wife — offered to adopt the child in the event that Gladys didn't want her to be taken out of California. Then for some days all parties waited patiently for word from the state sanatorium.

Both requests sent Gladys into a deep depression; she saw a threat to the only relationship of any value in her life. When she was rational — as she was occasionally — she informed the Giffens and the Carrolls that Norma Jean was not up for adoption.

With all outside offers to help frustrated, Norma Jean was taken to the Los Angeles Orphans' Home Society at the age of nine.

The main building, housing the office of the Directress and the huge communal dining-hall, is not formidable. It has graceful proportions and is vaguely colonial in design, built of old brick with white trim. But Norma Jean could read the sign on one of the columns clearly, and she knew she was not an orphan. Her mother was alive. Someone was making a terrible mistake.

She refused to walk in and they had to drag her all the way into the central hall. *"I'm not an orphan!"* she screamed. Her cries could be heard by several of the children nearest the tall arched doorway at the rear; it was their dinner hour. Some children's faces turned; Norma Jean became embarrassed and fell silent.

CHAPTER FIVE

If it is true that Marilyn, the woman, wanted everyone to love her and took enormous satisfaction from the public adulation she received for over a decade of her life, surely that need had its origins in the twenty-one months beginning on September 13, 1935, that the girl, Norma Jean, spent within the walls of Los Angeles Orphans' Home Society. When she was finally liberated a few weeks after her eleventh birthday, the pattern of life, a continuing quest for affection that seemed an end in itself, had been set.

In her first weeks there she felt terribly isolated. She would make serious inquiries attempting to resolve the "mistake", seeking some information about her mother. Marilyn remembered approaching a Matron, who told her. "You're better off not asking, Norma Jean. She's away. She won't be coming back."

"Do you mean she's dead?" the girl then would ask.

The answer is in doubt. Marilyn could not remember specifically whether she was told her mother was dead. But it is possible there was no answer and she took the woman's silence for confirmation of the dread fact.

The institution on El Centro Avenue in the heart of Holly-

wood was originally founded in 1880 as a non-sectarian home
for children. Its wealthy founder set up a trust for the care of
the children whose parents or parent were unable to maintain a proper home for them. There were a few true orphans,
and a number of half orphans like Norma Jean, as well as
several children who weren't orphaned at all but whose homes
were afflicted by illness, extreme poverty or disharmony. Tech-
nically, only those who came as orphans and those whose
parents died while they were in the care of the Home were
true wards of Los Angeles County. Others were given a tran-
sient status. Any stable parent or guardian could remove them
upon application to the Society.

"We are one big family," the Directress would say. "We
try to give each child as much love and attention as we can."
But this was a relative thing, and for Norma Jean it simply
was not enough. The rules – and there had to be many in
governing more than fifty children – cancelled out what little
love the Directress could parcel out. According to Marilyn's
recollection, she got none from the matrons.

She lived in an old dormitory behind the colonial main
building in a room with twenty-six other girls. The boys were
in another section, although all activities including meals and
sessions at the nearby public school were carried out together.
There was an honour system in the dorm room, and through
good behaviour, Norma Jean could work her way to the
"honour bed" next to the door to the corridor. At one point,
she did manage to move close to the bed of honour but her
individualism asserted itself and she was bounced back to the
twenty-seventh bed. Early one morning she just didn't feel
like marching down with the others to breakfast and lingered
near the window instead, looking down across the play-yard
to the huge sound stages and water tower of the RKO Studios.

"What's wrong with you, Norma Jean?" the matron wanted
to know.

Norma Jean stooped down and began working at her laces.
"I haven't tied my shoes yet," she said. She was demoted that
day and she never again made the effort. "What was the
point?" she said years later. "A bed is a bed."

Guardian Grace McKee attempted to instil in Norma Jean
some awareness that there were people outside who cared
about her. She would come two or three Saturdays each
month and take the girl out for a few hours. They would go

shopping in downtown Los Angeles and, in a few rare and wonderful instances, Grace would permit Norma Jean to try on her lipstick. As she approached her tenth birthday, she was tall for her years. She was so pleased with her new image in the ladies-room mirror that Grace was moved to inquire if she wanted to have her hair done.

She was taken to a beauty parlour where her straight "dirty blonde" hair was given a Marcel, or water wave. They would often end such afternoons at a movie house, when Norma Jean would forget the Home and pretend for a couple of hours that life hadn't altered so much.

But reality moved in on her again. Weekdays, the children would rise at 6 a.m. and make their beds and tidy up the dorm before breakfast. Then they would be off to public school four blocks away. There were no uniforms, but they would walk in a group down El Centro toward the school building. Passing adults often gave them a look of compassion that was especially onerous to Norma Jean. She liked to pretend that in her plaid skirt and wool sweater she was like other girls at the school. She attempted to dissociate herself from the Home children once inside the school building. She made a few friends among the "outside" girls, but this attempt to change her status was aborted every time they walked back to the Home and some schoolboy passed and said knowingly to his chum, "*They're* from the Home."

Marilyn has said they were paid for their chores and once mentioned a figure of five cents a month. The Society insists that this was not the case, that each child was given a small allowance, and that the chores were done by turns so that Norma Jean might sometimes find herself in the kitchen helping with the dishes "as in any large family", according to the Directress. This was a familiar chore; she and Lester had often been asked to do the dishes by the Bolenders. At the Home, there were stainless spoons and forks to wash, and mugs and plates; never any glassware. That only appeared at the matron's table, a small detail that etched itself deeply into Norma Jean's mind. Perhaps it was an accumulation of such omissions that made her sense of separation from the normal world so acute.

Grace McKee must have told the Directress how much pleasure Norma Jean had taken from having her hair done and wearing lipstick, for that lady – whose sensibilities were

more easily touched than the Matrons' – called Norma Jean
into her office one Saturday. She sat behind a highly waxed
walnut desk in a corner office at the front of the main building. Marilyn remembered there was a Pekinese dog near her
feet. Norma Jean feared one of the Matrons had reported
her for some misdemeanour and she tried to recall just what
might have provoked this confrontation.

"You have such a lovely skin, dear," the Directress said.
Norma Jean, embarrassed by the compliment, went crimson
and stooped to pet the dog.

"Stay that way for a minute," the lady told her, and she
took out a powder puff and began applying a delicately frag-
rant powder to her face. "Now look in the mirror," she said.
Norma Jean got up and walked to an antique mirror on the
wall. Her face was soft, alabaster smooth as her mother's had
been.

"Since it's Saturday, you may wear it all day, Norma Jean."

The girl left, feeling a love for the Head that far outdistanced for a time her regard for Grace McKee, perhaps
because the Head was always there, like God. Norma Jean
was buoyant for days. But as time passed, and the Directress
didn't repeat the audience, she began to wonder if it had ever
really happened.

In succeeding months, her sole link with the life she had
been forced to leave was "Aunt" Grace. It was she who sent her
the only birthday card received on June 1, 1936. It showed a
girl in a party dress with a bow in her hair walking into a huge
"ten". On the following Saturday Grace took Norma to an
ice cream parlour.

Rescue became an obsession in Norma Jean's mind, and
she discovered she was not alone in her desperation. One of
her closest girl-friends at the Home had decided in her eleventh
year that she was getting too old for anyone to ever take into
their home. The two girls plotted their escape, an episode recorded in the Home records.

Running away at night was out of the question. Darkness
was too terrifying, and besides, the dormitory was always
locked at bedtime. They elected to go to the rest-room from
the playing field behind the buildings, a perfectly natural excuse to leave the others. A Matron spotted them from one
of the upper floors as they made their way from the rear dor-

mitory down the side of the building and then across the wide
expanse to El Centro Avenue. She called down from the window. "Norma Jean! Theresa!" The fugitives ran back toward the playing field.

The Matron intercepted them as they were about to join
the others. "Don't tell the Head," Norma Jean pleaded. "She
let me use her face powder. Don't tell her, please. She let me
pet her dog."

But, of course, a report was made, including Norma Jean's
plea, but nothing was said about it except to Grace McKee.
Grace decided she would have to do something soon about
the girl.

At the time, Grace was being courted by a man ten years
younger than herself. He was Erwin "Doc" Goddard, a man
recently divorced and given custody of his three children, two
girls and a boy. One of the girls, Beebe, was two years younger than Norma Jean, and there was five-year-old Josephine,
and John, whom they called Fritz, aged seven.

Grace introduced Norma Jean to the Goddard family one
Saturday. Beebe and Norma Jean became immediate friends.
As Beebe's father, Doc Goddard, remembered it, they discovered they liked the same movie stars and apparently both
girls had scrap books of their favourites. They disliked school
with equal intensity. What Doc did not care to remember was
that both had come from broken homes and were extremely
sensitive about it. Like Norma Jean, Beebe had lived in a few
foster homes when it was inconvenient for Doc to keep all
three children with him; her disjointed childhood was to leave
its mark in later years.

Grace's own indecision delayed her marriage to Doc for a
time. She worried about the fact that, as a mother to Norma
Jean and the step-children, she would be an old woman by
the time they reached maturity. In many ways she was much
like Gladys, though far less vulnerable.

Doc recalls that Grace had promised Gladys on one of her
visits to Norwalk that she would take Norma Jean away from
the institution. The present Directress, Margaret Ingram, confirms that it was decided by all parties at the time that Norma
Jean needed a family situation. "Some children don't respond
as well as others to the environment of the Home. We do all
we can to give them affection and individual attention, but it
doesn't always work."

CHAPTER SIX

There was a small baseball diamond behind the main building of the Home. The hangar-like sound stages of RKO Studios were visible at the farther edge of the vacant lots adjoining the playing field.

On a muggy Saturday in late June 1937, there was a baseball game going on. The boys against the girls. Norma Jean, now in her twelfth year, wasn't the best girl athlete in the Home, but she was among the best. She preferred to be out-of-doors when she wasn't able to go to the movies, and had no interest at all in such feminine skills as sewing or making Indian beads into belts or headbands. She was now five feet three inches tall and still growing, and becoming slightly self-conscious about being so much taller than the others, including many of the boys. It made her appear to be one of the *ad-girls* or advanced teenagers, young ladies who were not yet through high school and had no home but this one.

Norma Jean later confided to her first husband, Jim Dougherty, that she liked to lose herself in group sports whenever she had the chance. It was a rare confidence. She almost never talked about the Home at that time of her life, perhaps because she still felt too close to it.

On that morning, she had just knocked the ball into the outfield and run to first base, then had dared to make second. She was a girl who never hesitated to run risks if the rewards seemed sufficiently tempting.

The Directress appeared on the steps behind the dining hall and then walked towards second base, where she conferred quietly with Norma Jean. Grace was waiting for her in a small sitting-room at the front of the building.

Grace had warned her a week or so earlier that she might not be able to provide a home for her immediately, that she must be patient. But Norma Jean had allowed herself to believe that her world would brighten perceptibly upon her rescue by Grace and even hoped the woman might see her eager expectancy and make room in her own home for her.

Grace McKee was too practical for that. While she was quick to do a kindness, she could never permit her life to be

upset by one. Oddly, Grace was more like the woman Norma
Jean was to become than the child's own mother. Her personality was slightly unstable and would become more so as
her comforts multiplied, almost as though she needed the bal-
last of some hardship or deprivation to keep her on an even
keel. She was keenly intelligent but not an intellectual, and
the core of selfishness in her nature was often obscured by
impulsive acts of generosity.

The Directress said goodbye and embraced Norma Jean,
then turned away. Two of Norma Jean's girl-friends watched
as she walked down the steps of the main building, and as she
turned to glance back, one of them began to wave and she
waved back.

She was taken to the first of a series of temporary family
"situations". The first was in the home of a couple in Comp-
ton who sold furniture polish made by the husband. The wife
spent most of each day with Norma Jean by her side in a
battered old Chevrolet. It was summer, and the girl was to
remember that vacation as one spent mostly rocking back
and forth over back roads seeking out small hardware stores.
If Grace and the Directress had agreed that she needed the
nearness of a parent substitute over an extended period of
time, Norma Jean was surfeited in a matter of days. There
was no escape. While she dawdled over her breakfast, the
woman was in the garage loading up the back seat of the car
with white bottles. Later, Marilyn recalled, she would hear
the offensive sound of the old engine revving up and the
woman's voice crying out the same words every morning,
"Norma Jean! Let's go! Lock the door as you come out."
In less than a month, Norma Jean knew the name of every
village in Los Angeles County.

Meanwhile, Grace had married Doc Goddard and moved
into his small house in West Van Nuys. Doc was a towering
man, about six feet two, in ruddy good health. When he was
not at work as a research engineer of sorts for the Adel Precision Products, manufacturers of aeroplane parts, he was in
his workshop inventing things. He often spoke of "selling his
patents" for a fortune. By the time of their marriage, Grace
was no longer deluded by his dreams and realized that was
his way of adjusting to life.

It is not easy to discover just why Norma Jean was sent by

Grace into a second temporary home soon after Norma Jean complained she was "wearing a callous on her behind". However it happened, Norma Jean was wretchedly unhappy there and even asked Grace if she wouldn't have her sent back to the Home. The Goddard family was shamed by the situation and it was decided that Norma Jean would join them prior to the spring term of school. Early in 1938 she made the transition to what she believed would be her final home where her status would not be in doubt. Initially, she had a room of her own since Beebe was then staying with her own mother. When a year or so later Beebe returned to her father's house, the girls shared the bedroom.

That February, Norma Jean entered Emerson Junior High School in the first half of the seventh grade, a term behind most children her age because of the irregularity of her school life. Beebe would join her there the following year.

Life at the Goddards' was strongly reminiscent of her year with the English couple. There was hard liquor in the house at all times, and while Grace drank sparingly, Doc seemed to enjoy his Scotch as much as George Arliss's stand-in did his bourbon.

Their nearest neighbours to the rear were the Doughertys, who had two sons at home and another son and daughter married. Edward Dougherty belonged to the working class and liked to putter around with masonry and carpentry in his spare time. The Doughertys and Goddards became rather close for a time. Norma Jean and Beebe thought one of their unmarried sons, "Jimmy" as they called him, extremely handsome.

Grace had been cautioned by her Aunt Ana, who had taken an interest in Norma Jean, not to give her any chores that might remind her of the Home, such as washing dishes. Instead, she kept their bedroom straight, while Beebe occasionally helped in the kitchen. An easy democracy prevailed in that household.

Aunt Ana, a widow who lived alone in a low ranch house on Odessa Avenue in Van Nuys some distance from the Goddards, was quite different from her niece. Many years later, Marilyn was to say that while she was "very fond" of Grace Goddard, she "adored" Aunt Ana Lower, and kept in close contact with her until that lady's death in 1948. Norma Jean was in close contact with Ana Lower for a period of more

than ten years, much the longest association of her life, ex-
ceeding by several months her relationship with Arthur Miller
(they met in December 1950, and separated permanently in
November 1960). And it was, also, one of the healthiest close
relationships she had in her lifetime. Ana was outgoing, relatively selfless, a "liberal" Christian Scientist who gave Norma
Jean a copy of Mary Baker Eddy's *Science and Health* which
she would treasure long after its tenets had lost their efficacy
for her. She began spending nearly every Sunday at Ana's,
accompanying the ageing woman (she was then in her early
sixties) to the local Christian Science Church. Affectionate by
nature and deprived of love for so long, Norma Jean responded to that creed's ethic – Love as God and the underlying
principle of the universe – with blind enthusiasm. She was to
remain a faithful member of the Church for over eight years,
the only really solid religious connection of her life.

It is difficult to say whether the Church failed her or if she,
in the end, could not bring to it the necessary belief. When in
the last decade of her life she most needed the relief Science
is supposed to bring, she had long since abandoned it.

Perhaps the significant heritage of Norma Jean's years with
Science was her lifelong ability to seem innocent, to appear
never to see evil in anything ("Evil is the awful deception and
unreality of existence"). It may well have been through
Science that she acquired the facility of never feeling guilt
over anything she did. This quality was basic to her screen
image and, as we can see from its background, there was nothing false about it. What is regrettable is that Ana Lower's
Church could not have remained the anodyne for Marilyn, for
in a very real sense, she was to be destroyed by her belief in
and reliance upon drugs and medications.

CHAPTER SEVEN

For some months after rescue by Grace, Norma Jean was
called "The Mouse". She often appeared in a room, listened
intently to whatever conversation might be going on there, but
never announced her presence by so much as a cough. Like
many other children from troubled backgrounds, she felt her

opinions were of small value. This feeling was to persist through many years, and while she might come in time to trust her own judgment, she still would be reluctant to express it verbally.

Alone in her bedroom when Beebe was not around, she was liberated from this sense of inconsequence. Her Saturday movie-going – which had lapsed only while she was in the two temporary homes just prior to coming into the Goddard household – continued unabated.

It was 1938, and perhaps to escape the ominous blight of Nazism spreading across Europe, Hollywood was in a period mood. Two of the most visually stunning productions were Metro's *Marie Antoinette*, with Norma Shearer baring her lovely white throat to the guillotine, and Warner's *Jezebel*, which Bette Davis turned into a *tour de force*.

Marilyn seemed to enjoy recounting certain incidents from this period but would go silent when asked leading questions about other events and circumstances of the time, including how she really felt about Grace Goddard or her absent mother. She readily confessed that she kept a smiling studio portrait of Clark Gable tacked to her bedroom wall for some months following her rescue from the orphanage. Gable was, she would tell her younger and more credulous friends, her secret father, a fabrication which must have taken some of the sting out of her growing awareness of her illegitimacy.

Marilyn also occasionally spoke of her primitive attempts at acting, long before she determined to enter films. Norma Jean would shut the bedroom door and act out all the parts, male and female, of the latest movie she had mastered through several Saturday afternoon screenings. She pretended she was the arrogant Jezebel or, more effectively, luckless Marie Antoinette saying goodbye to her lover, played by Tyrone Power and re-created, as Marilyn recalled, "on my knees on the bed. I wanted to make the hero seem to tower over Marie Antoinette, but if I stood on the bed, it became ridiculous." She would weep as she said farewell to her children before climbing into the tumbrel (again the bed) that would take her to the place of execution. Years later when filming *Bus Stop* and asked to weep on cue, Marilyn managed it so well that she was furious with Joshua Logan, her director, when she learned that most of her tear-drenched close-ups had been cut from the film. Logan blamed Buddy Adler, then production head at Fox, for the excision, saying, "As for me, I wouldn't cut a frame of Marilyn's."

As Norma Jean approached her fourteenth birthday, these solitary amusements or exercises apparently were put aside permanently. She was becoming a person of significance in her own right. People, especially other young people, were suddenly aware of her. It had something to do with her physical development, for she was becoming a young woman. But it had more to do with the self-assurance she quickly acquired when she realized she was no longer a lanky, over-tall schoolgirl, but someone attractive enough to make heads turn for another look.

She was not endowed by nature with great beauty, but when she began to take on a few contours she exercised some of the *will* to be beautiful that was to become the remarkable conjuration of her later years. Grace or Ana gave her home permanents to curl her straight hair; her physical health was at its peak; she never suffered from the facial blemishes characteristic of teenagers. She was careful what she ate and washed her face as often as fifteen times a day. In June 1940, she became fourteen. She was a big girl, having reached her full height of five feet six, and she was about to enter the final term of the ninth grade that September.

The Goddards moved during the summer into Aunt Ana's ranch house on Odessa Avenue. Ana had bought another, larger house on Nebraska Avenue in West Los Angeles with a rental unit on its first floor. Grace was buying the Odessa house from her aunt in instalments and it seemed a happy arrangement all around. Set on half an acre and surrounded by tall trees, it was for the children a great step upwards in the world. There was no more crowding in tiny rooms, and for Norma Jean it had an added appeal as "Ana's house". She was beginning to enjoy some continuity in her life.

But it was a greater distance from Emerson Junior High School, more than three miles and much too far to walk. It was arranged by Grace, who always managed such things with skill, that Norma Jean and Beebe would walk from the junior high school to the Dougherty home just behind their old residence, and wait there for Jim to return from his day shift at Lockheed to drive them home.

Jim Dougherty at eighteen was still relatively naïve. Out of high school for a year and "an uncomplicated kid", as he was later to call himself, it did not occur to him immediately that Grace Goddard had something more than a favour in mind.

Jim was earning nearly as much money as his father. A new blue Ford coupé caught his fancy in a show-window, and within a week he was driving it back and forth to his job. He had everything needed for popularity: a handsome Irish face, a sporty car, youth and money. As Jim remembers it, at the time he was going with the recent queen of the Santa Barbara Festival, Judy Drennan, who soon met Norma Jean accidentally and asked Jim what he was doing "hauling a little sexpot like that around in his car".

He was to ask himself the same question when a few months later Grace called to ask if he would take Norma Jean to a company dance being held by Doc's firm, Adel Precision Products, the next Saturday. He was surprised to hear himself say "Yes, that would be all right," and then she asked him to find a date for Beebe also.

Finding a boy-friend for Beebe was more difficult. It was not that she was unattractive, but she was withdrawn and quite tense most of the time, although being around Norma Jean had helped her enormously. Norma Jean had acquired an engaging and contagious sense of assurance in little more than a year's time. It was to remain as a surface cover throughout her lifetime, although it would mask an increasingly complex inner self once she got involved in films.

But the double date was finally arranged, with Jim and his buddy calling for the girls in time "for a drive and a malted" before going on to the ballroom. Grace was already there with Doc and seemed pleased that Norma Jean not only behaved like a mature young woman but appeared to be relaxed and enjoying herself. Later, Marilyn described herself as being always able to "feel gay" when the occasion called for it. Doc, now known as "Daddy" to Norma Jean as well as his own brood, told Grace, "Maybe there's something there."

What that something *was* is in some dispute. The Doughertys, including Jim, maintain that the romance and subsequent marriage of Jim to Norma Jean were arranged by Grace with some encouragement from Ana Lower. It was, Jim insists, a "loveless", planned courtship that led to real affection only some months after they were married.

Doc Goddard contends that it was apparent very soon after that very first date that Norma Jean was in love with Jim; that she was, in a way, the aggressor, and sought Grace's aid in getting Jim to propose.

The dispute would cause a falling out between Doc Goddard and Marilyn a year or two before her death when Doc called to tell her he was planning to publish his version of "the truth" of her early years so that the world would know, in case it cared, that the Goddards had not pushed her, as a matter of convenience, into an arranged marriage. Apparently, Marilyn at first failed to understand Doc's motive in undertaking this venture and was distraught, but she had later learned that he had decided not to publish the story without her permission. Doc himself says that he declined to visit Marilyn in her final residence on Fifth Helena in Brentwood "out of pride".

CHAPTER EIGHT

Early in 1941 Ana Lower and her niece Grace agreed that Norma Jean should move into Ana's home on Nebraska Avenue in West Los Angeles. It was probably Ana's idea originally and may have been inspired by an episode with Doc that had thoroughly frightened Norma Jean. There were times when Doc was frankly drunk, and Norma Jean would be aware of it. But on this occasion, as she later told Jim, Doc entered her room, embraced her, and kissed her in such an intimate way she felt violated.

There was little or no prudery in Norma Jean, as there would be none in Marilyn. Secure in Ana's house, she gave "Daddy" an affectionate hug when he dropped by with apparently no memory of the earlier encounter. Her fondness for Doc survived the "spat" over whether the Doughertys' version of her first marriage, which by 1960 had been published in several magazines, or the Goddard version was correct.

Ana and Norma Jean shared the second floor of the two-storey house on Nebraska Avenue. There was an outside stairway leading up to their quarters, and below them a four-room apartment Ana rented out for additional income. It was much the happiest move of Norma Jean's life. Only once again in her lifetime would she be surrounded by such a secure ambience of affection (with Arthur Miller in Connecticut in 1957). She transferred to a larger and more prestigious school, University High School, in West Los Angeles, and she had her own room on a permanent basis, or so she believed at the time, an important luxury to an involuntary gypsy of her sensibilities.

As Norma Jean's guardian, Grace was still receiving regular support money from Los Angeles County for the girl. At first Norma Jean was able to put this charity aspect of her situation out of mind since "Aunt" Ana had told her she would pay for her maintenance herself "in a minute" if she was not an old lady with limited funds. Norma Jean must have known that Ana really meant this.

But the idyll would end in 1941, some months before the attack on Pearl Harbor brought the country into the war. If Grace had known that tragic event was imminent, it might have altered her plans for Norma Jean, since they involved turning over the girl's future to a young man in prime physical condition, certain to be an early candidate for the draft.

Doc had been advised by Adel Precision Products that he was in line for a promotion but that it would mean his relocation. He was offered a plant assistant managership in Huntington, West Virginia, and Grace immediately urged him to accept. She knew she would have to terminate the county assistance for Norma Jean's support and that some other arrangement – marriage – would help ease her own conscience.

Norma Jean was never to completely forgive Grace for this. Interestingly, she blamed neither Doc nor Ana for instigating the plot, and Jim Dougherty later concurred in the belief that it was entirely Grace's idea. On one rare occasion after they were wed, Norma Jean rather tearfully complained to Jim that Grace always thought of herself first and that she had abandoned her.

There is some truth both in Norma Jean's complaint and in Doc Goddard's defence of his family's position on the matter. When Grace, who had persuaded Ana to accompany her, proposed to Mrs. Edward Dougherty that her son marry Norma Jean so that Grace could leave Los Angeles with a clear conscience, both Jim and Norma Jean agreed that it might be a satisfactory resolution. No one actually pressured

them into it, but they were young and pliant. And if in truth
Norma Jean was abandoned by Grace, it was not permanently. Some years later when the Goddards at Grace's behest
returned to Los Angeles after the young Doughertys were
divorced, Grace was still officially Norma Jean's guardian
and had to sign the papers allowing 20th-Century Fox to place
her ward, who was not yet twenty-one, under contract to that
studio.

It was a strange sort of courtship. For weeks after the plan
had been agreed to, Jim continued seeing his other girl-friends.
A virile young man as well as a responsible one, perhaps he
was sowing the last of his wild oats, knowing that marriage
would be the end of any casual relationships. But then as
spring approached, Jim recalls that he informed his regular
dates that he was about to get married and he began seeing
only Norma Jean, several times a week.

Most of Jim's interests were out-of-doors. Even today in
his middle forties he enjoys nothing better than taking a re-
modelled pickup truck with sleeping accommodation and an
improvised galley down to the Arizona desert or up into the
mountains surrounding Los Angeles for a weekend or more
of hunting.

Always a good athlete as well as a good sport, Norma Jean
joined him in horseback riding. Once, as they rode back to
the stable at dusk, she wanted to know how the horse could
see in the near darkness, and Jim half-seriously suggested she
turn on the headlights. "Where are they?" she asked childishly.
Sometimes they would go to the beach at Santa Monica. Norma Jean had no fear of the water, having learned to swim at
the orphanage.

She put her interest in movies under wraps for a while. Jim
remembers that they went no oftener than once a month.
They both loved to dance, and it was often a matter of choice
whether they would visit with friends, go dancing, or to a
movie. Norma Jean's world had expanded with her marriage,
although Marilyn has said that it had not been happy. This
statement came nearly two decades after her first marriage
and was considerably coloured by afterthought. Jim believes
that she tried very hard to make a success of their life together. She even suppressed her feelings for animals to the
point where she could skin and cook a rabbit Jim had shot.

Ana Lower and the elder Doughertys planned the wedding. It was to be held at the comfortable home of Chester Howell, a Dougherty friend, in Westwood – possibly because there was a winding staircase into their central hall which Norma Jean could descend as the wedding march was played.

Marion, one of Jim's older brothers, was to be best man, and Ana would give her sixteen-year-old "niece" away. The Goddards wired their love and regrets from West Virginia, but the Bolenders were sent an invitation at Norma Jean's behest and came up from Hawthorne for the ceremony.

There was no possibility of Gladys attending. She had left the Norwalk sanatorium a year or so earlier, gone north to San Francisco, suffered a relapse and was now institutionalized in the Bay Area. There was no sentimental bond evident between mother and daughter that day, and no one overheard Norma Jean wishing her mother there. With Ana and Ida Bolender in attendance, perhaps she felt she had all the family present that mattered.

The wedding took place on June 18, 1942, three weeks after Norma Jean's sixteenth birthday. Norma Jean wore a white wedding gown given her by Ana, and Jim wore a rented white-jacketed tuxedo. There were about twenty-five guests, many of them friends of the Doughertys. Norma Jean had dropped out of her classes in the first term of the eleventh grade in May, which might explain why only a few of her University High School friends were there, but one of them – whose name seems to have been lost – was Norma Jean's maid of honour.

The reception was held in the Florentine Gardens in Hollywood, an Italian restaurant where a waiter spilled a bowl of tomato sauce on to Jim's white jacket, the only mishap of the day.

There was no honeymoon. Jim had not told his foreman at Lockheed he was getting married. Norma Jean didn't ask why. There were numerous questions bottled in her mind those first few months she chose never to articulate. But the ceremony had been conventional enough to satisfy her notion of how such rituals should be managed. It was the first wedding she had ever seen performed and the uniqueness of it had a narcotic effect upon her. There had been a modest shower of rice supplied by Jim's married sister, Billie, as they ran to the Florentine Gardens parking lot, and they were pursued a few blocks by horn-blowing friends. Everyone knew they were headed for their new home in Sherman Oaks.

Jim had rented a studio apartment on Vista del Monte north of Ventura Boulevard. It was a one-room affair with a pull-down Murphy bed, but it contained new equipment in the kitchen and modern furnishings supplied by the landlord. Norma Jean was ecstatic about its gleaming newness and ran around the room, bathroom, and kitchen turning on all the lamps, the radio, creating her own sound and light show.

If Norma Jean never really loved Jim Dougherty as she was later to say repeatedly, then everyone around her, including Jim, was deceived. But Marilyn once spoke of her ability to quickly assimilate local speech patterns so that when making an appearance in the South, she acquired a southern accent within a few days – protective colouration perhaps. Her declarations to Jim may have come out of the twilight area of truth.

In place of their honeymoon, they settled for weekend trips to Sherwood Lake. There they fished from a hired rowboat, Jim tossing the catch to Norma Jean, who dropped them into a wicker basket. She sat in the back of the boat, never looking down into the depths where there were living things that moved among the swaying reeds, where animal life was threatened by their presence. With some shame she later acknowledged that Norma Jean, the champion of all living things, saw the anomaly in her new life as Mrs. James Dougherty. She was never able to take a fish off the hook, but once home, could clean and pan fry them. On other excursions, they went into the mountains, where Jim would gun down rabbits with his shotgun. Later, when she was given another name and another life, her reaction towards animal life could again be all compassion, but not without some glaring contradictions.

In the closing years of her life as Norma Jean, life was kinder to her than she knew. In Jim Dougherty, she had as a husband and lover the only man in her life who was at peace with himself. But there were unhappy signs even then that Norma Jean was not able to be at peace with herself. Dougherty himself has said that if Norma Jean had remained with him through another decade or more of her life, she still might have broken down even without the strain of terrifying public exposure. In all likelihood he is referring to her tenuous

hold on her identity, her actual and deliberate lack of antecedents (she almost never referred to her mother), her abortive effort to become one of the Doughertys. When the war
took Jim away from her and she went to live with her in-
laws, she saw her failure at once. She was an alien passing as
the young Mrs. Dougherty.

When she became Marilyn, contrary to all the glib declarations by some of her associates that she was an invention, she
invested that new creature with a sense of reality and purpose
she had never felt in her previous life. Perhaps there is some
clue here to her later disillusionment. There were *two* Marilyns: the actress and the woman, and the public and her film
colleagues were always confusing the two.

But in Sherman Oaks there was a veneer of high spirits that
glossed over the tensions. Teasing is the handiest weapon to
keep an uncertain situation from getting out of hand. Most of
Norma Jean's teasing was verbal. She would say astonishing
things in a casual manner, and only when she giggled behind
her hand would Jim realize she was joking. One time when
they couldn't decide whether to go out or stay home on a
Sunday evening, she tried to settle the argument by getting
into a new cotton print dress. Jim recalls that it was a white,
tight-fitting garment with pink rosebuds. Earlier in the week
they had quarrelled briefly over the money she was investing
in her wardrobe. He studied the dress for a moment, then
said, "What's so special about it?" "It's shrinkproof," Norma
Jean answered, rubbing her hand down her mid-section. She
regretted having answered, for he picked her up bodily and
carried her into the bathroom, and held her under the shower
for nearly a minute. She shrieked and laughed, and after she
had dried her hair, conceded it was a very amusing comment.

There were frequent protestations of affection. When Jim
was switched to the night shift at Lockheed, there was a note
in his lunch pail nearly every night. "My darling. When you
open this, I will be asleep and dreaming of you." When she
forgot, which might happen once or twice a week, he would
think she was angry. But it was nearly always an oversight.
"I knew when you left that I'd forgotten something," she
would say the next morning.

Apparently they were good comrades as well as lovers.
When their car broke down while Jim was driving it through
Los Angeles and it had to be towed for repair to a city garage,

Norma Jean later asked how they were going to fetch it back to Sherman Oaks. Jim waggled his thumb in answer, and she told him she would wait near the roadside to make sure he caught a ride.

Jim waggled his thumb until it ached. Then Norma Jean joined him at the edge of the road and smiled at an approaching Cadillac. Brakes squealed. The grey-haired driver was fascinated by Norma Jean, and they had a lively, parry-and-thrust conversation all the way into Los Angeles, with Jim smiling to himself from time to time.

Jim's protectiveness precluded her working. She was a "housewife", as lonely on weekdays as a single parakeet chattering to himself. Falling lint was caught on the wing and carted to the garbage can; a fly's life could be numbered in seconds after its arrival on the premises. She spent far more time than she cared to listening to radio serials, marathon record programmes. Planning the menu for dinner began right after breakfast.

Both she and Jim made contributions to what was an essentially innocent, even "moral", life. She took him off to the Sherman Oaks Christian Science Church every Sunday morning; he never smoked and rarely drank. When she was living her own life some years later, she discovered she had an innate aversion to smoking, but liked wines, which she had never tasted as Mrs. Dougherty. If she liked them to excess, perhaps it was compensatory.

Yet some of her behaviour at the time would indicate she longed for rescue. There was a staleness about her weekdays that worked on her nerves. She often took a bus down to the city and visited with Ana for the day, but after a few months even these excursions did not alleviate by much her dissatisfaction with her free time. Jim sensed this and began looking for something better.

They moved to a small house in Van Nuys. With the wartime housing shortage limiting choices, it wasn't terribly desirable, but there was a small bedroom and a walk-in kitchen along with a modest living room and a bathroom with a sit-down tub. Norma Jean was now able to add long and indolent soaks to her other modes of escape.

Sometimes, on an oppressively hot day, she would throw together an improvised picnic lunch – a couple of cold frank-furters, a tomato, half a lettuce – and take a bus all the way to Santa Monica and "Muscle Beach". Jim had shown her where it was one Sunday. He believed in keeping fit and did some calisthenics every day, but told her, "These muscle boys have gone around the bend". When one of the young men tried to make conversation, she raised her hand with her wedding band, then smiled, just to show there were no hard feelings. And when this gambit failed, she walked into the surf next to the stand of the lifeguard who kept a sharp eye out for her as she swam. Her solitude must have been brightened by such contacts, however impersonal. Certainly her ego was given a lift, and her life began to change course.

Jim's parents and brother Marion moved fom their house on Archwood Street in Van Nuys to a large Spanish bungalow in North Hollywood. Their Van Nuys house had three bedrooms, a wide front porch, and a spacious living-room. Jim and Norma Jean quickly abandoned their tiny cottage for the larger house, even though their landlord offered to sell them the place for $5,000. Maintaining the Archwood residence was nearly an all-day chore for her. A compulsive housekeeper, she cleaned thoroughly each day.

Possibly to make her seaside jaunts less tempting, Jim bought Norma Jean a collie. There had never been any discussion of having children and they exercised some precaution in that direction. (Jim believed she was afraid of the pain of childbirth, but he was mistaken in this.) So Muggsie, the collie, became Norma Jean's first pet since the ill-fated Tippy and filled a long-empty void. She kept her as carefully groomed as the house, bathing her twice a week, and felt considerable parental pride whenever someone commented on how immaculate Muggsie was.

The war began pressing in on them. Everything was rationed – gas most hurtfully – and there were no more weekend excursions. Norma Jean managed with less sugar in her cooking, but the meat ration was something else. She devoted a great deal of time to inventing casseroles.

But there was something distressing the couple far more than food. At twenty-two, Jim was beginning to feel conspicuous out of uniform. He applied for and got a job as an instructor in physical training with the Maritime Service on Catalina Island.

This move had a sense of adventure about it for Norma Jean. They would be moving by truck and then boat to the island. Muggsie went with them and they moved into a large two-bedroom apartment near the Maritime Service Training Base. There was a gallery on the second-storey apartment with a fine view of the Pacific nearby. The extra bedroom was to be Norma Jean's retreat whenever Jim might have some of his Maritime Service buddies by for a game of cards. This was her way of informing Jim that she would not be playing poker with his new male friends, even though she played a fair game after being taught by his brother Marion. She would backslide a few times, however.

She apparently felt somewhat defenceless during the day whenever she left the apartment because of the predominance of men. Immaculate Muggsie went with her on many of her walks and the dog was much admired by the sailors-in-training.

There was apparently no undercurrent of reciprocal feeling in these casual encounters with men. Jim was convinced that she was completely faithful to him throughout their time together. Her instinctual ability to arouse males through her walk and her dress had more to do with her basic need to feel loved and admired than with any provocative drive. For company while Jim was away during the day, she had a few close girl-friends, among them Mrs. Lynn White, wife of the master-at-arms in the Maritime Base cafeteria, and Mrs. Jim Patton, a neighbour. On weekends when Jim was home, Howard Carrington, an instructor from the Base, would stop by to teach Norma Jean how to lift weights. Her single-minded attention to these body exercises made her girl-friends wonder, but if she had a career in mind, she kept it very much to herself.

Jim recalls their Catalina period with considerable emotion. On the mainland, Norma Jean's status as a young wife had seemed more an act of charity than love to far too many people. Even Doc Goddard had managed to visit Norma Jean in the little Van Nuys house when he was reporting to his home office. There were simply too many ghosts around.

But on Catalina no one knew anything about their background nor cared. Norma Jean's growing affection for her young husband ripened there. In one instance, Jim remembers, she even threatened to jump off a pier if he were ever to leave her.

There were street dances nearly every Saturday night. They could do a mean lindy (an acrobatic sort of jitterbug that had its origins in the Savoy Ballroom in Harlem and which Marilyn would perform with Eli Wallach in her last finished film, *The Misfits*) although Jim never tossed her around as some of her other partners did. One night she was wearing a white summer dress that seemed over-tight to Jim. He made it a point, however, never to criticize her appearance and nothing was said.

Time after time, Jim would observe sailors and their oblivious partners dancing near them, the sailors staring frankly over their girls' shoulders at Norma Jean. Jim's disapproving expressions had no effect. Finally he'd had enough. "Let's go home," he said.

"But why?" Norma Jean wanted to know. "You've got to tell me!"

"I'm tired," he said, and they left. In the weeks to come, Jim chose to ignore the tension that was growing between them over her increasing sexuality and tried instead to live with it.

PART TWO

Goodbye, Norma Jean

CHAPTER ONE

Time was running out for the Axis partners by early 1944, but there were terrible periods when it seemed the Germans or the Japanese had again seized the initiative. Allied shipping losses on the world's embattled sealanes were appalling. On Catalina, Jim Dougherty began to feel the squeeze as the merchant fleet's need became more critical. "I can't last very long in this place," he told Norma Jean. "If I'm taken as a sailor, you'll have to move in with Mom."

The war had altered lives and relationships throughout the world. The young Doughertys had been luckier than most, having spent nearly two war years together. It is even conceivable that the war treated them kindly by separating them, for there would soon be an inevitability about Norma Jean's actions that would exclude Jim entirely. Jim looks back on his years with Norma Jean with no regret and considerable nostalgia, while Marilyn a year or so before her death spoke of Jim as "a nice man, kind to me always, but I haven't seen him since then because we have nothing in common".

In his high school days Jim had thought of becoming a school athletic coach, but since he hadn't gone on to college that career was closed to him. At the merchant seaman's training base on Catalina, Jim was a good instructor, probably a valuable one. But he had nothing to cement his relationship with the school or its command beyond his efficiency. He didn't drink with the rest of the staff. He hurried home to Norma Jean after each day's duty and he saw no more than half a dozen of the permanent personnel, underlings like himself, in off-duty time, often with their wives in his home or theirs with Norma Jean. It required a certain sycophancy to become a permanent, secure member of that élite, those who would never leave the States or the base, and that was simply not in his character.

Norma Jean was very like him in this. When she turned her physical assets to advantage, there was an innocence about it, often followed by a smile when she realized she was catching someone's attention. As Marilyn, eventually there would be the complicating factor of enormous public acceptance and all the pampering that salutes it, but she accepted this as her due, as a child of privilege, still innocent.

Norma Jean was being completely honest when she told Jim that he was the most important human being in her life. It is even possible that he spoiled her for other men who entered her life later on, and she resented this a little. Jim was at home with his manhood, his maleness not a studied thing. There was a perfect naturalness about their love-making she would never find again, perhaps because she would soon find herself in a world where this kind of man was nearly non-existent and because she was herself changing, developing into a narcissist of a peculiar sort. And, too, Jim was both a lover and father confessor, probably not a rare combination when a slightly older young man marries a girl as uncertain and undefined as Norma Jean.

Marilyn's narcissism was not conventional. There are some who knew her (but not intimately) who swore that her unpunctuality was due to her inability to leave her dressing-table and her mirror, that she was hypnotized by her own beauty and image. This could not possibly be true since she was not naturally beautiful, her face being disproportionately large (as is often the case with actors) above a body that ranged during her lifetime from magnificent to stout. Her public image was a contrivance of great skill and her will to be beautiful. When she spent an hour or more at her vanity table, she was often doing and re-doing her eyes or her mouth or her skin make-up to achieve the right effect. Rather than in love with her own image, she was fiercely dedicated to its perfectibility.

When Jim finally left on a freighter, the *Julia S. DuMont*, destination Townsville, Australia, Norma Jean did not seriously question the immediate future he had mapped out for her. She closed down their apartment and prepared to ship their belongings back to his parents' home.

At first her letters to Jim were frequent and loving. She took the time on that final day on Catalina to express her thoughts, although the note would not catch up with him until six weeks later. The rainy season had begun and she complained that she could "see nothing from the porch but fog". A curious and unaccountable winter was setting in.

Before he left for West Virginia, Doc Goddard had found Mrs. Ethel Dougherty, Norma Jean's mother-in-law, a defence job with the Radio Plane Company in Van Nuys. In her early fifties, the elder Mrs. Dougherty felt she needed the money. All of her sons would be gone soon except Marion, who contributed a modest sum to the running of the house. Her husband was semi-retired as he approached his sixties.

When Norma Jean moved in with her in-laws on Hermitage Street in North Hollywood, her days were to be spent much as they had been, cleaning an empty house while Mrs. Dougherty and Marion toiled nearby and Mr. Dougherty worked at building an addition to his daughter's home in Thousand Oaks.

According to one of her letters to Jim, there were more door-to-door salesmen than she could count, and she wondered just what was wrong with those who were not too old for service. She was offered china sets, encyclopaedias, and family plots in memorial parks. She rarely bought anything but she usually held the salesmen in conversation for a few minutes. When she did buy it was likely to be something monumental, such as a sterling silver service for twelve, purchased on time at four dollars per week. Her instalment buying would soon cut deeply into the allotment cheques the government was sending to her out of Jim's pay.

Jim's freighter had gone on to New Guinea where it joined a convoy hauling supplies to MacArthur's troops. In Italy, the Germans had the Allies pinned on to the Anzio beachhead, cutting them to pieces, and the liberation of Rome seemed remote.

Norma Jean asked Mom Dougherty to see if there was a place for her at Radio Plane Company. At first she joined an assembly-line in the chute room, where she and others carefully packed parachutes which, when attached to target planes operated by remote control, brought them down without crashing. To illustrate how easily and often Marilyn was later vilified by journalists, one was to write that she lost her job in the chute room when one of her chutes failed to open and *the pilot* died. She became quickly bored by assembly-line

methods, and asked for a transfer. She was moved along to
the dope room where liquid plastic, or "dope", was sprayed
over the cloth that became the fuselage for target planes.

Life became more congenial. Often on a Sunday she would
drive the Ford Jim had left with her over to Ana's house in
West Los Angeles. Ana had become increasingly important to
her. It would seem that Ana knew before Jim or the Doughertys of Norma Jean's growing need to be a free agent, of
her awareness, now that they were seprated, of the true status
of her marriage.

Evenings were spent with Mom Dougherty and Marion. She
resumed her poker playing and became more proficient at it,
keeping her penny winnings in a large storage jar. Sometimes
another brother-in-law, Tom Dougherty, more solemn than
Marion and religiously inclined, would drop by with his wife.
If he came alone, he and Norma Jean would hold lengthy
conversations in the kitchen. At those times she would recall
her past, the life at the orphanage (in terms less grim than
she would employ later on), the Goddards and her growing-
up years with the Bolenders. She appeared to be sorting out
her life but with little indication of what it was leading up to.

The next time Marilyn was to see Tom was at a chance meeting in Malibu in 1961, after her divorce from his brother. Tom
appeared to be delighted by the encounter and asked her to
come over for a visit sometime soon. Marilyn suddenly
turned cool and asked him, "How much is it going to cost me?"
It was the last she would see of any of the Doughertys.

Norma Jean had inherited her mother's restless energy.
Within two months of her arrival in the dope room she won
a commendation from her employers who handed her an "E"
certificate for excellence on the job.

Her co-workers, all women, must have felt her zeal unrea-
sonable. She rarely spoke to anyone, saving her conversation
for her mother-in-law whom she would meet during the half-
hour for lunch, which they ate from identical black boxes.
Marilyn was to recall in some detail the afternoon the certificate was given to her during an informal ceremony in the
dope room. There were numerous unfriendly asides and she
felt the room charged with hostility. Her bosses ignored the
reaction. They were used to handing out these citations to
unpopular workers.

That night she laid out the big "E" parchment on the dining-table for Marion and her mother-in-law to admire, then burst into tears. "The other girls are going to make life hell for me," she told them. "They've already started." Mrs. Dougherty suggested that it might be jealousy. "No," Norma Jean insisted. "It isn't jealousy. It's something else. I've felt it since I was in high school." She seemed convinced she was in for a rough time again.

Marilyn recalled that the next day as she moved back across the large factory room after getting more dope, one of the other girls jostled her, making her spill the refilled can. Norma Jean glared at the girl, but said nothing. But as she later told Marion, she was determined to remove herself "from those premises" from that moment on.

An army photographer by the name of David Conover was destined to help Norma Jean in her liberation. He had been sent to Radio Plane's plant in Van Nuys to do a photographic essay on women in war work for *Yank* magazine. The army private cased the plant for interesting angles. When he came across Norma Jean in the dope room, unhesitatingly he approached her foreman and asked if he might use her as a model. Credit must go to Conover for discovering Norma Jean Dougherty and to Emmeline Snively. What might have happened had not David Conover come to Radio Plane? Marilyn's last press secretary, Pat Newcomb, insists that Norma Jean would have created her own opportunity. She may be right.

The camera sessions lasted for three days. She was photographed spot-welding, folding parachutes, and spraying dope. And she was smiling, giving a few suggestions of her own, entirely the mistress of this new situation and new world.

A friend of Conover's, an older photographer, Potter Heweth, was so excited by her naturalness that he sought her out and made an appointment for a weekend of outdoor shooting. He made a number of colour transparencies of Norma Jean in a country setting. In one she is seen in Levis and a straw hat. Heweth, in turn, showed his colour shots to Emmeline Snively, then head of the Blue Book Model Agency in the Ambassador Hotel in Hollywood. Miss Snively sent Norma Jean a brochure describing her three months' modelling course with a handwritten note suggesting that she was wasting her time and talents in a defence plant. The vague direction Norma Jean had seen briefly at the beach at Santa

Monica and then among the sailors at Catalina was becoming sharply outlined. She called in sick the following Monday and drove to the Ambassador Hotel.

She was wearing a white sharkskin dress carefully ironed to a high gloss, which was, in Miss Snively's words, "in an excellent state of repair". A crisply efficient professional of the game, Emmeline cautioned her, "Never wear white on a modelling job. It's just no colour."

Norma Jean was informed the course was a hundred dollars, but Emmeline told her, "I may get you a job right away. You're very girl-next-doorish. They're looking for someone like you at the Pan Pacific Auditorium. The Holga Steel Company at the Industrial Show."

Norma Jean said nothing about being married and did not mention she was playing hookey from her job. Later that same afternoon she was interviewed by one of the salesmen for Holga Steel and hired at once for a ten-day stint as one of the hostesses. The pay was ten dollars a day, and since she was still drawing wages on her "sick leave" at Radio Plane, she was able to pay Emmeline the full amount for the course long before it was due.

That evening, she told Marion and her mother-in-law what she had done. They were naturally interested in her plans, but not terribly enthusiastic. Mrs. Dougherty proposed that Norma Jean write Jim and get his opinion. "Oh, there's no time for that," Norma Jean said. "I'll ask him later."

For the next ten days, she worked at the Auditorium days and spent her evenings at Emmeline's school. Nearly all of the visitors to the Industrial Show were men and they thronged about the Holga Steel booth, asking the salesmen questions about their product with the same indirection the sailors on Catalina had shown with Muggsie on her walks. A few were not so indirect and these Norma Jean fended off with some finesse.

When the Industrial Show was over she was faced with the distasteful prospect of returning to Radio Plane, and she must have felt the frustration some artists feel when the egocentricity at the heart of their work appears to be gross selfishness to others. The Doughertys did not openly state their disapproval, but there was about the house an air of mourning as though Trust had died.

There is some evidence that Norma Jean still believed she

loved Jim and would have to extricate herself slowly so there would be no total breakdown in her relations with the Doughertys. Her letters, which were turning up on his ship in the Far-East with less frequency, indicate that she thought she did. He was, after all, a benefactor as well as a husband, and neither Norma Jean nor her alter-ego, Marilyn, ever dismissed a benefactor from her life who had done her no wrong. There were always reasons, some of them tenuous, for permanent breaks.

She confided some of her anxieties to Emmeline, still not revealing her married status for fear her chances might be destroyed. Uncertainty often made Norma Jean and later Marilyn dissemble. Emmeline remembers telling her, "Don't worry, Norma Jean. Go back to the plant. You're lucky to have some security during this early period. Some girls who don't know typing or shorthand just starve. I'll have you out of there for good in less than six months."

Jim was not especially critical when he answered her letter that began, "Jim, I must tell you something. . . ." His answer seemed tolerant. The truth was, as Jim remembered it years later, that he was used by then to the unpredictable young woman he had married and was in love with. It had taken time for this strong emotion to develop, but it had, and now it must have hurt him rather badly to see she was making a claim for some kind of life of her own. He can't recall ever having blamed her for his predicament; if anyone was culpable, it was Grace Goddard. He would come in time to agree with Marilyn about that.

As Norma Jean's involvement with her new career deepened, time became more precious than sleep. She would work her eight-hour shift at Radio Plane, then drive to Hollywood for evening classes. Dinner was eaten on the run. There was one helpless victim of all this rushing. Muggsie. The Doughertys had problems of their own; all of them were out working during the day and Muggsie was left to fend for herself from early morning until Norma Jean got home late at night. A year later, the pet was dead.

Norma Jean heard about Muggsie's death by way of a phone call from Mrs. Dougherty. By then she had returned to Ana Lower's apartment in West Los Angeles to live, a move the Dougherty family must have considered a prelude to her leaving Jim.

CHAPTER TWO

When Norma Jean's first lay-out appeared, its captive army audience was enchanted. David Conover, who had done the photography, sent Norma Jean a note suggesting she consider modelling as a career and forget the defence work.

But she had already quit Radio Plane; several magazine covers and a few calendars for Earl Moran had given her the courage to give up her job. Conover's note arrived about the time Norma Jean was becoming one of Emmeline's busiest models.

There were two jobs for Douglas Aircraft at twenty-five dollars a day, and she was given the *star* treatment. They picked her up at Emmeline's headquarters in a new station wagon, drove her out to their vast installation, escorted her to the executive dining-room where she was viewed with considerable interest, and returned her seven hours later to the Ambassador Hotel.

"Lower your smile," Emmeline instructed Norma Jean. A photographer in New York who had been sent some shots of her had found a flaw in her appearance. Her nose was too long.

Emmeline recalled that Norma Jean seemed puzzled and held up a profile shot as proof of the man's mistake. "It's the shadow, dear," Emmeline explained. "There isn't enough upper lip between the end of your nose and your mouth." And then she walked around Norma Jean, studying her face, holding her chin in her hand a moment, and nodding to herself.

"Try smiling with your upper lip drawn down."

Norma Jean's mouth quivered a little with the effort, but she managed to lower her smile a notch.

"*There!* Now your smile keeps your nose in place. Just practise that a while so you don't make the mistake again. You can do it tonight at home before a mirror."

Norma Jean was never to feel entirely secure with that smile. Years later, after stardom had come, her lips would still move uncertainly as she smiled, and the movement would become part of her style.

She had already begun talking with Emmeline of the movies

as a possibility. Emmeline told her that most of her "better girls" would find more security in a stock contract at a studio than in photography assignments. "Otherwise," she said, "you'd better learn secretarial work or else get married."

"But I *am* married," Norma Jean confessed.

"Well it isn't the first time I've been fibbed to," Emmeline recalls telling her with a tinge of disappointment. Norma Jean looked distressed. She preferred to believe that she was an open, even a candid, person.

"I know," Emmeline said consolingly. "You were afraid to tell me."

"He's away. In the war. A nice man. I was living with his folks until a few weeks ago."

"And what does *he* say about your modelling?" Emmeline asked.

"Not much. I guess if he wrote me the truth, he'd say he didn't like it."

The next day she brought in her wedding pictures to show Emmeline. "He has a nice Irish face," Emmeline said.

The war had ended in Europe by the time Norma Jean moved in with Aunt Ana, but there was no possibility of Jim's early return. At the moment when the Enola Gay B-29 dropped its awesome pay-load over Hiroshima on August 6, 1945, changing the world's course irrevocably, Jim was off the coast of Argentina. His ship went on to Montevideo and Trinidad and finally ended its long cruise in New York Harbour. Once ashore, he tried to reach Norma Jean by phone, but Ana told him she was "somewhere", she wasn't sure just where. "You know she isn't home very much, Jim."

Something in the casualness of Ana's voice aroused Jim. He was certain she knew far more of Norma Jean's plans than she was saying. He decided to leave the Maritime Service and catch a plane back to Los Angeles and his busy wife. But his application for discharge was rejected. There was no one available to replace him, and every ship the United States owned or could commandeer was being put into service in a massive effort to bring the troops home.

It has been said that Norma Jean discarded Jim Dougherty with ease. The truth was that she did not. Life with Jim had a simplicity that safely anchored her. Love-making had been as easy, as pristine really, as washing her face, and she knew before leaving the Doughertys that there were grey wolves

and cunning foxes running through the scrub and back alleys
of the Hollywood hills. She must have experienced some fear
of the unknown ahead of her. Besides Aunt Ana, whose health
was failing, there was no one to reassure her. Her decision to
leave Jim was much the biggest gamble of her life so far, although there would be greater risks taken later with much
less hesitancy. One wonders how much strength she drew
from the frail reed of Ana's "I believe you've done the right
thing."

Ana Lower was then in her late sixties, but she ran her
household with little or no outside help, and when her blood
pressure mounted she retired to her bedroom with *Science
and Health*.

Norma Jean had been given her own room. She had a bedside table with a lamp for reading in bed. During her first
week with Ana she went to the nearby Westwood branch of
the public library and took out a card.

The two women attended services at the Christian Science
Church five blocks away every Sunday morning. For Ana,
there was also a Wednesday night testimonial service. Norma
Jean didn't wish to hear a recital of other persons' ills and
triumphs.

Doc and Grace Goddard returned to Los Angeles from
West Virginia in 1946. Doc remembers that Grace went
straightaway to Ana's and then waited for Norma Jean to
return from a modelling appointment.

"I've heard from your mother," Grace told Norma Jean.
"She's spoken with her doctors. They say she's well enough to
come out." Grace explained that she was taking Gladys in
with them "because she has to have a place to stay or they
won't permit her to leave".

While waiting for her mother's return to the city, she visited
the elder Mrs. Dougherty and Marion. She seemed to them
more relaxed, more in control, than she had ever been in her
life. It was only when she mentioned her mother's imminent
arrival that her mood seemed to darken.

Her mother-in-law told her amusing anecdotes about Radio
Plane, and now Norma Jean could laugh about it, sustaining
her high level squeak for quite a long time, rather like a
trolley-bus grating on its rails.

Soon after that visit, she learned that Jim was coming back

for reassignment. He had written Norma Jean and his mother the same week, giving them dates and telling them a few things he wanted to do. And then he arrived, blessedly before Gladys did. He was on leave from the base camp where they were holding him for transfer to another ship. With a yellowish tan acquired from atabrine and months of duty around New Guinea, he showed up at Ana's first, just to keep things straight.

Norma Jean sat on his lap and they kissed unashamedly with Ana rocking in a nearby chair, delighted to be part of the reunion. It was later, Jim remembers, that he saw the small pile of unpaid bills for dresses, shoes, sweaters, and blouses from Bullock's and other stores. "What happened to my allotment?" he wanted to know.

"It always goes," she said airily. "All that is an investment in myself. I've got to have these things when I go out on a job. If you're dressed well, they pay higher fees. If you're in a hand-me-down, they'll try to take advantage of you."

"Sure, Norma," he told her, trying to mask the discomfiture in his voice. "Sure. That makes sense." There was something over three hundred dollars in his wallet, savings from crisscrossing the China Seas and the sea lanes around New Guinea, winnings from gambling, savings from beers and women he'd declined to have. It was intended for one long blast with his wife, a night at the Coconut Grove, a lunch or two at the Brown Derby, and, yes, even a *new outfit* for her. He had imagined handing her a fifty-dollar bill and telling her, "Blow it all on some clothes, honey."

When she took the money she wept a little in gratitude. "I know it's a lot of money, Jim. I'll make it up to you some way."

Gladys phoned Grace Goddard from the bus terminal in San Francisco before boarding the express to Los Angeles. The nine hours the trip required enabled Grace to phone Norma Jean and make some plans. "We'll pick you and Jim up and then we'll all go to the depot," Grace said.

When the San Francisco express pulled into the Greyhound station, Gladys was one of the last to get off. Jim recalls that she was wearing a white summer dress and white shoes. Except for her flowered hat, she looked like a nurse going off duty.

Grace went up and embraced her, then brought her back to the others. The mother looked at her daughter, barely recognizing the young woman she had become. Norma Jean seemed uncomfortable and attempted a smile that failed. They didn't kiss, although Gladys shook Jim's hand.

An awkward dinner followed at the Goddard home. Even Doc seemed at a loss for anything humorous to lift the pall. There was such a large blank to fill in for Gladys that no one knew where to begin. But Grace managed a monologue, telling Gladys of their recent life in West Virginia and of her stepdaughter Beebe's sudden and unfortunate marriage.

Once Gladys was settled in with the Goddards, Norma Jean relied upon the telephone to keep in touch. "I'll be over as soon as Jim goes back to sea," she told her mother.

There were some modelling appointments she couldn't break during the next week or two, but she and Jim managed to spend just enough time together to make her uncertain again. She needed Jim physically; there was an ache when he left from which it took her days to recover. And she was troubled by the ease with which he glossed over her indebtedness. She had expected a quarrel but got compliance instead. She seemed unaware of the depth of his disappointment.

Jim went back to sea deeply disturbed. He was certain he was losing Norma Jean, and he was disgusted that he seemed to have tried to buy her back with his savings. He felt helpless to deal with this cruel dedication of hers. There was no other way to describe it. And he knew this was only the beginning.

With Jim gone again, Norma Jean decided she might make a better daughter than a wife. The three-room apartment below Ana's place became vacant, and Norma Jean rented it and brought Gladys in with her.

It was not a happy arrangement. Nothing involving Gladys could be. But neither was it disastrous. Gladys had become interested in Christian Science while in the last sanatorium, and the two older women and Norma Jean attended the services nearly every Sunday morning. Occasionally, Norma Jean had been on a late date Saturday evening and would sleep through, prompting Gladys to awaken her. But Ana gracefully intervened and made Gladys see that sleep was crucial for her daughter.

One winter afternoon early in 1946, Gladys left their apartment without a word to anyone – at least no advance word to Norma Jean, who had left in the morning rain for an early modelling appointment. Gladys got into her white dress and shoes and a new picture hat and took a taxi over to the Ambassador Hotel where Emmeline Snively had her agency.

Emmeline has a vivid memory of that unexpected visit. She was startled by the apparition, but recovered quickly, and the two ladies spent half an hour seated among the palms of the lobby, discussing Norma Jean's career. When Gladys got up to leave she took Emmeline's hand and said, "I only came so I could thank you personally for what you've been doing for Norma Jean. You've given her a whole new life."

Gladys stayed with her daughter for about seven months. There is no doubt about the mother's ambivalent feelings concerning her daughter's "new life". She was excited about its growing success and frightened by its perils. When Norma Jean was asked by the photographer André de Diennes (who already had shown through the pensive flowers he was sending that he was interested in the young woman as well as the model) to accompany him for a week of outdoor shooting in the Northwest (they would live in his trailer), Gladys was distressed and told her daughter as much, but Norma Jean went. And, naturally enough, many of Norma Jean's evenings were spent having dinner with men she met in her work: photographers, illustrators, actors, and agents.

Before the end of summer, Gladys had fretted herself into a state of nerves no palliatives could soothe. She asked the sanatorium to take her back, and she disappeared from Norma Jean's life. Although Marilyn's visits to her mother would be infrequent, those who were her closest friends always met Gladys. Paula Strasberg recalls the one meeting she had with the mother, who by then had married a Mr. Ely on one of her lengthy excursions into the world outside. Marilyn had taken Paula to Rock Haven Sanatorium, a private nursing home, and Paula later said: "I was amazed to see how much Mrs. Ely resembled Marilyn. It was uncanny. She was still a beautiful woman despite the ravages of her illness."

By mid-spring 1946, Jim was in Shanghai, and he left his ship to go into the city to look around. It was his first real glimpse of China, and he recalls the excitement he felt when he saw the hordes of Chinese choking the streets. The war had driven hundreds of thousands of refugees into the city and many of them had remained there, having no homes to go back to.

He recalls one day when he finally broke free of the side-streets and entered a shopping arcade festooned with lanterns. He was relieved to see a number of other American sailors around him, all fingering the jade pieces, tinkling the glass hangings, and rubbing the hand-carved boxes and figurines. He saw a carved wooden camphor chest, ideal for handker-chiefs, scarves, old letters, and photographs, and he bought it for Norma Jean.

When he reached his ship around four in the afternoon the men were having mail call and, as he came up the gangplank, his name was called out. The mail clerk eyed him peculiarly as he handed him a letter. The return address on the envelope was that of an attorney in Las Vegas.

He gripped the letter so tightly, he had to smooth it out below deck before he could read it. Then he tossed the camphor box on to his bunk and tore open the letter, half know-ing what it would say. It began "Dear Mr. Dougherty:" but it was a *Dear John* and the words were impersonal, dead words.

He lay back in his bunk, his eyes squeezed shut, hot with anger and the conviction that he was a damned fool, but he remembers, too, that he was full of anxiety for the future of Norma Jean.

CHAPTER THREE

Las Vegas, Nev.
May 25th, 1946

Dear Miss Snively,

I'm having lots of rest and I'm getting tan. It's very warm and honestly the sun shines all the time.

Las Vegas is really a colourful town with the Helldorado celebration and all. It lasted for five days, they had rodeos and parades every day.

Roy Rogers was in town making a picture. I met him and rode his horse "Trigger" (cross my heart I did!). What a horse!

I was walking down the street one day last week and noticed they were shooting a movie so like everyone else I

stood and watched. In between shootings a couple of fellows
from Republic Studio walked over to me and asked me if I
would please come over and meet some actor (I don't remember his name. I think his last name was Cristy or something like that). Anyway he wanted to meet me so I did and
I met most of the studio people including Roy Rogers and
I rode his horse, gee he is nice.

They asked me to have dinner with them at the Last
Frontier and then we went to the rodeo. What a day! Ever
since I've been signing autograph books and cowboy [sic]
hats. When I try to tell these kids I'm not in pictures they
think I'm just trying to avoid signing their books, so I sign
them.

They've gone now. It's quite lonely here in Las Vegas.
This is certainly a wild town.

Miss Snively, I would love to hear from you and hear
what's new.

Please give my best regards to Mrs. Snively and Miss
Smith, also to Dick Miller if you see him. I hope [he] has
been able to sell some of those pictures, he is so nice.

Is John Randolph or Paul Parry back in town yet? How's
Mr. Bloom? I wonder if Eccleston Agency is ever going to
pay me? Do you ever hear from Mr. Willinger about me?

I didn't know six weeks could pass so slowly.

I will write again soon.

Love,

Norma Jean.

She had taken a furnished room and felt lucky to get it.
The town was crowded with tourists coming in for the rodeo
and other events. Hotel space was quickly snatched up. Bug-
gsy Seigel and friends had not yet constructed The Flamingo,
and there was no such thing in those days as The Strip.

At nineteen, she was probably among the youngest divorce
candidates in residence at the time. She felt no bitterness; all
of her memories of Jim were pleasant ones, and if she never
saw him again, she could look back on her life as Mrs. James
Dougherty with few regrets. But apparently she *did* want to
see him again. She indicated to Emmeline Snively and others
she was in touch with at the time that she hoped she could
remain friendly with her ex-husband when she got her decree.

The stock movie contract Emmeline had discussed was behind the whole ordeal. Norma Jean's feeling that she was cutting herself off from her past must have been acute, but only a trace of the loneliness she must have felt crept into the letter to Emmeline. She later told Jim that she was being treated as an out-patient at Las Vegas General Hospital for a bad mouth infection that made eating difficult. She had several bad attacks of nerves.

But she felt compelled to go through with it. Few studios would sign up a married potential starlet for fear she would become pregnant before the expensive training period began to pay off. To Norma Jean, the contract was worth any sacrifice. Not only would it groom her for stardom, but it would fill in the cultural blanks she so keenly felt. Meanwhile, though she knew she would be financially and emotionally undernourished, she was increasingly preoccupied with the question of her final success. Everything started and ended with that.

Two decades after she left Las Vegas with her divorce decree, Jim Dougherty was shown Norma Jean's letters to Emmeline. He recalled she had met Roy Rogers earlier with him in a western goods store near Van Nuys where Jim was buying some boots. "He kidded with her for a while when I was trying them on. He probably isn't aware he had two encounters with Marilyn Monroe."

Back in Los Angeles with her decree, Norma Jean found Emmeline full of plans. She privately believed her protégée's hair needed altering. It wasn't really blonde enough. It was also kept so tightly curled by permanents that on one occasion when a pillbox hat was placed on her head, the effect was comical. "I have a call for a light blonde, honey or platinum. Wavy, not curly hair," Emmeline told her.

The change was accomplished in one session at the beauty salon, and the shampoo client had helped create a new and more negotiable Norma Jean.

Before Emmeline could send her to the Paramount lot for what was actually a second visit (she had spoken with one of the executives there before her Las Vegas trip), a rush call came through from a man at the Goldwyn Studios. Marilyn recalled the details in later years, frequently telling the story and punctuating it with laughter. Emmeline apparently blocked the whole episode out of her memory.

The man at the Goldwyn Studios was of indeterminate years and pasted his black hair to his scalp with scented oil. More distressingly, he was wearing the sort of plaid jacket Norma Jean had always associated with track followers.

Marilyn remembered asking him if he had summoned her for a particular part but he said "I'll ask the questions." He was nervously bouncing up and down on his heels and looking up in some alarm whenever footsteps were heard along the corridor outside. She wondered if his authority to hire people might somehow be in question.

Then the man said, "Now I'd like to see a little more of your leg."

"All right," she said, her voice more uncertain than the man's credentials. "But only if I have my hat on." And she placed a wide-brimmed hat on her head.

At this point a woman wearing thick glasses peered inside. She seemed to be astonished by what she saw. The man shoved past her and fled down the hall.

Emmeline, although she put it out of her mind as quickly as she could, was very angry with herself. To remedy the damage, if any, she spent all of that afternoon lining up appointments for Norma Jean. Marilyn remembered her saying something about "exposure" being what she needed. Then both women began laughing.

Emmeline managed it for Norma Jean. Covers appeared on *Laff* and *Peek* and *See*, as well as *U.S. Camera*. It was the great era of the photographic essay, launched by *Life* and its less sophisticated rival, *Look*, accompanied by a boom in amateur photography. And Emmeline was not above practising a bit of press agentry on Norma Jean's behalf. She recommended that she reverse her first name, adding an "n" to create a new surname. "Who wants to see Dougherty on a marquee?" she asked. She composed a publicity item and sent it off to Hedda Hopper and Louella Parsons: *Howard Hughes must be on the road to recovery. He turned over in his iron lung and wanted to know more about Jean Norman, this month's cover girl on Laff Magazine.*

This fiction came at a time when Hughes was receiving worldwide attention following a near-fatal plane crash on the Los Angeles Country Club fairway. Emmeline had been inspired by his recent successful promotion of the monumental Jane Russell, whose single film at the time, *The Outlaw,* was causing critics and vice squads alike to form outraged posses to bring its makers to book.

So effective was this invention (both gossip columnists published it the same day to their horror), inquiries began coming in at once. Norma Jean was never quite sure that Hughes *hadn't* seen her cover. More than a decade later, Marilyn related the episode to an interviewer as a factual part of her background.

In late 1946, Jim Dougherty at last won his discharge from the Maritime Service and decided to go into business in Van Nuys. There was a succession of new women in his life, but he couldn't shake the spectre of Norma Jean. His deep affection for her was something he couldn't put out of his mind, and then, less romantically, she was causing him personal annoyance.

Blithe about such humdrum things as restricted parking areas, Norma Jean always parked as near to a photographer's studio as she could get with the Dougherty Ford. The result was a string of parking tickets. She had in mind paying the first two or three when she caught up on her bills. But when she had a dozen, she became frightened and successfully blocked them from her mind.

Jim was still listed with the state as owner of the car. The Los Angeles police notified him that he was a "scofflaw", and a date was set for a hearing.

Before that day rolled around, Norma Jean ran into the rear of a priest's car, demolishing it. The priest wasn't injured, nor was Norma Jean. But the following week an attorney representing the clergyman called on Jim.

"I'm divorced from Mrs. Dougherty," Jim told the lawyer. "My only suggestion to you is to file suit against her as driver of the car." There was a grey area of the law involved here. Norma Jean had never made any effort to have the car's registration changed to her name, but Jim was no longer responsible for any of his ex-wife's obligations. The attorney said he would discuss the matter with his client, and, as it turned out, that was the end of it.

Norma Jean's indebtedness was a serious problem. Although her modelling fees were going up and her jobs were keeping her busy nearly every day, she was running huge bills at dress shops, a fur salon, and a Westwood book shop. She

sold her sterling silver service and her engagement ring. Jim
decided he must straighten out the tickets with Norma Jean,
and he phoned her at Ana's. She seemed delighted to hear
from him and asked that he come right over. When he reached
Ana's house, Norma Jean was waiting for him at the top of
the outside stairway. She took his hand in hers and seemed
genuinely happy to see him.

Once they were in the living-room, Norma Jean sat across
from Jim, quietly studying him for a minute or two. "You
look so different, Jim. I guess you are different."

"Maybe it's the clothes," Jim said. "You remember me in a
sailor suit." He recalls he was wearing a light-blue nylon suit
and striped tie.

"Maybe," she said.

Confronting her like this in the flesh, some of Jim's determination left him and the void was filled at once by the old
protectiveness. "Are you doing all right, Norma?" he asked.

"Have you seen any of my covers?" she wanted to know.

"Yeah. They're great," Jim told her. "But I mean you, not
your work. Are you happy?"

The question seemed to have caught her by surprise. Jim
recalls that she considered it for a minute or two, and then
said, "I guess I should be. During the day, I'm fine. But sometimes in the evening, well I wish there was someone to take
me out who doesn't expect anything from me. You know what
I mean?"

Jim knew what she meant and wondered if she would ask
him now to take her out or wait a few days and call him up.
The idea that she would drop him as a husband because he
was in her way and then talk about her loneliness angered
him. He brought up the matter of the parking tickets and
mentioned the visit by the priest's attorney.

"I'll pay the tickets," she said without hesitation. "In instalments, like everything else. About the priest, I'll wait and see
what happens."

Finally Jim got up to leave. As he stood in her doorway
she said, "We could go out sometime. I know I'd like that."

Jim said, "Okay. Sometime. Goodbye, Norma."

"Goodbye, Jim," she said. And Jim Dougherty walked
down the stairs and completely out of her life.

The Hughes story had reaped a harvest of propositions,

varying in legitimacy. To Emmeline, the publicity had made it a dead certainty that Norma Jean would be approached by one of the studios. Although most of her successful models wound up in films, movies were out of her field.

"I want you to see a friend of mine," she told Norma Jean. "I'm not up to handling a thing like this. It has to be done right. But I have a connection, Helen Ainsworth. It's her line, and she does it every day of the week. I was telling her about you while you were in Vegas."

Helen Ainsworth was a huge woman (over fourteen stone) in charge of the west coast branch of a talent agency with the unlikely name of National Concert Artists Corporation. She very carefully screened the best prospects from Emmeline, rather like an industrial recruiter on a college campus. Miss Ainsworth had been briefed by Emmeline in the basic facts of Norma Jean's past. She knew she was recently divorced and was a favourite of photographers and artists. When they met, the agent was encouraging and turned Norma Jean over to one of the agency's talent representatives, Harry Lipton.

Lipton interviewed her and later said that she was "so unsure of herself – that terrible background of hers had done it – it gave her a quality that set her apart". She was signed on as a client with Lipton in personal charge.

On July 16, 1946, Norma Jean, emboldened by her agency contract, paid a call on the Fox studios and received her first disillusionment. There was no glamour visible in the guard room. It was much more like a factory entrance. There were ashtrays of the garbage can variety and a cracked leather sofa. She walked up to the guard sitting behind a glass window (she later described it as being "bulletproof") and asked to see Ben Lyon, head of casting for Fox.

Lyon's secretary asked the guard if she had an appointment and Norma Jean volunteered the information that she did not, but that "my agent recommended that I see him". Lyon recalled that his secretary relayed Norma Jean's message and he said, "You know you don't have to have an appointment to see me. Send her in."

Norma Jean walked into Lyon's office and he was at once struck by her beauty – golden hair falling to her shoulders, the smile of an innocent child, an inexpensive cotton print dress encasing an astonishing figure.

"What can I do for you?" Lyon asked.

"I want more than anything to get into pictures," she said.

"Honey," Lyon told her, "you're in pictures."

Ben Lyon's instinct for movie talent had been developed through more than two decades of steady employment on both sides of the camera. He had been a film star of some magnitude some eighteen years earlier during the first years of talking pictures. He had had the sleek good looks of a well-groomed spaniel, his face perhaps too balanced in its proportions. His last important film had been *Hell's Angels* for Howard Hughes, and it was at his suggestion that Jean Harlow replaced the unintelligible Scandinavian, Greta Nissen. During World War II, Ben and his ex-screen-star wife, Bebe Daniels, had established themselves in England with their own programme on the B.B.C., *At Home with the Lyons*. Their popularity was highest at about the time Gracie Fields was at the peak of her celebrity.

During the interview that followed, Norma Jean was asked about her background and training. Apparently there was a pause as she considered the vast and empty reaches of her past, but then she said, "I've tried to pick up all the camera experience I can around the photographers who've used me." Lyon, grown slightly cynical during his career, wondered if the innocence – the uncertain smile, the unpretentious, nearly inconspicuous dress – was a pose, but when he asked her where she lived and she told him "the Studio Club", he knew that she was not playing the Hollywood Game, that she was obstinately relying upon her own ability and promise.

Before Norma Jean left Lyon's office, a test option for contract was set up and Lyon handed her the script of a scene which Judy Holliday had used earlier in *Winged Victory*. On the following day, Lyon got in touch with Harry Lipton and they agreed upon the terms, subject to the studio's approval of the test. Norma Jean's prospective salary – $75 weekly – was less than she was making during a good week of modelling, but she was ecstatic about it. The contract was renewable on a six-months' option basis with increases each time of $25, rising to a ceiling of $1500 during the seventh year.

Lyon called Walter Lang who was shooting a Technicolor film with Betty Grable, and asked if he would shoot colour film of Norma Jean when he finished his day's work. Lyon explained that Darryl Zanuck, production chief at Fox, might be disappointed in the black and white test since the girl had never performed before – even in high school. "She can't miss if Zanuck sees the colour," he explained. Lang understood and it was agreed.

Lyon then escorted her to the wardrobe department, where the head personally selected a gown for her to wear, then on to the principal hairdresser, and finally to the make-up man. By six o'clock both Lang and Lyon were on their own time but felt enthusiastic enough about Norma Jean not to care. Lang sat her on a stool in front of the camera and shot 100 feet of silent film, talking quietly to her all the while to ease her nervousness.

The following day Lyon ran off the test and saw that Norma Jean was all he had hoped she would be on the screen. He secretly placed the test in Zanuck's projection room where the production head screened his films at night. Less than a week later, Zanuck was on the phone telling Lyon that he had seen a test of a "gorgeous girl" and asked if the studio had a contract with her. Lyon said, "Yes. The test was for an option." Zanuck told him to exercise the option.

Norma Jean's composure cracked when she was given the good news by Lyon. She wept convulsively, shaking her head in disbelief. When she got herself in hand, Lyon told her. "We're going to have to do something about your name. I don't think 'Norma Jean Dougherty' sounds very much like a movie star, do you?" He reached for a casting directory and flipped through the pages. Finding nothing of any use, he closed his eyes for a moment of concentration. Then suddenly he said, "I knew a girl in New York named Marilyn Miller. She was a star in the musicals *Sally* and *Sunny*."

"That's a lovely name," Norma Jean said, after repeating it aloud.

Lyon nodded and observed, "To me, you're a Marilyn, and Marilyn Miller is dead now."

"But I don't want to take her whole name," Norma Jean said cautiously. "She must have been pretty famous and people will remember her." Then she bit her lower lip, covering the action with her fingers, a habit while thinking that would persist. "What about using my grandmother's last name, Monroe?" she asked.

"That's it, then," Lyon said. "You're Marilyn Monroe."

Before leaving that day, Marilyn, in some embarrassment,

asked Lyon if she could have an advance of $15 on her salary
to pay two weeks' back rent at the Studio Club. Lyon explained that such an advance would not look very good at
the front office, but he reached into his wallet and handed
her the money. Later he was to tell some friends that Marilyn
was one of the few people he had loaned money to who ever
paid him back.

She was always grateful. A half-dozen years later, when
Harry Lipton and Emmeline were seemingly forgotten, she
sent Lyon a photograph inscribed:

"You found me, named me and believed in me when no one
else did.

"My love and thanks forever."

PART THREE

Marilyn

CHAPTER ONE

Only rarely does a stage or film name give its owner an entirely new identity. For Marilyn Monroe, it meant the abandonment of a hand-me-down kind of existence.

When Grace Goddard signed Marilyn's contract, consenting to the terms of her ward's employment by the film studio, both parties knew it was only a formality. Marilyn quickly turned her back on Norma Jean and Norma Jean's associates and began to identify totally with her new self, her role as a film actress. It has been an enduring myth that Marilyn suffered from loss of identity. The truth was that she soon felt completely at home with *Marilyn*. The only uncomfortable element in her life was the intrusive past, the ghost of Norma Jean. At times Marilyn would regress to a giggling young woman and Norma Jean seemed about to reappear, but the point had to be conceded eventually – it was *Marilyn* giggling. The new person of Marilyn was to be accepted finally as half-child, half-woman.

To make this transformation required considerable will. On those few occasions when it happened to others, success had made it easy to forget an earlier life. Harlean Carpentier was quickly buried when Jean Harlow emerged from a year or two of walk-ons and comedy bits to become the sensation of *Hell's Angels*. But success was not to come to Marilyn for another four years.

During the year between August 1946 and 1947 at the Fox studio, Marilyn walked through the vast acreage of the company with all the apprehension of a traveller through an alien land, whose papers aren't quite in order. She expected her presence, so largely ignored by the management, to be challenged at any moment and a dismissal slip to appear in her next pay envelope.

There were reasons for this disregard. Aside from Marilyn's pitiful lack of dramatic training, Betty Grable was reigning queen of the Fox lot and, short of abdication, there seemed small likelihood she could be nudged from her throne. Not only was she in excellent health, but her box-office appeal had grown with the recent war, during which she and Rita Hayworth had vied as the favourite pin-up of the soldiers. When she was Marilyn's age, twenty, Grable already had completed a tour in vaudeville with Wheeler and Woolsey and a small role in the much-revived Rogers and Astaire musical, *Follow the Fleet*.

In the wings was June Haver, another shapely blonde, who would achieve a certain fame before renouncing Hollywood for an abortive try at sisterhood in a convent. All of Ben Lyon's early enthusiasm echoed hollowly in Marilyn's mind as the weeks passed.

And yet things were happening, however inconsequential they may have seemed. There were studio classes in voice and body movement. There was the usual ritual of swimsuit shots, appearances at restaurant openings and conventions. Marilyn brought to these an excitement that was to create a demand for her services in that peripheral field.

There was also, finally, a film early in the second six months of her first stay at Fox. June Haver was given a rural romantic comedy, *Scudda Hoo, Scudda Hay,* in the wake of the success of a rival studio's film version of *The Egg and I*. Marilyn was assigned with another starlet to go boating in one scene. There were one or two close shots of the girls in their rowboat, which were later edited out of the film. An additional scene in which she appeared in the foreground was also removed, probably because her identity in the film was by now obscure. As released, Marilyn was a remote and faceless figure on the far horizon. She discovered that a film editor wielded enormous power. Once one of your scenes was cut and your role diminished, the excision widened like a ruptured wound and other bits spilled out. It was a difficult lesson to take, but one she was never to forget.

Then for some weeks there was nothing but her studies, the public appearances, and her determination. The latter gave her a semblance of success. She carefully chose what she would wear each day, preferring things as form-fitting as possible or loosely diaphanous. She managed a smile for everyone who looked her way and got on a first-name basis with most of the grips, the property men, assistant directors, and occasionally a member of the studio hierarchy.

One of these encounters on a studio street would help to shape her future. Joseph M. Schenck, then an executive producer at Fox, was leaving the lot in his limousine when he passed Marilyn, who recognized him as one of the executives and gave him a friendly smile. Joe Schenck asked his chauffeur to stop the car and called Marilyn over, asked her name, and learned that she was on the studio payroll. Handing her a card on which he jotted down his home telephone number, he told her, "Call me about dinner around this time next week."

It is unlikely that Joe was in any sense Marilyn's sponsor. She was hungry for a decent meal and he had seen something of the Orphan Annie helplessness and endearing bravado that had won over nearly everyone Norma Jean/Marilyn met face-to-face.

Joe was still a figure of considerable power in the Hollywood he had helped create when he had followed his colleagues – Sam Goldwyn and Cecil B. De Mille – west. He had negotiated the merger of 20th Century Pictures, a new producing company he had formed with his brother Nicholas, William Goetz, and Darryl F. Zanuck, with Fox in 1935.

Joe Schenck was born on Christmas Day, 1878, in Rybinsk, Russia, a village on the Volga where his father was in the wood fuel business. His family emigrated to New York, and when barely out of his teens Schenck was already a success, having created the still-existing Palisades Amusement Park in New Jersey.

Schenck and Marilyn had much in common. They shared a feeling that the senses were more reliable than the intellect. Curiously, three years later when she first met Arthur Miller, Marilyn did not trust her instincts. She wrongly assumed that he had to be an intellectual and thus created needless problems for herself. Schenck was perhaps the first important film producer to realize that the public wanted to know who was in a film more than what it was about or even how good it might be. He helped create the star system, signing the Talmadge Sisters, Fatty Arbuckle, and Buster Keaton.

This is not to suggest that Marilyn was not as eager to improve her mind as she was her dramatic ability. But her approach to culture was through her feelings, abstract ideas

always remaining outside her grasp. Joe Schenck had even
fewer pretensions than Marilyn. There was almost never a
book around his house, at least none that bore evidence of
having been opened. His approach to life was tactile. He was
a sensualist whose life would become less tolerable with the
onset of age. But even then he had a keen appreciation of
women. He prized a beautiful woman the way certain men
prize fine stallions.

Within a few weeks, Marilyn was a regular at Schenck's
small dinner-parties. Having already achieved the combinations of curves and blonde innocence that the public would
know during the following decade, she was careful about her
appearance whenever she visited him. She would arrive in the
echoing, barely furnished entrance hall to his hill-top home,
usually a little breathless to cover her tardiness, and then
would give him a kiss that was something more than show-
business affection, where everyone uses terms of endearment
in wholesale fashion and kisses are *de rigueur* upon greeting
acquaintances after first meetings. But it was also something
less than passionate, and it was as close as she would ever come
to fulfilling the charge that she was mistress to this man nearing his seventieth year.

Schenck never permitted women to use him, although his
dogged devotion had allowed one or two to abuse him. Norma
Talmadge, for whom Schenck entered movie-making, resented
his cigars and cronies right up to their divorce. But she had
come through as a successful film commodity and the returns
were great for both of them.

A man of average height and sturdy physique who in his
youth and middle years had the slightly hunched look of a
beefy wrestler, Schenck was not handsome. He had a perpetual
squint and his smile was upside-down, perhaps from biting
down hard on so many cigars. Now in his sixty-ninth year, he
had outlived his wives, his flesh had lost its tone, and he was
beginning to resemble an ageing Chinese warlord.

During the several decades of his total engagement with
life, he had been game for anything, and often on impulse
would take half a dozen of his friends to Paris or Palm Springs
– distance didn't matter. Even as he moved into old age, he
continued to dissipate in a healthy way: late hours with congenial friends, liquor and cigars in moderation. Only when he
was approaching death in his eighties did he show signs of

senility. He became overly anxious (for a millionaire) about the cost of things, worrying over the price of meals at Chasen's or Romanoff's.

Joe Schenck once said he had to buy his friends. It is not improbable that Marilyn, listening late into the night as Schenck made this comment, remembered it. As Marilyn's income began to rise in the next decade of her life, there were to be few friends who weren't in some way added to her payroll.

Schenck's genius had been in manipulating money and people, not ideas. The wisdom Marilyn was to value so much in him came, among other things, from the disappointments of his life. On one mantel stood a photo of one of those disappointments, actress Jean Howard, whom he had loved desperately but who had chosen to marry Charles Feldman. Feldman was an agent who would represent Marilyn for a time before he became an eminent producer.

Another wholly gratuitous hurt, Schenck felt, was his jailing for income-tax evasion in the early forties. He had served four months and five days at the U.S. Correction Institute in Danbury, Connecticut, and he had been granted a full pardon by President Truman only two years before he first met Marilyn. The charge and conviction constituted a clear case of manipulation of justice by the government and had outraged Truman when he learned the details of it. What had landed Schenck in this imbroglio was his payment of $50,000 a year in bribes to union racketeers Willie Bioff and George Browne, rulers of the stagehands' union. The payoffs were covered up by trusted bookkeepers over the years. When Schenck co-operated in the government's case against Bioff and Browne, an income-tax evasion charge was dropped and he was convicted of perjury for lying about the matter in the first place. Hollywood studio heads, equally guilty, closed ranks behind him. This solidarity and affection were not totally unselfish, of this Schenck was fully aware. He frequently advised Marilyn to be alert to the pretence in Hollywood, and it was probably he who taught Marilyn not to trust easily studio executives.

With Marilyn, Joe Schenck developed a closeness that time – old age in fact – made comfortable for both of them. Her new life as Marilyn was not yet a year old, but there were few allusions made to her years as Norma Jean in his presence. He pretended disinterest, knowing there was remembered hurt there.

Curiosity and concern may have led him to ask at one point

for a showing of Marilyn's test. If he did, he could not have been very impressed, for there is ample evidence that he never interceded on her behalf at Fox either to improve her status, to give her more exposure in films, or to prevent her from being dropped in August 1947. He was far more interested in her as a human being than as an actress.

There are numerous witnesses to Marilyn's flashes of rage or periods of cool disdain. These sudden shifts in mood resulted in break-ups of relationships and associations thought to be lasting. Some people are convinced that she was a plunderer, one to tap a relationship, drain it and then cut the party dead. Among these "victims" Joe Schenck would be listed, along with coach Natasha Lytess and her future partner Milton Greene. In time Schenck and Marilyn's closeness did suffer, but it was through distance and her determination to remove herself both physically and spiritually from the Hollywood of her Greene-Miller period. But this behaviour is understandable. Even an average person, looking back upon a decade or two of active life, will see his probably more limited landscape littered here and there with dead, discarded, and neglected friendships.

Several weeks before Fox declined to pick up her second option, Marilyn was given a role of slight dimension but an advance over her fleeting appearance in *Scudda Hoo! Scudda Hay!* The film was *Dangerous Year's* and in it Sol Wurtzel, the producer, and his director, Arthur Pierson, were the first to get the image by which she came to be recognized on the screen. This had been a recurring vision in her mind's eye ever since Emmeline Snively had first discussed films with her, her face ghostly-white lighting the screen, her eyes moist and slightly larger than life, the whole shimmering as though reflected in dark water. Most of the luminous close-ups of the years ahead – in *Bus Stop, The Prince and the Showgirl,* and *The Misfits* – were projections of this old memory of Marilyn's. She was able to project what she aspired to be.

The film, released in early 1948, was a melodramatic exploitation of juvenile delinquency, at that time a theme newly discovered. Marilyn played Eve, a waitress in a jukebox parlour patronized by teenagers. She was not seen on the screen more than a few minutes, but she was assured by director Pierson that she looked fine in the rushes. Apparently he meant it, for he was to use her again two years later when he was doing another low-budget film, this time for Metro.

During that summer, too, Marilyn was referred to the Actors Lab, a drama school for film players operated by Morris Carnovsky, the character actor, and his wife, Phoebe Brand, both former members of the Group Theatre in New York. For the first two months, Marilyn's studio subsidized her training there. The Carnovskys, along with Paula Strasberg, Marilyn's last coach, were all cited as former members of a Communist cell within the Group Theatre during a session of the House Sub-committee on Un-American Activities in 1952. Doubtless Marilyn was aware of their political beliefs – there are few secrets in show-business – but she could not have been upset by them. Her attitude towards Communists was expressed by her answer to a question in the mid-1950s: "They're for the people, aren't they?" She often would respond with another question, and in this instance it gave a clue to her future nonconformity. If she preferred and seemed to attract persons of the political left, it was not an accident. This is not to say she was an activist. She did not come fully awake as a political being until her years with Arthur Miller, and even then it was an uneven and rather haphazard attachment to individuals rather than to causes.

By September 1947, Marilyn was out of work again. Inexplicably, she was let go, although her first film had not been released. Perhaps they reasoned that her role was so small it would be impossible to tell what public reaction to her might be.

Some years later she recalled her frustration during that bleak season and said that she had gone to the front office, a long two-storey structure conveniently next door to the studio hospital. She walked along the centre corridor, scanning the name plaques on the doors until she found the right one, Darryl F. Zanuck. She couldn't believe that she was the victim of a slap-dash system that sometimes resulted in waste and blunders. She refused to accept she was somebody's mistake that would be soon forgotten.

A secretary in an outer office informed her that Mr. Zanuck was out of town, "in Sun Valley". This sounded false to Marilyn, but she knew she couldn't call the girl a liar and expect to succeed in her mission, which was simply to have a confrontation with the overlord of the whole operation.

She wasn't absolutely clear as to what she would say to Mr. Zanuck if and when she reached him. She would play that by ear. But her stubborn will made her persist, and a day or so before she was to leave the studio, she dropped by Zanuck's office again. "He's still in Sun Valley, I'm afraid," the girl said, dismissing her. Marilyn remembers being angry with herself, and deciding that any girl who sought to know why she was unwanted was only asking for another grievous wound to her ego. Wholly dedicated to herself, unable to relate to others in any real way, without any steadying outside support for her ego, it might be expected that Marilyn would give way to despair, especially in a community such as Hollywood where there are nearly as many human islands as there are aspiring actors, and even attempt to put an end to existence. Although suicide was not infrequent under the circumstances, she did not give way, this time.

Marilyn was given occasional modelling assignments by photographers and artists such as Tom Kelley and Earl Moran. Her sense of being unwanted had strengthened her resolve to excite others and become more appealing than ever. She hid her anxiety and refused to complain. She lived on thirty cents a day, subsisting on hot dogs and coffee brewed in one of the several furnished rooms she rented during that period. She was determined to succeed despite her insecurity, her hypersensitivity, and her mistrust of others. These brought to the surface a tremulousness that – when caught by the camera – became a negotiable commodity. She had an extraordinary knack of turning everything that came her way to advantage. Small opportunities became wide-swinging doors; disasters, personal triumphs.

Marilyn was running up a substantial bill of overdue payments at the Actors Lab, but whenever a modelling job came through she would pay something on it. The Carnovskys must have been used to indigent actors. Her talent, however, was not especially visible to them after several months of work with her. She remained near the back of the class much of the time and had difficulty concentrating and relaxing. These problems plagued her through much of her career, prompting her first important director, John Huston, to remark: "I was far more taken with her in the flesh than on the screen when we first worked together. I had no idea that she would go so far so fast."

Still, she was not lacking in initiative. She tried out for the second lead in a comedy entitled *Glamour Preferred* at the Bliss-Hayden Playhouse and won the part. It was her first professional appearance in the theatre, but no studio talent scout in the audience on opening night chose to get in touch with her agent, Harry Lipton. Lipton himself seemed to have been more impressed that evening by the fact that multimillionaire Huntington Hartford met her after the performance, and as such things are judged in Hollywood then and now, Lipton was right in considering this social contact of more significance than Marilyn's acting debut.

Often her insufficient diet was supplemented by substantial dinners at Joe Schenck's or in restaurants along Sunset Strip with fellow actors who would invite her. One night in early 1948 when she was dining at his mansion, Schenck surprised her by saying, "I think it's time you started making movies again." And then he asked if she would mind if he called Harry Cohn, a fellow pioneer from his earliest Hollywood days.

Marilyn had already been suggested as a screen possibility to Cohn, head of Columbia Pictures studio, but she was too fearful of hurting Schenck's feelings to mention it. When Schenck brought up the matter during a Saturday night poker session with Cohn, he nearly queered the deal, Cohn telling Schenck not to pressure him. "I've got Max Arnow (talent head at Columbia) looking into that right now," Cohn said. By the first of March she was under contract to Columbia Pictures.

CHAPTER TWO

Joe Schenck was not the only Samaritan on the scene at the time of Marilyn's arrival at Columbia Pictures' Hollywood studio. In late 1947, shortly before Schenck had called Harry Cohn, the studio had arranged for her appearance as a "starlet caddy" at a celebrity golf tournament in Cheviot Hills. There she had met a studio talent scout, Lucille Ryman, and her actor-husband, John Carroll. Carroll strongly resembled Clark Gable and had recently won his release from Gable's studio, Metro, possibly because of this resemblance. He had a fine singing voice and appeared as leading man in several full-length musicals of the early 'thirties. Marilyn was wearing a pair of shorts and a tight sweater at the time, but Carroll and his wife saw at once the helplessness behind the eye-catching façade.

Miss Ryman, like John Huston a little later, detected no great talent in Marilyn, but when Carroll said, "We're going to take her home with us," she raised no objection. "She struck us," Miss Ryman later said, "as being a little alley cat that had come to our door and turned out to be more kittenish than a pampered thoroughbred."

She was then living with a family in Burbank close to Warner Brothers' studio. At one point during the summer, she had the house to herself while the owners were on vacation. Returning late from dinner with friends, an off-duty policeman followed her home. She locked the screen door and minutes later the policeman cut through the screen and entered the house. Fortunately, houses in that block were very close together and Marilyn's screams brought neighbours into the street as the would-be rapist made his escape through a back door. All of this unwelcome excitement was reported in the next day's *Hollywood Citizen-News,* scarcely the sort of publicity Marilyn was seeking during her enforced sabbatical from her film career.

Carroll was alarmed by Marilyn's recounting this near brush with sexual violation. He told his wife, "We must help this little girl." Miss Ryman agreed, and began doling out sums to meet Marilyn's room rent and other expenses. On December 4, 1947, the couple signed a personal management contract with Marilyn. Through a few months of close association with her, they finally had seen glimmers of screen possibilities. The only signatory on their side was Carroll, but Miss Ryman was very much a party to the agreement. Marilyn's agent, Harry Lipton, was to continue to receive his usual 10 per cent of anything that came in, so she was now legally bound to hand over a considerable share of any earnings in the future.

The transaction had been concluded by Marilyn without prior consultation with Lipton. He was bitter about it, since he had developed – to no one's surprise – a strong protectiveness towards his client. Listening attentively to Marilyn's defence of her new sponsors, he was convinced that Marilyn's cause was taken up with such energy by Miss Ryman out of fear of losing her husband. Doubtless it hurt him, too; that

Marilyn would feel the need of additional help to further her career. His own contribution to her eventual rise to stardom is not easy to assess, but he had given her hope and encouragement when she needed both desperately to hold herself together as a human being. Phoning Lipton once or twice a day and often at three in the morning gave Marilyn reassurance that she did in fact exist, that she was an actress whom Lipton had recommended to Metro or to an independent producer, to anyone, it didn't matter, so long as Marilyn Monroe was being offered to someone needing a blonde.

After Marilyn was "adopted" by the couple, Lipton was spared the constant phone calls. Marilyn began making them to either Miss Ryman or her husband. She would call him on the set where he was performing for Republic Studios. He attempted to make the conversations brief, but never scolded her. Miss Ryman, however, warned Marilyn not to bother him when he was working. From then on most of the calls were made to her office as head of Metro's talent department. "She would call to ask, 'Do you think I should wash my hair today?'" Miss Ryman remembered. "Or she might call to tell me, 'Do you know what I did today? I used a new hair rinse.'" Miss Ryman finally had to urge Marilyn to attempt to solve her own problems and reserve her significant announcements until they met later in the day.

By this time, Marilyn had given up her Burbank room and, in Miss Ryman's words, "She was invited to share our apartment at La Cienega and Fountain Avenues, known as the El Palaccio. We knew we would be away a good part of the time since we were then building a ranch house in the Valley. It seemed like a good idea and safer for Marilyn." The couple was also underwriting her acting classes and Carroll gave her occasional singing lessons.

Their flat was on the third floor of the luxury apartment building. It was decided, however, that Marilyn should join them at the ranch, which was ready for occupation. Carroll's mother was also a permanent guest at the apartment, and some friction is recalled by Miss Ryman: "She didn't get on too well with Marilyn. Marilyn would walk around in a wraparound robe with nothing on underneath. This was not wrong to her, but John's mother was old-fashioned enough not to appreciate this and thought it was hard on her son to be around something like that all the time."

Complications mounted. Carroll gave Marilyn an amethyst ring, which promptly disappeared. It could have been pawned or lost, since Marilyn had managed to shake loose most jewellery she owned in one way or another. She disliked much of it anyway; its value was always lost on her, and, if needed, costume jewellery served her equally well. Marilyn took Miss Ryman aside one day and said, "Lucille, I want to have a little talk with you. You don't love John. If you did, you wouldn't be off working all the time. I think I'm in love with him." This announcement, Miss Ryman asserts, caught her completely by surprise. Whether or not Marilyn had been encouraged by Carroll to get the matter into the open is unclear, but she then asked, "Would you divorce him so we can marry?"

When Miss Ryman recovered from her shock, she asked Marilyn what had prompted all of this, and Marilyn is said to have answered, "No one who is that good to me could *not* be in love with me." Miss Ryman then terminated the discussion, saying, "If John wants a divorce, he can have it."

No divorce resulted from this confrontation. The crisis passed with no one outside the Ryman-Carroll household observing any special melancholy in Marilyn. She decided independently that she could afford a place of her own with her Columbia salary, her take-home pay then being around $100 weekly. A strange little Hollywood house was leased over the objection of some of her friends who insisted that it had to be haunted.

Throughout her six months at Columbia, she moved around, as agent Lipton recalls, "like a flea on a griddle". Giving up her haunted house, she stayed for a time at the Bel Air and the Beverley Carlton hotels, then a motel, and finally settled in again for a long stay at the Studio Club, a residential hotel in the heart of Hollywood for young women seeking something more luxurious through the unlikely path of stardom. It was a pleasant, well-managed branch of the YWCA, with tasteful, printed curtains at the windows and a good restaurant where Marilyn was seen regularly.

A naïve and unfinished young actress with an affinity for trouble to Miss Ryman; a beloved but complicated child to Ana Lower; a restless and impatient starlet to agent Lipton – Marilyn seemed only to herself a whole person who knew where she was going. To the other guests at the Studio Club who rose as early as she did (six-thirty), she was an exercise addict without a weight problem who regularly ran around the block once or twice. The girl who shared her room was aware of her indifference to the young actors who sometimes picked her up in the evening for dinner or a movie, and her almost painful concentration on the handful of books she was acquiring, among them Lincoln Steffen's autobiography and Versalius's book on anatomy. She had opened a charge account at a nearby bookshop on the day she was put under contract by Columbia.

Her friends overlooked her obvious difficulty at concentration. She would seem to be listening to something said to her, but her remote look made it evident the words had come through – if at all – as little more than the shushing sound of the surf.

At Columbia she made an effort to be wholly involved in what they were doing with her. There wasn't the sense of anonymity at this studio she had felt at Fox. The studio itself was more compact and there seemed to be a conscious effort on its part to succeed where Fox had failed.

Credit must be given to the studio's foresight. Her aspirations outdistanced her abilities by far at the time. Despite her many months at the Actors Lab, there was a pretentiousness about her acting. In fact she was ill-equipped to do much more than decorate a set. Much of this difficulty was due to her instinctive withdrawal when compelled to function as a professional actress before a movie camera, and an accompanying insecurity. It was not until fame overtook her two years later that she was able to relax in front of a movie camera. Then it became apparent to her directors that the lens of a movie camera was the collective eye of vast millions to her. While she was uncertain of that audience, she was wooden and artificial, but once she knew she was accepted it became an assumption on the part of everyone associated with one of Marilyn's films that the single object she could cuddle up to on a movie set was the camera lens. Much, much later, a veteran British stage actress who was doing a film with her would say that Marilyn had a natural ability for acting before a camera. Usually secure in her lines and able to relax, she was only fully realized as a person at such times. Her emotions were definable, not submerged or flattened, her attention was engaged as much as it could be, and sometimes during the years ahead a luminosity would appear that seemed to limn her spirit.

Marilyn's musical background was scant. Her piano lessons from Miss Miller while with Ida Bolender had vanished from her memory at a distance of fifteen years, with the sole exception of "Chopsticks". But she had a voice of sorts. It was warm and sensual, although so unsubstantial it needed amplification to be properly heard.

At least one Columbia executive was impressed enough with her singing, following a brief audition, to send her along to vocal coach Fred Karger. "We've signed this girl," he told Karger, "and we're thinking of putting her into a musical. See what you can do."

Upon meeting Karger, Marilyn lost some of her usual abstraction and gave him a scrutiny that could only have been flattering. She clearly was not seeking a protector as she had been in John Carroll; her mood at the time was far more reckless.

Marilyn's reactions to others were not always spontaneous. But she could not help responding to this musician, with dark hair neatly barbered, and with a smile that was at once broad and tentative, betraying a nature almost as unsure as hers.

For his part, Karger, believing her platinumed hair natural, asked if she was Swedish.

"Not that I know of," Marilyn answered.

Later that day, Karger told the Columbia executive he was certain that Marilyn would be fine in musicals. A second thought prompted him to add, "If her voice isn't good enough for the songs by production time, we'll dub it."

If there are some readers who cannot quite accept a Marilyn of considerable virtue and discrimination in sexual matters, who believe she was a hedonist who bedded down with one male after another when she was between husbands and sometimes during marriage, it is nevertheless true the men in her life, from Jim Dougherty to Arthur Miller, do not believe she was promiscuous. This statement is made in the face of glaring contradictions, especially those supplied by her behaviour; in at least two recorded instances Marilyn spent all or part of several nights in the company of a man other than her husband at the time. Her husbands themselves have defined these departures from propriety as escape from loneliness caused by some separation.

The truth was that Marilyn was too self-absorbed to respond to men much of the time. Karger was one of the exceptions. Sharing some of Marilyn's need to be admired and loved, he was aware of her reaction to him and responded.

Divorced from his first wife, Karger and his daughter Terry shared a bungalow on Harper Avenue in Hollywood with his mother, the widow of Max Karger. Max, who died when his son was five years old, was one of the founders of Metro. A divorced sister, Mary, and her babies were also part of that tightly knit family.

The mother, Anne Karger, Boston Irish with a surface toughness that belied a warm and generous nature, had maintained open house in the old Hollywood Hotel during the year of Norma Jean's birth. The Karger hotel suite was the gathering place for nearly everyone who mattered in the days of the silent camera. Jack Pickford, brother of Mary and something of a playboy, was a close friend as well as Valentino and Nazimova. One of Valentino's marriages was performed in their rooms by a Hollywood clergyman whom Anne had found.

Fred Karger was soon moved by Marilyn's deprivation, not so much that of her past as that resulting from her mounting burden of debts. In the interests of cutting down on expenses and keeping her figure, she would pick up a raw hamburger across the street from the studio, taking it back to her Studio Club room as dinner to be washed down with black coffee. "Is that your regular diet?" he recalled asking her.

"Well," she said, "I have grapefruit and coffee for breakfast, and cottage cheese for lunch. Some days I get by with just a little over a dollar a day for food."

Karger was dismayed. "Would you like to have dinner at my house?" he offered.

Marilyn smiled and squeezed his hand. It was the most childlike acceptance of an invitation he had ever experienced. The following evening he drove her to the Karger home on Harper Avenue.

"This is a little girl who's very lonely and broke," Karger told his mother by way of introduction. Anne instinctively liked Marilyn and embraced her. Thus began a friendship between the two women that was to outlive her romance with the son and last through Marilyn's life.

Mary and Marilyn, nearly the same age, spent a good part of that first evening in conversation, with Karger and his mother listening. Mary's babies were asleep in an adjoining bedroom and before Marilyn left, she asked to see the sleeping children. "You love children, I can see," Anne said. Marilyn smiled wistfully and nodded.

When Marilyn had left with Karger, who drove her back to the Studio Club, Anne remarked to her daughter, "I don't know whether Freddy is serious or not, but she's a good girl. I'm going to make it clear to her that this is her home whenever she wants it." And then remembering her son's attitude, which was basically uncommitted, she added, "The children are crazy about her."

Marilyn pursued two men during her lifetime, and a third if one believes Yves Montand when he says that Marilyn "threw herself" at him. It is not easy to grasp why a young woman so richly endowed physically, with such potential – often realized – for striking beauty, would choose to pursue anyone. Perhaps Karger's polite disinterest in anything more than a casual relationship had become a challenge to her.

Saddled with her fundamentalist upbringing, she believed to the end that love meant marriage. When she realized she was in love with Karger soon after that first dinner she felt she must persuade him to marry her. That he didn't seem about to do so was a reality to which Marilyn finally would resign herself. Fred Karger was to have the singular distinction of being the only human being whom Marilyn attempted to disarm and yet who was resistant up to the end.

It was not for lack of help. Anne Karger was anxious to give her blessing to the match. Possibly a little too anxious. With his mother's and sister's encouragement, a kind of affair developed between Karger and Marilyn during those months of 1948.

While his interest then was not deeply serious, Karger for a time gave Marilyn much of what she wanted – affection, an interest in her continuing self-improvement and her career; and he reawakened her to the pleasures outside the studio – seaside suppers in Malibu, dancing at a club on the Sunset Strip, lying on a beach at Santa Monica, visiting the hoary old mining town of Virginia City, Nevada, and having drinks at the Bucket of Blood Saloon.

Alcohol was of small importance to Marilyn then. On

Christmas Eve, Karger organized a Christmas party for the staff of the music department at Columbia Pictures, and Marilyn was invited to be the hostess. Karger dispensed the drinks, pouring one for himself at every round. Marilyn declined, sticking to ginger ale and whispering to him, "One of us has to be sober to get us home." His fellow workers were impressed. "Please invite Marilyn to come back," they said.

The truth was that Marilyn's ambition frightened Karger and made him withdraw.

Anne Karger's kindness when Marilyn decided she could no longer take her son's indifference made of her a permanent friend, a member of an élite group whose number could be counted on the fingers of one hand. There seems little doubt that Karger's pride was bruised by her intelligent refusal to go out with him again, and he almost at once began courting his next wife, an actress who had come much, much further than Marilyn at this point.

Marilyn could now once more concentrate on herself and the advancement of her career. She learned that her vocal training was not to be wasted. Producer Harry Romm was grooming her for an important role in his musical, *Ladies of the Chorus*.

Despite the termination of her affair with Karger, her vocal progress under him was rapid. She had an intuitive grasp of a lyric's mood and meaning, and her own skilful exploitation of her native sensuality was total and extended to her voice. Even Marilyn herself, usually mistrustful of her talents, was impressed with the sound of it in playbacks, and she was to give Fred Karger much of the credit for this. Her gratitude for that survived her infatuation by a number of years.

As a budding actress, there was only potential to measure. While Columbia had no deliberate intention of permitting her to be idle, their casting directors had come up with only the one musical throughout her six months there, and their story department spent much of its time seeking solid properties for the studio's most valuable asset, Rita Hayworth, who exercised a certain royal authority on Gower Street. That these two women, Hayworth and Marilyn, should be under contract to the same shrewd vulgarian at the same time was an accident of fate and of no special import. Except for one audition in his office – made comfortable by their mutual interests in

Christian Science – Harry Cohn himself was very nearly ignorant of Marilyn's presence on the lot, although his frustration when she was long gone and a great star would impel him to seek out a fair substitute in Kim Novak.

But the potential abilities of Hayworth and Marilyn were very much alike. They shared a plastic ability to be only as good as their directors, and in the right hands that was very good indeed. In time Marilyn would move beyond this dependency, while Hayworth never considered herself an actress; she was a *star*, which is something else altogether. Much later, in *Separate Tables*, she would achieve a performance of depth and persuasiveness, just as Marilyn would in her final series of films beginning with *Bus Stop*. But Hayworth's private life, which was to be lived on three continents, and her stardom were enough for her. She was never to know the agonies of Marilyn's obsession with growth as an actress. And if Marilyn finally fell short of her goal, robbed of fulfilment by private demons, it was astonishing to see how far she would go. Billy Wilder was to say that Hayworth, Marilyn and Clara Bow all shared a quality of "flesh impact" on the screen. "Their flesh is warm and alive even in black and white." And interestingly, each was an archetype in the three separate decades of their stardom.

Marilyn still respected Karger's opinions, even those having nothing to do with her singing voice. Now she asked Karger, as the shooting date on her first film musical approached, if there was anything wrong with her appearance. One thing they had always had in common was a preoccupation with how they looked to others. Karger was as fastidious about his clothes as Marilyn was about her face and body. With a certain amount of guilt and a sharpened sensitivity to her needs, he looked at her dispassionately and observed a flaw. When she smiled, especially in profile, her upper front teeth protruded a little. She gamely and gratefully accepted the appraisal. "I'm going to see an orthodontist," he told her, "and see what he'll do for you."

Dr. Walter Taylor was a ranking specialist in cosmetic dentistry in the Los Angeles area. Karger knew that the cost of any such repair would run into hundreds of dollars. So Dr. Taylor was approached on a benefactor basis. "She doesn't have a cent," Karger told him. "But she's worth helping."

Joshua Logan, perhaps the most perceptive of her directors,

has explained something of her initial appeal: "Luminous and completely desirable. Yet naïve about herself and touching, rather like a little frightened animal, a fawn or a baby chicken." Most of Marilyn's Samaritans could not resist helping her upon first contact. They were often people with problems of their own. Dr. Taylor was an alcoholic who periodically fell from grace and then was able to recover his practice after drying out.

Marilyn was given a detachable retainer which she wore faithfully whenever she wasn't before a camera. During her brief time at Columbia, the protrusion receded and she was able to abandon the retainer at about the time of Dr. Taylor's final retreat from sobriety.

She seldom failed to phone the inactive orthodontist at least once or twice a week. When he contracted pneumonia, his organs gravely eroded by alcohol, he lingered near death for days at the Veterans' Hospital; Marilyn went to see him every day and she was there on the afternoon he died.

Marilyn had only been unemployed six months between her Fox and Columbia contracts, but it had made her feel expendable, an unwelcome reaction from which she took several years to recover. But when she was fired during the final summer of her life, discharged from a film which she believed was contrived for her from the outset, it is known from things she said at the time that it was almost impossible for her to accept the fact that she, Marilyn Monroe, could ever be expendable.

There were cogent reasons for her shock at the time of her abrupt dismissal from her film at Fox in 1952. One of them was the reassurance that she was unique, that she was an original worth any amount of fuss, an opinion expressed to her by several key persons in her life, beginning with a woman she was to meet that summer of 1948. Her name was Natasha Lytess and she was head drama coach at Columbia. At the time Marilyn was assigned to *Ladies of the Chorus,* it was thought by producer Romm and talent chief Max Arnow that the demands of her role were beyond Marilyn's present capabilities. Miss Lytess was consulted, and she agreed to do what she could to give the young actress whatever technical skill possible.

Miss Lytess was not very hopeful at their first meeting. In her memoirs she has written that Marilyn appeared in her

cottage office wearing a knitted red-wool, hip-clinging dress
that was cut too low. She described it as looking like a
"trollop's" outfit. She went on to write that Marilyn had such
a vacuous expression, such a lack of distinction, that she appeared to her on that first day as "utterly unsure of herself.
Unable even to take refuge in her own insignificance."

Marilyn recalled that the woman who opened the cottage
door was unsmiling, intense, and Slavic-looking with large and
rather intimidating dark eyes, a thick mane of greying hair,
and an emaciated figure that hinted at some terrible illness.
Small wonder that she was insecure on first contact with
Natasha Lytess. Then, too, Miss Lytess was annoyed over her
tardiness, but Marilyn had considered their meeting important enough for her to drop by the make-up department first
and have her face and hair gone over. No one there had said
a word about her dress being wrong.

Natasha Lytess has described Marilyn's voice as a "tight
squeak", but this is in conflict with Fred Karger's memory of
it, as well as those of the musicians in his department. It may
be that Natasha's memories were coloured by her bitterness
over the rupture that was to occur between them over seven
years later.

But seven years is a long time, and in Hollywood whole
careers are launched and buried in fewer. Despite her seeming
vacuity, Marilyn was keenly sensitive about the impression
she was making. She felt her disapproval and glanced about
the study-office for some clue that might save her. "You have
a wonderful library," she told Natasha.

Apparently Natasha dismissed this with a wave of the hand,
but when Marilyn began talking about her shortcomings as an
actress, she saw some originality peek through. Most actresses
she had coached before had tried to minimize their shortcomings. Natasha was provoked to make some inquiries into
her past. The version of her background Marilyn gave to
Natasha coincided with the story she gave producer Lester
Cowan in 1949 when the movie-going public was to "learn"
that Marilyn was an orphan native of Hollywood. Later, as
Marilyn began to trust Natasha and to move into her life, the
drama coach was to be told the truth.

Who moved in on whom is difficult to determine from the
facts at hand. There seemed to be a mutual awakening to the
potential in the other. Natasha soon began to see that Marilyn

was something more than just another starlet, and Marilyn quickly realized that Natasha's opinions were backed up by years of experience in the theatre and that her presence on a movie set gave Marilyn self-confidence to such a degree that she was unable to perform without her.

All of the spring and summer of 1948 Marilyn toiled like a nun in an over-taxed charity hospital. Having seen herself a lifelong recipient of various forms of public and private assistance, she was now earning her own way in a field to which she felt a calling as strong as that of a novice to a sisterhood. All of the benefits, and they were considerable, were hers and hers alone. That her mother was a ward of the state in a mental institution at the edge of Los Angeles was a fact of her life she accepted without any loss of sleep. Gladys had never been more than a troubling enigma to her. Grace Goddard was seeing her mother regularly, and even Marilyn had accompanied her mother's friend to visit Gladys during the Easter holidays. Grace had given the woman all of the exciting news of Marilyn's new contract and Gladys had asked to see her daughter. She had already begun as a starlet, a year in which she spent little time before the movie cameras but reaped a harvest of publicity stills.

Although the frail and greying ghost in the institution never evoked any close, filial response, Marilyn was not lacking for mothers. There was a wistful sense of dependency in her that aroused most older women, as well as men of almost any age. When Marilyn's fame was greatest, there was an astonishing number of grandmothers and middle-aged women among her staunchest fans. Besides motherly Anne Karger, who was concerned that Marilyn ate right and got enough rest, there was Natasha, whose concern soon became all-encompassing.

Natasha had come to the United States from Germany with her novelist husband, Bruno Frank, in 1937. She and Frank had fled Europe at the height of the exodus of Jewish and other intellectuals. Frank was a brilliant historical novelist and playwright whose works were available in translation and who was embraced at once by the writing community of Beverly Hills, where he and Natasha rented a home.

In 1945, at the age of fifty-eight, Bruno Frank died and Natasha was left a widow with a child and a living to make. Frank's fame had been greater than his royalties, and on the strength of her years with Max Reinhardt, Natasha was recommended for a job at Columbia Pictures.

At the time Natasha took over responsibility for Marilyn's dramatic training and intellectual advancement, reduced income had forced her to give up the Beverly Hills home and move with her five-year-old daughter, Barbara, to a large apartment on Harper Avenue in Hollywood. It was by chance at an angle across the street from the Karger bungalow.

While Natasha missed the luxury of her former home, she was by no means uncomfortable in her new home. She had five large rooms, allowing her to have occasional guests, including Marilyn, who was finally to move in permanently for slightly less than a year. There was a Negro maid who kept house and looked after Barbara during the day.

Natasha became a controversial figure in Marilyn's life almost immediately. Both Anne Karger and her son, Fred, disliked the woman, although they acknowledged that she was being helpful to Marilyn's career. Perhaps her chief faults for them was in being so totally absorbed in the life of the theatre. This meant that she was not the sort who could leave the studio and forget about the business of training young performers in the craft of acting. She would spend her evenings with other members of the European theatrical community surrounding Hollywood; the dancing Schoop sisters were close friends as well as several former actors from the Reinhardt repertory company. She had a huge library on the performing arts, much thumbed and constantly referred to for Marilyn's benefit as well as others. She took an inordinate interest in the private lives of her pupils. On numerous occasions she would exhort Marilyn not to see any more of the men who dated her "because they were interested in her as a human being and not as an actress", and to wear undergarments. She was able to convince her about her men friends but never about the underwear. Marilyn could never tolerate constricting clothing.

Whenever Natasha's intrusiveness became too much for Marilyn, she fled to the Kargers. Anne's friendship survived Natasha's by at least six years. She could breathe more freely there among less complicated natures.

Ladies of the Chorus gave Marilyn her first role of any length; but it had little, if any depth. As Peggy, daughter of a former burlesque star, she becomes a burlesque queen in her own right and meets a young scion of society; the backstage tale turns into a Cinderella story, with the youth's own mother as Fairy Godmother.

Natasha asserted that Marilyn failed to make the most of this chance because the director would not permit her to remain on the set during Marilyn's scenes. However poorly Marilyn may have done with the questionable dramatic scenes, she was effective enough as a musical performer to have one of her numbers, "Every Baby Needs a Da Da Daddy", lifted from the film three and a half years later and spliced into a war film, *Okinawa*.

To Marilyn, *Ladies of the Chorus* was far from being a failure. When it was released she drove several times past the theatre where it was double-featured. She later confided that she was never to feel a similar excitement again, not even when she saw her skirt-flying likeness nearly fifty feet tall on the front of the State Theatre Building in New York, an advertisement for *The Seven Year Itch*. Adele Jergens had top billing as her clothes-shedding mother, but Marilyn's name was on the marquee.

A story about her Columbia troubles – roughly based upon some trivial incident during her days there – was printed in 1954. Allegedly, studio head Harry Cohn had made a proposition to her and she had rebuffed it. His rage, the story went, was so awesome that he ordered her dropped at option time no matter how she came across in her first film with them. Actually, his anger came four years later and was directed against himself for having made such a blunder as dropping Monroe.

Her dismissal came in September 1948, six months after she had begun. Probably she was a victim *both* of her insecurity as an actress and of Cohn's shortsightedness. Cohn's opinion when option-review time came around, a ritual in which he always took a personal interest, was that Marilyn could not act. Significantly, despite her personal interest, Natasha Lytess did nothing to persuade her employer that he was mistaken. Marilyn's progress had not advanced far enough as yet for her to take any such risk.

It was not simple doggedness that drove Marilyn to make the rounds in the Fall of 1948. There was simply no return. She had no identity other than that of film actress. The one tie she valued from her past, Ana Lower, was soon to be broken by Ana's fatal illness. With Ana buried, Marilyn appeared to be finished with Christian Science. There was no practitioner around who could "unmake" the evil days that had come upon her. She divined that she would have to unmake them herself.

But she couldn't bear the thought that she was now without a sympathetic ear. Natasha seemed to believe that she was malleable clay, that she was whatever Natasha chose to make her. Marilyn rarely confided in her and almost always regretted it when she did. Since Joe Schenck had set up her contract with Columbia, she was embarrassed to contact him now. She had been done a favour, unsought, because he felt sorry for her, but it hadn't done any good.

She asked Anne Karger what she could do "to pull myself out of the dumps". Anne advised her to go to church, "any church. It's good. You'll get some comfort out of it". Marilyn went to nearby St. Victor's Catholic Church where she sat silently for two and a half hours.

When she came out, she hurried back to Anne's both comforted and confused. "I wasn't wearing a hat, and I felt wrong about that, and I wasn't sure what I should do." Anne told her just to pray to God and to give her thoughts to him. She said many years later that she never failed to pray for Marilyn right up to the end. "She was groping her last few years," Anne Karger said. "She was so ill." But Marilyn never went back to St. Victor's.

CHAPTER THREE

During that second period of retrenchment, Marilyn had numerous allies, several of them – Karger and Natasha at Columbia and Lucille Ryman at Metro – highly placed in the industry. Her agent had considerable film footage on her to help in tracking down new offers, and finally Lipton kindled a spark of interest in producer Lester Cowan. Cowan needed a girl for a brief scene with Groucho Marx in *Love Happy*. She was to enter the office of private detective Grunion (played by Groucho), and with an anxious look behind her, say: "Some men are following me." Groucho glanced at Marilyn when she came on to the set and nodded to the casting director that she would be satisfactory.

How Marilyn walked into Groucho's detective office was more important than the way she delivered her few lines. It was the first broad sketch of a walk she later could have had heavily insured by Lloyd's, if such a transaction did not carry with it the suggestion that her sexuality was more valuable than her talents as an actress. Emmeline Snively, interviewed years afterwards at her modelling school, was to attribute Marilyn's ambling gait to weak ankles. Natasha Lytess claimed that it was something she taught her. Marilyn herself said that she had always walked like that.

However· it was arrived at, with *Love Happy* there was beginning to be some public curiosity about who she was. While the comedy was in production in February 1949, producer Cowan called Louella Parsons, the Hearst movie columnist who was for over four decades either a scourge or a friend to nearly everyone of significance in American films, and told Louella that Marilyn was an orphan raised in foster homes "right here in Hollywood". This was sufficiently unusual to rate a mention in the columnist's farflung syndicate and created enough interest on Louella's part to make her an early champion of Marilyn's. In the years to come, she would often find Marilyn's behaviour on films difficult to defend, but somehow she usually managed to "explain" the background for some of Marilyn's actions, lending her column a strange tone of religious absolution since her pronouncements on any subject were accepted as gospel in Hollywood. In a very real sense, they had to be, for Louella wielded as much power over her ancient fief as the Queen of Hearts in Wonderland. Within another eighteen months, a reporter would confront Marilyn with the stumbled-upon fact of her mother's existence and the orphan apocrypha would fall out of the legend.

On her own, Marilyn came across the second fortuitous assignment of that risky year of enforced independence. Photographer Tom Kelley on one occasion had advanced her five dollars for a cab fare after she had crashed her yet unpaid-for convertible into another vehicle. She abandoned her car by the kerb, where it was pushed by sudden male volunteers, including Kelley himself, and continued on to a modelling appointment by taxi. During the summer of 1949, Kelley called to ask if she would pose nude for a calendar short. She had no misgivings about nudity, but she was concerned for her movie career. Finally she agreed to do it, in gratitude for Kelley's good turn.

Kelley paid her fifty dollars for the day, and after Marilyn's rise, the calendar sold in the millions. He was convinced that she had a genius for sensing what the camera saw as she posed and likened her natural grace to that of a snake or a panther. The calendar came close to being banned from the mails. Pornography was much on the minds of the Post Office at the time, and Kelley was compelled to have the better of the two final shots analysed by a committee of well-known artists, whose considered judgement was that it was a work of art in perfect symmetry. Marilyn was enormously proud of it and some years later asked Kelley for the transparencies that were too frank in their nudity (her pelvic area was visible) for calendar use. She gave them to her new husband at the time, Joe DiMaggio, as her wedding gift to him. By then the original transparency used in the calendar, "Golden Dreams", had been stolen from Kelley's studio.

At about the same time, Marilyn was cast as one of a small troupe of chorines incredibly shuttling through an embattled area of Colorado during the Indian wars. The movie, *A Ticket to Tomahawk,* starring Dan Dailey, was to take her back to the Fox lot, but her role was so insignificant, no one there seemed to have been aware she had returned as a freelance actress. Little of her incandescence came through in this brief appearance, but the film went into release in May 1950, a few months after *Love Happy.* While no one seemed to care who the smiling blonde was in the Fox western, nearly everyone who saw the Marx Brothers' film was impressed by the blonde with a problem.

The call that came to agent Harry Lipton from the William Morris office in Beverly Hills was not unexpected. Occasionally, as performers rose to some prominence under his management, they were plucked from his modest roost by one of the powerful agencies, MCA, William Morris, Famous Artists or GAC. He attributed this ill fortune to the unwillingness of his firm, National Concert Artists Corporation, to expand their West Coast operations. Now Johnny Hyde, one of the most influential talent representatives in Hollywood, was on the line, asking for details of Lipton's contract with Marilyn.

Johnny Hyde had brought comedienne Betty Hutton from obscurity as a band vocalist to enormous popularity as a film star. He had been instrumental in elevating Rita Hayworth to prominence. Lipton, who at various times had represented such performers as John Hodiak, Howard Keel, Guy Madison, and Dale Evans, realized that Hyde's interest was a genuine break for Marilyn. He felt for Marilyn's sake that he could do nothing but discuss the terms of a settlement, and Hyde, whose style was low-pressure anyway, had an offer ready. It is not known precisely what percentage the Morris office agreed to share with Lipton in taking over Marilyn's representation, but it was probably between two and three per cent.

Hyde was a native of Russia who had been brought as a child to the United States with his parents' vaudeville act, the Nicholas Haidabura Imperial Russian Troupe. After a few years of success on the Keith circuit, the family dropped the Haidabura name, and young Hyde, still in his teens, joined the Loew vaudeville booking office as manager Jake Lubin's assistant. Sometime after his twenty-first birthday, he joined the Morris office as a junior executive, where he rose quickly through his gentle and civilized manner of handling talent. He was able to demand huge sums for the stars he managed, and turned singer Al Jolson into a millionaire despite the performer's profligacy.

For some years Hyde had been a vice-president of his firm, helping its West Coast head, Abe Lastfogel, with its film operations. He was himself a millionaire, and like his client Jolson, not without his expensive weaknesses. These were not those of a glutton or show-off but of a man at home with himself and with his life. When compared with the strange and often outrageous taste of many Hollywood folk, he was a reborn Prince of the Renaissance. His impeccable sense of what was right for any situation, whether it was a wine for dinner or an allowance for his four sons, was one of the qualities that had attracted his wife, Mozelle Cravens, an *ingénue* he had liberated from Republic Pictures' westerns.

His gift for doing the right thing was also his undoing. In what is known as the "flesh" business, very few men do not succumb to extramarital diversion. Much of their business is transacted over drinks, lunches, and dinners, and many of their clients are actresses in constant need of affection and reassurance. If any of Hyde's girl friends, all of whom he met through his work, erred in any direction, be it make-up, wardrobe, personality, or even character, he persuasively led them

into reform, sometimes subsidizing the change with his own
cheque-book. This was too much for Mozelle Hyde. In her
own words, "I tried to take it for a long time, but in the end,
it was impossible. I'm a tolerant person, but there is always a
limit. I remember once Jimmy (their son) was down in the
cellar looking over some old things of his father's and he
found Marilyn's nude calendar. He brought it upstairs, but I
was so annoyed over that whole business, I made him get rid
of it."

The "business" began at the Racquet Club in Palm Springs,
a spa in the heart of the desert managed by the silent film idol,
Charlie Farrell. Hyde could often be found there, sitting fully
clothed in a canvas chair by the poolside, bemused by the
frolics of other film people in and out of the water. The Racquet Club was his escape valve right up to the end, and it was
there he first saw Marilyn in the flesh. He had seen *Love
Happy* at a private screening and now he was caught by her
shrill laughter, which seemed to suggest insecurity and hilarity
at the same time. Later, they had a few minutes of conversation together and he had given her his card.

At the time, Marilyn was staying with Natasha and her
daughter. Natasha later wrote that Marilyn exploited and deluded Hyde by constantly reminding him of his importance
to her while she was really not attached to him at all. At 3
A.M., Natasha insisted, Marilyn would phone Hyde with the
request, "Say something nice to me, so I can go to sleep thinking of you."

But Marilyn made several clear declarations on the subject
of Johnny Hyde. Until her own death, she acknowledged him
as the architect of her fame. They were friends upon first meeting, and she could see that he had more style and taste than
anyone she had met until then and that these came not from
inheritance but from self-refinement, which she found encouraging. Back in Palm Springs, she had thought him a small,
compactly built man, but she said that upon seeing him in
his office on the day they discussed her contract, he seemed
about ten feet tall. Photographs of Hyde taken at the time
reveal a man with a carefully barbered, velvety look, and if
small in scale, certainly well proportioned.

She did feel considerable panic when Hyde got to his feet
and took her by the arm, propelling her through his secretary's
office out to the corridor. Secretary Dona Holloway, who is

now an executive producer, can still remember Marilyn's look of astonishment until Hyde said, "I'm taking Miss Monroe out for the afternoon. I'll ring in later."

Soon after their first luncheon at Romanoff's, Hyde sent her to Saks in Beverly Hills for some new gowns and shoes. Natasha at first believed that Hyde, like herself, was merely grooming Marilyn for more important things. "He spent thousands of dollars escorting her around Hollywood," Natasha wrote. "Yet when it came to personal gifts to Marilyn, his tight-fistedness was almost bizarre. . . . When I helped her to choose two pairs of earrings . . . 'My God!' he shouted, '*Two* pairs of earrings – how many ears have you got?' "

Very soon after getting to know her, Hyde realized that Marilyn was self-invented for the purpose of becoming a screen star, that she was yet incomplete, and that life outside films held little meaning for her. While he was falling in love with her, he must have known, too, that he stood for recognition and appreciation in Marilyn's life. There was also the bitter awareness that these virtues were more important to her than personal happiness or wealth. And Hyde sensed that she would be fatally wounded if success didn't come to her. He could not know that the creature she had created and whose recognition he was attempting to ensure would begin to come apart when she realized that success was simply not enough.

Warned by his doctor to slow down because of a failing heart, Hyde accelerated the pace to get Marilyn firmly on her way. There were at least half a dozen or more star clients to attend to, and this was enough to keep him occupied during a working day, but he spent every spare moment discussing Marilyn with studio heads or taking her out on the town where she could be seen. When it was becoming common knowledge that Marilyn was Johnny Hyde's "girl", his wife Mozelle spoke with him about her. Hyde was not devious. He told his wife a little sadly, "It's happened, and I can't do anything about it." Mozelle, considering any attempt at reconciliation hopeless, filed for divorce. A sensitive and handsome woman, an American of exotic looks not unlike Ava Gardner, she was saddened, too, to realize that the eldest of their sons, Donald, was nearly as old as Marilyn.

There were muted cries of despair and frustration on both sides – surprising, because Johnny Hyde was not a man to be deprived of anything he sought. If his position of power in the film world failed to achieve an ambition, nearly always his art of persuasion did. With Marilyn, he was gently let down time and again. She said she couldn't marry him because that would be dishonest. All of his arguments that love would follow marriage failed to convince her. Oddly enough, Marilyn, too, was deprived occasionally during their close association. There were frequently times when Hyde simply could not take Marilyn to an affair. "The big man wants to talk to me about a deal tonight," he would tell her, and Marilyn would settle for having cocktails with him as he readied himself for an evening with a major producer or studio head. When it came time for the Academy Award evening in March 1950, Hyde explained to Marilyn that it was impossible for him to escort her. Marilyn phoned an actor friend who escorted her instead, and picked him up in Fred Karger's new car, which she had borrowed for the evening.

Marilyn's attachment to Hyde had ended her disappointment at not becoming Mrs. Fred Karger. Her affair with Hyde had an even more significant compensation – there was a limit to what Karger could do for her; reassure her at public appearances (she often asked him to accompany her to military bases and theatres where she was to perform a song or two); escort her to a party; and discuss confidential matters she needed to talk out with somebody. But Hyde could perform all of these functions admirably, and there was simply no ceiling on what he could do for her career. When in love with Karger, anything that threatened their relationship would throw her into a deep depression. Now with Hyde solidly backing her up in every way, she seemed suddenly mature, incapable of panics or hysteria. There is a glimmer here of the elusive spirit inhabiting Marilyn. New Galahads were full of such promise to her; past defeats and frustrations lost their sting.

The last confidence she uttered in her whispery voice to Karger was about Hyde. She seemed eager to spill out to him all of her anxiety when it appeared that Hyde was showing signs of deep, personal involvement. She said that she knew it was true, for his face had tightened painfully when she told him recently that she had a date with Karger and couldn't accompany him to an opening at the Coconut Grove. The thought that Hyde might have some claim upon her time simply mystified her.

Marilyn and Karger were in a taxi at the time on their way out to El Toro Air Base. She seemed concerned about their privacy for such an important conversation and whispered to Karger that she couldn't talk freely in the presence of the taxi driver. Then she leaned forward and asked, "Don't you have a window that separates the front and the back?" There was none visible, but perhaps she expected that one might rise out of the back of the driver's seat.

The taxi driver turned and said, "Miss Monroe, I promise I won't listen and if I do hear anything, I promise I won't repeat it."

"We'll trust you to keep your word," Marilyn said solemnly. Then she turned to Karger and told him that she was sure that Hyde was falling in love with her, but she didn't know what to do about it. "He's so sweet," she said. "I love him dearly. But I don't feel the way he does."

Karger could not counsel her, nor could anyone. She was to say substantially the same thing to Natasha and perhaps these confidences were warnings to herself. But then she apparently put aside her reservations and drifted into an intimacy that was only a step removed, if that, from sexual entanglement. There were many in Hollywood who began to call Marilyn Johnny Hyde's mistress.

After Hyde's separation from Mozelle, he bought a house several blocks away from her but convenient enough to see his sons whenever he wanted to. He established a bachelor home for himself with a cook-housekeeper, butler, and a chauffeur-valet. Marilyn did not as yet move into the new house on North Palm Drive, but she was there much of the time. Six years later, she moved into a large English Tudor cottage down the same block with Joe DiMaggio.

There were a few executives at William Morris with little faith. They were convinced that Marilyn was overrated by Hyde, that his obvious affection for her had clouded his judgement. The iciness she encountered from these sceptics following Hyde's death was her first knowledge of there being any difference of views about her talent at the agency. This disaffection was to become endemic following the funeral; some of them shocked by her unravelling at the rite and others feeling that she had contributed to the death of their executive vice-president.

To those who had come close enough to see beyond the terrible ambition, she was thought to be deserving not only of Hyde's nearly total consideration but their own, too, within limits. Among these, Lucille Ryman was probably the least deserving of Marilyn's neglect. While the friendship had been allowed by Marilyn to deteriorate during the months of her close association with Hyde, possibly because of some rift which neither woman would ever discuss openly, Miss Ryman came across a film role in the course of her daily routine at Metro that seemed absolutely right for Marilyn.

The perfect role was that of a guileless young woman bedding down with a criminal lawyer old enough to be her father. If Miss Ryman saw any parallel between reality and the part of Angela when she was given the script of The Asphalt Jungle, it was never articulated. John Huston, who was to direct the film, had wanted Lola Albright but found she was unavailable.

Huston had by then already made his break with the film establishment. He was, in his way, as much of an original as Marilyn was to become. Considerable wealth had accrued to him through a series of notable films for Warner Brothers, including The Maltese Falcon and Treasure of the Sierra Madre. He felt himself nearly a free agent in films, his daring permissible because of his past reputation. When he bought W. R. Burnett's original novel, which was a savage view of the criminal mind, he planned to direct it for Metro, where production chief Dore Schary had given him his head, without adulteration.

A script was sent to Johnny Hyde and a cursory glance confirmed that Lucille Ryman had been right. On Monday, Marilyn phoned Miss Ryman to tell her in some excitement that she was testing that day for Asphalt Jungle. The contract was temporary and their friendship was not renewed again. What had happened to the personal management contract between Marilyn and Miss Ryman and her husband is unknown, but it was no longer in force, either abandoned by agreement or allowed to die.

Huston remembered Marilyn from her Columbia days as a "lovely, simple blonde" whom he and John Garfield had wanted to test. They had, in fact, set up an early morning session with her before the cameras on the sound stage housing the production of We Were Strangers, a Cuban war film in which Garfield was starring. But S. P. Siegel, the film's producer, who had suddenly been apprised of the secret project, began citing to Huston the cost of such a test in film, footage, processing, lighting, equipment, not to mention the energy of his star, Mr. Garfield. "Are you prepared to pay for all this?" he asked first Huston, then Garfield. The test was called off.

In its realism, *Asphalt Jungle* would be very nearly a documentary of crime – a safecracking job – from its inception to its failure. Angela Phinlay is the youthful blonde mistress of a lawyer down on his luck, a role already assigned to Louis Calhern, who was often cast as a business tycoon-type with a fatal flaw. Nearly all of the parts were to be played by actors chosen by Huston for their ability to create three-dimensional roles rather than for their prominence. The film finally would launch Marilyn and it would re-establish the waning career of Sterling Hayden who was cast in the role of a petty gangster with an alcoholic hang-up and a sentimental regard for his old farm home.

Marilyn went into seclusion at Natasha's apartment and spent the weekend going over Angela's scenes with her coach. Marilyn also studied the entire script, for she wanted to know who Angela was and how she had got involved with Lawyer Emmerich in the first place.

Early the following week, Marilyn told Hyde she was as ready as she'd ever be, although she was uneasy about facing John Huston. With Natasha and Hyde, she was driven to the Metro lot in Culver City and waved on to the sound stage where Huston was waiting.

Huston is a gentle-voiced man and those who have worked with him usually find him a well of encouragement. He recalls the day in these words: "I was not too surprised when she asked if she could sit on the floor. I'd been told that she was unusual. I told her that would be just fine, and the cameras rolled. When it was over, Marilyn looked very insecure about the whole thing and asked to do it over. I agreed. But I had already decided on the first take. The part of Angela was hers."

No supporting actress had ever come to one of Huston's sets (or possibly any set) accompanied by her own personal drama coach, but Natasha was too involved in Marilyn's life and career to back away. She quit Columbia as soon as the film went into production to devote all of her time to Marilyn.

Sterling Hayden, who had no scenes with Marilyn, remembers her as being terribly frightened, and he did what he could to reassure her. Huston himself was an important factor in allaying her fears. He knew that his film, and her first major production, was pivotal to her career. Of course, he could not have known then that he would also guide her through her final major film in *The Misfits*, but it was fitting that he should have had both these fateful assignments for it is probable that in less capable, less sensitive hands, she would have gone down in defeat on both occasions. By 1960, she had come full circle. The terrors that plagued her on *Jungle*, successfully submerged through nearly a decade of film-making, would surface once more in the Nevada wasteland where *The Misfits* was located.

Noticing her nervousness on the first day of shooting, Huston came up and told Marilyn in a low voice to glance at veteran actor Louis Calhern. "See how he's shaking?" Huston asked. "If you're not nervous, you might as well give up." Many years later, Lee Strasberg would bring to mind those words of Huston when he told her that "nervousness" was the energy-source that propelled a sensitive actor.

It was Jim Dougherty who was assigned by the Los Angeles Police Department to keep an eye on the fans behind the barricades when *The Asphalt Jungle* had its world première at Grauman's Egyptian Theatre. When he had the chance, which was seldom, he would glance at the celebrities disembarking from their black limousines. But he saw no sign of Marilyn. The fact was that she had attended a sneak preview at a neighbourhood movie house with Hyde who saw no reason for her to appear at the première. "*After* the fans have seen you in this, they'll cheer you when they see you in person," he advised her. "Now they're not quite sure who you are."

And Hyde was partially right. Critics applauded the film, and some singled Marilyn out. Howard Barnes wrote in the New York *Herald Tribune* that Marilyn contributed "a documentary effect to a lurid exposition", which was precisely what Huston had hoped to achieve with her.

Johnny Hyde had become a vital part of Marilyn's life. Mid-morning, he could expect a call in her breathy voice wondering what she should wear to lunch, whether the date was with him or not; wondering if he really thought she should do the second feminine lead in Mickey Rooney's rollerdome film, *The Fireball*. "The part has no lines, Johnny," she'd pro-

test. And he would spend ten or fifteen minutes of his valuable
time reassuring her.

Although he'd had numerous affairs with actresses, his
relationship with Marilyn was untypical in ways far more
significant than the money his secretary saw being paid out to
hairdressers, dress shops, and eventually even to a plastic
surgeon. There had been a boundary to his romances, a mutual
give and take. He had helped a few starlets advance their
careers and they, in turn, had given some amusement and
satisfied his need to be seen in the company of beautiful women.
But he was far more protective of Marilyn than he had been
with his previous liaisons. She was not to be criticized, patronized, or ignored. His friends walked on eggshells where she was
concerned and speculated endlessly on how this change in
Johnny had come about. Few of them, with the possible exception of Sam Berke, his business manager, and his friend Ben
Thau at Metro, saw the potential actress in Marilyn that he
did, and a number of them felt her helplessness to be an artifice.

When it was discovered that she had refused to marry
Johnny, several of his closest associates felt she was holding
out for material reasons; that she was interested only in his
making her a super star. But two or three intimates such as
Dona Holloway and Joe Schenck knew the truth, which, in
Marilyn's words was, "I love him, but I'm not *in* love with
him." Hyde sensed Marilyn's absolute dependence on the
security he gave her and pressed her to marry him. Knowing
of his heart condition, it is believed that she refused, saying
that should something happen, life would be unbearable without him. It is known that he then asked Joe Schenck to inter-
cede, believing that Schenck's paternal attitude might be a
decisive factor in changing her mind.

Johnny Hyde was the person most instrumental in the making of Marilyn's fame and subsequent legend. He gave her no
false notions about her potential. He didn't compare her to
Garbo or Duse, but rather to Jean Harlow and Clara Bow.
He seemed sure that she would become a representative of her
time as Clara Bow had been of hers. He spoke of hard work
and apprenticeship rather than of genius. He made her realize
that the right director and cameraman were more important
than all her co-stars put together.

He persuaded Joe Mankiewicz, then casting *All About
Eve*, to hire her for the part of Miss Caswell, an empty-headed

young lady with a cynical tinge, mistress to an acid-tongued drama critic. Even though the lines were few and her exposure would be limited to two or three scenes, Hyde assured Marilyn that it would be better to play a minor role than wait for a more important one in a film directed by a less talented man.

And he was proved right in November 1950, when *All About Eve* went into general release. Its brittle humour and fresh dialogue made it an enormous success in urban areas around the country and gave everyone connected with it a boost. Bette Davis was to call it "a charmed production from the word go". Every performer in it became almost instantly in demand.

With the release of *The Asphalt Jungle*, offers had begun coming in for Marilyn's services. Prior to that she had done a series of small parts in two films for Metro, *Right Cross*, starring Dick Powell and June Allyson, and *Home Town Story*, a newspaper melodrama with a capitalistic message, written and directed by her old friend from *Dangerous Years*, Arthur Pierson. As a result of her rush of activity in 1949-50, she would have six films in release in one year, four of them set up by Hyde.

Perhaps Hyde felt the approach of death. In any event, he spent much of his last month sifting through the properties offered Marilyn, talking deals and terms with studio heads. He never assumed at any point that Marilyn was incapable of making her own decisions. He respected her native intelligence and would act upon her suggestions when he agreed they were logical. When, after *Eve*, she complained about being strait-jacketed in dumb platinum-haired roles, he discussed with Metro chief Dore Schary the possibility of her playing Grushenka in a new adaptation of *The Brothers Karamazov*. Almost anyone who knew what Marilyn was capable of doing and who saw Maria Schell in the final film production agreed that Grushenka's earthiness could have come through with Marilyn in the part. But Schary, like Harry Cohn and Darryl Zanuck, thought Marilyn basically a mindless commodity of limited potential, and failed to renew her option once *The Asphalt Jungle* was completed; and this despite the intervention of both Lucille Ryman from his talent department and his production associate, Hyde's friend Ben Thau.

When word first leaked out that Marilyn was interested in the Dostoevsky novel, the reaction of the trade papers and then the dailies was incredulity. Finally her aspirations became a public joke; one that she was sensitive about to the end of her life, for Marilyn knew better than any of her detractors how well she could have played Grushenka. The general amusement, as circulated in the press, indicated that her recent successful films had brought Marilyn very much before the public eye.

Johnny Hyde's brother Alex, who was on the staff of Metro's music department, went to him to caution him about Marilyn. Apparently he warned him that he was being taken over by a guileful young woman incapable of fidelity. He was assuming that Marilyn was Hyde's mistress and probably had in mind Fred Karger or, even more implausibly, Joe Schenck. It seemed inconceivable to the Hyde family that Marilyn might have rejected Johnny's proposal of marriage, for that would suggest a naïveté that defied comprehension. On the basis of the evidence at hand, his ex-wife, Mozelle, had little to do with this confrontation. By this time she was already divorced from Hyde and philosophically resigned to his weaknesses.

Hyde shrugged his brother's warning off, or appeared to, since he was a man who always presented to the world an unruffled exterior, but his friends believe that the criticism made its mark. From then on, for a critical period of time, he felt constrained to prove he was physically up to being Marilyn's consort. Rather than spend his time resting about his comfortable home as he had been doing for some weeks, there were frequent weekends in Palm Springs together and too many nights "dressed up", as Marilyn termed it, touring the Hollywood clubs. Soon, the strain began to show.

When his bantam weight began to drop alarmingly, his heart specialist warned him not to climb stairs. His chauffeur, Fred Waldemar, had to carry him up to the master bedroom each night.

With each encroachment upon his independence and sense of manhood, his concern for Marilyn's future grew. He had felt for some time that minor plastic surgery would be beneficial. In his last weeks, he attempted, with some urgency, to get out of the way as many refinements to his blueprint for her career in Hollywood as he could manage. He arranged for the operation and she came to convalesce in his home. While earlier photographs of Marilyn compared with those made

after 1950 reveal little or no change in her appearance, it is
believed the surgery removed a small lump from the tip of
her nose, previously masked by cosmetics.

She was given her own room on the second floor of the
house. Hyde's family was outraged by this flagrant disavowal
of all their principles, not to mention their earlier advice. But
for a week or more, Hyde ignored the tempest and spent as
much time as he could spare from his other clients with Marilyn. Then, perhaps because the furore finally got to him,
around the 10th of December he complained of difficulty in
his breathing and his doctor sent him to Cedars of Lebanon
Hospital, where it was found he had suffered a mild coronary
occlusion.

Dona Holloway recalls that Marilyn seemed aware of his
family's hostility towards her presence in the house during his
illness. She suggested that it might be best for her to return to
the Beverly Carlton Hotel, where she had a studio apartment,
but Hyde sent word that she was to stay.

Within three or four days, Hyde felt well enough to talk
about leaving the hospital and going up to Palm Springs for a
few days. His doctor saw nothing wrong with this, and just
before leaving town Hyde had a conference with his close
friend and business manager, Sam Berke. He told Sam he was
having no luck in persuading Marilyn to marry him and said
something about the tremendous pressure he was under from
his kin to terminate this intimate association.

"They have no cause to criticize you, Johnny," Berke told
him. "You're divorced, and they're not close enough to you to
know you're not sleeping with Marilyn. But what if something
should happen to you? With their attitude, I'd say Marilyn
would be out in the cold altogether."

"You mean change my will?" Hyde asked.

"That's the only way Marilyn will get anything unless you
do marry."

That was the first and only time Berke recalled seeing any
evidence that Hyde feared an imminent death. He clenched
and unclenched his hands. Then he told Berke, "I've been
feeling a pricking sort of pain in my fingers the past day or so."

They talked seriously about his leaving Marilyn one-third
of his estate, after providing for the education of his sons.
"Something negotiable. She likes the house, but she wouldn't
know what to do with it."

He had his chauffeur pick up Dona Holloway, whom he had asked to stay with him until Marilyn could join him. Since the onset of the pain in his fingers, he was afraid of being alone. And then he went on to Palm Springs, confidently expecting Sam Berke to have a draft of the revised will around the time of his return.

Four days passed. The dry desert climate, usually so beneficial, did nothing for him. A constant but unspecified anxiety gripped him. Dona, who was married to a busy physician, was getting anxious to return home. She phoned Marilyn at the North Palm Drive house and urged her to come down. Marilyn told Dona she would come down the moment she could get away from her various commitments.

Marilyn had fully recovered from her operation but was involved with costume fittings for her next film. She was also busy posing for publicity stills, one of which would appear in the January 1, 1951, issue of *Life*, the first of many appearances in that magazine. In a light-hearted photo essay devoted to starlets, she would be called a "busty Bernhardt [who] at twenty-two seems to have her future assured. After small but pungent roles in *Asphalt Jungle* and *All About Eve,* her studio, 20th-Century Fox, is convinced she will be a fine dramatic actress too."

Hyde had worked out the final details of a seven-year contract for Marilyn with Fox, which in less than a year would be paying her $750 per week. It was signed late in November and was already in force. She was to appear in *As Young As You Feel* with Monty Woolley, David Wayne, Albert Dekker, Jean Peters, and Thelma Ritter. The Lamar Trotti screenplay was an adaptation of the first Paddy Chayefsky story to reach the screen.

That Friday evening, Marilyn drove her new Pontiac directly from the studio to Palm Springs to rejoin Hyde. It was a death watch, and doubtless Hyde sensed it despite his pretended annoyance at any fuss made over him.

Johnny Hyde's final heart attack occurred in the late afternoon of Saturday, December 17. Marilyn asked the staff to help her get him to his room at the Racquet Club. She did not give way to hysteria then, but her anxiety was so deep she may have been in a state of shock. The house physician put in a call to Hyde's doctor and it was decided to get him back to Cedars of Lebanon Hospital immediately.

Marilyn followed the ambulance directly to the hospital. The attendants treated her with all the kindness accorded a critical patient's kin. Dona Holloway joined her in the vigil, and at one point when Marilyn left the room for a moment, Hyde signalled for Dona to come closer to his bedside. He was in an oxygen tent and his breathing was laboured, but he whispered to her, "Be sure that Marilyn is treated as one of the family."

But this was not to be, for on Sunday Johnny Hyde died, and his last words were ignored by his brother and other members of his family. Their ultimatum was conveyed to her by a lawyer's call to the North Palm Drive house. She was told to get herself and her things out immediately.

Marilyn went into seclusion at Natasha's; Natasha kept a discreet distance from her, but rarely left her alone in the apartment. Marilyn lay on her bed much of the time. It is the first recorded instance when someone close to Marilyn felt that she could not be left alone. At intervals, Marilyn would emerge from the bedroom, swollen-eyed, and go to the bathroom or the kitchen to sit silently hunched over a cup of black coffee. The first day, she had been given several stiff shots of whisky to insulate her from the shock, and later was sedated with pills.

The studio was called, although Natasha said nothing about the pills. Everyone understood, for everyone had known the situation, although there was some disagreement over the nature of Hyde's and Marilyn's relationship. Had she been his mistress? Or had Johnny been too ill to make demands? No one was quite sure, but all were moved by her stricken state. All but the Hydes.

Word went out to Marilyn that she was not to appear at the funeral. Johnny's sons would not understand, and if she had really cared for Johnny she would make this sacrifice.

But Hyde's closest friends and associates – producer Ben Thau at Metro, Dona Holloway, and business manager Berke – thought differently. Hyde's last words were directed to Marilyn's welfare. And so it was decided that Marilyn would go with Dona and her husband.

Nearly two decades later, Hyde's second youngest son, Jimmy, himself a well-established agent at William Morris, had this to say about his father's funeral at Forest Law: "All I can recall clearly is Marilyn screaming my father's name over and over again. It shook everyone."

Some who were close to her believed her grief would soon be forgotten, but they were wrong.

CHAPTER FOUR

While world fame was ahead of her, by December 1950 Marilyn was becoming a success at the only thing that still mattered to her – acting in films. Rupert Allan, who was then western entertainment editor for *Look* magazine, came to her Beverly Carlton apartment to interview her. He was impressed by her lack of pretension. The studio apartment was simply furnished and she had tacked up several reproductions of paintings by Matisse and Cézanne she had cut from magazines.

Her aura of wholesomeness and innocence, so natural upon the screen, were facets of a character and personality she insisted were her own. But these attributes seemed to have emerged as dominant partially to cover her insecurity. She was shaky about so many things: modern art, authors' names, acting. She knew what she liked and had a sure instinct for what was good. But while she could retreat behind her mask of innocence whenever she was uncertain, she still loathed being patronized. Anyone who made this mistake would be excluded from her circle of friends.

The executives at Fox seemed to have been won over to the late Johnny Hyde's point of view and now felt that she could handle bigger roles than those of Miss Caswell and Angela. Studio head Darryl Zanuck will not discuss Marilyn, so one can only come to a conclusion about his influence in the further shaping of her career through others. What seems undeniable is that Zanuck did not believe she was an actress. She was a new personality he felt was marketable. So long as he was in command, Marilyn's roles would all be fundamentally the same, vacuous, innocent, sometimes working, sometimes married, sometimes drifting, but always in need of help. It *was* a negotiable commodity and perhaps Zanuck's shrewd showmanship contributed substantially to Marilyn's quick rise to stardom. What made these two – actress and employer – implacable foes was his lack of faith in her potential.

As Young As You Feel was the first step in Zanuck's programme for Marilyn. She was to play a private secretary to a corporation president, Albert Dekker, who had recently been forced by company policy to put out to pasture one of his ageing underlings, Monty Woolley. The film was a vehicle for Woolley, whose career as a film star had begun in his sixties with *The Man Who Came To Dinner*.

The studio had instructed screen writer Lamar Trotti to give Marilyn as much exposure as her role would permit. Good lines and the capable direction of Harmon Jones contributed to Marilyn's success in the film. Bosley Crowther writing in *The New York Times* was in the advance guard of her admirers: "Marilyn Monroe is superb as his [Dekker's] secretary." Crowther later became soured by the publicity hoopla surrounding her.

Marilyn had met Elia Kazan some months before Hyde's death. Kazan, who seemed to have been fascinated by blonde actresses at the time, liked Marilyn's simplicity and wit. Some of Marilyn's friends of that era speak of his "love" for Marilyn, convinced then that it was only a matter of time before he proposed. Marriage would not have been a simple matter, however, since Kazan had been married for over eighteen years to Molly Thatcher, the sensitive and intelligent mother of his four children. Molly Kazan was not a background person. She was writing works of rare humour and perception during her spare time and would be launched as a Broadway playwright before her death.

Even if Kazan had become serious, Marilyn was never interested in the director romantically, or so she asserted on several occasions, although she respected his talent and was aware of him as a man.

With Kazan interested in Marilyn so early in the game, it does seem remarkable that they never were to make a film together. The best explanation is that Marilyn's career up to the milestone of *Bus Stop* consisted of variations on a theme that held no interest for Kazan. By the time she made *Bus Stop*, she was about to marry one of Kazan's closest theatrical colleagues, Arthur Miller, but Miller and Kazan were still on the outs following events which occurred in 1952. Yet Kazan could not get Marilyn out of his mind. Some years after their first meeting he answered a question about his success by saying, "All that matters is the actor. That little human thing you want to get at – that little moisture in the girl's eyes, the way she lifts her hand, or the funny kind of laugh she's got in her throat." A better description of Marilyn would be hard to find.

Late in December 1950, Kazan appeared on the set of Marilyn's first "co-starring" film during the second week of shooting. He was there ostensibly to see how his former film editor, Harmon Jones, was making out. This was Jones's first major job of direction. Arthur Miller accompanied him – he was in Hollywood to sell a waterfront locale screenplay. Marilyn was involved in walking across a huge crowded room, possibly a ballroom or salon. Miller, who tells the story, can't remember the specific details.

What he does remember is that he and Kazan walked back towards the dressing-rooms when Marilyn ran off after completing a take. They didn't find her there, and director Jones wasn't sure where she had gone. "She goes off to a corner sometimes to be by herself," he said. "She took Hyde's death pretty hard." The two men found her in an adjoining studio warehouse alone with papiermâché gargoyles and Egyptian artifacts of plaster and gilt.

The immediate impact of that first meeting between Marilyn and her third husband can only be speculated upon. Miller said that they met again during that week at a Hollywood party given by Charles Feldman, then an agent on a par with the late Johnny Hyde. They were able to talk with some privacy during the evening, and it may have been then that Marilyn first realized Miller was the kind of man she had been seeking ever since her divorce from Jim Dougherty.

Still temporarily with Natasha during that critical period following Hyde's death, she came home from the Feldman party and described her rather unique impressions of Miller. "It was like running into a tree! You know – like a cool drink when you've got a fever. You see my toe – this toe? Well he sat and held my toe and we just looked into each other's eyes almost all evening." Then she said he had talked about his next play, and Marilyn had told him she longed for someone to admire, that most people can at least admire their fathers, but that she had never had one.

Later that week, a long letter arrived from Miller. It said in part: "Bewitch them [the public] with this image they ask for, but I hope and almost pray you won't be hurt in this game, nor ever change. . . . If you want someone to admire, why not Abraham Lincoln? Carl Sandburg has written a magnificent biography of him." The first part of this letter seemed not to have impressed Marilyn as much as the last, for she bought the volumes by Sandburg on Lincoln and began reading them. Her admiration for Lincoln carried over to the author himself, and within a few years she had met Carl Sandburg and become his friend.

Foremost among the apocrypha published about Marilyn has been the assertion that she was attracted by Miller's mind. This could not possibly have been the case. Miller, relaxed among friends, was not given to witticisms, pithy observations, or any other form of intellectual exercise. He was more apt to be a quiet and attentive listener or to ask someone like Marilyn a few uncomplicated questions about the movies that might have come from anyone's lips. The deceptively serene sense of being at home with himself which he radiated was not too different from Jim Dougherty's masculine stability.

Undeniably, his fame and the halo of his success did set him apart from anyone else she had met. But his boyish smile also seemed to suggest that he wanted to be liked.

Miller's visit to Hollywood was brief. Despite his renown as a prize-winning playwright, his first screenplay had not sold. In the letters that followed during 1951 their correspondence must have taken a serious turn, for soon Marilyn was telling Natasha that she was in love. There were also numerous phone calls and at least one or more meetings in New York.

During the next three years, they met half a dozen times in the East and Marilyn came to regard Brooklyn, Miller's birthplace, as a kind of earthly Elysium. For her, it was a place with lovely bridges, an international harbour, and families of every shade and origin living together harmoniously. Immediately following her ten months' marriage to Joe DiMaggio she told Dave Garroway in a radio interview: "I want to retire to Brooklyn." And when Marilyn had an unrealized ambition, it was not soon abandoned.

Marilyn's relationship with Arthur Miller as friend, lover, and wife would span an entire decade. Prior to their marriage there were periods when they were completely out of touch, but the ties that bound them were never really severed. Miller felt at once her extreme sensitivity. He moved cautiously, probably giving her little hope at first that his family situation would be resolved. He was aware, too, early in their relationship, of her sense of futility. While her intentions were plain – and Marilyn was rarely devious when approaching something of great importance – he knew that if he were to marry her at some future date when he was free he would also have to save her and instil in her some confidence.

There were other friends in her life, usually back-of-the-camera people assigned to her such as Allan "Whitey" Snyder, her make-up man; Agnes Flanagan, who styled her hair; and Rupert Allan, who was in the process of resigning from *Look* to become a press representative for film stars. Marilyn was one of his first clients. In the years ahead she became extremely close to these people and a handful of others. Nearly all of them felt free enough with Marilyn to occasionally give her advice, to disagree with her, but in the background their status as employees was firmly defined. If anyone crossed the line and became involved in her life – such as Natasha Lytess had done – they became vulnerable to dismissal from it. Miller was perceptive enough to see this very early, although human enough to forget what he had seen once they were married.

Her years with Miller were the ones that defined her as a person and as an actress. With his help, she attempted to live like other people even though the legend was growing.

Despite the bitterness that followed in the wake of their divorce, Marilyn saved all of her letters from him. Immediately following her death in 1962 they were found in a small chest in her Brentwood home by her mother's guardian, Inez Melson. It is not easy to determine what moved her to preserve them when she had cut out of her life every tie with Miller except his father, Isidore. She was sufficiently aware of her fame and his place in American letters to realize their value, but I suspect that it was not history she was thinking of but those not so distant days when hope had supplanted futility and happiness seemed almost possible.

Fox released three films "co-starring" Marilyn in 1951. The best of them, *Love Nest*, immediately followed *As Young As You Feel*. I. A. L. Diamond, who later collaborated with Billy Wilder on Marilyn's most commercially (and some say, artistically) successful film, *Some Like It Hot*, had written a sprightly screenplay around the flimsy idea of a young man returned from the war to his wife and her renovated brownstone house in New York. He is expecting the imminent arrival of an army friend, "Bobby", who turns out to be a woman recently discharged from the WACs. The lines were bright and amusing, and the film itself held up better than most other early Marilyn films, excluding the classic *Asphalt Jungle* and *All About Eve*. It suffered mainly from its other performers' anaemia: June Haver, the wife; William Lundigan, her husband; and Jack Parr, playing a family friend who makes several awkward passes at Marilyn, as the ex-WAC, were all, unfortunately, bland screen personalities. Whatever flavour the film had was given it by Frank Fay, who played a rascal with decent instincts, and Marilyn, who emerged from this production as an actress able to instil more excitement into a role than it deserved.

There were sessions with the Fox publicity staff for a press release. Her studio biography was to go through a series of alterations, each a little more honest than the last. Her mother was deceased in the first one, an invalid in succeeding versions. Her father remained anonymous throughout.

Some months back in her Beverly Carlton studio apartment, Marilyn seemed to enjoy a period of sustained emotional well-being. But while her third Fox film, *Let's Make It Legal*, was being edited in the Fall of 1951, she suddenly decided to have a confrontation with the man she believed was her real father, possibly because the emphasis on her waif status was bringing Norma Jean back to life in a way that was disturbing. She knew then that her reputed father once worked with her mother, that his name was Gifford, and her last information on him was that a friend of her mother's had seen him on the Paramount lot.

Gifford was located on a farm, The Red Rock Dairy, just outside of Hemet, a rural village near Palm Springs. The following Saturday, Marilyn phoned Natasha and asked if she would drive to Hemet with her. "I'm going to do it," she said. "I'm going to see my father."

Natasha then wanted to know if she had been in touch with him.

"Oh no! That's the whole point," Marilyn told her. "I'm going up to his farm and see him, talk to him."

Natasha had little to say to this. She knew Marilyn well enough by now to realize that opposition or advice frequently made her more determined. "Why don't you say something?"

Marilyn asked. "You agree, don't you? I mean, that I must see him? Tell him who I am and everything?"

With some reluctance, Natasha agreed to accompany her.

After serving in World War II, C. Stanley Gifford had remarried. Through some luck in investments, he had a considerable sum of money at the time of this second marriage. He reinvested a good part of these earnings in real estate, first in some cabins at a resort known as Gilman Hot Springs, a mineral spa. Soon after this venture, he bought ten acres just outside Hemet, where he established his dairy. This was successful almost from the very beginning. He moved there with his second wife, but shortly thereafter, illness disrupted his life. His new wife died of cancer within a few months and he himself began having heart trouble. He suffered two attacks within a period of a few months. In between these two illnesses, he remarried once again. His last wife, a few years younger than he, ran the dairy after his second attack. Marilyn was unaware of most of this history.

The highway from Los Angeles to Hemet and Palm Springs runs eastward across the date-palm country. Natasha recalled that Marilyn was silent much of the way, almost in a daze, but it did not appear to affect her driving.

When they passed Riverside, she pulled over onto the shoulder and stopped. A highway phone booth was a few yards ahead. "I'm going to phone him," she said. "I can't just barge in on him this way."

Natasha recalled that she quickly agreed, and as she watched Marilyn run to the booth and deposit a coin, she prayed silently, *Treat her kindly*.

Marilyn repeated the jarring conversation later to one of her trusted confidantes: "Hello," Marilyn said. "Is Mr. Gifford there?"

"Who's calling him?" a woman inquired sternly.

"This is Marilyn. I'm his child . . . I mean, the little girl years ago. Gladys Baker's daughter. He's sure to know who I am."

"I don't know who you are," the woman said, "but I'll tell him you're on the phone." Natasha recalls that there then followed a minute or two of silence, during which Marilyn leaned back, eyes closed, seemingly fighting an impulse to hang up.

Finally the woman came back on again. "He doesn't want

to see you. He suggests you see his lawyer in Los Angeles if you have some complaint. Do you have a pencil?"

"No," Marilyn said in a defeated tone. "I don't have a pencil. Good-bye." She walked back to the car and slumped over the wheel.

CHAPTER FIVE

During that frantic year of 1951–52, when Marilyn was rushed from one film to the next, film critics were mostly kind and tolerant of her rough edges. A certain protectiveness began to develop among a few of them, important because their praise and acceptance of her as a serious actress were the chief factors that made Marilyn's films as popular with intellectuals as with the majority of movie-goers. Marilyn was beginning to say something of significance to these people. Two of them, Alton Cook in the New York *World Telegram and Sun* and Otis L. Guernsey, Jr., in the New York *Herald Tribune*, appeared to have become increasingly mesmerized by her screen presence.

Some of the parts, such as her role as a gold-digging hanger-on at a fashionable hotel in *Let's Make It Legal*, were brief and not important enough to do much for her career, but these pictures were made before the production executives at Fox became aware of the impact of her appearances in such films as *As Young As You Feel* and *Love Nest*. Her earlier sensation in *All About Eve* was still winning her new fans well into 1951 since it ran for months both at home and abroad. Marilyn was often a stricter critic of her performances than most of her critics and fans. She would sometimes become physically ill while viewing a completed picture.

Occasionally Marilyn felt frustrated in the hands of un-creative directors and insisted that one of them did nothing more than read parts of the script back to her like a parrot. But basically she was unhappy with her situation as an actress. In time, as her rage and frustration grew, this would lead her to seek psychiatric help. At this earlier stage, she realized suddenly and to her horror that she had become a studio commodity and that she was being assigned indiscriminately all of the dumb-blonde roles and that often her inclusion in a movie was just an afterthought inspired by her growing popularity.

She felt helpless without Johnny Hyde. The William Morris Agency treated her shabbily almost from the day of his funeral. To Marilyn, it seemed as if they blamed her for his death. When in early 1951 she dropped by their Hollywood offices she was treated with icy disinterest. She then phoned Harry Lipton to complain that "all the Morris Office cares about is Betty Hutton". She told him she was thinking of leaving and asked what he thought about Hugh French at Famous Artists Agency. Lipton assured her that French was one of the best and that she was probably right about the Morris Office.

With the groundwork carefully laid by Johnny Hyde, Marilyn's film career began to ignite under Hugh French's management. He was able to get her contract upgraded within a short time and for several years was an able mediator between Marilyn and her studio.

But there were limits to any agent's ability to help shape the career of an actress under a long-term contract to a film company. In the decade of Marilyn's contract with Fox (not counting her rebellious year of 1955), she was given sixteen film roles of which only four could be considered worth doing: *Bus Stop, Gentlemen Prefer Blondes, The Seven Year Itch*, and *How to Marry a Millionaire*. The others vary from dreadful (*Let's Make Love*) to passable (*Niagara*), and responsibility for Marilyn's poor handling must be assumed by the Fox hierarchy.

There were notable properties and original writers around throughout this period, but with the four exceptions cited above, little was done to see that the studio's top female star be given anything choice. She admired *Pillow Talk* as crisp and funny. She knew she could play the female lead expertly, but its authors were committed to Universal and Doris Day's own film company. With the single exception of *Bus Stop*, her finest films, *Some Like It Hot, The Misfits*, and *The Prince and the Showgirl*, were made outside her home studio, and all four followed her declaration of independence and the formation of Marilyn Monroe Productions.

Much of the trouble emanated from the industry itself and its ills. *Play it safe* was etched deeply into the minds of the studio heads. While her European counterpart, Brigitte Bardot, moved from one fresh and daring film to the next, Marilyn was stifled by unoriginal and musty old scripts. Her final "illness", which led to a total breakdown in communication between herself and the studio on *Something's Got To Give,* grew directly out of her conviction that she was being forced to play in a retooled and dated marital farce under equally outdated contractual terms (she was to be paid $100,000 while the studio was paying Elizabeth Taylor over a million for *Cleopatra*). As proof of her contention, if any were needed, the same script would later let down even the unsinkable Miss Day when it was finally shot as *Move Over, Darling.*

Had Hollywood properly forecast the future of the experiments in film being made in Europe and assigned Marilyn to medium-budget films that strived for new insights and excitement, she might have survived not only her final summer but most of her personal hang-ups. With a few notable exceptions such as *Sunset Boulevard* and *The Three Faces of Eve,* excitement and originality had been dead or dying in Hollywood throughout Marilyn's rise. In the last months of her life she was aware, however, of the changes in the air and was plotting her own participation in that new scene.

Yet in spite of all her misgivings, Marilyn was not totally immune to the Hollywood syndrome. When her last film, *The Misfits,* was in preparation she was disturbed by the decision of director John Huston, producer Frank Taylor, and finally even Arthur Miller to make the picture in black and white rather than colour. "All of my important pictures have been made in colour," she complained, forgetting that her greatest success had been the black and white *Some Like It Hot.* She and Miller had substantial financial interest in the film and she was afraid to take chances, but she was persuaded by these gentlemen that colour would destroy much of the film's impact.

Despite her dedication and tenacity, no one at her studio really took her seriously as an actress at any point. Pampering her and later giving her a certain amount of power were scarcely compensation for their contempt. When she wasn't furious, Marilyn might try to smile at this disrespect, but the smile was more than a little wry. And there was always a reporter on *their* side around who would ask when she intended playing Lady Macbeth.

Jack Palance, whom Marilyn had met during her final months at Columbia (where he had made an overnight success of the romantic villain in *Sudden Fear*), found himself in an equally shaky position in 1950. He was greatly in demand, but felt his roles to be limited not only by his lack of craft but also by his cadaverous appearance. To improve the former he had a choice of several established and respected acting schools. He finally chose that of Michael Chekhov, nephew of the Russian playwright and one of the two men (the other was Joshua Logan) who had studied under the great Stanislavski who were also to become instrumental in furthering Marilyn's career. Palance and his actress wife spent an entire summer in Chekhov's class. When he next met Marilyn he unhesitatingly recommended the class to her.

During the decade after he left Stanislavski, Chekhov had remained in Russia, refining his own theories about the craft of acting. These studies resulted in a definitive text, *To the Actor*, used nearly everywhere in the world. Unlike the directors of the Actors Studio, who also were indebted to Stanislavski, Chekhov preferred to use the classics exclusively, especially *King Lear, Hamlet*, and *Twelfth Night*.

Marilyn became excited by Palance's enthusiasm and enrolled in the Fall of 1951. Within a few months she was playing Cordelia to Michael Chekhov's King Lear. The transformation of her teacher into the old and forsaken King never ceased to amaze her. "That is what I find most exciting about acting," she declared. "The illusion that became reality. Mr Chekhov *is* Lear."

Chekhov's widow, Xenia, remembers clearly how impressed her husband was with the sensitivity of Marilyn's Cordelia, and he reinforced Marilyn's own growing suspicion that she was being wasted in most of her screen roles. Unlike her late teacher, Lee Strasberg, Chekhov never once discussed the stage as a possibility but believed her future was in roles of increasing depth and dimension on the screen.

She kept Chekhov – who soon became fond of her – and Natasha Lytess in separate compartments of her life. They were never to meet. This branching out may have been unsettling to Natasha. "I taught her how to walk, how to breathe," Natasha later wrote, but Marilyn was now declaring her independence from her in everything but script study.

Sometime during 1952, Marilyn gave Chekhov an engraving

of Abraham Lincoln, and said, "Lincoln was the man I admired most all through school. Now that man is you." Having a talent for espying odd treasures in shops and galleries, Marilyn gave her ageing teacher an old and quite valuable ikon of St. Nicholas for his last Christmas in 1954. In such small but touching ways she endeared herself to the Chekhovs. Marilyn remained in close touch with them until Michael's death in September 1955, and on her last Thanksgiving Day in 1961 she paid homage to his memory by giving his widow a fine tape recorder. She believed that thanks should be given on that holiday to friends to whom she was grateful.

As with all her close associates, there were moments when she became a trial to the Russian teacher. She often made an appointment then failed to keep it or else arrived so terribly late she conflicted with someone else's lesson. At one point, Chekhov told her that it might be better for her to forget her lessons for a while. The strain had become too much for him. The matter was resolved by a touching note from Marilyn:

Dear Mr. Chekhov:
 Please don't give me up yet – I know (painfully so) that I try your patience.
 I need the work and your friendship desperately, I shall call you soon.

> Love,
> Marilyn Monroe.

Before summer arrived in 1952, Marilyn had made half a dozen films under her new contract for Fox and one on loan-out to RKO which became more important to her career than any of her early Fox films. The RKO production was an adaptation by the novelist-playwright, Alfred Hays – who had been called to Hollywood following his successful war novel, *The Girl on the Via Flamina* – of Clifford Odets's *Clash by Night*.

The realistic story bears a superficial resemblance to Sidney Howard's *They Knew What They Wanted* in that it is set in a working-class environment in a town resembling Monterey and concerns an adulterous affair between a married woman and a stranger which leads to violence. In Odets's story, the wife's situation is complicated by her brother, a stern young man of high ideals, who is engaged to a fish cannery worker, played with enormous persuasion and naïveté by Marilyn.

The troubled husband and wife were played by Paul Douglas

and Barbara Stanwyck; the stranger by Robert Ryan. None of them was especially pleased to find their young supporting actress in frequent conferences on the set with her personal drama coach, Natasha, and all of them were professionals with years in the theatre or films who found her failure to report for a scene on time unprecedented.

Some explanation is needed for Marilyn's notorious unpunctuality. It got worse from this film on and led to uneven and often strained relationships with her employers. Until 1956 and the filming of *The Prince and the Showgirl* her lateness had nothing to do with her use of barbiturates to fight her chronic insomnia. She would rise before daybreak and begin getting ready to leave for the studio. Before seven she was usually on her way, sometimes catching some more rest en route if she were in a chauffeured limousine supplied by the studio. In her dressing-room, she would sip at black coffee while Allan "Whitey" Snyder made her up, and a hair stylist worked over her hair, and Margie Plecher arranged her costuming. All of this required something over two hours. Then she would review her lines with Natasha, and if they weren't right she would barricade herself in the dressing-room for another half-hour or hour.

Her closest associates called her a perfectionist, but there was a strong element of insecurity in her behaviour. As the films became more important and her scenes more numerous, her uncertainties mounted so much that her last six years were even more disturbed by the additional factor of sedatives and tranquillizers.

When *Clash by Night* went into release, all of the New York film critics were in agreement that Marilyn was sensational. Alton Cook, one of the most astute of them, said she was "gratifyingly good" with "an abundance of girlish high spirits. She is a forceful actress, too, when crisis comes along ... a gifted new star, worthy of all that fantastic press agentry".

The opening of this film in February 1952 was well timed, for the favourable notices served to counterbalance the bad publicity occasioned by the discovery of her poses in the nude. The calendar she had done for Tom Kelley had been seen by a wire-service reporter Aline Mosby. Miss Mosby was convinced the model in "Golden Dreams" was none other than Marilyn Monroe and contacted Jerry Wald, the producer of *Clash by Night*.

Marilyn had no one to guide her through this ordeal. Ever since Hyde's death she had sought opinions from the handful of associates she felt that she could trust; Whitey Snyder, columnist Sidney Skolsky, Natasha. They all advised her to acknowledge that she was "Miss Golden Dreams", which was what Marilyn had wanted to do from the beginning.

The public's favourable reaction to her admission encouraged Marilyn to follow her instincts from that time on. A few years later she was to do her bedroom love scene in *Bus Stop* in the nude with only a sheet draping her for the camera. In *The Misfits* there was a scene with Clark Gable during which she bared her breasts to the camera. She attempted to persuade John Huston to use the uncut version for European distribution, but without success.

Among her Fox films of this period are two comedies that were great box-office hits; the first was a film of the omnibus type made popular some years earlier by *Tales of Manhattan*. It was written and produced by Nunnally Johnson, who was one of Marilyn's favourite writers until he did *Something's Got to Give*. *We're not Married*, which went into release in July 1952, was an episodic and rather irreverent treatment of marriage strung together by Victor Moore, playing a justice of the peace, who discovers too late that he has no legal authority to marry anyone. Marilyn played opposite David Wayne to whom she was wed by the dubious Mr. Moore. When she discovers that her marriage is not valid, she enthusiastically competes for the Miss America prize – which she wins – with ex-husband Wayne cheering her on from the sidelines, their son in his arms. This sequence very neatly parallels Marilyn's own ability to turn disasters into personal triumphs and the film played holdover engagements throughout the country.

The other substantial success of this time was *Monkey Business*, released in September 1952, in which she played opposite Charles Coburn and, to the amazement of her employers, displayed a remarkable skill as a comic actress. She turned in an equally funny performance with this same droll gentleman a year later in *Gentlemen Prefer Blondes*.

But Marilyn was to have a distressing failure in *Don't Bother to Knock*, where she was required to play a mentally-ill baby-sitter who becomes more interested in the hoodlum across the air shaft than in her charge. The script was implausible and director Roy Baker seemed uncertain as to how Marilyn's role should be played. The decision was left to Marilyn and Natasha to work out on their own. When the film was premièred in New York in August 1952, nearly every critic suggested that Marilyn return quickly to comic roles.

Both Wilder and Lee Strasberg had said much the same thing: that Marilyn had to find the key or "handle" of a role in order to play it convincingly, and unless a director was able to hand it to her, her performance would suffer. It is possible that Roy Baker and, two years later, Otto Preminger, were both unable to communicate their grasp of the roles she was to play for them. Marilyn had an intuitive sense of character motivation, and if it was faulty no amount of explanation by her director would make it work for her.

When she grasped the key, the result was pure joy. Montgomery Clift, the most brilliant of all Marilyn's co-stars and the one New York-based film actor she wanted to meet when she moved there in 1955, was to say in a most candid interview shortly before his death: "Marilyn was an incredible person to act with ... the most marvellous I ever worked with, and I have been working for 29 years. But she went over the fringe. Playing a scene with her, it was like an escalator. You'd do something and she'd catch it and it would go like that, just right up."

By the time Fox was shooting their fifth film with Marilyn (since her return to them as a stellar performer), she finally seemed at home with her new life and identity. In O. Henry's *Full House* she played opposite Charles Laughton, and while at first she likened this to an audience with God, he quickly put her at ease and she was able to bring tender pathos to her interpretation of a young and sensitive street-walker. Her performance emanated from her own understanding and was to be a preliminary sketch for Roslyn, another bruised innocent she was to play, in *The Misfits*.

Marilyn now, with the security, albeit temporary, of a woman who believed she knew who she was and what she was about, was able to question the motives of some of her closest associates, notably Natasha Lytess, something her previous insecurity had made impossible earlier.

Two incidents provoked this reappraisal within the space of a year. The first was a strange illness of Natasha's. She complained of throat trouble and informed Marilyn that her doctor suspected a malignancy. Although Marilyn was earning $750 weekly, she was hardly in a position to underwrite an operation of this nature.

Marilyn felt genuinely obligated to Natasha. Long after the woman had gone from her life, whenever her name was mentioned she would say "Poor Natasha!" Mentor and coach, Natasha had taken Marilyn under her wing when she was between contracts and had offered her the refuge of her apartment during the early stages of Marilyn's career. She had nurtured her talents with great care and intelligence, and deservedly took much of the credit for making Marilyn a star of the first magnitude. With this debt weighing heavily upon her as well as genuine concern for Natasha's survival, Marilyn sold her mink coat to pay for the operation. When Marilyn confided to some friends that she was puzzled by Natasha's quick recovery, they suggested that Natasha had exploited her with a hard-luck story.

Fortunately Marilyn said nothing of her doubts to Natasha, for some months before Marilyn's own sudden death, Natasha's health began to fail rapidly. In 1964, she left a comfortable apartment in Rome to enter a cancer clinic in Switzerland, where she died within six months.

When the mysterious business of Max Reinhardt's manuscripts occurred, Marilyn was convinced that Natasha was something less than a selfless friend. Marilyn had bought the manuscripts at auction, having become interested in Reinhardt through Michael Chekhov and Natasha, who had once been a member of the Reinhardt acting ensemble.

Once it became known that Marilyn owned the folios, university drama departments expressed some indignation. Why should a feather-weight actress like Marilyn own such valuable theatrical memorabilia? At that time Natasha came to Marilyn with the news that Reinhardt's own son was living in reduced circumstances nearby and desperately wanted the manuscripts returned to family hands. Through Natasha, Marilyn promptly sold them to the young Reinhardt for what she paid for them.

Some months later, according to her press representative Rupert Allan, who had been appalled by this abuse of her good will, Marilyn discovered that Reinhardt had resold the annotated playscripts to a university at considerable profit. Immediately, Marilyn regretted her gesture and began feeling deep and permanent mistrust towards Natasha. Had the woman acted as a broker and shared some of Reinhardt's profits? Marilyn never did find out. Natasha stayed on the Fox studio payroll and saw Marilyn through six more films, for Marilyn still felt helpless without her on a sound stage, but there was little socializing after hours and none at all following Marilyn's second marriage to Joe DiMaggio.

By this time Marilyn had found other confidants. One of them was the movie columnist Sidney Skolsky, who spent much of his time sitting in a section of Schwab's Drugstore on Sunset Strip several blocks above the apartment on Doheny Drive in which she now lived. She had also become close to her new business manager, Inez Melson, who had assumed the burden of guiding Marilyn's affairs when it had become clear that Marilyn simply could not live comfortably on her salary and was sinking deeply into debt. Doc Goddard, who had volunteered to manage her money when she first began her climb to fame, had by then given up the chore and subsided into the background with those few friends she would call from time to time, perhaps to remind herself that she had once lived quite a different life as Norma Jean. Now that she was secure in her new identity, she could afford to peek occasionally at the ghosts from her past.

But apparently she was never going to be able to accept the tragedy of her mother's existence. Marilyn had until 1952 permitted the State of California to carry the burden of caring for her mother in a public institution just outside Los Angeles. But when this arrangement became general knowledge and an obvious embarrassment, Mrs. Melson suggested that the state appoint her (Mrs. Melson) as Conservator of Gladys's estate. This was tantamount to a guardianship. Within a few weeks, Gladys was quietly moved from the state hospital to a private nursing home managed by Agnes Richards, one of Gladys's old friends from her film-cutting days. From then on Marilyn had to face this not-too-recognizable phantom from the past. She visited her occasionally with Mrs. Melson, and carried the financial burden of Gladys's care until her own death when this need was met by Marilyn's estate.

CHAPTER SIX

Marilyn was beginning to experience a new kind of fear. This is not to say she became morose; she could usually subdue her anxieties to the point that her friends were often unaware of their existence. Much of the time her gaiety, wit, and even her temper covered the real emotions just below the surface. But her make-up man, Whitey Snyder, who had entered Marilyn's life with *Clash by Night*, and Arthur Miller were to learn much about Marilyn's internal turmoil. Snyder detected immediately Marilyn's nervous sensity and soon began wondering if she should not quit films before it was too late. He felt she was too genuine to surround herself with the phonies and hangers-on who by now had encircled her life. "The trouble with Marilyn was she didn't trust her own judgement, always had someone around to depend on. Coaches, so-called friends. Even me."

Miller has agreed with Snyder's judgement, and said, "She had this fear of any involvement which would endanger her personally. People in her situation are either victims or else they're the aggressor – which they can't bear the thought of." Because of her early deprivation it would be easy to decide that she was a victim, but that would be a shallow judgement. As time went on, Marilyn rapidly dismissed people from her life whom she thought to be deceitful. Her community of friends was constantly changing as she advanced in her career, and as her interests grew and diversified. From as early as 1952 until a few months before her death, she conducted an unrelenting series of experiments in adapting herself to her life and world.

Marilyn had recently undergone an appendectomy and had discovered the temporary isolation from the growing pressures of her screen work rather of a restorative tonic. Although she continued her sporadic reading in such works as *The Prophet* by Kahlil Gibran, it could not be said that much of her time was spent in introspection. Marilyn herself has given a fairly comprehensive account of these periods. Once in her white-carpeted living-room, she would kick off her shoes and turn

on the record player. She preferred Ella Fitzgerald and Mel
Torme, known as "the Velvet Fog", as well as such moody
instrumentals as "I Cover the Waterfront". She would usually
turn up the volume for companionship.

On one such evening in April 1952, Marilyn recalled, the
phone rang just at the moment she had got into blue jeans
and was relaxing over a martini. It was a girl-friend who was
persuaded that Marilyn was becoming a recluse. "Did you
forget our date? We've been waiting for nearly an hour. He
isn't just anybody, you know."

Marilyn had indeed forgotten the plans made only the day
before. She said she was sorry and that she knew the man she
was supposed to meet wasn't just anybody. He was a baseball
player. A Yankee. "But can't you make my apologies?" she
asked. "I've already changed and I'm exhausted. I look terrible."

"This isn't Romanoff's," her friend had insisted. "You can't
let me down."

Marilyn knew nothing about baseball beyond the games she
had played against the boys at the orphanage. She had heard
of the name *DiMaggio* however, probably ever since 1941
when he was known as Joltin' Joe, the Yankee Clipper. She
would call him her "Slugger" soon and until she died.

She liked him on sight. "He was different," she later told
a reporter who cornered her in New York when rumours were
spreading that she and DiMaggio were headed for divorce.
Her denial was an elaborate one, going into some detail about
the circumstances surrounding their first meeting. "I was
afraid when I heard he was a ball player and part of the sports
crowd, he might have slick black hair and wear flashy clothes,
but he was very conservative. Like a bank vice-president or
something. His hair had a touch of grey in it. I liked that. And
I could see he was as shy as I was. No jokes that I can remember. Not then. Not even any compliments. My exhaustion left
me all of a sudden."

She did not know that he was a native Californian like
herself. She had somehow assumed that he was from New
York. "I still live here in San Francisco. I come down once
in a while," he told her.

Marilyn said she had gone to San Francisco once to do publicity for a movie she would like to forget. "Did you like the

place?" DiMaggio wanted to know, and Marilyn thought his question sounded more eager than polite.

"I liked the view from the hills," she told him. "But it was a little chilly the day I was there."

Then DiMaggio explained that this was the great thing about it. "They call it the air-conditioned city."

"Yeah," Marilyn agreed, "but you can't turn it off."

Then Marilyn remembered that DiMaggio laughed. Sometimes he would weep when he was laughing.

In noting that he looked like a bank executive, Marilyn had put a finger on one of DiMaggio's character traits: a constant quest for dignity, a quest she complicated seriously. Not that Marilyn was undignified. She was by now *Marilyn*, take it or leave it, with a variety of moods that ranged from the very proper to the outrageous.

DiMaggio admired clothes more than she did, and had an extensive wardrobe with an entire closet devoted to sports attire. He liked dark shades in his business suits and vivid blues and blazing reds in his casual and golfing apparel. He enjoyed being recognized by the colour of his jacket, and at thirty-seven he was in magnificent shape, with the exception of a spur in his heel, which would provoke occasional gasps of pain.

Marilyn soon discovered that DiMaggio enjoyed his popularity nearly as much as his privacy, and that his celebrity was as pervasive as her own was becoming. When he attempted to turn into a home-body for Marilyn's sake, it was foredoomed to failure.

As DiMaggio gradually became her most intimate friend, her protector against the sharks of Hollywood, the exploiters, and false friends, all contact between Marilyn and Miller ceased. It seemed that he could not bring himself to make a break with his family, knowing his wife would get custody cf his son and daughter. He says that he was making a final effort to save his marriage and during the next two years immersed himself in the writing of *The Crucible*.

When it was all over between DiMaggio and Marilyn as husband and wife, and prior to the closeness that was to develop during her last years, DiMaggio gave in to occasional waves of self-pity. John Conley, Anne Karger's brother, remembers an evening when DiMaggio called them and asked if he could come over. By chance, Marilyn's early escort, Fred Karger, was there, and finding conversation with DiMaggio

difficult, Karger began to play the piano. DiMaggio listened
for a while and then he held up his strong, large-boned hands
and said bitterly: "These hands! They're only good for hit-
ting a ball with a bat." There was a deep vein of operatic melancholy in him at such times, but this was a self put-down
of extraordinary proportions.

During the week of their first meeting, DiMaggio escorted
Marilyn to dinner at least three times. Natasha scolded her,
privately believing "she could do better". Her memoirs make
very clear her feelings about DiMaggio. She was convinced
that Marilyn would vegetate with such a man, and perhaps
sensing the disapproval, DiMaggio disliked her on sight. Natasha was perhaps the first in a long line of Marilyn's associates
with whom he felt no personal warmth.

Before 1953 was very far advanced, DiMaggio was deeply
in love with Marilyn, and the feeling was returned, guardedly.
He had expressed his strong disapproval of nearly everyone
she knew with the exception of Inez Melson, her business
manager, and Whitey Snyder. There were occasional evenings
out with Whitey and his wife and several Sundays spent on his
boat off Malibu. Cutting through pretensions with the skill of
a man who had known his way around the Broadway crowd
for years, he eliminated most of the phonies and "leeches".
Marilyn, rather a loner herself, voiced no serious objections.

Both of them made an effort to enjoy the other's special
interests. Marilyn enjoyed their fishing trips and they reminded her of her pleasanter moments with Jim Dougherty.
She presented DiMaggio with a collection of books, a selection Natasha Lytess described as including "everything from
Mickey Spillane to Jules Verne". DiMaggio came from a
family of fishermen, and the sport was as natural to him as the
swing of a bat. But reading was an acquired taste of Marilyn's,
and DiMaggio may have believed there was a tinge of pretension about it.

In September 1952, the last of Marilyn's co-starring films
opened at the Roxy Theatre in New York. *Monkey Business*
had been written by Ben Hecht, Charles Lederer and the re-
sourceful future partner of Billy Wilder, I. A. L. Diamond.
Its stars were Cary Grant, Ginger Rogers, and Charles Coburn, and its antic suburban nonsense descended in a direct
line from one of Irene Dunne's earliest comedies, *Theodora*

Goes Wild. Early in that film a prim spinster is revealed to have written a racy best-seller and goes on to utterly destroy her image as village old maid. In *Monkey Business*, the spark that ignites the story is a research monkey who gets out of his cage and into Cary Grant's laboratory, where he proceeds to mix a brew that apparently is the magic youth restorer Grant has been seeking for a long time. The potion is dumped by the monkey into the water cooler and in time all of the principals except Marilyn, as Coburn's secretary, have imbibed and regressed to juvenilism. The film's formula, that of reducing conventional behaviour to absurdity, worked well for its stars and did as well at the box office as Marilyn's earlier *We're Not Married*. A latecomer among the critics discovering Marilyn was Paul V. Beckley writing in the New York *Herald Tribune*: "Not having seen Miss Monroe before, I know now what that's all about, and I've no dissenting opinions to offer. She disproves more than adequately the efficacy of the old stage rule about not turning one's back to the audience."

Just after completing *Monkey Business* in the late spring of 1952, Marilyn's studio bosses finally decided to put her into a starring vehicle. She was summoned to a conference concerning the film attended by its producer, Charles Brackett, who had in 1950 collaborated with Billy Wilder on *Sunset Boulevard*, and Henry Hathaway, assigned to direct the upcoming film. She had been told something of the story by Brackett earlier. The studio had come to feel that Marilyn deserved a monumental setting for the first picture tailored to her particular abilities and had decided upon no less than Niagara Falls. Brackett had retooled a script by Walter Reish and Richard Breen in which Marilyn would be playing a seductive villainess in love with a young man who is supposed to murder her husband. The studio rightly assumed that there was no need to fuss over details since the audience would come to see Marilyn and, possibly, the Falls. The film's central situation was adulterous: Marilyn as Rose Loomis was married to a brooding older man, played by Joseph Cotten, recently released from a mental hospital. Most of her scenes with her lover were to take place in such uncomfortable places as the rock shelter beneath the thundering falls. All of the adultery was hosed down by torrents of water with the lovers encased in chaste slickers.

There were to be at least two weeks of location shooting at

the Falls for *Niagara*. Marilyn flew to New York before going to Buffalo with her co-stars, Joseph Cotten and Jean Peters and her support cast, including Casey Adams as the garrulous and square husband of Miss Peters, and Richard Allan, the lover of the amoral Rose Loomis. DiMaggio was already in Manhattan, and he took her to Toots Shor's, where she met Toots, a longtime DiMaggio friend, and George Solitaire, a Broadway ticket broker who had become as close to DiMaggio in the East as bartender Reno Barsocchini was on the West Coast. Marilyn liked Solitaire at once. He was years older than DiMaggio but she must have sensed his deep loyalty to the Yankee Clipper. Solitaire became one of three older men who thought of Marilyn as a daughter – Joe Schenck earlier, and Isidore Miller, Arthur's father, four years later.

Director Henry Hathaway was already aware of Marilyn's emergence as the publicly accepted successor to Harlow. Several things had crystallized in her screen personality. Her voice had dropped to a lower register (where it would remain) and its breathy sexuality could be edited and husbanded for maximum impact, as exploitable as her provocative buttock-swinging gait, her moist-lipped open mouth, and her ash blonde hair. Sewn into a skin-tight red dress, Marilyn was followed by Hathaway's camera in a long tracking shot as she walked across a wide tourist vista. His focus was frankly vulgar. Marilyn's red-clad bottom, swinging in a pattern of movement few could duplicate, transcended this vulgarity and offended only the most puritanical of the film's vast audience. Somehow Marilyn's ingenuousness made innocent what Mae West earlier had burlesqued.

Upon its release in February 1953 the film elevated Marilyn to the élite of top-grossing stars. While studio executives frequently abused her verbally ("Hasn't that bitch left her dressing-room yet?"), there was respect, especially in the New York office, for her earning powers. Spyros Skouras, studio president at the time, was probably chiefly responsible for the soft-glove approach in handling Marilyn which began at this time. In one sense, this coddling had an adverse effect upon Marilyn's life: she needed the tension of opposition for she had moved against contrary forces most of her life. When the studio on three occasions disagreed with her, she walked out, and each time was taken back, welcomed back. The crisis of her final summer had its beginnings in that winter of 1952–53

when Skouras began sending west his memos on how to keep
Marilyn happy.

She had become fluid in her work and in her life away from
the cameras. She was open to change, to doing something a
little differently and a little better than before. But the studio
by now saw her as a highly commercial product of Hollywood's assembly line.

DiMaggio as a ball player had also aimed for the intoxicat-
ing plateau of success where the fans expect miracles and get
them. He had retired only the previous year, in 1951, and
his legend had begun ten years earlier when the Yankees had
lost four in a row. DiMaggio sparked a winning streak for his
team and a remarkable series of hits for himself, breaking the
record of George Sisler established in 1922. The New York
Yankees won the pennant that year, going on to win the World
Series as well.

Perhaps there is some reason why those who turn a skill
or a talent into something splendid and breathtaking have
such difficulties with their private lives. When DiMaggio retired he was earning $100,000 a year. He had been in nine
World Series, but he seemed withdrawn and incapable of happiness away from the diamond. His first marriage, to actress
Dorothy Arnold, had ended in divorce, although his boy, Joe,
Jr., remained one of his few joys.

The same thing was already happening to Marilyn. Nearly
all of her ego and energy were being funnelled into her career.
If one is to make a judgement based upon the lives of these
two, it would seem that ego-driven successes have very little
to offer their companions after hours. What Marilyn needed
away from the camera was a challenge, a stimulus to shake her
out of her exhaustion.

In the Fall of 1952, the studio announced that they had
bought the Broadway musical version of Anita Loos's *Gentlemen Prefer Blondes*. They could not say in that first announcement that it had been purchased for Marilyn since an elfin-
like but big blonde named Carol Channing had created the
role of Lorelei, making her an original and very funny parody
of an opportunistic but loveable innocent. During a season
or two at the old Ziegfeld Theatre, Miss Channing had played
to standing room for months. There were film offers coming
in and it was expected by nearly everyone in New York that

when Miss Loos's reincarnated heroine sang "Bye, Bye Baby" from the screen, Miss Channing's ample mouth would be forming the words. But Fox had bought the property for Marilyn, and word was conveyed to her that she was not to be concerned about newspaper speculation concerning Carol Channing's debut as a film actress, at least not in *Blondes*.

Marilyn made two new friends during the production, which lasted fourteen weeks in the winter of 1952–53. Jane Russell, her co-star, remained close to her for many years. Miss Russell was married at the time to a former football player, Bob Waterfield. From what Miss Russell can recall of that first season of their friendship, Marilyn had been proposed to by DiMaggio and was very undecided about what she should do. She wanted to know what it was like being married to an athlete, but Miss Russell made it clear that her husband's gridiron fame had not affected her decision to become Mrs. Waterfield. This left Marilyn pretty much where she had been, and she was to defer her answer to DiMaggio until late 1953.

The other professionally based friendship was struck up with the choreographer assigned to the musical, Jack Cole. Later, at Marilyn's request, he was to guide her dances through two more films, *River of No Return* and *Let's Make Love*. When Marilyn encountered a thorough professional with whom she could work, she declined to give him up. Her professional family now included Whitey Snyder for make-up, Rupert Allan, who handled press relations, Inez Melson, her business affairs, Gladys Rasmussen, her hairdresser, and, of course, Natasha Lytess who, at Marilyn's instigation, had now become head drama coach at Fox where she worked steadily when Marilyn was between films.

When *Gentlemen Prefer Blondes* had its première at Grauman's Chinese Theatre on Hollywood Boulevard in August 1953, both Marilyn and Jane Russell were invited to place their palm prints in the cement of that famous front patio where Norma Jean had gone so many Saturday afternoons and attempted to fit her feet into those of the stars of the thirties.

Marilyn had come a long way as a comedienne by this time. *Blondes* was her sixth comedy if one excludes her brief appearance in *Love Happy* but includes her Miss Caswell in *All About Eve*. Otis L. Guernsey, Jr. wrote in the New York *Herald Tribune* that Marilyn looked "as though she would

glow in the dark." What he was doubtless saying was that she
had by now acquired a distinctive image on the screen. Strasberg was later to describe it as both luminous and "gauze-like"
and comparable to the effect of seeing Jeanne Eagels on the
stage. She had, in sum, wrapped up the film and made the public forget even the magnificent Miss Channing.

Marilyn's photographers have given a clue to Marilyn's
photographic quality. Richard Avedon once said that "she
understood photography, and she also understood what makes
a great photograph – not the technique, but the content. . . .
She was more comfortable in front of the camera than away
from it. . . . She was completely creative. . . . She was very,
very involved with the meaning of what she was doing, in an
effort to make it more, to get the most out of it." Philippe
Halsman, whose *Life* magazine cover of Marilyn, her first,
in April 1952 had helped considerably to persuade her studio
that she was an important asset, suggested that "the only way
she knew to get herself accepted was to make herself desired.
Her behaviour in this direction was so strong that it even
worked with the camera".

Marilyn, who was not a natively beautiful woman, was able
to work a transformation. The audience was now seeing what
she wanted it to see. It was an act of witchcraft. Relaxed at last
before a movie camera, she was able to exercise some of the
vast experience she had stored away on the camera's uses and
possibilities. Elliott Erwitt, who, as a still photographer on
her last film, *The Misfits*, was to say that "even though she was
overweight at that time, she didn't look fat in pictures, which
is amazing. Very often, people who look attractive in person
look like hell in pictures; but she was the opposite". He said,
too, that "she was a very bright person, an instinctive type,
especially when the situation seemed right. Very rarely does
one meet a truly witty woman. Marilyn Monroe was one".
Marilyn's wit and alchemy had wrought the incandescent image that was to be seen from now on in her final nine films
after *Blondes*.

Spring of 1953 was a difficult time for Marilyn. Not only
was she being rushed from one film to another, but she was,
through the Chekhovs, exposing herself to all the theatre she
could find that would be useful to her. Mrs. Chekhov had
taken her to Lotte Goslar's Turabout Theatre that spring, and

Marilyn had liked Mrs. Goslar's staging of one of Anton Chekhov's plays so much that they went backstage to congratulate the lady director. When Marilyn learned that Mrs. Goslar was conducting a class of mime she asked to be enrolled.

Marilyn's very real need to be alone much of the time was now apparent and the need increased as she advanced into the period of her greatest fame and the pressures mounted. Nathanael West's image of Hollywood as a place of grotesques and a parody of American ambitions was not off the mark. If he had been writing in 1953, he might have used Marilyn and the friends she began gathering around her as models for the characters in *The Day of the Locust*. There was something savage in the hostility she was beginning to arouse in some quarters, countered by an equally fierce protectiveness.

Mr. Zanuck seemed satisfied that Marilyn had stood the test well when measured against the impressive competition of Niagara Falls. He and his associates now were very eager to see Marilyn stretched across the wide screen they had acquired under the name of Cinemascope. Nunnally Johnson, who had done well by Marilyn in *We're Not Married*, was asked to adapt a couple of old plays Fox had acquired years earlier into a major property to fit the title of a best-seller they had bought by Doris Lilly, *How to Marry a Millionaire*. They had thrown away the contents of the book as unsuitable for adaptation. The film, which would turn out surprisingly well, had yet another interesting sidelight; it brought Marilyn together with the former queen of the studio, Betty Grable.

Miss Grable was basically a healthy personality. As she moved close to her forties she seemed undismayed by the certainty that her pin-up days would soon be over. Unlike one or two of her contemporaries, Miss Grable was prepared to graciously step aside and leave the most spacious dressing-room suite on the Fox lot to Marilyn.

Marilyn's part was not enormous, but public interest was. On the first day of production, a small platoon of newspapermen and photographers converged on the set, all looking for Marilyn. Miss Grable glanced out of her dressing-room door and knew what they were after.

Lauren Bacall, the third female co-star, remembers that day when the three leading ladies were holed up in Miss Grable's dressing-room, the two older stars attempting to calm Mari-

lyn's jangled nerves. Betty Grable looked out at the dozen or
more newsmen and said, "They're looking for you, Marilyn."
Then she carefully scrutinized the young *arriviste*. "You can't
go out there looking like that," she said, reaching for a bottle
of nail polish. She stooped down and began re-doing Marilyn's toe-nails, visible in her gold sandals.

Most of Marilyn's memories of that film were pleasant.
Both Betty Grable and Lauren Bacall came to feel they had
to take care of her. This was not easy, for often she did not
arrive before the camera until 11 A.M. "She's frightened," Miss
Bacall told director Jean Negulesco. "She's absolutely terrified
of stepping before the camera." This statement, which conflicts
totally with the opinion of most of Marilyn's cameramen, only
reinforces the belief that Marilyn was a kind of living abstraction. She was what you believed her to be.

Lauren Bacall had first met Marilyn in 1950 at Romanoff's.
She was having lunch with Johnny Hyde, and Hyde brought
Marilyn over to Bogart's booth, where in addition to Lauren
Bacall Bogart, Marilyn first met the Nunnally Johnsons. It
was not easy for Miss Bacall to take up Marilyn socially, for
there was a certain amount of tension on the set because of
her behaviour. Apparently, from late 1952 onwards, there always would be. When she was not barricaded in her dressing-
room, she was looking beyond director Negulesco to Natasha
to see if she had done her work to that lady's satisfaction.

But Negulesco was a gentle, patient man and there were no
scenes. He accepted Marilyn's troubling insecurities and didn't
allow them to upset the other actors. Miss Bacall was impressed and came in time to adopt his attitude as her own. On
one occasion she invited Marilyn to spend the evening at the
Bogart mansion in Holmby Hills and her husband remembered
their earlier meeting at Romanoff's. Bogart, who had a splendid contempt for the studio hierarchy, liked Marilyn, but after
the evening was over apparently Lauren Bacall told her husband that it was not meant as anything more than a gesture of
friendliness, that she was not about to take up Marilyn as a
steady thing. "She's confused," Miss Bacall said. "She wants
to be happy, but she's not. I'm not even sure she's an actress,
but she wants to be."

There would be one other evening with the Bogarts when
How to Marry a Millionaire had its première in Hollywood
seven months later and the Nunnally Johnsons invited them

all to dinner. Bogart had spent much of that spring on location in Italy with John Huston, filming Truman Capote's final draft of *Beat the Devil*; even with Bogart gone there had been no real socializing between the women. But there was an occasional conversation on the set. Miss Bacall, who had once given Warner Brothers a few scares of her own, got fed up with some of the grumbling about Marilyn that she overheard from the studio heads. She warned Marilyn not to allow the studio to push her around. "I'm a little of a rebel, too," she told her. "And I know that when you stand up to them, the bastards back off." Once Marilyn came up to her and said, "Let's talk. There's nobody else I can talk to." Lauren Bacall was both moved and frightened, but she recalls that it wasn't easy to talk with Marilyn. There was little real communication, so involved was Marilyn with her own personality and its protection and advancement.

But if Marilyn was moving into an increasingly private world of her own making and cutting herself off from her peers, there were compensations. Her salary had been adjusted upwards almost to her satisfaction, and Nunnally Johnson's lines were bright, although she would be forced to bowdlerize Dorothy Parker's famous quote about girls who wear glasses. This came in the first scene between Marilyn as Pola Debevoise, a near-sighted blonde who bumps into things, and David Wayne as her landlord.

"Men aren't attentive to girls who wear glasses," Marilyn recited blankly to Wayne, while Jean Negulesco smiled encouragingly. It is possible the foreign-born director was unaware that all snap had been drained from the quotation.

Marilyn had welcomed Wayne as an old friend and good-luck token. It was to be his fourth and final appearance with her, for no reason other than chance.

To the uninitiated, it should be explained that four minutes out of every five spent on a movie in production are passed in waiting by performers and crew. During one such long wait, Miss Bacall remembers sitting idly on the set while her son, four-year-old Stevie, turned somersaults on a mattress used later in one of the bedroom scenes. Marilyn chanced upon him and ran over to watch the boy turning over and over. Her interest in children was always acute, especially if they belonged to someone she liked, and she usually had no difficulty communicating with them.

But on this occasion, something went wrong and she couldn't get through. She stood silent above the mattress until Miss Bacall called over to her son, "Stevie, this is Miss Monroe."

"Hi!" said Stevie as his head appeared.

Marilyn showed no concern over Stevie's determination to continue playing. "How old are you, Stevie?" she asked.

"Four," he said, as his face again bobbed into view.

"My!" she told him, "you're so big for your age! I would have thought you were two or three."

Stevie continued somersaulting, unperturbed, while Miss Bacall pondered over the remark.

During the season of Marilyn's romance with DiMaggio, each tried to join the other's orbit. He brought some of his suits down to Marilyn's Doheny Drive apartment and she gave over one of the closets for his "spare" clothes. Before Memorial Day arrived, DiMaggio was staying with Marilyn whenever he was in town, and it was impossible to keep their relationship a secret. Word spread that they were already married. They had endless discussions about it. She would soon be travelling to Banff, in Alberta, Canada, on location for a new film being done by Otto Preminger; it was agreed that DiMaggio would join her and they would come to a definite decision. In all that open space up there, miles from the Hollywood DiMaggio detested, surely they would know what to do.

CHAPTER SEVEN

The Preminger film had to be shot during the summer months when there was a maximum of sunshine in the rugged Canadian province. Marilyn seemed eager to leave Hollywood. The truth was she was never very happy being a member of any group, and even though she had now stepped into the inner circle of the highly famed and valued it was none the less a group.

She wanted to be liked, especially by men. She drew a measure of delight from the affection of her fans, but it was all too impersonal. In Hollywood, she had to be *on* much of the time at any gathering. While she seemed to enjoy drawing a circle of men around her, being courted and amiably kidded, it was a strain.

A serious rupture had occurred between DiMaggio and Marilyn shortly before she was to leave for Banff. Its origin is unknown, but it must have been particularly upsetting to her when she had counted so heavily on talking seriously with him in Canada about the possibility of marriage. In any event, DiMaggio came by the Doheny apartment and quietly picked up his clothes while Marilyn was away at the studio.

But the breach was healed over, and DiMaggio flew to Banff to join her. He had not yet lost out in his valiant attempt to save her from those he was afraid would destroy her.

By May 1953, Marilyn was nearing the end of her seventh full year as "Marilyn", a person with few determinable antecedents. But there were claims from the past. Her mother, Gladys, was still in the private sanatorium called Rock Haven in Verdugo. She had written *Marilyn* a stark note of seven lines – Norma Jean was blessedly dead for her, too, and she spent much time showing news clippings of her daughter to others in the institution – pleading for a letter and complaining about Rock Haven, telling her that she wanted to move away as soon as possible and saying that she would like to have her child's love instead of hatred.

There was a twinge of conscience in Marilyn. She asked Inez Melson what could possibly be wrong with Rock Haven. It was certainly costing enough. She had made it clear a long time ago that she couldn't manage to take Gladys in with her. "It didn't work when I tried it. It will never work," she told Mrs. Melson, and then confessed that it upset her terribly to visit her mother. But she said she would try to answer the letter.

It would be another fourteen years – five years after Marilyn's death – before Gladys won her freedom, spirited out of a state hospital by a friend and then on to Florida to her daughter Berneice, where she would remain. Her flight was the kind of escapade that Marilyn would have appreciated – Mrs. Melson ignorant of her departure and stunned, a lawyer appearing from nowhere to break the news; total silence from Berneice, and Mrs. Melson finally seeking help from the courts to free her of the responsibility.

Marilyn has often been charged with ingratitude towards those who had helped her achieve success. Her road to world fame, they alleged, was strewn with the dead bodies of friends and Samaritans. The truth was that she kept a careful ledger in her mind of what she gave and what she owed. If she was becoming something of a "taker", it was because she was often rapped for her charities. It was not infrequent for associates whom Marilyn had discarded to forget that she had once helped them financially and in other ways as well.

Although she rarely saw her, she felt some link to her mother from whom she had inherited not only the looks but some basic character traits as well — like Gladys she felt an instinctive mistrust of nearly everyone, fear of the insanity that ran like a dark thread through the family, the conviction that nearly every man not a fool was a philanderer, and a fear of death.

More tangibly, she owed to Gladys the seven years of financial support when she was with the Bolenders. If this would seem to be the least a mother could give a child, Berneice and Jack had received much, much less. Marilyn looked upon the Bolenders as well-meaning religious zealots who had needed her mother's twenty-five dollars monthly.

Although she felt no obligation towards them, she decided on impulse to contact them.

Later she told a friend she wasn't sure why she had done it. Albert Wayne Bolender, however, remembered that final contact with Norma Jean more distinctly than that misty time more than twenty years earlier when she had entered his household, and he recalls her saying, "I just wanted to know how you were."

"You come see us, Norma Jean," he said. It was impossible for him to call her Marilyn. He had never known Marilyn Monroe, and would never know her.

And then suddenly she reverted to her stammer. "Well, I . . . uh . . . I th . . . thought you wouldn't want to see me now I'm in the movies."

"You know better than that, Norma Jean. We love you as much as we ever did. You come see us." But she did not, and that phone call was her last attempt to reach back to that part of her past.

She knew she owed something to the Goddards. Grace had died suddenly at the end of summer, mysteriously, Marilyn thought. Doc was evasive about the cause, although she learned it had been "sudden" and that Grace had not been ill. Marilyn became convinced that Grace had killed herself. And it was frightening because it made her see how little she knew of the woman with whom she had lived during a critical time.

With Grace gone, she began to worry about Doc. When she broke up her apartment on Doheny, she gave him her bedroom furniture, including a delicately carved oak dressing-table with a marble top, one of several choice antiques she had acquired.

To the executives at Fox, she felt she owed a measure of revenge. Her stardom had been accepted by Darryl Zanuck as a fact of his studio's life. While she resented him – and personal confrontations were limited – Zanuck knew she was worth all the pampering she required. A year or so later, when Zanuck stepped out of his post for independent production and Buddy Adler moved over from Columbia Pictures, there was hope that the recriminations would stop, that this urbane, white-haired gentleman with his patrician features and charm might persuade her of his respect and admiration.

But what neither executives realized was that excessive abuse of her innate sensibilities – for Marilyn plunged soul and body into each film – eroded her emotional stability. Within a few years, her work undermined her physical balance to such an extent that her personality and behaviour were noticeably affected. Years after her death, Billy Wilder would say, "Hindsight is nearly always twenty-twenty. If I knew then what I came to learn later of her problems, I would have handled her differently." Had Buddy Adler lived (he died of a heart attack in the summer of 1960), he might have concurred.

Marilyn felt she might come to some final decision about sharing her future with Joe DiMaggio while working in all that unending wilderness near Banff. At first she overlooked her mounting difficulties with the studio and Natasha, problems which became apparent in that isolated location.

She was not enthusiastic about *River of No Return* from its inception, but she had no script approval. There was, however, the side benefit of getting away from Hollywood and her fame for an interval.

Marilyn tended to avoid her director, Otto Preminger, remaining secluded in her rooms at the lodge much of the time before DiMaggio's arrival. When he showed up he came laden with a new outdoor wardrobe, plaid shirts and lumberjackets, and considerable fishing paraphernalia. Now DiMaggio's love of fishing would be useful to them, for it would permit them to get off by themselves when she wasn't on call.

DiMaggio had also brought along his old New York friend, George Solitaire. If Marilyn was disappointed to realize Di-Maggio always had a crony around, she didn't let on because Solitaire brought out in DiMaggio a spark of humour so often lacking. The two men seemed to be a couple of New York sports off on a lark, and Solitaire's gravelly laughter was infectious.

Natasha was unnerved by DiMaggio's presence. She and Marilyn had already had a tiff over Whitey Snyder. Snyder had come to dislike the woman even more than DiMaggio did, but unlike him, Snyder could not escape her. Natasha knew that every morning Snyder would have half an hour or more in which to talk privately to Marilyn while he made her up, and this was to her a great disadvantage. She felt his suggestions to Marilyn about abandoning her career as being "too tough for a thin-skinned dame" were undermining all she had invested in "creating Marilyn".

Natasha brought up the subject of Snyder after one of their evening script sessions. "I mean it, Marilyn. Either he goes or I do. It's one or the other."

For a moment, Marilyn believed that Snyder had resolved one of her problems. But all she said to Natasha was, "Let me think about it." And in the end, he remained on Marilyn's films until the last, while Natasha survived only two more.

Like Marilyn's, Natasha's feelings were very close to the surface. She knew Marilyn was unhappy over the present film and she had done all she could to enliven the dialogue with some sense of reality. But now Marilyn was off in a corner somewhere a good part of the time, screeching with laughter at the locker-room jokes of Solitaire and DiMaggio. Very likely it was Natasha's irritability that precipitated the crisis with Preminger.

When she returned to Hollywood, Marilyn was to tell Anne Karger of an episode involving the youngest actor in the cast. Child actors are seldom welcome on a movie set. They are likely to be unlovable creatures of fanatically dedicated par-

ents. When ten-year-old Tommy Rettig arrived on the set to
play an abandoned waif who joins forces with Marilyn in the
wilds of the Northwest, the rumour was that he was a sensitive
lad who wanted to be liked. But for the first three days of
shooting at the studio before they left for Canada, the boy
would do his scenes with Marilyn with deftness and warmth,
and then be bundled off by his mother without a word to anyone.

Marilyn was hurt by the boy's strange unwillingness to
speak to her off camera. Near the end of the third day she
was determined to find out the reason for his chilliness. Waiting for a rare moment when his mother was not in his immediate vicinity, she went over to him. "Tommy, could I speak
to you for a minute? You've been avoiding me for three days.
We've never met before this picture, so I couldn't have done
anything to hurt you. What is it?"

The boy studied her for some time with a frightened but
penetrating scrutiny. Finally he managed to say, "It was my
priest. My priest told me I could work with a woman like you,
and it would be all right," implying that to fraternize off
camera would not be.

Marilyn remembered that it was as though an unseen
gremlin had kicked her stomach. Tommy became acutely
embarrassed, and from then on went out of his way to smile
at Marilyn in a shy, hesitant manner that beseeched forgiveness.

In the weeks to come, she became fonder of Tommy than of
any of her other co-stars. When DiMaggio arrived, the boy,
seeing them together, was thoroughly convinced of her purity
of heart (how could the great DiMaggio be so deferential towards her otherwise?). On at least one occasion, the three of
them went off fishing together.

Tommy was more secure professionally than Marilyn. He
rarely fluffed a line and had that quality often found in child
actors – he was able to repeat an action or emotion, even to
crying real tears, on cue over and over again. This ability
endeared him to Preminger. Marilyn was having difficulty remembering her lines. This failing seemed to have less to do
with her memory than with her nerves. If she felt comfortable
with herself, she was often able to do a scene on the first or
second take. But this seldom happened.

A crisis developed on Preminger's Canadian Western that
had nothing to do with Marilyn. Tommy Rettig had arrived

on the outdoor set-up in a very edgy mood. It had never happened before and Preminger recalled that he was rendered so uneasy by the surprising show of temperament that he found himself shouting before the cameras had even begun to turn.

When shooting began, young Rettig blew his lines. They went on to a second take, then a third. Sensing the child's discomfort, Marilyn tried to reassure him. This reversal so upset the boy he burst into tears.

"What's wrong, Tommy?" Preminger asked, but his words were not soothing and they came out like a regimental command. "What's the matter today?"

Tommy was too worked up to answer but his mother, always only a step away, spoke up. "May I speak with you privately?"

Mrs. Rettig and the director walked off the set. "It's Miss Lytess, Mr. Preminger," Mrs. Rettig explained. "Yesterday she said something to him and he's been upset ever since. I don't think he slept at all last night."

Preminger's patience with Natasha had been eroded steadily by the woman's empathetic reactions to Marilyn's tensions. Indeed, tension would ricochet and strike all three in quick succession. Whenever he, through superhuman effort, controlled his temper and tried with all the persuasion he could command to coax Marilyn into the mood of a scene, she would sense she was being patronized, glance in martyrdom at Natasha, who would, in turn, shoot a murderous glance at Preminger.

"What did she say?" Preminger wanted to know, and he repeated the question.

"She may have meant well," Mrs. Rettig said with little conviction. "But she told him that all child actors lose their talent by the age of fourteen."

"Eine herzlose Frau," Preminger said, half to himself.

"She said that unless they take lessons and learn to use their instrument . . ."

"Their *what*?" Preminger asked incredulously.

"Their *instrument*. That's what she called it. Unless they learned that, their talent leaves them." Mrs. Rettig had gone pale in the telling, while Preminger's blood pressure rose. "Tommy's been too busy working to attend any dramatic school regularly," she added.

"Leave this to me," the director told the woman, and seeing

his altered features, his heavy-lidded eyes almost squeezed shut as he looked beyond her towards the group near the camera, she must have become concerned by the fury she had unleashed in the man. "Like I say," she repeated as he moved away from her, "she may have meant well."

Natasha, seated near Marilyn in a folding director's chair, had been watching suspiciously the conference between Mrs. Rettig and Preminger. Preminger came over to where they were sitting. Standing above Natasha, he looked at her as though she were something vaguely obscene. "Miss Lytess," Preminger hissed. "This is not a pleasant thing for me to say to *anyone*. I am a patient man, but there is a limit. I know what you told young Rettig, and now I want you to get up from that chair and just disappear."

Natasha looked pleadingly at Marilyn, hoping perhaps that she would go into a rage and the stunned Preminger would back away, licking his wounds. But Marilyn seemed to be out of reach. Although only a few feet from Preminger and within touch of Natasha, she was miles away.

Natasha closed her copy of the script, and got to her feet. She stared at the ground.

"From this moment on, you're barred from this set, and that includes the sound stage back at Fox when we leave location," Preminger continued. He savoured his words in a manner that suggested he was rather enjoying the scene, but that might have been due to his previous experience at the role.

Marilyn sighed loudly and allowed her hands, which were clasped together in her lap, to fall to the edge of the chair. It was the only comment she was to make to Preminger about his ultimatum.

"I'll see you back at the Lodge," Natasha told Marilyn before leaving the location.

Within two days, Preminger received a wire from Darryl Zanuck, cataloguing all the favours done the director by the studio head and ending: "And now I need a favour from you. Let Lytess come back to the set. She promises she will not talk to anyone."

Preminger realized that Marilyn had contacted Zanuck with the demand that Natasha be reinstated. It is highly probable that she was hoping to find Preminger so inflexible she might have an excuse to walk out on the film. But if that was in her mind, Preminger had no intention of letting her get away with it.

Preminger later recalled that he summoned Natasha to his office and made it clear that his opinion of her behaviour had not changed. "Someone – Marilyn, I suppose – has been in contact with Mr. Zanuck. He has personally requested me to permit you to return to the set. But your silence is a vital part of the bargain. Can you agree not to talk to anyone?"

Natasha, humbled momentarily, nodded. The crisis ended as the woman maintained a rigid silence with everyone except Marilyn. They always spoke in whispers when they were in one of their huddles.

What is important about this contretemps is that Marilyn was so committed to Natasha she would take a grievance such as this immediately to the head of her studio. It was not a personal commitment; within a year she would terminate her association forever with her coach and show not a tinge of regret. But she sensed that Natasha was a vital, if troublesome, part of her professional life. She could not imagine how she could function without her, although she would be quick to dismiss her when a suitable alternative presented itself. This clash with Preminger was only a pale foretaste of what Marilyn would have to do to defend Natasha's successor, Paula Strasberg, from abuse at the hands of producers and directors.

Marilyn was ill-equipped to wage such battles. But when cornered she would fight, feeding her temper with the slightly worn injustices of her childhood. There would be times when that ancient bile would spill out on a shocked director in such a torrent that they feared for her sanity.

DiMaggio must have had a grudging admiration for the way Marilyn handled the reinstatement of Miss Lytess, even though he detested the woman. For him this constituted proof that Marilyn was not wholly blinded by the picture business. He already knew how she felt about Zanuck, and she had equally vivid complaints about Preminger now that the film was nearly finished. Preminger was outspoken in his denunciation of Marilyn in turn, but curiously he was to announce after her firing by Fox in the summer of 1962 that he was ready and willing to direct a film with Marilyn any time he found a suitable property.

It is conceivable that DiMaggio hoped that with Marilyn's

deepening disillusionment with films and their makers she might be induced to retire from the screen. Her retirement seemed a necessary part of their future together.

CHAPTER EIGHT

In September 1953 there was a party at Gene Kelly's. Small by Hollywood standards, there were perhaps twenty guests, all very animated and rather noisy. As it was popular in those days, the group was engaged in the Saturday night pastime of charades.

The game was a challenge to the lethargic and a field day for the cynical show-business crowd who would express their originality and release their hostilities at the same time. Marilyn, who could be very good at mime and usually displayed an inventive bent, was too exhausted by the final scenes on the Preminger film to come very early. She had badly sprained an ankle at Banff and hobbled around on crutches.

But she was quietly ebullient that evening as only she could be when nursing a secret, for she had decided to marry Di-Maggio. It had taken her over a year to make up her mind, but now she was sure.

Marilyn rarely acted on impulse or without getting opinions from others. She still seriously distrusted her own judgement. Important advice had come once more from the man on location whom she could consider a true friend, Whitey Snyder.

"Why don't you marry that Dago and raise a dozen kids?" he asked one evening as they were returning on the slow, antiquated railway train Preminger had chartered for the several weeks of their stay. They were on the rear end of the caboose and Marilyn was leaning on the rail, looking out at the rural countryside.

"Maybe I will," Marilyn answered. Back in Hollywood she told DiMaggio she would marry him, but they agreed to make no announcement until things were more definite.

Around ten in the evening she entered Gene Kelly's living-room, wearing black slacks and a snug black sweater, over which she wore a polo coat. She kissed her host and accepted a glass of champagne.

Before the evening's end it appeared that Marilyn had not come to play charades. Among the guests were the New York photographer Milton Greene, and his bride of a week, Amy. Marilyn embraced them warmly, which surprised some of the film people there since the Greenes were new to Hollywood and had only recently met Marilyn.

Amy, then a brunette with a fashion model's languor, continued to play charades, which she did brilliantly, while Marilyn sat talking in a corner with her husband.

Little attention was paid to them, since they had moved away from the centre of activity. There was nothing untoward in the heads-together, whispered conversation. Greene appeared to be happy with his well-bred, slender bride, and everyone knew that Marilyn and DiMaggio were together nearly everywhere but at Hollywood parties. There was some speculation that DiMaggio might take her off permanently to San Francisco and New York, where all of his cronies and interests resided.

Greene was handsome enough to arouse curiosity about his sudden rapport, given other circumstances. He had large, very dark, melancholy eyes, his black hair was closely cropped.

They had met earlier in the week when Greene had come to the Fox lot to photograph Marilyn for the Christmas issue of *Look*. Rupert Allan had set up the appointment. "You'll like Milton," Allan had told her. "A very warm and sensitive guy."

Amy was not so sure she was all that wild about Marilyn at that time. She couldn't imagine what her new husband found so fascinating in her. He was not the sort of man who went out of his mind over a sexy dish. A woman had to have something more to interest him, and besides, weren't they on their honeymoon? Greene had completed another assignment for *Look* that same week, doing a layout on Audrey Hepburn. Amy might have understood more easily if *they* had become friendly and found that they still had things to talk about after the photographic session.

After their wedding, the Greenes had flown to New Orleans, where he was to photograph the incoming Broadway production of *Kind Sir* with Mary Martin, and directed by Joshua Logan. They had stayed on in the French quarter for a couple of days; Greene's Bohemianism was an interesting contrast to Amy's taste for elegance.

They had flown on to Los Angeles where Greene was to photograph Rudi Gernreich's first big collection of gowns and ensembles. At the time Greene was so hot in the field of photography, they had no choice but a "working" honeymoon. Amy loved it nevertheless. She adored the theatrical and the fashion world and her husband was now important in both.

Amy was soon to learn that her husband and Marilyn had a great deal to talk over. Within a little over a year, Marilyn would be moving into their spacious Connecticut home and very much into their lives.

The legend had only just begun. Marilyn had been accepted as an original – a rebellious creature who struck terror into studio executives' hearts in the manner of Hepburn, Bacall, and Davis; a misadventurous innocent who had an affinity for trouble; a young woman who had achieved an enormous success in two years but who attracted empathetic souls and compassion like an underdog. Yet, within a year, her legendary celebrity, eclipsing that of any other film star before or since, except for Chaplin and Garbo, would be an established fact.

Milton Greene may have had some prescience of what was about to happen when he had his initial discussions with Marilyn. His personality was exactly the sort to interest her: an apparent diffidence masked youthful audacity; the detachment of an outsider was combined with a considerable insight into her standing with the studio. Either he had been well briefed or it was one of those instances where two congenial people fall into a profound rapport upon meeting.

He had no practical experience in the industry but this did not seem to bother her. She was caught by his enthusiasm, by the impeccable taste shown in his opinions of her performances and in what he considered to be suitable screen properties, and by his courage. Greene did not seem to be a businessman. He was a creative human being like herself, she believed, anxious to make a contribution to the screen.

"Producing a movie isn't all that different from what I'm doing now," he told her. "I have half a dozen assistants in my studio back in New York. I'm forced to job out a lot of my work, so in a sense, I'm already a producer." He had persuaded a Wall Street financier to become a partner with him in an independent film company, so he had some backing.

His preparation for this meeting suggests it did not happen by chance.

There is some slight confusion over who proposed what to whom, but Marilyn was then ready to listen to any intelligent proposal that might liberate her from the bondage of her contract with Fox. She was making only $1500 a week under her seven-year contract drawn up in late 1950, although she had been cast as the feminine lead in a top-studio property, *The Seven Year Itch*. Her leading man was the star of the Broadway original, Tom Ewell, and the director Billy Wilder, whom Marilyn later considered the most talented of all her directors.

Her contract hadn't accorded her script approval, director approval, or the kind of money Doris Day was making from her own productions. No one could dispute the fact that she was now the biggest draw on the lot, but there was stiff resistance to giving her any accompanying privileges. Her lack of education and her semblance of naïveté had persuaded most of the executives that she didn't have the intelligence to guide her own career.

How Greene's own proposed film company became Marilyn Monroe Productions must remain something of a mystery. The name itself would later cause considerable legal concern as a too-obvious tax haven (which it was not designed to be); too personal to embrace other projects with other stars, and too special to attract such outsiders as recording talent.

In succeeding meetings, Greene was definite in his proposals to Marilyn. He was ready to commit himself and his finances, but he needed to have some guarantee from her that it would not be time, energy, and assets invested in vain. He soon wanted to know what would happen if she married DiMaggio and was asked by him to leave the movies. Marilyn answered Greene's question during an impromptu press conference on her wedding day. "I intend to remain in pictures," she told the reporters, "but I'm looking forward to being a housewife, too."

CHAPTER NINE

DiMaggio and Marilyn were married on January 14, 1954, in his home town. The corridors of San Francisco's City Hall were jammed with over a hundred reporters and photographers. Inside Judge Perry's chambers, about a dozen friends of the groom witnessed the ceremony, including Reno Barsocchini as best man, DiMaggio's brother and sister with their spouses, George Solitaire, and DiMaggio's first baseball boss, Lefty O'Doul. None of Marilyn's friends were there, although she had spoken the day before with Anne Karger and Whitey Snyder. Natasha was apparently not invited.

For luck, DiMaggio wore with a dark suit the same polka-dot tie he was wearing the night he met Marilyn. She matched his conservatism by wearing a high-collared brown suit with an ermine collar. "Save those low-cut things for the movies," he had suggested. And Marilyn wanted to please him.

Glowing and euphoric, they emerged from the chambers into the corridor and DiMaggio obligingly kissed the bride for photographers. Then they ran, the newsmen lining the walls. They sped away from a cheering throng in front of the building in DiMaggio's blue Cadillac, headed for the freeway south of the city, "down the Peninsula".

Early in the evening, not more than four or five hours from their starting point, DiMaggio spotted a motel on Highway 101 on the edge of Paso Robles. Early the following morning the DiMaggios left the main highway and headed eastward. Late in the afternoon they reached a friend's mountain lodge not far from Palm Springs. There was snow above them and mild desert weather below.

While DiMaggio and Marilyn were on their honeymoon, her lawyers and agent were involved in a marathon conference with Fox. She was on suspension for walking out of *Pink Tights*, a musical film, which had been slated for production a month earlier. She had told Frank Sinatra, who was to play opposite her for the first time, that there was nothing personal in her move but she thought the script was *lousy*. Fox believed the script was not at issue, that she really wanted a revision in her contract and a stronger hand in guiding her own career in films. Somehow it was settled and a temporary truce arranged with her salary adjusted upwards. She even won her fight against *Pink Tights*, which was shelved permanently. For better or worse, she was winning most of her studio battles now.

There is ample evidence that at that moment, Marilyn and DiMaggio were persuaded they were in love, and DiMaggio would keep that feeling, but they were opposites despite the accepted view that they had much in common. As Whitey Snyder was to comment later, "They made better friends than husband and wife."

They came back briefly to a handsome two-storey house belonging to DiMaggio's family in the Marina district of San Francisco. His sister, Marie, came in to handle the cooking and run the household. She had been told discreetly by her brother that any time Marilyn wanted to cook dinner to just pretend there was nothing unusual about it and get out of the way.

Marilyn did lots of hiking up and down hills away from the level Marina district. Joe Jr. came in from school to meet his father's bride, and he and Marilyn went out to Seal Point and Cliff House, and then to the Zoo hard by that rocky shore of the Pacific.

After this brief introduction to what was intended to be her new hometown, Marilyn and DiMaggio left on their wedding trip. DiMaggio had agreed to go to Japan with Frank "Lefty" O'Doul, who had hired him as a rookie on the old San Francisco Seals. It was typical of DiMaggio to see nothing wrong in combining that obligation with a formal wedding trip. O'Doul had married only a few weeks before. Marilyn and O'Doul's bride, Jean, could spend some time together while the men visited the ball teams around Tokyo, Osaka, and Yokahama, lecturing, appearing on television, and generally spreading the word.

Marilyn was determined not to let their careers conflict. So this was to be DiMaggio's business trip and her wedding journey. She'd always wanted to see Japan. The other country she wanted to visit was, perhaps because of DiMaggio, Italy.

The belated honeymooners flew first to Honolulu, where they were mobbed by Marilyn's fans. They had neglected to seek any security against the public's wild enthusiasm. Di-

Maggio got his second and more frightening taste of his future as the husband of the most famous blonde in the world when the plane touched down at Tokyo's International Airport. Crying "Monchan" (precious little girl), hordes of "little Japanese" (as DiMaggio was to remember it) came rushing towards them. Some threw flowers. Others reached out to touch Marilyn, several of them grasping at her hair and threatening to pull it out by the roots. Marilyn's frozen smile masked the greatest fright of her life, and she felt she was paying dearly for her reputation as the most "monchan" since Shirley Temple.

The two couples settled into adjoining suites at the Imperial Hotel. After a week or so of trips by limousine to Fuji, religious shrines, and villages, the DiMaggios were invited to a cocktail party given by the international set of Tokyo. There were numerous high-ranking American army officers there. At one point an officer approached Marilyn and proposed that she consider a quick visit to the American troops then fighting for the United Nations in Korea.

Marilyn was thrilled and she crossed the crowded room to tell DiMaggio, who was surrounded by sports fans. He was less enthusiatiç and thought it was pretty dangerous. "But it's the least anyone can do," Marilyn is reported to have said, and DiMaggio agreed finally.

With Jean O'Doul and a contingent of brass, Marilyn was flown into Seoul as snowflakes swirled about the runway. From there she was airlifted by helicopter towards the war area where the First Marine Division was already gathering on a frosty hillside, warmed by the prospect before them.

Corporal C. Robert Jennings, assigned by *Stars and Stripes* to cover the frontline visit, recalls that Marilyn asked the 'copter pilot to fly low over the soldiers on the ground so she might wave to them. She managed this by lying face down on the floor of the 'copter, lowering her body outside the sliding door, secured only by two accompanying soldiers sitting on her feet. While all of the men in the field knew of the imminent arrival of Marilyn, the sight of her dangling from a helicopter, waving and blowing kisses, must have been an astonishing, if not a frightening sight. Jennings remembers that they were more than a few minutes late arriving at the Division Headquarters because Marilyn apparently asked the pilot to make several passes over the troops.

Several thousand Marines broke ranks and crowded around the small landing area. These men cheered wildly as the 'copter came down, and Marilyn was thrilled by the sight of soldiers clinging to radio and water towers, with additional hundreds held back from the field by armed Air Police. Corporal Jennings said that as she climbed out, her hair was tousled by fierce Siberian blasts and looked as unreal as if it had been plucked from the head of a doll. Impromptu road signs in the vicinity had gone up reading "Drive carefully — the life you save may be Marilyn Monroe's".

With Jean O'Doul assisting her in the wings, Marilyn changed from an olive-drab shirt and skin-tight pants to an equally clinging gown of plum-coloured sequins, cut so low it exposed much of her breasts to the frigid winds. She was decked out with rhinestones to go with her first song, "Diamonds Are a Girl's Best Friend". Her singing voice was slight and was always amplified many times to ensure that its provocative warmth was properly audible, but now she had an ordinary mike. In mid-performance, she stopped singing and walked over to a soldier in the wings who was about to snap her picture (Marilyn's visit to Korea was more thoroughly recorded by cameras than any event on this planet up to that time). She leaned towards him and gently plucked a lens cover from his camera, saying, "Honey, you forgot to take it off." The soldier blushed and appeared about to swoon as his thousands of comrades roared approval, many of them applauding the gesture as well. Although a bit wavery, fighting inadequate equipment and gusts of wind, her song came off all right, and the wild enthusiasm of the enthralled soldiers carried her securely into the next number.

That evening, there was a dinner for Marilyn in the General's Mess, a lavish arrangement of several quonset huts. The Signal Corps had arranged a telephonic greeting from her new husband back in Tokyo and the dessert course was highlighted by an Army-planned but slightly embarrassing conversation overheard by the fifty guests, with Marilyn asking "Do you still love me, Joe? Miss me?" In subsequent phone calls from her insulated tent that night, she begged DiMaggio to join her, but he explained that he had made so many commitments in Japan, he couldn't possibly make it. This imbalance of warmth and eagerness from Marilyn and DiMaggio's frequent bland lack of enthusiasm was to become more marked in ensuing months. Following that day, she cut down on her communications to DiMaggio, letting him know only that she was all right. She basked in the most concentrated adulation of her entire career.

By the time Marilyn reached the Third Division a pattern was beginning to emerge as she moved from one unit to the next. The officers had become aware of considerable grumbling from the men that the brass was monopolizing her, so that from now on, much to Marilyn's satisfaction, she was surrounded by enlisted men even at mealtimes. A dozen or two representative types were rounded up from foxholes and bunkers and hustled to whatever mess happened to be feeding her, where the fried chicken and steaks were democratically consumed by all.

When she reached the 160th Regiment's amphitheatre, a light snow began to fall on Marilyn's head and shoulders, but she didn't seem aware of being cold at the time. Many of the Regiment's troops were so moved by her physical presence, they stormed towards the stage, snapping through the wall of military police, and the performance came to a jolting halt. Colonel John Kelly, their commander, rushed onstage and declared he would stay there guarding his valuable charge and effectively blocking the troops' view until "every last man moves back". At other places, there were smaller riots. A trampled soldier had to be rushed from the scene by ambulance.

As Marilyn's plane waited to take her back to DiMaggio in Tokyo two days later she told the officers and men in the airport farewell party, "This was the best thing that ever happened to me. I only wish I could have seen more of the boys, all of them. Come to see us in San Francisco," and then she darted inside.

Hanson Baldwin, writing in *The New York Times*, sternly complained that Army Secretary Robert Stevens and Chief of Staff General James Ridgway should "correct the weaknesses in service morale epitomized by the visit of Miss Monroe to Korea. On two occasions during the visit of the motion picture actress, troops rioted wildly and behaved like bobbysoxers in Times Square, not like soldiers proud of their uniform".

Marilyn became feverish on the flight back to Japan, and by the time she reached the hotel her temperature had risen to 104. Someone in Korea had called the Army Medical Department stationed in Tokyo and before DiMaggio had Marilyn safely bedded down, an Army doctor was on the phone inquiring about her. The doctor diagnosed Marilyn's ailment as a mild form of pneumonia. She lay in the hotel room for four days, taking antibiotics and resting, with Joe to nurse and comfort her, and Jean and O'Doul for company. As memorable as her Korean visit had been (during the last year of her life she was to say again that it was the high point in her life), she was exhausted and her brief stay in bed gave her time to think about her career. She made up her mind about a couple of things. She was certain that her acceptance of Milton Greene's proposal was the only way she could continue in films, and she would try to make a go of it with Di-Maggio in San Francisco. While these decisions were in conflict, she occasionally relieved her anxieties by saying "yes" to two parties in opposition.

When Marilyn recovered fully, she and DiMaggio toured the rest of Japan. She fell in love with the country and the tidy look of its houses and landscape. There was still something of the compulsive housekeeper in her.

There was a quiet family celebration upon their return to San Francisco in the Marina house. Marie stayed on to run things, but Marilyn didn't seem to mind that arrangement. DiMaggio spent an hour or so every day at the family restaurant on Fisherman's Wharf, and Marilyn went with him a couple of times, but she became at once the focal point of all interest on the Wharf and tourists came on the run.

Some mornings, they would go out early in DiMaggio's cabin cruiser, *The Yankee Clipper,* Marilyn in slacks and a floppy hat and huge dark glasses to keep her face from getting burned by the hazy sun. One Sunday, he drove her up to the small village across the bay where he had been born over thirty-nine years before.

San Francisco respected Marilyn's privacy for the most part, smiling in a proprietary way, but not moving in on her. Tourists, who sometimes outnumbered natives, were another matter. On one occasion, twelve-year-old Joe Jr. had to fight off a mob of out-of-towners who seemed about to overwhelm them as they got out of a cable car. Marilyn received a rebuke from DiMaggio about this and agreed to move about town by car.

Apparently, Marilyn disregarded this sensible advice only once. The episode, recounted later to a Hollywood friend, was as amusing as it was mysterious. It was a foggy night and DiMaggio was out somewhere. Leaving her sister-in-law fretting, Marilyn moved in her moccasins silently through the fog-shrouded streets. She said she was enchanted by the feeling of detachment from the world. Attracted by the dim glow coming from Coit Tower, she ascended that slope and stood for a few minutes looking down at the city through patches of grey. A young man approached her, probably out on a lonely prowl himself. About six feet away from her, the man appeared startled, peered through the mist towards her a bit more intently, then hurried off, swallowed at once by fog. She told her Hollywood friend, "He either thought he was seeing things or I've become a femme fatale."

Relieved of the pressures of her Hollywood life and the tensions of courtship the DiMaggios had a good, clear view of each other. The first significant quarrels started in San Francisco. DiMaggio seemed to be sinking back into a comfortable semi-bachelor existence. Sometimes neighbours would catch a glimpse of Marilyn standing alone on the back patio at night wearing a light raincoat and bedroom slippers.

But DiMaggio's love for Marilyn was so profound even he would not realize its intensity until after he had lost her. When disillusionment moved in as an unwelcome third party, much of the give-and-take of the early weeks of their marriage disappeared.

A new film was scheduled for Marilyn, something the studio hailed as a tribute to the songs of Irving Berlin. *There's No Business Like Show Business* was certainly a shopworn bouquet for the composer, but Marilyn was to be surrounded by a clutch of expensive entertainers from Ethel Merman to the phenomenally popular "cry" singer of the period, Johnny Ray. Even though the script – which concerned a showbusiness couple and their three grown children, their squabbles and affairs – was written by skilled hands Phoebe and Henry Ephron, from a story by Lamar Trotti, it was a makeshift and often preposterous framework for the songs and dances. Marilyn was cast as Vicky, a singer and dancer with the same opportunistic tinge of her earlier Rose Loomis in *Niagara*. Vicky is courted by one of the song-and-dance offspring, Tim, played by Donald O'Connor, whom she brings into a Broadway show along with his father Dan Dailey. Marilyn had one dazzling number, a spectacular version of "Heat Wave", in which she was costumed like a blonde Carmen Miranda.

Even though she knew the script to be vastly inferior to *Pink Tights*, Marilyn suddenly agreed to return to Hollywood. She and DiMaggio left San Francisco in April and found a rented house on North Palm Drive in Beverly Hills not far from Johnny Hyde's last home.

The "Elizabethan cottage" was not private. It was Marilyn's selection and the most accessible of any star's home, only three doors removed from busy San Vicente Boulevard. It was also something of a mess. The last tenant had neglected to clean it before vacating, and the kitchen was filthy. Marilyn phoned Inez Melson to wail: "The kitchen's so dirty, it must be full of germs! It will be terrible for Joe's ulcers!"

His ulcers were worsening, but his condition had nothing to do with germs. Nevertheless, Mrs. Melson went to the empty house with her secretary and spent the better part of a day scrubbing down the floors, walls, and appliances. When Marilyn learned what they had done she showed her gratitude by inviting Mrs. Melson to share their first dinner, prepared by Marilyn herself.

On the following Monday, Marilyn went back to the Fox lot to begin work on the musical. DiMaggio was to visit the set only once and Marilyn had turned that occasion into a kind of open-house day to which she had also invited Emmeline Snively. The gamble DiMaggio had taken already seemed to be lost.

CHAPTER TEN

On the morning of September 9, 1954, when the plane ramp was secured at Idlewild Airport in New York and the door opened, the chaos below Marilyn appeared to dismay her for just a moment. She recovered quickly and beamed at the excited multitude below her. Police had set up barricades to keep the mobs back. Milling about in front of the police lines were dozens of photographers, reporters, and men in white overalls, airport employees who had run from their jobs to catch a

glimpse of her. This was the year of Marilyn's romance with
the public. It would not always be so, although there would
continue to be echoes of it from time to time; hand waves to
passing taxi drivers, special smiles for surprised men emerging
from manholes.

She had quarrelled with DiMaggio before the plane took off
from Los Angeles. The filming of *There's No Business Like
Show Business* had been done *at home*. Now, he was anxious
from the first, about her location trip to New York for Billy
Wilder's production of *The Seven Year Itch* and kept insisting
she was in a position to tell the studio heads and even the public to go to hell if they insisted on imprisoning her in this jazz-
baby image and then setting her loose to emote on a public
street in New York. For one terrible moment, she was afraid
he was coming along as a kind of chaperon.

Apparently, too, she was upset about one of his several
business associations. He had considered going into a holding
company being set up by an industrialist. The business man
had suggested to DiMaggio that it might be helpful if Marilyn
would appear on occasion at certain affairs planned by the
new company – sales meetings, conventions, and possibly
stockholders' meetings. It had troubled her that DiMaggio
had not declared himself opposed to the idea when it was first
broached to him.

She had learned to master the crowd, such as the one which
awaited her at the St. Regis, but she had failed to still her private torments. This is not to say she had given up on DiMaggio, but the shrillness and indignation of her complaints to
close associates such as the Greenes were clues to the tottering
state of her marriage.

Two days later, DiMaggio suddenly appeared at the hotel.
The crew on *The Seven Year Itch* heard the news of his arrival
with concern. But DiMaggio made an effort to keep out of
the way of the movie in progress most of that weekend. When
Marilyn and Natasha were together going over the first scenes,
he slipped out of the suite to run over to nearby Toots Shor's.

If DiMaggio believed that he could take things in hand and
see that Marilyn was treated with some dignity in her street
scenes, which he correctly anticipated would be watched by
thousands, he had overlooked his wife's stiffening resolve. He
had felt only a touch of it in California.

Shooting began with Marilyn in an apartment set-up the

studio had subleased on a daily basis from two tenants of the building with special permission from the landlord. It was an attractive four-storey walk-up on a fashionable block of East 61st Street. A barricade at either end of the block kept the crowd at bay, but the shouts forced the assistant director to decide to shoot silent and dub the few lines in later. Director Wilder concurred and went into a huddle with Marilyn and Natasha. He expressed his concern over Marilyn's slight look of fatigue. "How do you feel, Marilyn?" he asked.

She was drinking a glass of ice water offered her by an excited bachelor tenant. "I'm okay this morning," she said, which seemed to suggest she might not hold up through an entire day of shooting.

Wilder had begun his first film with Marilyn with some knowledge of her previous behaviour. Their first meetings had gone beautifully. DiMaggio, who was present, was bored to distraction by their talk of camera angles, set-ups, and dialogue. He disappeared in the middle of the first conference, not to return. Wilder attributed what he called her fuzzy connection with reality to some mental malfunction aggravated by alcohol. Since her return from San Francisco she had begun drinking champagne to excess.

But he considered her an absolute natural before the camera. And more importantly, she brought a freshness of approach to her work that was the key to her attraction, the audience reaction. The public immediately grasped whatever she was doing, no matter how strange or unexpected, and went with her.

When Marilyn's stand-in, Gloria Mosolino, appeared at the window as arc lights and other equipment were adjusted below, Marilyn could hear hundreds of bystanders shouting: "Where's Marilyn. We want Marilyn!" And then she heard a few shouts, almost drowned out by the others: "Where's *Joe*?" The possibility that he *might* be there seemed to trouble Marilyn. She moved to the window and looked below. There were some students across the street who had been allowed passage down 61st Street.

"Hey, Marilyn!" one of them shouted, and threw back his arms. Marilyn smiled and blew him a kiss. The youth pretended to stagger and faint. Down at the barricades, great cries went up. "Marilyn! Marilyn!" She waved and roaring cheers could be heard in response.

Much of the next day, Marilyn was in conference with Milton Greene. Her rebellion against the film industry was now being committed to paper, long legal forms of partnership bearing the exciting name, Marilyn Monroe Productions. Greene now had two attorneys, Frank Delaney and Irving Stein, working on the organization and filing of papers, as well as an accountant, Joseph Carr. They were all New Yorkers. Her very own company would have no taint of Hollywood whatsoever.

DiMaggio greeted Greene pleasantly enough in the hotel suite, but then went off to the adjacent bedroom and turned on the television set. Greene knew nothing about baseball so there was no kidding around about the upcoming series or even dead-level inquiries as to which team might win. Later, Amy Greene met DiMaggio and talked half through the night about averages and fanouts and other matters peculiar to the ball game.

Around midnight, Marilyn was driven by limousine to the Trans-Lux Theatre at 52nd Street and Lexington Avenue. As with East 61st Street, the studio had cordoned off the block, and cameras and lighting equipment were moved in near the theatre marquee. DiMaggio had come along, and Marilyn was silent and brooding. She wore a sweater over her shoulders against the night chill. Her costume for the scene was to become one of the memorable ones, a backless white dress with a pleated flounce skirt, white shoes, and white panties, which would be plainly visible in one of the shots.

Nearly a thousand New Yorkers had somehow heard about the location and were lined up behind a barricade at the corner. They had earlier watched studio workers install a portable air blower beneath the subway grating in the sidewalk adjacent to the movie house. When a grip tested the equipment, standing over it while his clothing rippled in the blast, none in the crowd had to be briefed as to what Marilyn would be doing in the scene.

DiMaggio kept out of the way of the actors and of the film crew, but at some distance from the crowd. His expression was grim, unsmiling, his hands thrust deeply into his trouser pockets. Marilyn turned her head once to catch a glimpse of him and appeared disconcerted for a fleeting moment. Then she moved over to the grating and allowed the upward thrust of air to toss her flounced skirt well above her knees. Shouts of "Hurrah!" could be heard from the spectators. "Higher! Higher!" also became a dominant cry as the machine puffed and Marilyn straddled the grating.

DiMaggio appeared to turn to stone. While Marilyn rehearsed the scene with Tom Ewell, DiMaggio retreated to the other end of the block. He didn't see the newspapermen who had been observing him until he had stepped around the studio barricade to head west towards Toots Shor's.

"What do you think of Marilyn having to show more of herself than she's shown before, Joe?" one of them asked.

DiMaggio had no time to put a face on his anger before those men. He shook his head and walked away. Some of the newsmen realized they were uninvited witnesses to a profoundly private moment and declined to print what they had read in his face. One or two others waited briefly to see if there was any further excitement to report and then rushed to their typewriters.

Marilyn returned to the hotel around four in the morning, exhausted by retakes and all the commotion at the location site. Apparently, DiMaggio returned at about the same time or shortly thereafter.

Some shouting and scuffling was overheard by other hotel residents near by, followed by hysterical weeping. On the following day, DiMaggio departed for California.

A few hours after DiMaggio's departure, Milton Greene arrived with some papers for Marilyn to go over. He waited in the sitting-room for some time, which wasn't too unusual, but when Marilyn appeared she seemed very distant. She was heavily sedated.

When he began to discuss the intricacies of some of the documents, Marilyn was unreachable. Later, Greene learned the source of her distress. The marriage was over.

CHAPTER ELEVEN

Upon her return to Hollywood in the middle of September, Marilyn retained Jerry Giesler, whose legal clients were almost exclusively film celebrities who could afford his fees. Marilyn would no longer concern herself with being even slightly penurious. There would be no more used cars, small apartments, or clothes off a rack. When her money ran out, as it would on one or two occasions, her debts would become mountainous. But somehow, there would always be more money.

Inez Melson was at the Elizabethan cottage early on the morning Marilyn's separation from DiMaggio was to become legal. She realized that her friend and client was numb from emotional fatigue. New floods of tears ruined her mascara every few minutes, so Marilyn was obliged to spend much of her time in front of a mirror in her second-floor bedroom. Mrs. Melson suggests that the reason for Marilyn's preoccupation with her appearance that morning was because of a scheduled appearance with Mr. Giesler before the press.

DiMaggio was in the house that last day. He made some orange juice for Marilyn, which he insisted she drink. He was able to bear Mrs. Melson's presence with equanimity since he considered her a woman with decent instincts. For her part, Mrs. Melson recalls that she felt terribly sorry for DiMaggio that day. "He seemed so lost," she said. "So angry with himself. Not with Marilyn, but with himself and with what was happening to them."

Mrs. Melson was mercifully answering the phone and the door, turning away reporters and callers she knew were not close to Marilyn. Her mind was a catalogue of Marilyn's preferences and dislikes. She had a sombre and laconic nature. Perhaps that is how she managed not to get on DiMaggio's nerves. He must have known from Marilyn that the woman was not among the "leeches" who had attached themselves to the actress. Marilyn had ambivalent feelings about most of them; she knew some of them were bleeding her financially, but because of her insecurity she hesitated to shake them off. Unquestionably, it was this mutual respect that was to bring Mrs. Melson and DiMaggio together at the end to bury Marilyn.

On this separation morning, Mrs. Melson made an abortive effort to assure DiMaggio he was still her friend despite what was happening. "I liked Joe so much," she was to say. "When Marilyn asked if I would be a witness in her divorce, I told her, 'Only if Joe tells me it's all right with him.' Then Joe phoned to tell me to go ahead and I told him half as a joke that Marilyn could claim she was abused by him for not taking her to the race track at Caliente."

When DiMaggio was completely packed, his best man and closest friend from his home town, Reno Barsocchini, loaded gear into the trunk of a Cadillac parked in the driveway. Di-Maggio delayed making an appearance in front of the house as long as he could. Outside on the lawn were gathered about a hundred newspapermen and the curious, and Reno was duly photographed at his task by news photographers and newsreel men. Finally DiMaggio emerged from the house and joined Reno in the Cadillac. Asked where he was going, he told reporters, "Back to San Francisco. That's my home."

Marilyn went back to work later that same week when shooting resumed on *The Seven Year Itch* at the Fox studios. The Fox was therapeutic and director Wilder was relieved to find Marilyn more engaged with her work than before. Occasionally he would yell "Cut and print" after the first or second take, much to Marilyn's and Natasha's surprise. He hadn't known before what was wrong with her and had been caught totally by surprise when her separation from DiMaggio was announced. But he was too long in the business and too shrewd a judge of character to feel he was home safe with Marilyn. Their association on this and a subsequent film would be the most frustrating of his long career, dating as far back as 1929. Apparently neither a happy marriage nor a crisis-relieving divorce was any guarantee that all would be well with Marilyn.

In 1961 and 1962, DiMaggio was again seeing Marilyn regularly. It is highly unlikely despite the stories that circulated at the time that they were romantically involved. They knew one another far too well for that. Perhaps that was what Di-Maggio wanted, but Marilyn was "cured" and said as much to her friends.

There was one encounter in 1960 in Nevada when she and Miller, along with the Frank Taylors (he was Miller's producer on *The Misfits*), by chance ran across DiMaggio in a restaurant. Marilyn left her group and spoke quietly to him for a minute or so. To those present Marilyn's gesture was no more than a courtesy. When, in 1961, they became close again, Marilyn's life was much changed both by her break-up with Miller and by the difficult months that followed the divorce.

PART FOUR

An Experiment in Reality

CHAPTER ONE

Marilyn's break with Hollywood occurred when she completed *The Seven Year Itch* on November 4, 1954. She may have been anxious about the future, for now she was entirely on her own, but her relief was great. Almost any way she looked at it, it seemed the most intelligent move of her career.

She declared herself "no longer contractually bound to 20th-Century Fox", and left it to her lawyers to argue the finer points. Once again she had walked out on a film, this one, *How to Be Very, Very Popular*. During her year of absence, Fox shot the film with another blonde, Sheree North, who was, they said with little hope, their answer to Marilyn. There was some discussion as to whether Fox had or had not exercised an option, but that became academic once her mind was made up. To sue her, as the studio threatened to do, would have been pointless for she would never go back into the fold.

An agreement was reached with the owner of the Elizabethan cottage to terminate the lease and she moved into one of the bungalows of the Beverly Hills Hotel.

From her failure with DiMaggio Marilyn learned that she was on an irreversible course and she could not turn back. If she married again, and it is probable it was very much on her mind, her next husband would have to accept her fixed direction and, hopefully, make her way a little smoother.

Through a combination of circumstances she was winding up her Hollywood years. Her longest sustained effort to live like a normal human being with family ties and obligations, country places, close friends not involved in movies, took place during the next six years in the East. When she later returned to her native city, she discovered that she no longer fitted in. Hollywood doesn't accommodate itself to rebels easily.

As Fox became threatening, she was advised to go into seclusion until she was ready to leave for New York. She moved into the Voltaire Apartments near Sunset Boulevard with Anne Karger. Headlines asked, "Where Is Marilyn?" while Marilyn had a good laugh about them with her old friend in the heart of Hollywood.

For ten days she wandered about the spacious apartment, eating snacks much of the time and gaining weight. Milton Greene visited her there and they discussed plans for her future. Anne Karger recalls there was a great deal of talk about expected income and how it would be divided. Apparently, it was also decided that she would move in with the Greenes in Weston, Connecticut, out of the reach of newspapermen and lawyers.

In those closing weeks of 1954, Hollywood represented tyranny to Marilyn, while New York beckoned as the home of new friends, one very important old friend, and the hope of a new start in the industry with Marilyn Monroe Productions. In some manner, possibly by phone, she had been in touch with Arthur Miller and had become convinced that if they were ever to wed, she would have to be in his territory to persuade him to do it. That December was not only a time of flight for Marilyn, it was also a time of pursuit.

Some years after Marilyn's death, Miller was to say that his first marriage with Mary Slattery was dead or dying at least two years before their divorce became final in June 1956.

She flew to New York in early December. Although it was one of several new beginnings in her life, she was still too frightened to feel revitalized. Nevertheless, the auspices for some sort of fulfilment were more favourable now than ever before. Certainly her status as a performer had improved immeasurably. Even the most acid of her critics had to admire her courage. Most of the jokes about Marilyn ceased from that time on, and she was taken seriously by nearly everyone.

Moving in with the Greenes was not without its handicaps. She never felt at home with disciplined natures and Amy Greene was the most organized human being she had ever encountered. Even the simple act of emptying a brimming ashtray was transmuted to a graceful act. Trimly feminine, with a suggestion of submissiveness that concealed a sturdy will and endurance, Amy was an unlikely best friend for Marilyn in those first months of retreat and re-evaluation. Marilyn was to come to a conclusion which she later confided to Miller that Amy's subterranean strengths had a tinge of the devious, requiring permanent defences. Actually, it was probably one of the few times in Marilyn's life when she was forced by circumstances to spend an extended period of time with another woman of her own generation and with some of her own wiles. In Amy's case, those wiles had become refinements. In Marilyn's hands they remained rather transparent ploys.

The Greenes lived in a spacious hilltop house on eleven acres near Weston, Connecticut, a rural section of lower New England. Marilyn delighted in it. She took long solitary rambles over the acreage with one or more of three Greene dogs, two setters and a Kerry blue. When warm weather came, she attempted water-skiing in Long Island Sound. During those months, she was more intimately aware of the out-of-doors than she had been since her first months with Jim Dougherty.

Greene and Marilyn had formalized their partnership on the last day of 1954, and that New Year's Eve there were numerous toasts to the success of Marilyn Monroe Productions. There were 101 shares of stock in the corporation, giving Marilyn 51 shares or a majority interest. Later, when dissension and misunderstandings created a breach in their relationship, Marilyn and Miller, who had by then become deeply involved in her affairs, would feel she had been deceived by Greene over that division of shares. The by-laws were written in such a way that she had no controlling voice in the affairs of her own company. The other officers were Greene's associates and she could be outvoted at any board meeting on any issue.

But to understand why Greene was so desperate to protect his own interest it is important to examine how extensive was his stake in the corporation. Initially the impact on his finances was not oppressive even though his original partner, the Wall Street man, had objected to the risk involved with Fox, who were threatening to sue them, and had pulled out. Greene purchased a mild Broadway success by Terence Rattigan, *The Sleeping Prince*, by borrowing the money. And when Marilyn began to assert her independence and insisted they find her an apartment in town, he went more deeply into debt and subleased a small apartment for her in the Waldorf Towers from a lady about to depart for Europe. If he entertained any regrets by then, he kept them to himself. He was too deeply committed to do otherwise.

The Waldorf Towers was deemed by Marilyn a necessary adjunct to an important star. The Towers have a separate entrance on 50th Street with a carefully guarded elevator for the exclusive use of residents and their guests. Marilyn's self-esteem had not suddenly skyrocketed, but she felt compelled to show Fox that she was not merely a tasty morsel for hungry wolves. Prior to this display of affluence, Marilyn and the Greenes had shared a draughty old suite of rooms at a hotel on 52nd Street with faded carpets, huge Victorian furniture, and rumours of bats in the corridors, fine for a Connecticut family wishing a *pied-à-terre* in town, but not for a star in the public eye. Marilyn even jokingly invented an item for the columns: "Is it true that Marilyn Monroe, the slum child from Los Angeles, is now living in a run-down Manhattan hotel?"

She kept much of her wardrobe in the Weston house, but spent an increasing amount of time in town. There was continuing newspaper and magazine interest in her rebellion. To prepare for her interviews, there were visits to hairdressers, the Jax dress salon, and other shops. All of the bills were going to Greene and he somehow saw that they were paid.

Early in the year, Edward R. Murrow made an inquiry to Greene about the possibility of "visiting" Marilyn on his *Person-to-Person* television show, then a top-rated weekly programme on the Columbia Broadcasting System. The appearance was scheduled for March, and Murrow and his technical crew descended upon the Greene farmhouse.

Marilyn had developed a certain amount of self-confidence in handling a spontaneous interview. She was always good copy because she had the wit to see the human flaw in almost any situation. It was the edge she had over her rivals. But on that crisp Tuesday evening after the technicians had laid their cables and the cameras were all in place, she became terrified at the thought of being exposed to millions of viewers. Greene was hopeful that the technical preparations would be concluded in time for a brief rehearsal to mitigate her nervousness, but it was not possible.

Marilyn asked Amy to help her in any breach (silence) and Amy was to oblige by answering two or three questions direc-

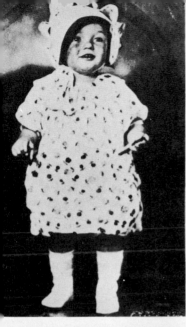

Above: Norma Jean and the Bolenders' model A Ford. (*Courtesy Ida Bolender*)

Left: Norma Jean in an ensemble run up for her on the Bolender "Singer" – the stance was one she often assumed at the front door.

Above: Marilyn on the Fox lot, 1947, when she was limited much of the time to work such as this outside their sound stages. (*Courtesy Culver Pictures*)

Left: Model coach and agent Emmeline Snively achieved considerable "exposure" for Norma Jean on all of these magazine covers, 1946. (*Courtesy UPI*)

It was inevitable that when Hollywood columnists wrote that Marilyn would look good in anything, someone would photograph her like this. The culprit was Earl Theisen.

(Courtesy Culver Pictures)

1953		JANUARY				1953
SUN	MON	TUE	WED	THU	FRI	SAT
				1	2	3
4	5	6	7	8	9	10
11	12	13	14	15	16	17
18	19	20	21	22	23	24
25	26	27	28	29	30	31

"Miss Golden Dreams"

Joe DiMaggio's face turned to stone while watching this scene from "The Seven Year Itch" being shot on a New York street before a crowd of fans. The pose became a trademark for the film (1954).
(Courtesy UPI)

Arthur Miller's favourite portrait of Marilyn. It was abandoned in his study at Marilyn's apartment following their separation.
(Photo by Jack Cardiff)

"Do you like this pose?" Marilyn asked photographer
Elliott Erwitt as "The Misfits" lined up for the camera.
Clockwise from Marilyn are Montgomery Clift,
Eli Wallach, Arthur Miller, John Huston and Clark Gable.
(Photo by Elliott Erwitt Magnum, courtesy Culver Pictures)

Above: The elder and younger Millers pose at the Roxbury farm on the wedding weekend, 1956. Father-in-law Isidore Miller and Marilyn already had fallen into a close rapport that lasted until her death.
(Courtesy UPI)

Left: Marilyn and Joe DiMaggio stop off in Honolulu on their wedding trip, February, 1954.
(Courtesy Wide World Photos)

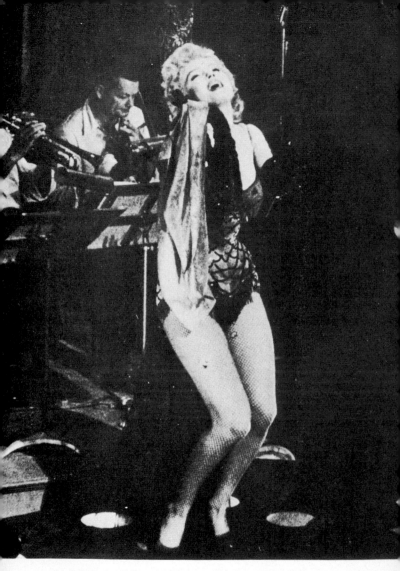

An off-the-set shot of Marilyn singing "That Old Black Magic" in *Bus Stop*, 1956. Note the large hole in her net stockings, a touch Marilyn added following her exposure to the Actors Studio and "The Method".

(Photo by Zinn Arthur)

ted to Marilyn. The result on the air was that she appeared to be of rather limited intelligence, as delightfully vacant and helpless as many of the women she had portrayed on the screen. From a publicity point of view, however, it was far from a failure. It succeeded in making thousands of sceptics into confirmed protectors of that "scared little rabbit" who was standing up to the crass businessmen and other Hollywood tyrants and making a good show of it.

On the surface, it seems that Amy was being drawn into much the same position as Natasha Lytess had been for nearly six years. But there was a considerable difference between Amy Greene and Natasha. Natasha was totally engaged in films and the theatre. Her daughter Barbara was immersed in it. There was little time for ordinary life in her world and while Marilyn's career was advanced and enhanced by it, her connection with reality was largely overlooked. With Amy, Marilyn was drawn into a semblance of reality: games with their infant son Josh, intimate evenings of conversation by the Greenes' hearth on cold winter nights, even an occasional argument having nothing to do with her career. Amy Greene would have had to be superhuman to have avoided some discomfort about Marilyn's status in her household. Marilyn represented the biggest gamble her husband had ever taken. Their whole future was tied up in her. In that period of transition, Marilyn was to acquire some of Amy's self-control. When she realized that it was the most difficult quality for her to assume, she went to extraordinary lengths to retain it. The *new* Marilyn was emerging during that year with a self-possession she had never shown before. The public, including members of the press (but not including private and professional associates), would never again see even the smallest evidence of insecurity or indecision in her.

She was also to learn something valuable about grooming from Amy. Already a professional in matters of make-up as well as a gifted subject before any camera, Marilyn had felt wholly dependent upon experts to prepare her for public appearances. (It turned out in later years that Amy Greene had a genius for such matters. She was to become in time fashion editor for *Glamour* magazine, one of America's best-dressed women, and adviser to friends in the theatre on their off-stage make-up and dress.)

Marilyn may have been one of Amy's first "projects" in

grooming. Possibly because of the background role she played in Marilyn's life, when she was with her she chose to wear simple things, sweaters and slacks and skirts, her dark hair unbleached and worn something like a schoolmarm's. Perhaps this was some of her "deviousness", but it helped to make her guest feel more at home.

It cannot be said that Amy's subtle suggestions to Marilyn in this area met with complete success. To the very end, Marilyn remained resistant to any idea of becoming celebrated for her attire. She was barefoot whenever possible, her hair left to blow in the nearly constant wind of that hilltop, and make-up was something applied only for outside appointments.

Marilyn could never remain isolated for an extended period. She went out of gear after a time when all demands upon her were removed. Even her interest in reading sagged when she found whole days yawning emptily to be filled in at her pleasure. She needed the pressure of a busy schedule. Being *busy* might mean she had one appointment of some importance, and she could devote as much as three or four hours preparing for it. She had to do everything unhurriedly or she went to pieces.

Miller having come back into her life, she was determined it was now for keeps. Because of his children, Robert and Jane, it was hard to make the decision to break up his fifteen-year marriage to Mary Slattery Miller. There were secret meetings at the homes of friends in Manhattan and Brooklyn Heights. There were none at the Greene home in Connecticut. According to Miller, he was not to meet Greene until late 1955 or early 1956. Marilyn, sympathetic to the needs of his children, did not insist upon an immediate rupture with his family.

As her interest in a bucolic life waned, New York became a symbol of promise to Marilyn. What had begun as her defiance of Fox had now become a whole new life. Her friends in New York were real people, and when they had problems, they were worth the worry.

She felt little satisfaction in what she had done up to that time on the screen. A sense of guilt had developed with the successful completion of *The Seven Year Itch*. She felt she was getting away with murder by playing The Girl Upstairs very much as she had played Lorelei Lee and before that the near-sighted member of the gold-digging trio in *How to Marry a Millionaire*. It was time to go on to something of more permanent value.

There were occasional painful episodes induced by her loneliness while living in her Manhattan tower. They would end for a time following her marriage to Miller within the year, but one of the worst occurred during the summer.

Columbia Pictures had brought Tyrone Power and Kim Novak to New York to do location work on *The Eddy Duchin Story*. Fred Karger had come along to help with the music, which was an integral part of the film. With the stars of the film he was in a suite on a lower floor of the Waldorf-Astoria celebrating the conclusion of their New York shooting. Karger, remembering that Marilyn lived in the Towers, phoned her around eight in the evening. She told him she would be down in half an hour; she only needed time to change.

In an hour, Karger called back, and Marilyn's voice was fuzzy with alcohol, probably vermouth, then her favourite insulation when fretful. Apparently the ghosts of her past had revisited her after Karger's call and she was trying to banish them. When, later, Karger went up to say goodnight, she was too far gone to care.

But there were other times when she was quite content to be alone. She frequently took a taxi across Brooklyn Bridge and have the driver drop her near the Esplanade, a wide walkway along the foot of the East River on the edge of Brooklyn Heights.

She had been on this pedestrian walk overlooking lower Manhattan and the bay at various times of the day and evening. Miller had told her where it was. Other times she would walk the brick-paved side streets of the Heights, examining the restored carriage houses along Love Lane, visiting the musty book stacks of Long Island Historical Society, pondering the outstretched arm of the statue of Reverend Henry Ward Beecher in the churchyard of what had once been his famed Plymouth Church. Since Miller was not supposed to be courting her, she carefully avoided walking through the predominantly Federal Period restorations that flanked Willow Street where he was still living with his wife and children in a brick house of modest proportions, set back a few yards from the pavement.

When Marilyn dined out, it was rarely in a public restaurant, but usually with some of Miller's friends in their apartments: Norman Rosten, also of the Heights, whose wife Hedda had become a good friend, and the Eli Wallachs. At one of these dinners she met the lady producer and director, Cheryl Crawford. Miss Crawford became interested at once in Marilyn's ambition to make her abilities as an actress equal her reputation as a personality. She spoke of the work being done at the Actors Studio and thought it might be a fine idea if Marilyn discussed her acting problems with its Artistic Director and leading teacher, Lee Strasberg.

Strasberg was then about as controversial a figure as could be found in the American theatre. He had come into it as an actor in his teens at the Chrystie Street Settlement House in New York where he had attracted the attention of Philip Loeb, then casting director for the Theatre Guild and later a star performer on *The Goldbergs* television series until he was blacklisted. It was alleged he had belonged to an actors' cell of the Communist Party. Soon after the programme's encounter with McCarthy's witch-hunters, Loeb killed himself. It was from such brushes with very deep and divisive undemocratic activity on the part of McCarthy's followers and heirs that Marilyn's political beliefs, such as they were, were forged and sustained.

Strasberg, after directing several plays for the settlement house and enrolling as a student at the American Laboratory Theatre (where he first came in contact with the acting principles of Stanislavski as taught by Richard Boleslavsky and Maria Ouspenskaya, former members of the Moscow Art Theatre), was cast by Philip Loeb in the Theatre Guild's production of *Processional*, which had its première on January 12, 1925. He was to remain with the Guild as an actor and stage manager until 1931, when he joined the Group Theatre, then building its company in a rustic Connecticut theatre.

Strasberg directed an exciting and well-received production of *Men in White* for the Group in 1933. For some reason, his recent efforts at direction have been almost without exception artistic failures, possibly because he seems to have been so impressed with certain theatrical moments from the past that the rather wide departures from tradition during recent years have had little effect upon him. This is something of an anomaly since his instruction of actors in the Method has contributed heavily to the breaking down of acting traditions.

He was to meet not only his future wife, Paula Miller, in the Group company, but also his future associates in the Actors Studio, Lewis, Kazan, and Crawford. It can be said that the Studio grew out of the Group Theatre, although it was not an extension of it. The Studio was to remain apolitical, while the Group Theatre was noted for its far-left activist works such as Odets's *Waiting for Lefty*. The Group expired in 1941, a victim of its own success. It had launched a number of prominent directors and actors besides those already named, including Morris Carnovsky, John Garfield, Lee J. Cobb, and Luther and Stella Adler. If it hadn't expired from its members' affluence and popularity, its political bias might have killed it.

Strasberg took the inner truth of Stanislavski a step further than the master. He encouraged such total involvement with self among his students, with their emotional memory and experience, they would often appear to outside directors as independent agents, unable to do a scene as directed until they grasped "the inner key". Strasberg also approved of his students entering analysis, the better to discover their total inner selves. All of this emphasis on self-involvement would be pivotal to Marilyn's future development both on and off the screen.

In Weston and even more so in New York, the problem of Marilyn's relations with the press became acute. At first the journalists wanted to know where she was and then what she was doing. Requests for interviews were more than Greene and his small staff could handle. Inexpert in the field, it was not easy for him to learn which newspaper or magazine or syndicate could be ignored and which should be given an appointment, either to see Marilyn or to photograph her. Greene had had some previous dealings with the Arthur Jacobs office of press representatives. Marilyn had also heard them highly recommended by her press-agent friend Rupert Allan. The Jacobs New York office was contacted and after some consultation, a staff member named Lois Weber was assigned to her.

Miss Weber was a plain-talking young woman in her early thirties whose blunt but patient manner seemed exactly right for dealing with veteran newspapermen who were all hoping for some exclusive on Marilyn's secret world. Miss·Weber

also yielded to the peculiar sense of helplessness and naïveté
that had disarmed everyone else who had come close to Marilyn. "I've never felt that about any other actress I've ever
worked with," she was to say. "In a matter of days I found
myself protecting her just like the others were."

As newspaper interest in Marilyn's rebellion waned, she was
about to give reporters something to speculate on for the
balance of her career: her declaration that she was a serious
actress.

The Malin Studios were a series of dingy rooms in a loft on
the second floor of a theatre building in the West Forties just
off Broadway. They offered acting classes and rehearsing stage
companies space rather than elegance, and it was here that
the original Actors Studio had held its classes and workshops
since its founding in 1947 by directors Elia Kazan, Robert
Lewis, and Cheryl Crawford.

Kazan was, as noted earlier, one of Marilyn's admirers from
her early days on the Fox lot and had introduced her to
Miller. The two men were not on the best of terms during
that year of 1955 because of Kazan's having informed on his
leftist friends before the House Un-American Activities Sub-
committee in 1952. It seems highly likely that Marilyn was
the catalyst in bringing them together again, for in January
1956, Miller was to deny in a letter to the *New York Post* that
he had ever sent a copy of his most recent play, *A View from
the Bridge*, to Kazan so that he would see "What I thought
of one who informs on communists." He denied having sent
the script to him at all and added that he would send a play
of his to Kazan at once if he thought Kazan was the right
man to stage it. Given the coolness between the men, the letter
seemed conciliatory.

Kazan heard from Miss Crawford of Marilyn's interest in
visiting the Studio, and he made a date to meet her there and
introduce her to Strasberg. She was, she told him, frightened
of the prospect and needed the presence of an old friend to
see her through.

"I think you should work with him," Kazan said to Marilyn
as she took the hand of the small, cat-like man. Strasberg
took her into his office to talk and Kazan left them alone.

Strasberg's sharply observant eyes bored into her and Marilyn flinched a little, a reaction he attributed to shyness. He

was struck by what he called her "luminousness" and he felt there was a talent here that could stand up on a stage.

Perhaps fearing that Strasberg would not accept her as a pupil unless she conveyed to him something more than the skimpy background of an actress strait-jacketed by her long series of giddy blonde roles, Marilyn mentioned that she had for some time, until her departure from Hollywood, studied with Michael Chekhov. Strasberg had already made up his mind to take her on but looked properly impressed. He had heard about Chekhov's association with Marilyn, possibly from Kazan.

Hoping to reassure her, Strasberg said that the sensitivity which she obviously had was innate. "All we can do is to help bring it out. It's like the possession of a good voice. You can't train a great voice. You've got to have it, but then it can be trained. I understand that Caruso and Flagstad were told by their singing teachers that they would never become singers. But none the less, it isn't the work that creates it. The work only brings it out."

Marilyn was always impressed by a good conversationalist. With Strasberg, one could barely voice a question, perhaps four or five words, before a great flood was unleashed, non-stop, that might last five or ten minutes. When Strasberg invited her to come to his apartment on Central Park West later that week for her first acting lesson, she must have been overwhelmed by the towering book shelves all around her. The foyer was lined with books. The library to its left was crammed with books to the ceiling and there were numerous floor-to-ceiling book shelves in the living-room.

After she was comfortably settled next to the mirrored-fireplace wall, Strasberg began baiting her. Questions that hurt, that were downright embarrassing, came one after the other. He wanted to see how she would rise to the stimulus of a loaded question and how she would respond. And, perhaps more importantly, if she would respond quickly and easily. He was also alert to see how much imagination was brought into play in her answers.

When she left, Strasberg went to his wife Paula and said that Marilyn had an extraordinary and seemingly inviolate sensitivity. This sensitive core should have been killed by all that he had heard had happened to her as a child and adolescent. But here it was, fresh and alive.

Although Norma Jean had been emotionally deprived, without a father, turned over to a succession of mother substitutes, except for her two years in the orphanage she was never without some kind of affection. The Bolenders, despite their stern sense of discipline, really loved Norma Jean, as had her mad grandmother in her own peculiar fashion, and Gladys Baker had lóved her daughter sufficiently to insure that she was never physically deprived. In early adolescence there had been the warm devotion of Ana Lower, and then the comfortable sanctuary that was her home as a bride with Jim Dougherty. What was missing, of course, was a father, whom Marilyn had sought since she was able to form the word. Lee Strasberg was then unaware that he was to partially fill that role.

Her first private lessons in his home made it clear to Marilyn that what Strasberg was going to work on was her ability to create the experience that is supposed to be happening to the play's character. Understanding the role was not enough, nor was any external projection of what the character might be like. Strasberg wanted her to sharpen her grasp of what was happening inside the character at that moment, and to be able to re-create it inwardly. She was told she must almost live through the experience she was acting. Concentration was her weak point, as it is with a great many actors, and Strasberg sought ways and means to sustain it through the twenty minutes or so of a scene from a stage work.

Whether by intention or not, Marilyn was becoming a Method actress. Strasberg objected to the denigration of the term (some called it "the sweat-shirt school of acting") and explained that it was simply one way of working, that there were other good methods as well.

But Marilyn, as she progressed towards the more powerful stage works, could only achieve the proper intensity of the scene at hand by tapping her own reserve of emotional experiences. Strasberg had taught her how to arouse this reserve and activate it into usefulness as part of her craft.

After a time, Marilyn was considered sure enough of herself to join Strasberg's regular class in the Paramount Theatre Building. The class met twice a week and had around thirty members. She sat near the back, never abandoning the diffidence that set her apart from some of the more extroverted actors in the class.

She was asked to work up a scene with a young dark-haired

actor by the name of Phil Roth. Before agreeing to meet with him outside the class she went over her lines by herself for a day or so. Finally, believing she had them committed to memory, she was ready to phone young Roth.

"Hi!" the soft voice came through to Roth over the telephone. "This is Marilyn."

As a joke, Roth recalled later to Strasberg, he pretended to draw a blank. "Marilyn who?"

In case she had dialled a wrong number, she explained, "You know, *Marilyn*. The actress from the class."

"Oh! *That* Marilyn," Roth said. And Marilyn showed up a little later, breathing heavily from the five-flights climb to his walk-up apartment. She glanced about the littered room, looking troubled. "You need some woman to look after this place," she said, and then she asked for a broom and waste-basket. Before beginning their assignment together, she swept the floor, put all the papers in neat stacks, and emptied the ashtrays.

Despite her chance for a new life, there were a few unattractive hold-overs from Marilyn's past. There was her bad temper, inherited from her grandmother. She knew no one in a position of power should permit his feelings to get out of control. But as president of her own company, she knew that her rages had to be dealt with. Amy Greene had helped polish her self-possession in public. It was her private furies she worried about now.

She also wanted a fuller life. Beyond a new marriage with the man she had pursued across the continent, she wanted children of her own. She hoped to create around her the ambience of family living she had never really known before. She could not know then, nor would anyone, that it would be physiologically impossible, that every pregnancy, of necessity, would be terminated.

And she knew without being told that she was too self-dedicated to be either a good wife or mother. This was not peculiar to her, but was an occupational malady, evolved from a lifetime of fighting for attention.

But Marilyn wanted to subdue this preoccupation, at any cost. An analyst, a Hungarian Jewess living on the West Side, was recommended to her, and soon that lady's bills, too, began arriving for Greene to pay. He and Miller were not yet in real contact, but had they been, they would have been in accord that it was a good investment.

In Strasberg's view, these sessions began to liberate Marilyn. The work in the class helped her analysis, and the analysis freed her in such a way that the class work took on another dimension. In the opinion of Whitey Snyder, Inez Melson, and a handful of others, her preoccupation with her "emotional memory", a term much used by the Actors Studio, triggered a disintegrating process, a fracturing of an ego that had only been reassembled with much pain a few years earlier.

CHAPTER TWO

On her rounds of appointments during the Summer and Fall of 1955 (her class with Strasberg, the sessions with her analyst, visits to nearby boutiques) Marilyn was often hailed by taxi drivers, and she would wave and return their greetings.

Her screen personality was something she could put to one side for long periods of time. Wearing slacks and an oversized man's sweater, a kerchief about her head, she liked to pretend she was an ordinary private person. In such a guise without make-up or dark glasses, she was unrecognizable. But when caught by the public, she underwent an instant transformation. She spoke in her screen voice and her expression altered sufficiently to persuade anyone that Marilyn was now present.

The poet Norman Rosten, an old friend of Miller's, was often pressed into service as an escort. Although happily married (a piece of luck Marilyn would never let him forget), there was enough freedom allowed him so that a warm friendship developed between himself and Marilyn. She was, he later said, a poet in her own special way. He only felt comfortable with her when she was casual, not wearing the mask of stardom. One evening in late summer of 1955, she attended a party in Brooklyn Heights given by some of Rosten's neighbours. When they reached the house and he introduced her as his "friend, Marilyn Monroe", nobody believed him and they went ahead with their drinking and conversation. Rosten, perhaps frustrated by the people's disinterest, reintroduced her several times only to get an unconvinced "Yeah, sure", from his host and others.

On another night that Fall, she was walking along the East River, shadowed by two of the Monroe Six – a group of her most ardent fans who were always near by but who respected her desire for solitude and never betrayed their presence at such times – and she stopped to look across the murky waters to Queens and its industrial skyline. A lone policeman walking his beat spotted her and came up beside her. "Are you all right?" he wanted to know. Perhaps he had recognized her and felt some apprehension about such a valuable piece of humanity wandering unguarded through the darkness, or it might have been she attracted the protection of strangers as well as those she met formally.

"Do you mind if I talk to you for a while?" she asked. That anonymous policeman spent an hour in her company, and they spoke of "Life" and what it all meant and why people did things.

When not involved in town, she often accompanied the whole Strasberg tribe, including some far-out friends with Studio connections, to their summer place on Fire Island. Relaxation was insisted upon rather strenuously, and no one was permitted to bring any work. Sometimes there was a kind of drawing bee and everyone sketched something. Marilyn, who hadn't drawn anything since grammar school, drew a skinny Negro girl with a pile of kinky curls and a flounced skirt and called it "Lonely". The Negro girl was drawn in a naïve and comic fashion (very much in the manner of Marilyn's screen roles), and her ability to see something in a freshly original way was strikingly evident. Strasberg rightly observed it was a projection of herself.

At this time, Marilyn was often seen by members at the Actors Studio monitoring a session. She came in very quietly just before the doors were closed. Strasberg barred any latecomers, no matter how dear to him personally.

One day in mid-autumn, her session with the analyst had lasted longer than she had planned, and she was late for her acting lesson. Fortunately she encountered one of the Studio officers, Fred Stewart, on West 44th Street near Ninth Avenue, close to the Studio's offices. When they found the doors to the main auditorium locked with the voices of actors echoing behind them, she became very upset. "Can't we sneak in some way?" she wanted to know. "I don't want to miss anything." Stewart led the way up an iron circular staircase to a concealed area above the stage where they crouched silently as mice in the walls until the scene was over.

In December, Strasberg pronounced Marilyn ready to do a scene before an audience of Studio members. He felt she needed to test her skills and concentration before a group other than her class.

When Marilyn protested that she would be terrified by a live audience, Strasberg attempted to reassure her. "A stage role," he explained, "is a totally different thing from films. You're on the stage, you have the lights, the audience is dark, nobody talks. You remember all those technicians and everybody standing around smoking and laughing back in Hollywood. You were very much aware of them, all that distraction."

His mood was messianic. He was preaching a new gospel to Marilyn and she was enraptured. "But on the stage, everything is very concentrated," he told her, his voice falling in a tremendous whisper. "There is a curtain between you and the audience. The curtain goes up and only when you are ready and not before. Whereas on a movie set, if you trip, if anything happens when you come on the set, everybody laughs. The mood is broken."

Strasberg's voice and manner had a soothing effect upon her. It would be unfair to say she was mesmerized by it. There was no Trilby–Svengali relationship. It was a hybrid association: she felt as close to Strasberg as she had to Michael Chekhov, and Strasberg had the same tense, challenging attitude towards those who did not understand her as had Johnny Hyde.

For the next two or three years, she would seriously consider the stage as a possibility since it was Strasberg's realm. Although it is no longer fashionable to assert that the theatre is a more important medium, there is small doubt about Strasberg's view on the matter. Apparently, he persuaded Marilyn for a time that she could do better than make movies. "In films," he was to say, "you do something well and that's it. No one is much interested in what you can do beyond that. That isn't any satisfaction to an actor." The thought of Marilyn making more exciting films was not much discussed. Hollywood was a place to make money, and not to be thought of as a rival to the Broadway theatre.

This premise has fallen out of date with the advent of the films of Bergman, Fellini, Godard, Kurosawa, Polanski, and Truffaut. Great artists frequently discredit competing media and Strasberg was a great teacher in his field, but he sidetracked Marilyn badly at a critical time in her career. Her next two films were adaptations of plays, just as her last had been, and Marilyn's creativity was hampered, if not damaged, in the process of making replicas of good plays. She sat through several performances of *Bus Stop* with Kim Stanley as Cherie, and she became terribly impatient with Sir Laurence Olivier when he directed her in *The Prince and the Showgirl* and she discovered that whenever he described the character of Elsie Marinj, he had in mind his wife Vivien Leigh's performance of the role. This is written more in regret than in criticism, for Marilyn's first film following her exposure to Strasberg's teachings, *Bus Stop*, is considered by most critics as her finest. It is clear from nearly all of her public and private utterances on the subject that the ambitions fanned by Strasberg were more of a hope than an eventuality, that her whole life was tied up in films. She was, through almost equal measures of will, emotion, and Strasberg's encouragement, coming through finally as an actress and not merely as a screen star who could command the best directors. There is reason to believe that the Strasbergs were persuading her that she should toil in the high-paying vineyards of Hollywood to support her higher goal – instilled in her chiefly by them – of becoming a polished performer in the legitimate theatre. This was unfortunate for she was led to believe she was a valuable property to the Hollywood studios because she was becoming a valuable actress. From 1956 onwards, largely at Marilyn's suggestion, there would only be major productions for her with as little risk involved as possible. The only exception would be *The Misfits*, but this too would be beefed up with the strongest support available. The bankers at United Artists, in basic agreement with her premise regarding her films, could not believe that a Monroe–Gable combination would fail at the box office.

By the Fall of 1955 it was decided that Marilyn would do a scene from *Anna Christie* before members of the Studio. Strasberg says it was not an audition for membership. Marilyn was never to become a Studio member, although she was for more than two years directly responsible for much of its publicity. Later, aware of her panic following her firing in 1962, Strasberg talked with Marilyn about her finally becoming a permanent Studio member. It was one of the things she planned to do that September she never reached and Strasberg was going to do everything he could to prepare her for it.

The scene finally selected by Marilyn was the same one that had inspired Metro's "Garbo talks" ad campaign when the Swedish star played Anna Christie in her first talking picture – the introductory scene with Marthy in the bar when Anna returns home.

Marilyn spent the next few weeks right through the holidays painstakingly studying the whole play. She wanted to know who Anna was, how she thought, what she wanted from life. She put some of her questions to Arthur Miller. *Was it an end to life Anna desired? Was it death?* She and Miller spent a couple of hours in her Waldorf Towers living-room going through the text, he taking the part of old Chris and sounding rather like a southern cracker with a Scandinavian accent.

As an exercise to prepare her for her audience debut, Strasberg had her work up a scene from *A Streetcar Named Desire* with his acting son, John. Blanche de Bois is a spiritual cousin to Anna Christie, and when the scene was done in class with John Strasberg in the role of the young man from the *Evening Star*, Strasberg was at once struck by the inner beauty of Marilyn's Blanche, her subtle realization of the kind of woman Blanche was.

In early February of 1956 she appeared at the Studio before a capacity audience of members. Her performance as Anna Christie caught everyone there by surprise except Strasberg. Her painful nervousness lent a tension to the scene that seemed right. He later said, perhaps a little generously, that she walked away with the scene despite the considerable talents of Maureen Stapleton playing Marthy. "It was stolen only by the sensitivity and tremulousness of her acting," he said. "I had stressed for the people who were watching what I call her courage, the actress's willingness to make the effort, which is quite something, to appear in public for the first time. Don't forget Marilyn had not. She had always dreamed of being an actress which meant appearing in public," he continued, "but she had appeared only on the screen. To appear in public with an actual audience there, and especially people from the Studio, is more terrifying. There are many people who perform in public and go through the difficulty of an opening night, who will not subject themselves to that. They just can't take it." He became terribly excited by her work that night and foresaw a long and rewarding career for her on the stage.

Eugene O'Neill did not give the actress much of a clue in his description or dialogue as to what sort of young woman Anna is. We know she has been ill and is coming back home. She doesn't know what's in store for her and she is edgy. Marilyn conveyed all of this. She became Anna, or perhaps Anna became Marilyn. It was difficult to tell.

Although he was not present for the actual performance, it was during those evenings spent with O'Neill's play that Miller fully realized how fiercely dedicated Marilyn was to her craft. He was to say of her grasp of Anna: "She had a real tragic sense of what that girl was like." When they first met he was caught by her vulnerability and was moved to want to protect the woman. Now he saw the actress beyond the woman and felt an obligation to protect her as an artist and to help her improve. He saw the potential for greatness in her. It was almost more than Marilyn had hoped for in her next husband.

After more than half a year of study with Lee Strasberg, she was beginning to reach deeper resources within herself. If Miller had small respect for the Strasbergs, even he had to concede that they were helping her build some sturdy defences about her talent. If they went too far and began to speak of her genius, it was done out of respect for her original style and thus, out of honesty. Her belief in her own work, never secure, was getting needed reinforcement.

Her imagination, always vivid, had been caught up and channelled, when she performed for Strasberg. She was giving play to some sixth sense, a sense of experience, out of a memory storehouse she had kept the lid on heretofore. In her previous film work she had created characterizations that had some semblance of truth in them but were composed of externals. While these performances, notably in *How to Marry a Millionaire*, *Gentlemen Prefer Blondes*, and *The Seven Year Itch*, had satisfied millions of her fans, she considered them inadequate.

But now she had been elevated to another sphere and had proved she belonged there. She was exhilarated by the reception accorded her Anna. She told a journalist that she hoped to become a character actress so she might continue acting when she was no longer known for her sexuality. She recalled Strasberg's words: "The art of the actor grows more rich with age, not less."

CHAPTER THREE

Hollywood's attitude towards Marilyn had hardened during her transitional year and would not change perceptibly during her lifetime. There was a feeling in Hollywood that she had rejected the place and the industry reacted accordingly. Even those who had known her fairly well were inclined to dismiss as unfortunate her pretensions to lift herself up culturally. It seemed a little sad to them, a little embarrassing. They could not be blamed for thinking this since Marilyn was constantly changing, evolving. She was now quite different from the Marilyn they had known.

Twentieth-Century Fox was a divided camp. The top executives in New York frankly missed the income she brought in and urged the men on the coast to a more tolerant position. The studio had been made the heavy in the eyes of the public and nearly everyone on the payroll felt the charge was undeserved. Of course, no one at Fox lost much sleep over this as the public was so fickle, its judgements of today were its equivocations of tomorrow. The world's movie-goers were even more divided than Fox. Some applauded Marilyn's public and private courage, her individual stance, while others deplored the Miller–Monroe rumours then beginning to appear in the gossip columns. These items suggested that Marilyn was a home-wrecker, and underlying them was the implicit reminder that Marilyn had never known a stable home so how could she have any standards?

It might be expected that Miss Weber would be asked to draw the shades on Marilyn's romance with Miller, but she found it unnecessary. "Marilyn was completely honest about it," she said. "When we heard her begin saying 'No comment' or its equivalent when asked about Arthur, we knew they were making plans to get married."

Before 1956 was very far advanced, Mary Slattery Miller had separated from her playwright husband, and it was disclosed that Miller had left their home in Brooklyn Heights and had moved into Manhattan.

"I have nothing to say about any so-called romance with Arthur Miller," Marilyn told reporters with as much emphasis as she could manage. She was suffering from laryngitis which she had contracted just after her success as Anna Christie. The motive for this hedging about their relationship remains obscure. Miller may have been a reluctant suitor when he finally saw the responsibility he would have to assume as Marilyn's husband. In addition to her profound insecurity, there were her moods that swung so precipitously from gaiety to depression; he was never quite certain just how he might find her. There was also her frightening ambition, so towering that it seemed beyond realization. But all that changed in weeks to come. He attempted to give all the support he could muster to counterbalance her insecurity. He met her depressions with lightheartedness even when he didn't feel it, and he already had joined in league with her ambition.

There was yet another complicating factor. Joe DiMaggio, his ego apparently badly bruised in the divorce, appeared occasionally at Marilyn's Waldorf Towers apartment. The old recriminations began as though their lives had not been legally separated. In one instance, Marilyn ran into her bedroom, bolting the door after her. When she called her press agent, it was difficult at first to determine just what was wrong since she was almost literally struck mute with fear, but the banging on her door in the background was unmistakable.

There was still another complication unrelated to Marilyn, at least in any direct sense. Miller's writing career was in the doldrums, and the outlook for any relief was remote at the time. When any writer is in a season of sterility he moves either recklessly or with extreme caution, depending upon his character. Miller was not the reckless type. His first move was to extricate himself from his family situation. When he recovered from that, he might have committed himself totally to Marilyn and hurried to the altar so as not to prolong his emotional turmoil. He wanted to get involved in his work again, but he could do so only if the theme he had decided upon was worth all the effort and concentration needed to write a serious play. It was several months before he even attempted such a project. Cannily aware of Arthur's agonies and indecision, Marilyn realized she might kill the spark if she piled on more kindling. It was a curious situation and an even more curious romance as they carefully threaded together the strands of their emotions and their careers.

Marilyn's former studio bosses were now insisting that they were not "former" at all and they still had a stake in her future whether she was incorporated or not. Buddy Adler dusted off a project that had been on the shelf for years, the life of Jean Harlow. He closed a deal with the late actress's mother, Mrs. Bello, and announced filming would begin in the late Fall. When Marilyn heard about the project and examined the script sent her by Adler, she was both angry and disheartened. She told her agent and her friends she would never do such a film. "I hope they don't do that to me after I'm gone," she said.

By mid-December 1955, negotiations between Milton Greene and Fox were nearing settlement. From now on the studio was to discuss terms not with Marilyn herself but with Marilyn Monroe Productions. Milton insisted that she have director approval, and a list of six suitable directors was promptly drafted (including John Huston, Billy Wilder, and Joshua Logan among others). The new contract would run for seven years and encompass the making of only four films, leaving her free to do outside productions. The first of the group, *Bus Stop*, had already been established as an enormous success on Broadway. It was one of several properties Greene had sought as a property for Marilyn.

Her corporation would be paid $100,000 for her services on each film, and retroactive pay was worked out for the period of her self-imposed exile. According to the terms of the corporation agreement between herself and Greene, she was to get $100,000 a year from February 1, 1956, in equal monthly instalments. Since her actual holdings in the corporation amounted to 51 out of a total of 101 shares, she would get only 50.5 per cent of the firm's profits, so she was really being paid a little over $50,000 per film. She would have to complete two films per year in order to earn her prescribed corporation salary, a prerequisite she would never fulfil as her own employer.

Greene was to receive $75,000 per year in equal monthly instalments, which if paid would leave little or no working capital for the firm even with two films annually. Theoretically, there was to be income from other sources: Greene's photography studio had been thrown into the hopper and would produce only $3,500 in profits for 1956 (a drastic drop from its customary income due to his involvement with Marilyn); phonograph records were often discussed but never made; film productions with stars other than Marilyn were another unrealized project.

At about the same time Marilyn's Fox contract was being drawn up, Joshua Logan finally settled a lawsuit over the film rights to James Michener's *Sayonara* by working out a separate arrangement with each of the three parties suing him. He was to retain his rights to film *Sayonara*, but he was to produce it with William Goetz, one of the parties to the suit. He was to direct a film for Metro, another party to the action, and he was also to direct a film for Fox, the third party.

Fox was ready with *Bus Stop*, the William Inge comic study of a youthful and innocent cowboy determined to carry back to his ranch the "angel" he sees singing in a tawdry Phoenix night club. The project interested Logan immediately when Fox added that they were working out details to have Marilyn return to the fold in the role of Cherie.

Marilyn was equally excited by the prospect of working with Logan. She knew he had studied with Stanislavski at the Moscow Art Theatre. He was, in fact, the only American prominent in the theatre who had ever spent any appreciable time with the Russian innovator. It was no accident, perhaps, that members of the original Group Theatre, who declared their work to be inspired by Stanislavski, always considered Logan's work to be a bastard spawned by ideas borrowed from the Russian master coupled with the most commercial aspects of the Broadway theatre.

These sour-grape criticisms of Logan's work, which Marilyn may have once heard from a former Group Theatre member, did not affect her to the slightest degree. If Logan had succeeded in combining these two dynamic forces so they would work he had achieved precisely what she was aiming for herself.

On January 4, 1956, Fox made the official announcement

that Marilyn and the studio had come to terms. She was headily triumphant; Greene was suddenly solvent. It was one of those rare moments in Marilyn's life when a calculated risk had turned out brilliantly.

CHAPTER FOUR

Marilyn's career was being guided by three very different men by the end of 1955: Lee Strasberg, Milton Greene, and Arthur Miller. The least involved at this point was Miller, who within less than a year would be the most intimately involved. Greene – sensing her deepening commitment to Strasberg – made a significant effort not to seem to be in conflict with the man, but Greene was too creative by nature to confine his interest to the business end of Marilyn's future. Within a few weeks, there would come the first major misunderstanding over whether Strasberg had or had not approved Sir Laurence Olivier as Marilyn's director on a film her company planned to do in England the following summer.

Marilyn felt impelled to go on with the work she had begun with Strasberg, the exercises, the concentration and focus. He had suggested that his wife Paula might be willing to help. She had coached others and had been a member of the acting ensemble of the Group Theatre.

Paula Strasberg was more specific in her application of acting principles than her husband. She went into great detail to set the mood of a line or a scene for Marilyn, and when she wanted to create a general atmosphere of elation or dejection, she employed a metaphor, such as "You're a bird, an eagle, and you're looking down upon the earth from very high in the sky" (elation) or "You feel like a wet soda cracker" (dejection). Sometimes in the future, when Marilyn wasn't feeling very "metaphorical", she could get no vital help in finding the key to a scene and would become terrified.

But the liaison was formed as simply as that. She wanted to continue to cultivate her inner resources as an actress, and Paula was ready to volunteer. It was to become one of the most controversial attachments of Marilyn's life and certainly one that Marilyn herself was to ponder over.

Milton Greene was sure that something could be worked out with Fox so that Paula could go on salary when the film went into production. His own feelings were neutral about the woman, but if Marilyn could perform better with Paula around, then it must be arranged.

Paula was to be called everything from "essentially exploitive" (by Arthur Miller) to "a warm Yiddisher Mama with words of advice and caution pouring from her in torrents, all out of love and interest" (by Joshua Logan). She soon made herself indispensable to directors on a Monroe film, for Marilyn simply could not act without Paula's constant help. Her work on a new picture began with this dependency very much in everyone's mind.

Joshua Logan, the first director to be affected by this new relationship, had heard that Marilyn's last coach, Natasha, used to sit well behind the camera, watch Marilyn do a scene, and then give her some kind of high sign as to whether she was fine or poor. This system might have worked had Natasha's judgement of when Marilyn was "fine" been infallible and had she weighed all the other performances in the scene for their effectiveness as well. But her sole concern was for Marilyn, naturally, and this meant that Marilyn might be perfect while one of the other actors sagged a little. Only the director of the film could be the final judge. Logan wanted complete control of his film and he brooked no interference on his set, be it from a dramatic coach or God. He recalled that Paula had been a sort of coach to her daughter when Susan had done a small role in his film *Picnic*, and he remembered Paula's constant presence on the set. Perhaps what he had been told about Natasha also contributed to his negative view. In any case, he sent word to Greene to inform Marilyn that he didn't want Paula on *Bus Stop*.

The Strasbergs were distressed and dumbfounded by Logan's attitude. Lee immediately phoned Logan on the coast and wanted to know why Paula was being rejected. He pointed out to the director how far Marilyn had come with her studies. During that conversation, it became evident to Logan that both Strasbergs had come to have an enormous respect for Marilyn's talent as well as her mind. This was surprising to him. The advance word on Marilyn was that she was rather dense, difficult, and unpunctual. Only George Axelrod, who had become acquainted with her during the filming of his play

The Seven Year Itch, had defended her. But now Strasberg was telling him that he had encountered two film personalities of really great potential in his work at the studio, Marlon Brando, and "quite as good as Brando is Marilyn".

Logan abandoned his objections. "As long as it's clear to Paula she is never to come on the set, why fine. Let her come."

There was some unfinished business for Marilyn in New York before she could leave for the West Coast and *Bus Stop*. Miller had suggested that they continue to deny all rumours that they would be married soon, possibly out of deference to his children. Marilyn asked a reporter, "How can they say we're having a romance when he's already married?" and her question was wholly in character with her public image at the time, while Miller called the report "absurd", and gratuitously added, "We have never been alone."

Mary Miller came to their aid with an avowal that Marilyn had nothing to do with their separation. This was an honest declaration as Miller had considered the marriage doomed for a long time.

John Moore, a designer for Talmack, a better-class manufacturer, was doing a new wardrobe for Marilyn. She saw much of him over a period of several weeks, and he introduced her to his mother. When she was ready to depart for the coast, she told John and his mother and her other new friends in the East how much she was going to miss them. "But I'll be back," she added, "when the picture is over. New York is my home now. Hollywood is just a place to work in."

It was painful leaving Miller, although they were to keep in touch by phone. She left behind, too, her press agent, Lois Weber, who was permanently attached to the Jacobs New York office. They assigned to her a slightly younger woman named Patricia Newcomb who brought with her some social distinction. She was the daughter of an Army judge advocate general, and much of her life in society had been spent in Washington, D.C. Marilyn and Miss Newcomb clashed during the production of *Bus Stop*, and the press agent was reassigned elsewhere. It was far from being their last contact, however. She re-entered Marilyn's professional family nearly five years later.

No one had mentioned Natasha Lytess when Paula Strasberg became Marilyn's new coach. It was assumed that she was long gone from Marilyn's life. This was not true; Marilyn was often careless in tidying up her life, possibly because important decisions were often deferred and then acted upon quickly, almost impulsively. Natasha was still on the Fox payroll as head drama coach for the studio. She had been given the post principally at Marilyn's behest. She was being paid handsomely and got even more when she was on one of Marilyn's films. There was nothing phoney about her status during Marilyn's hiatus. Natasha was kept busy with several contract actors, by whom she was highly regarded. She was living then in a Beverly Hills house which Marilyn had helped her to finance a year or so earlier.

Marilyn had not contacted her once during her Eastern sabbatical, and Natasha must have been aware that a break was imminent. But Natasha had said nothing of this to Fox, and since the studio was out of communication with Marilyn through most of that year, they were not aware of either her current favourites or discards.

"Natasha knows I've made other arrangements," Marilyn told the Fox executives. "It's been in all the papers. I haven't been in touch with her in months."

The Fox people told Marilyn to settle the matter herself. It is an unfortunate but understandable fact that many of those who were anti-Marilyn – and their number now included a great many salaried production personnel at Fox – saw her path to the extraordinary fame she now enjoyed littered with the shattered remains of those whom Marilyn had discarded, beginning with Jim Dougherty and now including, not too surprisingly, the "indispensable" Miss Lytess. One of them looked at a mock-up of a colossal likeness of Marilyn being prepared for a Times Square theatre during her year of absence and the release of *The Seven Year Itch*. He said, "There's Marilyn! But where are we?"

A telegram was drafted by a law firm Marilyn had retained on the East coast and dispatched to Natasha. Judging by her subsequent behaviour it is clear that Natasha felt great distress on the day the telegram arrived. She had committed herself to Marilyn through seven years of steadily increasing demands as Marilyn's roles became larger and her talents needed even more refining. Marilyn's career was neatly divided in half; the Strasbergs were to guide her for seven years, too.

There has been a tendency, because of the great stress journalists and writers of books have placed upon Marilyn's association with the Strasbergs, to minimize Natasha's contribution to the development of Marilyn as an original, and even
irreplaceable, screen personality.

In her memoirs, Natasha later declared that Marilyn needed
her like "a dead man needs a coffin", a singular description of
dependency. A dead man is beyond needs, but Marilyn was
not, and she needed more than mere assistance behind the
camera when she met Natasha. Lee Strasberg was surprised
when he first met Marilyn to find that her sensitivity had not
been destroyed by the devastating events of her earlier life.
What he was overlooking was the well of sensitivity that was
Natasha, and Marilyn drew on this source for years. This is
not to say that Marilyn was insensitive before she met the
woman. Natasha had shown how to make her own innate, if
not always visible, sensitivity work for her, giving her film
roles a seeming, if uncomplicated, reality. She awakened Marilyn to important authors at a time when Marilyn had just
met Miller and desperately needed to know who they were.
She had begun polishing the rough edges months before
Johnny Hyde came on the scene.

Billy Wilder realized when he was directing Marilyn in *The
Seven Year Itch* that she had developed into a skilled comedienne. Part of the credit for that performance must go to
Natasha Lytess. She would live approximately nine years following her dismissal from Marilyn's life.

Marilyn's return to Hollywood after a year's absence was
an event equally as epochal in the annals of filmdom as the
departure of Chaplin or the advent of Desilu to the old RKO
Studios. A swarm of reporters enveloped her as she left her
plane, so she held an impromptu press conference in the terminal building. When told by a lady journalist that she looked
different, she said the suit she was wearing was new but she
was the same person. She added that she now had director
approval. "That's very important," she said with a trace of
diffidence. She had the manner of one who has been given
great power, but who is in awe of it.

Despite the fact that she had become the hotly defended
pet of a great many people in and out of films, there were
numerous critics around, most vocal in Holywood, who were

eager to spread the word from a "reliable" source at Fox that she had come back to the studio practically on her knees since Milton Greene had run out of funds. As they told the story, the bills from her analyst, courturiers, hairdresser, and others were about to force Marilyn Monroe Productions into bankruptcy before it ever got around to shooting a foot of film.

There was an element of truth in this, but she had done something that had proved her value beyond any ordinary reckoning. As she moved through the air terminal, surrounded by reporters, she came as close as she ever would be to realizing that she was a film goddess.

Beyond her standing on Olympus, there *was* a subtle difference about her. Economic security (now that she could breathe freely again following Milton's close call with solvency) and a new self-confidence gave her every utterance the weight of a pronouncement and turned some of the Fox executives' blood to ice. They reasoned that, before, if she could drive them up the wall when she was plagued by uncertainty, now that she seemed to know where she was going they should brace themselves for something far more nerve-shattering.

When she was shown the elaborate costumes designed for her as Cherie, she let out a groan of displeasure. "They're terrible!" she said, holding up one of the drawings to Joshua Logan, who quickly agreed they were far too expensive-looking and out of character. "Let's find something in the wardrobe department," she suggested, and this provoked an incredulous but delighted grin on studio chief Buddy Adler's face.

Marilyn and Logan walked through wardrobe and she snatched up the sleaziest things she could find, including a lamé coat with monkey-fur trim. When she got her hands on the long net stockings for her night-club number, she began tearing holes in them and demanded that they be obviously darned. She was determined to make Cherie into a real person. It was clear that her studies with Strasberg had included a thorough investigation into how everyday people looked and behaved.

Milton Greene had been signed to design her make-up and lighting, and, more significantly, to be a peacemaker between the studio and his corporation president. His contribution to the success of the film was not meagre. He lent to the character of Cherie a pale, aspirin and black-coffee aspect, and one could believe that she was a creature who rarely saw the sun, who could sing badly night after night to cowboys who rarely listened and collapse in a hall bedroom at three every morning, and who stubbornly refused to concede that she was a failure. There was much of the early Marilyn in Cherie.

Marilyn and the Greenes rented a large place in Beverly Glen where Amy was to stay much of the time, supervising the household and, of course, her small son, Josh. The atmosphere of the place was altogether different from the homestead in Connecticut. There Marilyn appeared to be groping for a new direction, and her dependency upon Amy had bound them together. Despite her preoccupation with a sense of reality in her films, things were not always what they seemed in her private life. The Beverly Glen house was at once charged with the presence of an egocentrist in the throes of a new project. The phone rang constantly. Messengers appeared with scripts and photos. There was a steady army of servitors: hairdressers, masseurs, publicity men, and Paula Strasberg. Amy, who had quietly dominated her Connecticut household, was now very much in the background.

Marilyn was in prime condition, looking, as Amy Greene put it, like a "noodle". She had lost every ounce of excess flesh and she seemed to subsist on a diet of raw steaks and champagne. The champagne was taken in the evening with an occasional glass during the afternoon.

To Logan, she was the most constantly exciting actress he had ever worked with, and that excitement was not related to her celebrity but to her humanness, to the way she saw the life around her.

Once shooting began, Logan quickly learned that Marilyn turned on her incandescence only when she knew the cameras were running. Once he said "Cut!" she would amble off to the side and fuss at her hair, her concentration broken. An infinitely patient man with people he is betting on to produce the goods, he had the camera loaded with a thousand feet of film and permitted her to extemporize before the running camera. In this way he had a vast and valuable accumulation of takes on Marilyn to choose from: Marilyn reacting to disappointment, crying on cue, her eyes getting moist; Marilyn showing joy and exuberance, her face flushed. He treated her as something fragile that could be easily crushed or extinguished. He studied his moviola with the taut expectancy of a lepidopterist about to drop his net over a rare specimen. And through the very casualness of his approach, he captured on film a living, breathing Cherie.

But the executives at Fox, including Buddy Adler, were hardened critics of Monroe. Complaints reached Logan every day. They found Greene's stark-white make-up for Marilyn "freakish". They wondered why Lee Strasberg hadn't taught her to be more disciplined. They were, according to Logan, ignorant men who hated anyone who wouldn't conform.

Finally, when their criticisms extended to Don Murray, her leading man for whom this was his first major role, asserting that "he yells too much", Logan told them to "knock it off". "You hired me for this job," he told Adler. "Now tell these stupid bastards they either go with me or replace me." From then on, he was left alone.

Despite Logan's patience, Marilyn was in a state of nerves a good part of the time. She had a great deal riding on this first production since her freedom had been won. She had to prove she was worth all the trouble. She must somehow measure up to all the fuss.

She had studied Kim Stanley's performance as Cherie in New York. Having a flair for dialect, she practised a Southern accent endlessly with Paula until they agreed it was authentic.

She knew as well as some of her detractors that *Marilyn* was a flawed creation: her education was a patchwork affair with glaring omissions, a hand-me-down from Norma Jean: her torrential rages might possibly stem from tainted family genes. Some of her most trusted friends felt that she was too withdrawn and sensitive to succeed as an independent actress.

But knowing the odds, she was waging a fight on all these fronts. Through Miller and on her own, she had met literary figures, poets Norman Rosten and Carl Sandburg and soon Edith Sitwell, winning their friendship and loyalty at once. She was able in most instances to beat a quick retreat from any source of irritation so that her temper was kept bottled in her dressing-room or submerged by tranquillizers. She was heavily reliant upon Logan on the set and Paula off to prove that her sensitivity was the negotiable coin of her success as a free agent, though she would, when necessary, reveal that it masked a will of iron.

Her hysteria built up when the moment approached for her

appearance before Logan's mood-devouring camera. Often she grasped the arm of some friendly member of the production company, such as script supervisor Joe Curtis, and walked with him up and down the darkened periphery of the sound stage. If she was seen at such an embattled moment by some-one of the company waiting for her at the camera set-up, everyone understood that she was not to be approached, and Logan was too keenly aware of her problem to send anyone looking for her.

Sometimes her tension would not leave her during these walks and she would give up and come to the set nearly dis-traught with apprehension. On one of these occasions, she was required to flick the "tail" of her night-club costume over Don Murray's face, but in her nervousness, she swatted him with unnecessary force. Murray became furious and stalked away from her. Born in the theatre, the son of a stage man-ager, he was a veteran professional despite his youth, and he knew you didn't have to hit anyone that hard for an effect. But Marilyn was contrite, and the incident was forgotten.

When the love scenes were finally done, the camera worked in very close, and Marilyn had a very real response at work in the first kissing close-up. A string of saliva was visible just for a moment as her lips parted from Murray's. When she sat in on the rushes, she realized that Logan had cut out the saliva. In the name of realism, she insisted that part be used. She accused Logan of being less than a man in his "prudery". Later, Logan said that the cut was not made at his order but by an edict from a high studio executive.

Some of the rapport between Marilyn and her director dissolved as they moved to their first location in Phoenix to do the rodeo scenes. She was in seclusion a good part of the time and Logan could no longer rely upon a close, personal communication with her. Milton Greene was called on numer-ous occasions to talk with her and attempt to get her to the set.

In Sun Valley, where the exterior bus-stop scenes were made, the snow – a kind of magic powder for her – sweetened her temper for a time. She was often playful and she even man-aged some friendly conversation with the ingenue, Hope Lange, who had recently become Mrs. Don Murray.

But once she was back in the dusty acres of Fox's Beverly Hills lot, she caught a bad case of bronchitis and Greene drove her to Cedars of Lebanon Hospital, where she was admitted and treated for nearly a week.

Visitors were kept to a minimum. It is said that DiMaggio came on one occasion, and Nedda Logan visited her one afternoon. She reassured Marilyn that her husband had become "very fond and very protective" of her. The director's wife was a woman of quick-silver sensibilities who had been associated with the theatre all her life. The daughter of the late and esteemed actor Ned Harrigan, she had seen flare-ups of temperament from Jeanne Eagels to Mary Martin. Perhaps Marilyn was entitled to greater combustibility than the average star because she had fewer around to lean on, excluding her minions. Marilyn told Nedda ruefully that the hospital had sent someone around to take down her medical history and they asked who the next of kin would be in case they needed to be notified. "And there wasn't anyone I could think of," she said, turning away and staring at the wall. "Give them my name," Nedda told her.

While she was hospitalized, Logan shot around her. Much of the period was spent staging a fist-fight between Don Murray and Bob Brag, who played the bus driver. The fight took place in the cornflake snow in front of the bus stop, and Logan managed to string it out over a period of two or three days. The sequence was to have a certain notoriety as the longest fight ever filmed.

When Marilyn had recovered, and the film was nearing completion, it became evident that *Bus Stop* was the most nearly perfect film of her career. She was as good as she would ever be, and that was very good indeed. She was more than worth all the "fuss".

Logan was able to relax at last and he gave a cocktail party for President Sukarno of Indonesia, who was being escorted through Hollywood by Logan's brother, Marshall Nolan. Marilyn was invited, and the climactic moment came when the little men from the Far East gathered expectantly near the door for her entrance. She was instantly surrounded, and it reminded Logan of a scene with Edwina Booth in *Trader Horn*. He had never before heard such a spontaneous sexual roar as came from the excited throats of the diminutive Asians.

When the film was done, Logan escorted Marilyn to a dinner-party – he was totally her champion now that the worst was behind him, denouncing all of her detractors, both real or fancied, given the slightest provocation. He would be too disarmed to resist her unexpected attack the following summer in London when they met, an occasion when Marilyn lashed out at him for cutting from *Bus Stop* what she considered to be her most effective moments. The dinner was at the home of producer William Goetz, Logan's partner in the soon-to-be-produced *Sayonara*. Marilyn was as warm and considerate to Logan that evening as she had been during the first weeks of their association – she had not yet seen the final cut of the film. She was her own severest critic as has already been pointed out, and she knew instinctively that her work on the picture had been honest and convincing. From the rough, unedited cut she had just seen, she realized that Logan had made her wholly believable as a human being. There was nothing false about any of it.

The director had brought a 35-mm. camera along. It was a secret shared by only his closest friends that he was a photographer of professional calibre. Logan's portraits taken that evening in front of several of the masterworks in the extensive Goetz art collection reveal Marilyn's ability to fall into the mood of her surroundings and, as much as any still photographer ever has, her peculiar incandescence.

A few days later, Logan received a silver-framed earlier study of Marilyn, one she especially prized, along with a note reading: "This would look well with yellow roses next to it." She meant well, and she couldn't have known then that some of the shots taken that evening by Logan's candid camera would be better.

There had been numerous phone calls from Miller, who was then in residence near Pyramid Lake, Nevada, for his divorce. Before she was ready to fly back East, they had come to a decision about a possible marriage. They would wed just as soon as they were together again in New York and could make their plans. This decision was exhilarating to Marilyn and sobering to Miller.

PART FIVE

Marilyn Monroe Productions

CHAPTER ONE

There is a considerable body of Americans who are convinced that all writers who are not transparent hacks must be intellectuals. This is fast generalization, for the intellectual content of the American theatre has never been high, nor can we be especially proud of the original thought and ideas found in much of American fiction of recent years.

When Arthur Miller first took a magnifying glass to the American social scene, a couple of things were at once evident. Here was an often brilliant analyst and only a passable writer of prose. This is not stated in dismissal, for two of his plays, *Death of a Salesman* and *The Crucible,* have such evocative power and mercilessly clear focus, the playwright must rank as an American writer of importance and permanent value.

But a valuable writer is not necessarily an intellectual one, and Arthur Miller cannot, indeed does not, claim to be an intellectual. He pares down the content of his work several times in the process of creation, until he achieves the essence. An intellectual playwright, T. S. Eliot as a recent example, begins with an idea and then articulates it with dialogue, character revelation, and action, probably in that order of importance. The best playwrights of any age are almost never intellectuals and frequently their associates are disturbed to find them withdrawn and even inarticulate away from the theatre as though they are saving what wit and civilizing elements they possess for use in their work. On the two occasions, both recent, when Miller temporarily abandoned his simplicity and directness for philosophical reflection (*After the Fall* and *Incident at Vichy*), he came joltingly to earth in his own leaky gas balloon. In the first play, his intelligent grasp of theatre is apparent only in the clinical observation of the character he calls Maggie in her scenes with the verbose hero, Quentin. Quentin's ideas, which he delivers front and centre, are nearly all curiously threadbare and we are embarrassed for him as he plunges ahead, unaware of their obviousness. In the *Vichy* drama, we sit half-mesmerized by regurgitated recent history and keep hoping that we will be presented with some less familiar cry of outrage along the way.

The Misfits should not be overlooked when discussing the Miller canon. Certainly it ranks not too far below his *A View from the Bridge,* although this screenplay is flawed to a degree that prevents it from achieving the stature of *Salesman* and *The Crucible.* But here it was more the matter of adapting a fine short story into absorbing entertainment. Perhaps the amplification of Roslyn, who is entirely offstage in the story, into a major character has given the screenplay more delicacy and depth, while sacrificing the cruder but nevertheless beautiful masculinity of the short story.

Marilyn was accepted as a part-time member of the intellectual establishment. She did believe that Miller was an intellectual from the moment of their first meeting, and since she seemed to take some pleasure from it, he never really made an effort to disenchant her. Her own intelligence was often concealed beneath malapropisms, hopeless mis-spellings, and illogic. Her insecurity made many of her observations sound like questions. But Miller believed that he and Marilyn came to their courtship as equals, and she soon realized they were of nearly equal intelligence although she would always stand in awe of his intellect. Initially, she felt honoured to be associated with him. Later on, she made strenuous efforts to compensate for what she felt was her cultural inadequacy.

If she couldn't compete with Miller's intellectual friends, and there were a number of them, she could at least disarm them with her candour and ingenious wit. An avid reader, she "got more" out of books than most people, but never enough to feel assured that her impressions were accurate. Exceptions were certain biographies, and some screenplays, into whose margins she wrote tiny notes to herself, explaining and often motivating characters whom the screen writer had sketched in broadly. So astute were these annotations that Paula Strasberg was attempting to organize them into a book on the art of performing for the screen at the time of her death in March 1966.

All of this helped to make Marilyn's screen roles more considerable than they sometimes were. The role of Sugar Kane in *Some Like it Hot* was essentially a supporting one, but few in the audience who saw her perform carried away that impression. This background is not brought in to gloss over Marilyn's flaws as an actress. It is merely stated to reinforce the conclusion that Marilyn was something more than a plastic personality, an automaton totally in the hands of directors, or a mindless vacuum filled at intervals by miasmic fogs of despair and unreasoning fears. The imbalance of mental capacities often cited by writers exploring Marilyn's relationship with Arthur Miller simply did not exist.

In May Marilyn arrived in New York carrying a white Persian cat named Mitsou, then expecting kittens. In a special carrier on the same plane was a young basset-hound she decided to call Hugo.

Miller was still off in Nevada near Pyramid Lake, where he was sitting out the residency required for divorce. When Mitsou went into labour, Marilyn phoned her New York press agent, Lois Weber, who said she would be right over but who advised that she call a veterinarian.

By the time Miss Weber had reached the eight-floor apartment that Milton Greene had found for Marilyn at 2 Sutton Place, upon her return to New York, Mitsou had given birth to three kittens. "I've called three vets," Marilyn told her. "They think I'm kidding when I say 'This is Marilyn Monroe. My cat's having kittens.' They think I'm some kind of a nut and hang up."

The cat had chosen the white-carpeted hallway as her nest. Marilyn was on her knees, excited and involved in the event. All told, there were eight kittens of various hues that evening, and finally, by dint of keeping her identity a secret until the end of the conversation, she learned from the vet that goat's milk would help to supplement the mother's own.

Caring for the numerous felines and Hugo occupied much of Marilyn's time while waiting for Miller's return. There were also several sessions with the stills on *Bus Stop*. As always, her judgement – which could not be faulted in this department – killed a great many of them. There survived, however, a remarkable photographic record of the production taken by Zinn Arthur, a New York photographer assigned to the task by Joshua Logan. In these, Marilyn is seen in a variety of moods and attitudes, some strikingly beautiful and others quite human and less than perfect. Apparently, Marilyn saw few of these and had no control over them.

Those final days before her reunion with Miller was observed by her friends and associates, the Greenes, Lois Weber, the Strasbergs, with apprehension. Marilyn, they felt, had become totally vulnerable, had abandoned all of her defences, and thrown aside any wisdom she had gained from the past. She wanted to come to her forthcoming marriage cleansed of the past, and their fear was that in this purified state, whether fancied or real, she might easily be destroyed.

Marilyn had no such qualms. Her mood was gay, the weather was fine, and it was difficult for her to recall another time in her life when things were going so well. When she left her apartment building where that curious group who called themselves the Monroe Six were always waiting for her, she joked with them. Its members were all just out of high school, with no discernible employment or further schooling to distract them. None was over nineteen years of age. They had begun their vigil as individuals a year and a half earlier. John Reilley, a sober-looking red-haired Irish-American with dark-rimmed glasses, became fascinated by Marilyn's presence when she was staying at the St. Regis during *The Seven Year Itch* location work. Two members, Jimmy and Eileen Collins, were brother and sister, and there were three young ladies, Gloria Milone, Freda Hull, and Edith Pitts.

While she never heard of any of them being picked up for vagrancy, they always seemed to be near the foyer of her building when she came out. Often they would be waiting for her outside of a theatre she had attended or a friend's apartment building. They somehow discovered her itinerary for each day, a feat which amused and sometimes astonished Marilyn. In time, everyone around her had met them, Miller taking the dimmest view of their preoccupation. There was also a more aggressive loner named Jimmy Haspiel, who managed to befriend not only Marilyn but most of her circle as well. The Six and young Mr. Haspiel, after several years, collectively owned the most complete off-the-screen record of Marilyn made with still and home movie-cameras; they amassed the most comprehensive collection of press clippings and, through dogged attendance, were witness to sufficient aspects of the Marilyn drama to be of more than passing interest to any biographer. Their stakeout was endless. In cold weather one was chosen to run for coffee and then race back with it for fear of missing something.

Marilyn developed an easy familiarity with these special fans, treating them as younger brothers and sisters. A year later, she held a first reunion for them at Miller's Connecticut farm. There were hot dogs and a swim in the pond, and there was far more of Norma Jean than Marilyn visible that summer day.

CHAPTER TWO

It was early in June 1956, and Arthur Miller flew into New York at breakfast time, his divorce papers in his pocket. His time in Nevada had not been entirely wasted on the business of divorce. He was working on a new play, and he had met some down-at-heel cowboys near Reno who inspired him to write a short story, *The Misfits*.

Marilyn was waiting for a phone call in the Sutton Place apartment. That call was delayed nearly half an hour as Miller was cornered by reporters, all wanting to know when the wedding would take place. The newsmen were getting used to spilling out to the airport at an ungodly hour. About ten days earlier, Marilyn had brought them there at 7 a.m. when she had flown in from Hollywood. A reporter for the *New York Post* attempted to soften up Miller by explaining, "We only bother you about this because people want to know." Miller's answer was a reflection of what was to plague him for more than four years, "It is your job versus my privacy. That's a remorseless conflict."

The reporters had to be there. Public interest was so high that Miller's "no comment" rated page one in several newspapers along with a photograph. The lack of a denial *was* newsworthy, but he would not reveal any details of the wedding that was now a certainty. There were too many problems to unravel before they would know themselves when and where it might be.

Miller recalls laconically that Marilyn seemed pleased to

see him again. Other friends recall her inability to leave him alone even for a moment. Miller, who had always seemed reserved before, was equally abandoned with her among friends whom he trusted. They were entwined a good deal of the time and gradually their friends recovered from their embarrassment and accepted their behaviour as natural.

Conversation was limited mostly to plans for the future. Since Marilyn had already invited both Strasbergs to accompany her to England for the filming of her first independent production, *The Prince and the Showgirl*, because, as she told them, "I want everything to go right," she now urged Miller to meet with them.

Miller and the Strasbergs were not unacquainted. They had met through Elia Kazan. Miller had no admiration for the work of the Actors Studio and he was frankly sceptical of Paula's ability as a coach, but because of Marilyn's involvement he kept most of these opinions to himself.

He sensed that the Strasbergs had instinctively placed a finger on an exposed nerve in Marilyn and were making themselves her sole defenders in a crass, insensitive business. He was not in any haste to meet them on an intimate basis.

He was, he knew, among a silent minority. He discovered that Marilyn's press agent, Miss Weber, shared his view but she, too, felt herself in no position to say anything. Miller's actress sister, Joan Copeland, was nearly as enthusiastic about Strasberg as Marilyn. The teacher had become the guru for so many in the theatre that Studio actors' adherents were claiming nearly everyone of any talent in the business and believed those without the Strasberg master course had happened upon his tenets by sheer dumb luck.

Marilyn was always seeking support and reassurance, and Lee and Paula were supplying these wholesale draughts. She had no family to give a blessing to the marriage, and it was clear that the Strasbergs were her chosen substitutes. Miller felt obliged to comply with her wishes.

And so they met. Miller seemed stand-offish to the Strasbergs, more so than they had heard about or remembered. To Marilyn, his remoteness must have been a disappointment. There was no starting point from which to proceed to any closeness. She had hoped for something better. They appeared to have so much in common, so much to talk about, far more than she had, although she always managed. When she was with them, conversation not directed towards her career often centred upon family-type gossip: Suzy's acting career, just launched with *The Diary of Anne Frank*; their pets. And, when she felt most secure in the womb of their book-lined, cluttered apartment, they would even discuss Marilyn's early days.

Afterwards, Marilyn never alluded to the coolness of that first meeting, and included the Strasbergs in her wedding plans. Strasberg, in fact, gave her away. After their return from England, she spent frequent evenings with them at the Central Park West apartment and then around 11 p.m. disappeared to the study phone where she was sometimes overheard reassuring Miller, "I'll be there in twenty minutes, Pa." The Strasbergs imagined him skulking about nearby drug stores or bars, waiting, but adamantly refusing to become part of their cosy group.

Plans for their wedding shared top priority with the final arrangements with Olivier. Marilyn and Milton Greene were involved in costume approvals and fittings, interviews, and a review of the budget. Here again, Marilyn observed a kind of distance between Miller and Greene whenever the latter dropped by the apartment to talk about the movie. This was especially disconcerting to Greene, for he sensed disapproval.

There was a difference between Miller's attitude towards the Strasbergs and the way he behaved in Greene's presence. He seemed not at all interested in Greene as a human being, although he nearly always tried to half-smile upon greeting him, but he had an inexhaustible supply of questions to ask about Marilyn Monroe Productions. His intervention here would one day soon provoke Greene to cry out to him, *"Be a husband!* Leave the corporation to Marilyn, me, and our attorneys."

Miller was in almost daily conference with his own lawyers in his resolute struggle with the federal government to regain his passport denied in March of 1954 because of supposed Communist leanings. This preoccupation kept feelings between the two men fairly neutral prior to their departure for England.

The renewed action by Mrs. Frances Knight of the Passport Division had triggered some reckless and unsubstantiated charges by Congressman Francis Walter (Democrat, Pennsylvania) of the House Un-American Activities Sub-committee. If his object was blatant headline-seeking, then he was succeeding. *Paris-Match* had a twenty-four-hour stakeout on the Sutton Place apartment, and was attempting to rent a vacant apartment across the street on the same floor to keep a sharper watch on Marilyn's home. Other reporters came from time to time to watch for an appearance by one of the principals. Marilyn was inclined to blame herself for what was happening, but Miller's troubles were of long standing.

Senator Joseph McCarthy was dead, but his "ism", not quite decently buried, still boasted a few old dragons breathing fire from Capitol Hill. Moved to some caution by newly vocal guardians of the Constitution and its Bill of Rights, Chairman Walter issued a statement that Arthur Miller was wanted in Washington as a witness in their current investigation. Walter informed Miller's attorneys that testimony would be confined to examining the alleged misuse of passports by American citizens. They wanted to know why, he said, the writer had been denied a passport.

The question was merely rhetorical. In 1954 the State Department announced that Mr. Miller's application had been rejected under a regulation denying passports to persons believed to be supporting the Communist movement, "whether or not they are members of the Communist Party". The release went on to state that Mr. Miller had requested a passport to travel to Brussels for the opening of his play, *The Crucible*, on March 9.

At the time, Miller, then staying with his family in New Milford, Connecticut, denied that he was supporting any Communist movement. He went on to point up the speciousness of the government press release by informing reporters that he had withdrawn his application for renewal a few days after asking for it because by then it was too late for him to attend the play's opening. The State Department had acknowledged in writing many days earlier this request for withdrawal. But Miller was angered by the sheer destructiveness of the State Department's press office in releasing the item two weeks later, possibly for lack of anything more sensational for the newspapers that month. He said he could not understand how his presence in Europe could have affected the United States and hoped that his plays would make more friends for American culture than the State Department.

The Sub-committee had the whole story at its fingertips. But, Miller believed, and he is probably right, Congressman Walter and his colleagues had another matter in mind. They were not getting much space in the daily papers, and the world's attention was focused on their present witness because of his forthcoming marriage to Marilyn Monroe.

Miller felt it was disgraceful for the Sub-committee to abuse his rights as a citizen for such a shallow reason. It appears likely that one of Miller's attorneys told Chairman Walter as much, for when Miller finally appeared at the special hearing, Walter was no longer talking about passports. He wanted to know the names of persons Miller had seen attending a Communist-sponsored meeting of authors in 1947.

The question was not entirely specious. Four years earlier, the same Sub-committee had hit the jackpot with Elia Kazan when he identified his fellow party members by name. Chairman Walter could not have been ignorant of the falling out between Kazan and Miller over this, but it is likely he had missed the recent semi-thaw.

It is clear from the manner in which he handled the case that Walter's attempt, shortly before June 21, the scheduled date of the hearing, was a disservice to the Republic. He expected a declaration of principles from Miller, a refusal to betray his friends. Naturally, this would lead to an almost certain citation for contempt of Congress. To land one-half of the hottest headline pair on the current scene in the Sub-committee cauldron would be an achievement to rank with McCarthy's triumphs, or so the Chairman may have reasoned.

To establish for the historical record how ill-planned was Chairman Walter's attempt, Miller's lawyers in Washington were made a strange proposition. A Sub-committee member close to the Chairman had suggested that there was a strong possiblity Walter might find a painless solution to Miller's difficulties if a news picture were taken of Walter with Marilyn Monroe. Her compassionate interest in her husband's problems with the government might be enough to turn public sentiment in Mr. Miller's favour, or so the Sub-committee spokesman explained. This proposal evoked first incredulity, then outrage in Miller. His lawyers cautioned him to keep the suggestion to himself since no one would ever believe it.

On the evening of June 20, Marilyn accompanied Miller to Washington for the hearing. They went directly to the home

of Joseph Rauh, resident Washington attorney for Miller's
lawyers. The Rauhs did what they could to reassure Marilyn.

The next day, while Miller was closeted with Chairman
Walter and his colleagues, Marilyn managed to go outside the
Rauh home and meet with a covey of reporters who had dis-
covered she was there.

The dozen or so journalists, photographers, and newsreel
crew gathered near that front stoop were the first outsiders to
see the change that was occurring in Marilyn. Having completed what nearly everyone was saying was her finest movie
(*Bus Stop*) and able to relax in the happy knowledge of becoming Mrs. Arthur Miller in the immediate future, she projected a wholly unexpected contentment.

One reporter asked her if she thought this political difficulty of her fiancé would affect her career. She said she didn't
believe that it would. Another asked Marilyn how she thought
Arthur Miller would fare at the hands of the Un-American
Activities Sub-committee. "I believe he will win."

But if it was indeed a contest, it could not be considered
won that day. Miller told the Congressmen and their aides
that he would not hesitate to sign a statement certifying that
he had never been a Communist, but refused to co-operate
in the matter of informing on his fellow-writers. By the middle of the last week in June, he was again in the headlines and
in what appeared to be real trouble.

His Roxbury, Connecticut, farm was a retreat that was increasingly necessary to him. Miller and Marilyn fled there
early that last week of June along with his parents, Augusta
and Isidore Miller.

On Wednesday afternoon, Miller took a call from his lawyer in Washington, Lloyd Garrison, who was working with
Joseph Rauh on the passport matter which had by now bal-
looned into an inquisition. Garrison's news was not unexpected. The House Sub-committee had voted unanimously to
give the playwright ten days to answer its ultimatum to reveal
the names of his colleagues or face a contempt citation, which
it would forward promptly to the Justice Department for pre-
sentation to a grand jury. Conviction would mean a maximum penalty of $1,000 fine and one year in jail.

The New York tabloids seized upon the action in great glee,
making much of the possibility that Marilyn might have to

postpone her wedding until her fiancé cleared himself. Shortly before their flight to Connecticut, he had pleaded with the boys from the press to lay off, promising a press conference and "all the pictures you need" at the Roxbury farm. He would not commit himself to announce the date and hour, nor even the place where they would be married.

Earlier, just after the Washington hearing, Marilyn had hurried over to the Strasbergs and asked mournfully what they thought would happen to Miller. Strasberg recalls asking, "Do you want me to speak to him? Paula and I have been through this sort of thing back when Kazan was called to Washington. We don't have any axe to grind."

Marilyn said that she thought it might be a good idea. Strasberg then told Miller in a friendly way that Paula had been co-operative with the Sub-committee and nothing had happened, but that, of course, he must make up his own mind about such a thing, that he wouldn't presume to give advice in such an important matter. Miller stiffly said that he agreed with the principle, for he wouldn't listen to any advice on an important private matter such as this.

Within a week, pressures from abroad began to build. This cavalier treatment of one of America's most significant playwrights was intolerable. Editorials appeared in England and France. Then very quietly the State Department passed the word to the Passport Division: "Issue the passport".

CHAPTER THREE

Isidore Miller, a retired manufacturer who had lost much of his fortune in the crash of 1929, found Marilyn's determination to become one of the Miller family altogether disarming. He promptly fell in love with his future daughter-in-law and became in time one of the elder advisers in her life, a position he still held after her marriage to his son was dissolved.

If Marilyn was going to marry a Jew, she would become one. She had been ready for this new life with Miller for a very long time. Among his family and those of his friends who were Jews, she wanted to be thought of as a member of the *mishpacha* (one of the clan or immediate family), not as a *shiksa* (gentile girl). It was not too difficult for her to lay aside her Christian beliefs. Her drift away from Christian Science had been going on for over a decade and nearly all of her closest friends now were Jewish – the Strasbergs, Milton Greene, the Rostens, the Wallachs. It was nothing she had deliberately sought. It had just happened.

Miller had first brought Marilyn to his parents' two-family house in the Flatbush section of Brooklyn during that final crowded week before the wedding. She was struck by the unpretentiousness of the household. She commented to Miller that it fitted in with her earlier persuasion that Brooklyn was a place where people could "really live", and this feeling, this ambience of a family environment, must have been reinforced when she and Miller walked up the steps arm-in-arm. About a dozen neighbourhood children came running up to see them.

Miller recalls that Marilyn laughed and talked to the children for a few minutes, even giving out a few autographs, and then he gently detached her from them and led her inside. The children relaxed their vigil after a while and drifted away.

Miller called Marilyn's press agent, Lois Weber, early on the Thursday he had designated for their press conference at Roxbury. Miss Weber was asked if she would please come up to assist. "There may be five or so reporters," he told her.

"You're living in a dream world," Miss Weber interjected. "You'll be overrun. They'll be hanging from the trees." The press agent knew better than Miller that the imminent marriage had the public enthralled. Some of its obsessive interest may have stemmed from the apparent incongruity of their natures, but there was an additional excitement among those who had watched Marilyn's career closely for several years. They probably numbered in the hundreds of thousands, and they all knew that Arthur Miller was a long-range plan of Marilyn's about to reach fruition.

Some of their closest friends through an accident, the highway death of reporter Mara Scherbatoff, a foreign correspondent, while tailing Miller's car, precipitated the hasty civil ceremony in White Plains on Friday evening. Earlier, Miller and Marilyn had decided they would be married by a rabbi on Sunday, July 1, at the home of Kay Brown, Miller's literary agent, in Katonah, New York, just over the Connecticut line. Most assuredly, Miss Scherbatoff's fatal head injury when she was thrown from her companion's convertible made everyone feel that it was time to stop the carnival being staged around the couple by more than sixty accredited newspapermen and journalists. Their number surprised even Lois Weber. They were not only hanging from the trees on the Miller property, but stampeding over the lawn with lamentable effect as someone would cry, "They're coming!"

Miller would not permit Marilyn to leave the car when his cousin Morton, groaning despairingly, pulled their car over to the narrow shoulder of the winding road. They had all heard rather than seen the crash. Marilyn, chalk-white, was shaking her head mutely and seemed on the edge of hysteria.

Miller ran back to investigate. The small foreign car had failed to negotiate the last curve and had smashed into a tree. The driver, a young man, appeared to have no grave injury, but the French woman, whose publication, *Paris-Match*, had always had a keen appreciation of Marilyn, lay half-conscious, dying in a pool of blood.

Miller then returned to his car and Morton drove on to the farmhouse. Miller leaped from the car and raced towards the house and phone. Several reporters converged on the car, and when Marilyn failed to respond to their questions, Morton told them there had been an accident, probably fatal, down the road. This chilled even the most hard-bitten of them.

Marilyn made an effort to get out of the car and make her way towards the house, but she swayed so dizzily two reporters had to assist her most of the way.

It would be said later by some of Marilyn's friends and co-workers that her nerves were always at a delicate edge, but she managed that exhausting week in the glare of the world's attention – Miller's clash with Congress, a needless death, and finally marriage – with a surprising tranquillity. She was finally being saved by the one man she had had her sights on for years. The prospect gave her a grace that was impressive. If she was inwardly terrified that he might not succeed, the feeling was carefully contained.

As her private terrors increased their hold over her, her expression was that of a woman anchored safely in some faith. It was an illusion, of course, but the press, her fans, people in the street, taxi drivers would see this side of Marilyn only. She clung to the image with only rare lapses until her death, though it often required heavy doses of sedation to maintain.

As her marriage approached, Marilyn was privately given to unpredictable shifts in feeling and attitude. She saved her sunny radiance for Miller and his family, allowing her hirelings to taste the whip. Lois Weber, who was handiest at the time, bore the brunt of Marilyn's reaction when she saw the television reporters setting up their sound equipment at Roxbury. "I thought they understood there was to be no sound," Marilyn said, her manner that of a victim recovering quickly from a nasty, unexpected blow and matching treachery with venom. Miss Weber tried to explain that reporters, television or otherwise, were hustlers who always came prepared for more than they would probably get, but it was several days before Marilyn forgave this imagined perfidy on the part of her press agent.

The hasty civil wedding in the White Plains courthouse was arranged through a phone call by Miller to an attorney friend, Sam Slavitt. As soon as they had the time set by Judge Robinowitz, Marilyn phoned several of her close friends in New York and told them to meet outside the courthouse. These included the Strasbergs, John Moore and his mother, and Milton Greene. Miller had borrowed his mother's wedding band (the elder Millers were in the farmhouse that evening) and with his cousin Morton and his wife as their witnesses, they were off to their rendezvous in Westchester County. Early the following week, he bought a gold wedding band for Marilyn, having it inscribed "A. to M., June 1956. Now is Forever."

As Miller had predicted, the impromptu courthouse rites both caught the reporters and their readers by surprise. When the Millers journeyed from Roxbury to Katonah on Sunday morning for the official Jewish double-ring ceremony, only a handful of reporters were present. On this occasion, all of Marilyn's new friends from New York were there and Lee Strasberg gave her away. No one from her Hollywood days was in attendance, and her break with her past seemed complete.

Just prior to the ceremony, Marilyn was closeted with Rabbi Robert Goldberg, a Reform Rabbi from a suburb of New Haven and a friend of Miller's for several years. He instructed her for two hours or more in the general theory of Judaism; a humanistic approach. He explained his view that there was no after life. Embracing the Jewish faith was a sentimental thing with Marilyn and Rabbi Goldberg was trying to determine whether she was prepared to go through with it. When the indoctrination was over, Marilyn was persuaded that she was finally a Jewess. How profound this feeling was is difficult to know. A sensitive director could convince her that she was also an Archduke's mistress or a cowboy's simple-minded "angel". Even Miller isn't sure how *Jewish* Marilyn really became but he is inclined to accept it as part of her intense desire at the time to please him, to become a vital part of his life.

CHAPTER FOUR

Plans to film in England Terence Rattigan's play *The Sleeping Prince* – retitled *The Prince and the Showgirl* – had been settled by Milton Greene and Marilyn Monroe Productions since January. The first breakdown in communications between Greene and Marilyn had occurred when Greene announced that Sir Laurence Olivier was being assigned to direct as well as act the leading male role. Part of this empathetic failure was Marilyn's fault. She had passed along Strasberg's opinion that such a possibility "was a good idea", and Greene had cabled Olivier a firm offer. What Strasberg had really said was that "it was worth exploring and *might* be a good idea". When Marilyn learned of the cabled offer, she and Greene decided that they had no alternative, if they really wanted Olivier, but to let the cable stand, while she apologized to Strasberg and explained the misunderstanding.

After the contracts had been signed, Olivier flew to New York in February for a press conference held by Marilyn and Greene at the Plaza Hotel. At first Marilyn had appeared relaxed and comfortable with the two hundred reporters gathered in the Terrace Room. She was very proud of being associated with Olivier at that point and showed some pique when reporters, in their eagerness to get next to her, elbowed the British actor out of the way. To Marilyn, this rudeness seemed an abuse of royalty. She had felt honoured to be in his presence and was awed by his easy democracy.

Then almost without warning, the scene at the Plaza had turned into bedlam. Marilyn was wearing a sedate black sheath and one of its straps broke. For a moment, she was trapped.

She was backed up against a wall with press agent Lois Weber.
They both agreed later that they expected to be crushed by
the reporters, who seemed less ravenous for some fresh Mari-
lynism than half mad with curiosity. This had been her first
major press appearance since her flight from Hollywood and
otherwise intelligent men were reduced that afternoon to fren-
zied baboons. After the ordeal, Marilyn said they made her
feel like something in a zoo, but she wasn't sure whether she
was a specimen or a spectator.

Miller received his first shock at this sort of press reception
at the airport when they were about to depart for England.
Only then did he realize how vulnerable and exposed he would
be as Marilyn's husband. He and Marilyn and their party were
surrounded by hundreds of people, all supposedly with press
cards, and literally carried along, strange arms under their
elbows, to the waiting plane and safety. He recalls that it was
a little like drowning. There seemed to be no air to breathe,
voices became a muffled roar, and life stopped for the several
minutes it took them to reach the ramp.

Their first days in England felt to both of them like a long
hangover following the protracted binge of their wedding.
The actual celebration had been mostly in the press, and their
own private moments had the quality of uneasy respites.

It had been agreed that both of the Strasbergs would accompany Marilyn to London for the filming. Miller was unhappy about this since the journey was to be their wedding
trip, but he did not break his vow to himself about them. If
she believed she could not do without them, so be it.

Sir Laurence Olivier and his wife at the time, Vivien Leigh,
met the Millers at London Airport along with the usual army
of newsmen and photographers. Marilyn handled the reception with her new serenity and some journalists mistook it for
snobbishness. Her husband was silent, a stance he maintained
permanently in public with Marilyn. It was an effort for him
to show his smile to strangers and so published photographs
of their arrival show him as gaunt and grim. After that, he
sometimes made an effort to smile into the cameras and was
often convinced that the muscles he was using to lift the corners of his mouth were working all right – until he saw the
published photographs. In private conversation, he had a boyish, self-deprecatory grin that illuminated what he was saying.
It was very appealing, and one of the things Marilyn found

most charming about him; now he wondered if being alone was not part of a lost past.

Olivier embraced his co-star warmly. He had received half a dozen letters from Joshua Logan informing him how sensitive and magnificent Marilyn was as a performer. "She's worth all the trouble," Logan had written him, and his prescription for avoiding trouble seemed simple enough. "Load up the camera and put Marilyn in front of it, and keep Paula Strasberg, whom I love dearly and who seems to be giving Marilyn something she needs, away from the set."

Milton Greene had brought Amy along, though some of the closeness of that friendship with Marilyn had evaporated before the wedding. It is unlikely that Amy knew of the change at this early stage, for Marilyn was, on the surface, all cordiality with her. She had seen that Marilyn was immersing herself totally in Miller's life, and may have thought her own status was unchanged. Still, Marilyn knew, and it must have seemed an omen of sorts that Marilyn brought along Hedda Rosten, wife of the poet and Miller's friend, as her secretary-companion.

The Millers settled at once into a large rented estate at Egham some miles from the edge of the city. It was located near Windsor Park, a part of the royal grounds. Marilyn seemed enchanted by it and obtained a bicycle to ride through the royal preserve.

During the first week of shooting at Pinewood, Olivier began to feel deceived by Logan's reassurances. He made it clear to Miller that he was counting heavily upon him to help see Marilyn through. Later, Logan recalls, Olivier told him plaintively, "You never told me what to do when I'm explaining to Marilyn how to play a scene and she walks away from me in mid-sentence." This apparent rudeness, which happened several times, was due to her utter distraction, according to Miller.

The playwright today is far more tender and considerate concerning Marilyn than critics of his play, *After the Fall*, would have us believe. There is no sense that he intended then to exploit his intimate relationship with Marilyn, nor will he ever. So one must face the dichotomy. Miller, the ex-husband, approaches his past with Marilyn with considerable love. Miller, the playwright, looks at his craft and his work rather like a surgeon.

Olivier held frequent conferences with Milton Greene to
revise their shooting schedules when Marilyn failed to appear
on numerous occasions. Often, he or one of his associates (at
the highest level) called the Miller residence to inquire after
Marilyn. Miller invariably would get on the phone and tell
them he was doing all he could to get her on her way. The
pressure was on him throughout the filming to keep the production from collapsing.

Marilyn looked pained when Miller first mentioned that
they were calling him to ask about her. "Why are you getting
involved in this?" she wanted to know. This was a good question and one Miller often asked himself a film or two later.
He confessed some years after Marilyn's death that he wished
he had been less conscientious. Then he might have said, "Oh,
you're not going to work today? Well, here. Have a glass of
milk."

Marilyn told at least two of her press agents that she regretted Miller's close involvement with her work and career. Perhaps she did at the end, but it happened so gradually and so
casually that neither was aware of what it was leading to. A
group of stills was handed to Marilyn in her dressing-room,
and Miller's presence – he was less than six feet away –
prompted her to invite him to study them with her. They
decided on the kills (rejects) together. In time, her need for
his opinion became greater than that sought from the Strasbergs.

As the production moved ponderously along, it became apparent that Olivier was both too intrusive as a director and
too lax. Quite often he had elaborate notions about how the
script should be played. There was little room for Marilyn's
new feeling for spontaneity. Perhaps Olivier's memory of his
wife's performance in the original production was responsible.
In any case, he gave his Prince a thick German accent, a
monocle, and a rather tough exterior. If beneath all that heavy
make-up some gentleness had seeped through, all might have
been well, but his nervousness as Marilyn's director kept his
interpretation in the same Prussian key throughout.

More disastrously, Olivier saw that Marilyn was bringing
Paula to the set with her and he did nothing about it. Instead,
he complained to Greene and Miller that Paula was driving
him out of his "squeaking mind". Paula's presence did bring
about a situation that was humiliating to Olivier. If Marilyn

had some difficulty with a scene and Olivier corrected her in any way leading to an upset, she ran to Paula. And there were long waits while Olivier watched her and Paula in conferences that might go on for half an hour while her director waited for Marilyn to return before the camera. Halfway through the production he took action to rid himself of this unnecessary headache, but by then any semblance of a friendly working relationship with Marilyn had disappeared.

Since Marilyn suffered her first major emotional setback on *The Prince*, it would be easiest to blame Miller. But in the face of all evidence at hand, his only error, if such it be, was in his attempt to make his new wife recognize her worth. If Marilyn felt inadequacy was a permanent condition, Miller began to feel a permanent indignation. To him, it was an outrage that anyone should fail to see or appreciate her quintessential naturalness, her rare spirit and sensitivity, or her unique talent.

Miller's opinion might have been formed out of his very obvious affection for her, but he was not a man easily taken in even by his own biases. He agreed with the Strasbergs on one single point, Marilyn's potential for greatness.

So it was his intention to be her chief ally in her world where nearly everyone regarded her with suspicion or doubt. Even Olivier made the error of telling her during that first week of shooting, "All right, Marilyn. Be sexy." She fled to her dressing-room, trembling with uncertainty. It had been her hope, expressed freely to Miller and the Strasbergs, that Olivier had agreed to work with her out of respect for her talent. Did he believe that it existed only in her curves? She phoned Lee Strasberg at his hotel in London and asked in a voice flattened by anger and frustration, "Lee, how do you become sexy? What do you do to be sexy?" Strasberg, who recalls the incident, was very nearly as put out as Marilyn.

Having heard about Marilyn's witticisms long before ("What did you have on at the time, Marilyn?" "The radio."), Olivier was shaken to discover that her sense of humour was apparently lacking. What he did not know at this early stage was that under such circumstances, the only brand of wit Marilyn could produce from her fears and anxiety was a kind of gallows humour.

In the face of Olivier's maladroitness in handling his leading lady, Miller felt completely helpless. He knew that he was now the main prop in Marilyn's life. It would be cruel and futile to tell her that he had no answer to her central complaint, which was "Why are they doing these things to me?"

Imagine if you can a child – who has learned to use his innate wisdom and intuition to make others relate and react to him – suddenly walking into a salon of bewigged aristocrats, who move about in a choreography as rigid as a minuet, speak in ritualistic accents that only faintly resemble everyday conversation, and seem, in truth, like creatures from another planet. Such was Marilyn's reaction to Olivier's direction.

Her slide from partial ability to function to complete incapacity was so precipitous that Miller didn't know it was coming until it happened. Before, she had been troubled by insomnia partially relieved by pills. Now even they didn't work. As the night deepened, she became hysterical. He was unwilling to risk the amount of barbiturates that could drop her into a sudden slumber. Nightly vigils began.

There were a few days when he pinned her together after several hours of effort and got her to the studio only four or five hours late, but two or three days passed when he had to call in that she was ill.

"Oh, I'm sorry," Olivier would say, honestly concerned. "What seems to be the matter?" And Miller's hesitation, his unwillingness to put into words the sad truth, was answer enough.

As word seeped through the acting company that Marilyn was ill, some of her colleagues were genuinely distressed. Dame Sybil Thorndike, playing the Prince Regent's mother-in-law, surprised some of them by saying, "We need her desperately. She's the only one of us who really knows how to act in front of a camera." Later, Olivier repeated this to Marilyn to her astonishment and delight.

A week or so later, Dame Sybil was given ample motive for changing her opinion when Marilyn kept her waiting on the set for two hours on the day of the big scene between Elsie Marina (Marilyn) and the Dowager Queen (Dame Sybil), but she did not. The story of the affront was repeated by other witnesses, never by Dame Sybil. It was to become a much-repeated proof of Marilyn's lack of professionalism. Billy Wilder had the best answer for these critics when he said that he knew if he hired his Aunt Maude for a film she would show up on time, but the public was simply not interested in seeing his Aunt Maude on the screen. Marilyn never considered herself a professional. The word itself suggests something finished, something that runs smoothly. She often said that she hoped she would never stop learning, that she thought of herself as unfinished, and nothing on one of her films ever went smoothly, short of a miracle.

About six weeks after production began the Strasbergs came to Egham for the weekend. Marilyn appeared distraught to them. She was, Strasberg later said, in a state. When Arthur retreated to his study, Marilyn began weeping and told her friends that something terrible had happened.

A day or so earlier, she said that she had come into the living-room to pick up her script from the table, and lying open next to it was Miller's black notebook. She was so overwrought in telling the story it was not easy to determine precisely what the notebook entry had said, but Strasberg remembers there was indignation in her voice. "It was something about how disappointed he was in me," Marilyn told them. "How he thought I was some kind of angel but now he guessed he was wrong. That his first wife had let him down, but I had done something worse. Olivier was beginning to think I was a troublesome bitch and that he (Arthur) no longer had a decent answer to that one."

The Strasbergs were shocked. Why had Miller left the notebook open for Marilyn to see? They and half a dozen others who were to become close to Marilyn in subsequent years believe that her sense of having been betrayed in Egham was the seed of her later destruction. Miller, defensively perhaps, admits to the carelessness but minimizes its impact.

The truth probably lies somewhere in between these views. Quite often, an aggrieved partner to a deteriorating marriage will remember something from their wedding trip or first months together that was a devastating discovery. "I saw then what kind of a person he (she) was," they will say. It is likely that Marilyn began to construct a small mountain of betrayal around this incident. In years to come, she often became morose and embittered and would alter what Miller had actually written to declare that he had called her "a whore", leaving out any reference to Olivier. It was a close parallel to her inventions and exaggerations about her childhood, which was an emotional desert for her, but not really peopled by dirty old men with rape on their minds or brutal disciplinarians who would take a strap to her backside at the slightest provocation.

The Strasbergs, on that weekend at Egham, were in the position of in-laws who were reluctant to tell their weeping daughter to pack her bags and leave the wretch. Ironically playing the same game as Miller, they chose discretion as the most sensible reaction to her aggrievement since Marilyn had invested so much of her hope in Miller.

The incident was to haunt Miller, despite his disclaimers. Late in the play, *After the Fall*, Maggie refers to a similar wounding by her husband, Quentin. "What about your hatred!" she demands. "I was married to a king, you son of a bitch! I was looking for a fountain pen to sign some autographs. And there's his desk" – *She is speaking towards some invisible source of justice now, telling her injury* – "and there's his empty chair where he sits and thinks how to help people. And there's his hand-writing. And there's some words." *She almost literally reads in the air, and with the same original astonishment*. "The only one I will ever love is my daughter. If I could only find an honourable way to die." *Now she turns to him*. "When you gonna face that, Judgey? Remember how I fell down, fainted? On the new rug? That's what killed me, Judgey. Right?"

In the play, Quentin tells Maggie that he had written it, "Because when the guests had gone, and you suddenly turned on me, calling me cold, remote, it was the first time I saw your eyes that way – betrayed, screaming that I'd made you feel you didn't exist –" Maggie then angrily tells him not to mix her up with Louise, his previous wife. "That's just it," Quentin says. "That I could have brought two women so different to the same accusation – it closed a circle for me. And I wanted to face the worst thing I could imagine – that I could not love. And I wrote it down, like a letter from hell."

There are at least two of those who were intimate friends of Marilyn's who had been told of the incident by her, who swear that the notebook entry at Egham had included the reference to his daughter. Miller, however, cannot recall that it did and feels that they have the episode confused with the quotation from his play.

The lady psychiatrist whom Marilyn had been seeing back in New York was hastily summoned to England. Soon after her arrival, she visited Egham several times and then remained on call for an additional period. Her availability seemed to make a difference in Marilyn's behaviour, and shortly she was in shape to work most of every day.

Olivier took advantage of the doctor's presence to request that Paula Strasberg's services be dispensed with. Greene, working in close association with Olivier, knew that Paula's effect upon Olivier seriously threatened the quality of the film itself. It was not difficult to persuade Miller of this. If she was the source of strength Marilyn drew upon to sustain her performance, which Olivier seriously doubted, it was a risk they would have to take. She had frayed his nerves to a point where *he* was beginning to need reassurance and calming down.

There is a cloud around Paula's departure. Some close to the production insist that she was fired. Others believe that she was persuaded to withdraw for a time to permit Marilyn to re-establish some rapport with Olivier for the sake of the film. It is also possible that the psychiatrist, who knew Paula from New York, explained that her patient had become overly reliant upon her and needed some time to stand without support.

However it may have been, Olivier seemed like a boxer whose recovery between the rounds enables him to go to the finish and leave the decision in the hands of the judges. There was no diminution in Marilyn's performance as a result of the change.

But all was not contentment by any means. Greene had begun some informal discussions with Jack Cardiff, cinematographer on the film, to set up a British subsidiary of Marilyn Monroe Productions, and with funds or subsidy granted under the liberal Eady plan, to make British films with Cardiff as director. The cameraman had optioned several properties, including an adaptation of Henry James's *The Turn of the Screw*, which he would later direct for 20th-Century Fox with Deborah Kerr, using the title of the stage adaptation of the work, *The Innocents*.

Greene, whose enthusiasm for new productions often would subvert his judgement, made a small announcement to the press about his British plans. When Marilyn and Miller read about it in the morning paper, they were enraged. Or, more accurately, Miller was enraged and Marilyn allowed her bile to flow, too. She had already decided that her vice-president was far too friendly with Olivier to be trusted.

"Did Milton say anything about this to you?" Miller wanted to know.

Marilyn couldn't recall that he had, but because there were so many business details of some concern to her as president of the company, sometimes she would nod dutifully to Greene as he rattled on and turn her mind to more interesting matters.

Miller put in a call to Greene, but his anger was such that he was shouting into the instrument and all Greene could hear was an incoherent roar. He recalls his angry reply, "If you want to talk to me, talk to me. If you're going to yell, then I'm not going to listen." When the roar continued, he slammed down the receiver.

The British subsidiary was soon dropped as a viable proposition, although Cardiff went on to direct not only Deborah Kerr in *The Innocents* but a prize-winning version of D. H. Lawrence's *Sons and Lovers*. All of which, of course, falls into Greene's file of lost opportunities, although in Marilyn he had more than enough to occupy his full attention. But his intentions were laudable. He had promised to make their film company more than a one-star haven and he was still on a token basis by throwing his photography studio into the company assets.

There was one final note of triumph for Marilyn before she left England. She was invited by the Queen to attend a command performance. Before she had left America to make the film, the possibility of such an appearance had been discussed and Marilyn had asked her old friend Anne Karger how she should behave. Anne had counselled, "Look her straight in the eye and say to yourself, 'I'm just as pretty as you are.'" Whatever were Marilyn's private thoughts, she handled the confrontation with dignity and managed some idle conversation with Her Majesty.

And then it was all over. There was a certain stiffness in Olivier's farewell to Marilyn, and they were never in touch again. As for Greene, he was relegated to the equivocal position Natasha Lytess had been in following *The Seven Year Itch*. In the ensuing months of silence, he had to determine for himself where he stood in Marilyn's life.

CHAPTER FIVE

The Millers came home in October. Both needed privacy and they found it in a rented cottage at Amagansett, Long Island, where there were cloistered stands of trees to walk in and a sheltered beach nearby on the bayside. They needed time to live quietly.

Her insomnia was something she tried to live with. It was never to leave her, although there would be nights when her spirit had been insulated by an especially carefree day – and they were fairly numerous at Amagansett – permitting her to drop into slumber with only two pills. There had been no real crisis with Miller over his notebook complaint. Rather, it had left her at times fretful and anxious, her security with him threatened but not destroyed.

The cold winter in the creative career of Arthur Miller was not about to thaw. It had begun soon after he completed *A View from the Bridge*, the last work he finished while still with his family in Brooklyn Heights. It happens to most writers whose careers span a number of years, and it was only coincidentally that much of his barren time came when he was with Marilyn.

Beginning with his first efforts in the Amagansett retreat, he was cursed by false starts, plays that wouldn't germinate into something an audience could identify with, plays that were too internalized, or too filled with dialogue that didn't add up to a solid theme that was satisfying to him. Two entire manuscripts, consisting of hundreds of pages, were tossed into the fireplace during his four and a half years with Marilyn.

Once their lives were joined, there is no question but that Miller gave over much of his time to reassurances, investing nearly all of his energy, creative and otherwise, in Marilyn, the wife and the actress.

Quite aside from his frustrations as a dramatist, there were some splendid short stories from this period, many of them based upon an autobiographical fragment: *The Misfits* already mentioned, and *Please Don't Kill Anything*, a moving account of a husband and wife walking along the sands of a beach and coming across hundreds of unwanted fish left stran-

ded on the beach by fishermen. The young wife takes off a
sandal and attempts to flip a sea robbin into the water, but it
slips away. Then the husband is shamed into tossing back into
the water all of the sea robbins.

The story had grown out of Miller's discovery that Marilyn
was becoming obsessively concerned with death and things
dying. It was based upon an actual episode at Amagansett.

In Amagansett, Marilyn discovered she was pregnant. Unfortunately, the pregnancy turned out to be tubular, and Marilyn was in such agony and danger that by the sixth week Miller
rushed her into the city where it was surgically terminated. In
the wake of her loss, an unyielding despondency settled upon
her during her hospital stay. Attempting to cheer her, Miller
told Marilyn that he was going to write a movie for her, that
he had conceived of a way of adapting the short story *The
Misfits* into a screenplay by bringing the cowboy's girl-friend
onstage or on-camera and making her an integral part of the
action.

Marilyn was delighted by this unexpected gift. It sustained
her for several days, but when she was at home again hopelessness returned and she began swallowing Nembutals to
deaden its impact, to make her days even remotely tolerable.

Miller noticed late one afternoon that Marilyn had half
stumbled into a chair and immediately gone into a doze. Having roughly counted her Nembutals and listening now to her
laboured breathing, he realized that her diaphragm was becoming paralyzed by one pill too many. It was his initiation
into the most frightening aspect of his life with Marilyn:
there were times when the bleakness of her outlook was so
total that all external help, such as Miller's attentions and concern, was worthless and some compulsive black spirit within
her would seek oblivion. The sound of those sighing breaths
became the alarm with which he would have to live.

In such crises, Miller usually moved quickly without panic
and with heightened efficiency. He wasted no time in trying to
rouse her himself but sought immediate medical help. A crew
with some oxygen apparatus from a nearby clinic was summoned to resuscitate her. Miller's dispatch had saved her life
then as it would again.

For several days following one of those episodes, Marilyn's
affection for her husband, for the man who had saved her,
was limitless. As she came round and was able to recognize

him, she would reach for his hand and kiss it over and over again. There was an exquisite tenderness about her regard for Miller then. Perhaps being saved by him was an unconscious need. There is no evidence that she was actually courting death.

A large Connecticut farm adjacent to the Roxbury one which Miller had sold while in England came on the market. It was over three hundred acres and Miller wasted no time in acquiring it. He had Marilyn moved there from Amagansett in the early Fall.

The writing of *The Misfits* screenplay had begun on Long Island, and at the new farm Miller hastened to complete the first draft. He incorporated into it yet another instance of Marilyn's obsession with all living creatures (and conversely, with death) to which young Mark Taylor, fourteen years old at the time, was a witness.

The Taylors were Connecticut friends then living in Old Greenwich. Mark was one of their four sons. He and his brother Curtice, known as Tucky, were frequent visitors to the farm, where the Millers were in the process of renovating the two-storey frame house.

Their father, Frank E. Taylor, was a lean and oddly handsome book editor with greying hair and a youthful face. He stood as tall as Miller, with whom his friendship went back a dozen years or more to the time when Mary Slattery Miller was his secretary and he was Miller's editor. Miller's first and only novel, *Focus*, a study of anti-Semitism in New York City, was published in the same year as an enormously successful book on the same subject, *Gentlemen's Agreement*, and it had a modest sale. At about the time Miller had written *All My Sons*, a play that won the Critics Circle Award, Taylor had gone on to become editor-in-chief of the Dell book division of Western Printing.

Even more than Miller, Taylor had a deep interest in American films. In 1948, he was drawn into active film production by Dore Schary at Metro. Because of his literary background, Schary spoke at the time of acquiring the rights to Fitzgerald's *Tender is the Night* and having Taylor produce it. But nothing had come of this, and he was given a low-budget film as a starter. Miller sent him a copy of *Death of a Salesman* before its Broadway opening, and Taylor showed it to a Metro executive with some excitement. The man returned it, saying, "This is too downbeat for Hollywood. Some day you'll learn what will go and what won't out here." His faith in the movie industry shaken, before the end of 1952 Taylor was back in the East.

His son Mark had been invited by Marilyn to spend a week with them at the farm. It was late April and a warm spring had already arrived. In mid-morning, Marilyn and her young guest were out walking through the pasturage when they came across Miller's tenant farmer and his helper, loading a bull calf into a small truck.

Her interest was not especially caught by the sight. She thought the calf had been sold to someone, but she called out to the man: "Where is the black calf going?"

Mark recalls that the farmer laughed and told her, "He may wind up on your table next week as veal cutlets."

Her eyes widened in horror, and she turned to Mark. "What does he mean?"

"He's a dairy farmer," Mark said, knowing a little about such things. "He has no use for a bull calf. He'll only cost him money in feed, and he's already got two good breeders."

"Th ... then, he's going to the slaughterhouse?" she asked. A memory flashed through her mind, painful and dark, nightmarish. She could see Jim Dougherty stopping the car on a hunting trip when a deer he had shot suddenly horribly revived and moved its head. He reached into the back and began strangling it. "No! No, Jim!" she screamed, tugging at the back of his jacket. "Let him loose!" and a loud screaming "Please!" came from her throat. With the searing memory came doubt, too. Had this happened or was it one of those troubled dreams she had suffered time and again during her last months as Norma Jean when Jim was gone from her life, but not from her thoughts?

The dairyman overheard some of the conversation between Marilyn and Mark and was embarrassed by it. "I'm afraid that's where he's headed," he said, his face slightly flushed.

Marilyn then became frantic. "But you can't! He ... he *lives* here!" And she ran back to the house, Mark following her.

She entered the kitchen, where she stood in the middle of the room, trembling and shaking her head. "There must be *some* way," she said, mostly to herself. Running into the room she used as a study, she picked up her handbag. She emptied it and found only twenty dollars in cash.

"It isn't enough," she said hopelessly when she returned to the kitchen, the money clutched in her hand. Miller was in New York on business, so there was no hope of raising any more cash immediately.

"Even if it was enough," Mark told her, "it wouldn't be any solution. He gets a bull calf about every six months or so. You can't buy all of them, can you? What will you do with them? Keep them for pets? Go into breeding?"

Marilyn looked at the boy, some of her hysteria leaving her. "Smart guy!" she said, as though she were at last in on some joke on herself. She didn't go outside, but they could both hear the truck as it pulled on to the paved road and headed for Waterbury twenty miles away.

When Miller returned that evening, Marilyn related the incident, including the recalled nightmare or memory. Later, Miller made a note of the episode for future reference, and eventually it appeared with more point as the sequence in *The Misfits* where Roslyn attempts to purchase life and freedom for the mustangs from Gay Langland. Marilyn, the actress, trembled visibly as she played the scene in the Fall of 1960.

Miller had a brief spell of hopefulness. It was unexpected since she had shown no great interest one way or the other when he had sold his first farm. But with their settling into the new country place, she no longer seemed apathetic about the Connecticut countryside. Perhaps the first farm having been Miller's prior to his divorce gave the place a second-hand aspect. But the new farm was occupied together, renovated together. She spent days prowling about nearby towns for kitchen cabinets and accessories. She bought a device that appeared to have been invented by Rube Goldberg that was shaped like a long pipe with holes and was placed just under the fascia board of the roof over their large verandah. It was supposed to squirt insect repellent into the air adjacent to the porch, but a stiff wind would often bring the smelly stuff down on to the Millers as they relaxed there of an evening.

At Marilyn's suggestion, sliding glass doors, like those in her Doheny Drive apartment in Hollywood, were installed, opening up the low-ceilinged, beamed living-room to the broad verandah and beyond that to a wide sweep of hill and man-made pond.

When Miller realized the necessity of putting some distance between his role as paternalistic lover and his needs as a writer, he had a split-shingle cabin built on a knoll about thirty yards from the house. He listened carefully to Marilyn that Fall to detect her speech patterns, jotting down her feelings towards life and, even more importantly, towards death. If Roslyn is the most human and convincing of all of Arthur Miller's female characters, it is not by chance.

Yet there was a limit to Marilyn's love for the country. It was, Miller felt soon after introducing her to it, a way station at best. Perhaps some of her disenchantment stemmed from the proximity to death which was more open than in the city: expendable livestock being herded for the slaughterhouse, their cat dragging home a slain robin in triumph. But it was the everyday sameness that finally got her more than anything. She needed distraction.

When Marilyn proposed that they take an apartment in town and use their farm as a weekend place, Miller wanted to know what they would do with their basset-hound, Hugo, who was able to amble freely over the farm.

"I'll walk him," she said. "I always did like walking along the East River. Now I'll have some protection."

And so they moved with Hugo into what became known as Marilyn's apartment, just as Roxbury had become "Arthur's farm". It was on the thirteenth floor of a building at 444 East 57th Street with a fine view of the East River. Marilyn had it redecorated in white tones and had work begun on a study for Miller. She often shushed people and steered them away from the vicinity of Miller's workroom when he was closeted inside with an idea.

She resumed her classes with Strasberg. If Miller felt that he was something of a charlatan, he also realized that the director and his wife gave something important to Marilyn's self-confidence which had been badly bruised by her miscarriage.

Marilyn was convinced she knew both Strasbergs so well by now that she had seen their souls exposed, an intimacy that was rare in her life. She never condemned them, even though she had few illusions about Paula and her knack of alienating at least one key member of the production staff of every one of her films. At the very least, Marilyn felt, Paula's inter-ference was for a good cause, her protection.

But her relationship with Milton Greene had soured alto-gether. Since she was deriving not the slightest benefit from it that she could see, she and Miller determined to take steps to settle the situation to everyone's satisfaction. (For the past four years, Greene had been getting nearly one-half of all her earnings.)

Miller's lawyers sent one of their partners Robert (Bob) Montgomery to see Marilyn about terminating her contract with Greene. Montgomery remembers finding Marilyn in a highly emotional state which the straight vermouth she con-tinued drinking throughout their interview hardly alleviated. She launched into a long and scarcely coherent harangue about Greene's alleged shortcomings and then, pausing only to refill her glass, began telling the amazed lawyer how she had been violated at the age of nine by a grown man. (This story, which many accepted as the gospel truth, was denied by Jim Dougherty, who asserted that she was a virgin when he married her.) While, ostensibly, rape had little to do with the legal matter at hand, perhaps it was, in Marilyn's mind, akin to the ravaging of her future earnings.

When it was announced that Marilyn was breaking with Milton Greene and suing to take over control of Marilyn Monroe Productions, Greene was bewildered by the action. Early in 1957, he had been approached by one of the tele-vision networks offering the corporation a $2,000,000 deal for Marilyn Monroe series, and he had turned it down. "She isn't up to the strain of a series," he had told them, knowing that she was not. By so doing, he had lost whatever his share of the net would have been.

"It seems Marilyn doesn't want to go ahead with the pro-gramme we planned. I'm getting lawyers to represent me," Greene told the press, his feelings plainly hurt by this un-pleasantness. "You can't just make a contract with somebody and then say 'forget it'."

He had an additional reason to be distressed, for word had reached him that Marilyn, through Miller's lawyers, was at-tempting to have his name removed from the credits of *The Prince and the Showgirl* as executive producer.

A stockholders' meeting was called by Marilyn in the offices of Miller's lawyers. She issued a formal statement saying "My company was not set up merely to parcel out 49.5 per cent of my earnings to Mr. Greene for seven years. My company was formed because I wanted to make better pictures, to improve my work, to secure my income, and to help others make good pictures."

At the meeting, a new board of directors was named by Marilyn with the help of Miller's lawyers. The board met and elected new officers of the company, and Greene was out as vice-president.

Greene threatened a lawsuit, telling the press he might seek a claim for as much as $2,000,000. What was important about the possible suit was that it showed vividly how complete was the breakdown in communications with Marilyn. Greene held Miller largely responsible for this.

He felt that Miller had interfered and meddled in the affairs of the corporation from the time he became Marilyn's husband. Much of this charge was true, but since Miller had accepted total responsibility for Marilyn – he was constantly at her side reading script possibilities, helping her sort through photographs to "kill" the bad shots – it was entirely in keeping with his protective behaviour at the time to review every phase of her partnership with Greene. That Greene was still to be fully reimbursed for his investment in Marilyn during her year of voluntary exile never occurred to Miller.

Perhaps Greene had more imagination than befits a tough-minded businessman and hence was unable to answer Miller properly or pit himself against the hyper-realistic film men who considered Marilyn a risky venture. But he had brought *The Prince* through within budget and Joshua Logan had lauded his contribution to Marilyn's total effectiveness in the earlier *Bus Stop*. No one could fault Greene when it came to *class*. It is highly unlikely that his presence at the studio where Marilyn was to make her next film, *Some Like It Hot*, would have been a detriment. Indeed, it seems probable that Billy Wilder might have been able to spill his complaints to Greene rather than to the press. It is likely that Greene would have found a suitable property for her in the long void between her ill-fated pregnancy and the Wilder comedy. And, perhaps more important, he was a man who would have fought like the very devil to prevent Marilyn from making the tasteless and humourless musical, *Let's Make Love*, her next-to-last film.

But a settlement was reached at last. Greene was offered $100,000 to terminate his contract, a sum Miller's lawyers were surprised he accepted. They had anticipated having to go much higher. But as Greene was to say to anyone who would listen, "My interest in Marilyn's career was not for gain. She needed me at the time, and I put at her complete disposal whatever abilities I possessed."

The outside world moved in on the Millers again when Marilyn was hospitalized in late spring, 1957. It was announced that her disorder was gynaecological, and so it was, but she was also suffering from a depression too deep to allow her to be left alone.

Miller stoically resigned himself to the intrusion, while Marilyn's wounded spirit seemed to find some balm in the thousands of cards and telegrams, flowers, and other tokens of idolatry that poured in to her bedside. After all, it was the love of the multitude which had kept her going before they had married. It had been her best defence against Zanuck's callous disregard, her directors' impatience; in fact, against Hollywood itself.

Marilyn's appraisal of her public's admiration and its value to her emotional well-being was sound. The public had never let her down since it first discovered her. She was, if one is to make a judgement about the worldwide continuing concern about her, as close to being the earth's adopted daughter as she was a star. It is no exaggeration to say that when she was reported dead, a public far beyond the millions of her fans felt deep personal loss.

Miller knew by now that he must concede in matters which concerned the public. The wisest course was to appear as part of the background and patiently wait for photographers to have their fill. In spite of general interest in them as a couple, it soon became a fact of his life with Marilyn that he was ignored by the press and public. His own celebrity entered a certain eclipse, and it only partially came into daylight again when shooting began on his own screenplay written for her.

For over a year they were able to divide their time between New York and the country. Marilyn insisted that they must try again to have a child to complete their happiness. Miller agreed with her at the time, although he later said after much reflection that a child probably would not have altered the course of her final years. Meanwhile, there were Jane and

Bobby Miller, whom Marilyn had come to love as she did Joe DiMaggio, Jr. She looked forward to their visits like a child to Christmas.

Marilyn's interest in politics was never very profound. What political convictions she had were nearly all anarchistic or anti-establishment in essence, but the mere fact that some firebrand had taken a definite stand on an issue would not draw her to his support even though his cause seemed just. If she found him personally attractive, as she did Adlai Stevenson and later John F. Kennedy, or if they had met and he projected a friendly attitude towards her, then she became an enthusiastic supporter. But if they had met and he had seemed the least bit hostile, or if she found him personally unattractive, that ended the matter.

But she was an activist in her personal life almost to the end. When a friend or associate asked another, "What's Marilyn up to now?" it was not an idle question. She could be a dynamo of energy. It was almost as though she had to keep on the go so as not to lose that vital spark which would keep her from destruction. In the city, there was almost too much to do.

On one occasion, the Millers met the Frank Taylors in town for the Bolshoi Ballet. Marilyn, in a flame-coloured gown, was not exactly invisible as they made their way to their seats. She was very excited by the performance and stood with everyone else applauding Galina Ulanova, the first dancer of the company. But half of the audience in their section turned to look behind them at that moment and whispers cascaded down from tier to tier until nearly half the entire house had turned to stare at her, still applauding. It was a confusing moment. It was difficult to tell whether there had been a subtle transference of emotion from Ulanova to Monroe or a less complicated and more typical reaction of the public to Marilyn's presence. The management had to be called to seal off their section to ensure her safe descent to the street.

She had invested a small fortune in having one of the rooms on East 57th Street converted into a study for Miller. Posters and stills from his earlier plays were hung on its walls along with a large provocative study of Marilyn taken by Milton Greene.

But contemplation and reflection require more than four

elegant walls. Miller was having increasing difficulty finding either the time or the privacy to work. He would have liked to have pulled her away from excessive public attention, but he knew by now that away from it she would sicken quickly and lose all interest in life. Sometimes, rather than disturb him, she would run across town to the Strasbergs, where she would receive commiseration rather than help. Despite the deep inroads her problems made on his time, Miller always wanted her to come to him so they could sit down and have a heart-to-heart talk. But communication was frequently short-circuited between them, leaving only the consolation of the bedroom.

It was easier for both of them at the farm. There she was usually able to conceal her anxieties, especially when people she cared for came to visit. Weekends with Miller's children passed without incident. Bobby and Jane Miller had lowered their guard and a genuine affection developed between them. Sometimes she even chided Miller about his casual attitude towards fatherhood. At such moments, she projected a very real maternal response, and he was relieved to see the woman he had hoped he had married surface again.

There were writing projects he had to take care of. Norman Rosten was adapting *A View from the Bridge* to the screen, and he and Miller were in frequent conference.

Somehow on those extended weekends in the country, Miller was able to make real headway on *The Misfits*. It was to be his one enduring tribute to his wife, and because of the nature of the theme and the character of Roslyn, Marilyn's frequent panics and pronouncements of defeat and betrayal fed his creative impetus instead of crushing it.

The Taylors sold them their riding horse, Ebony, and their son Mark went to the Miller farm to instruct Marilyn how to ride the rather nervous animal (and to visit his horse). Altogether, she mounted the skittish beast no more than two or three times, always with apprehension and certainly with more fear than pleasure. She was not to get astride a horse again until she was forced to do so in a scene with Gable on location in Nevada.

To Marilyn, the Taylors were much the liveliest and most congenial of Miller's married friends. She came in time to confide in both Frank and Nan Taylor, and this acceptance led

Miller to propose very soon that Taylor become executive producer of *The Misfits*.

Other visitors to the Miller farm believed her to be *home safe* at this apparently calm time. Neighbour Alexander Calder, whose mobiles hang in nearly all contemporary galleries around the world, dropped by frequently, and Marilyn knew him as "Sandy". Eli Wallach and his wife Anne Jackson were frequent visitors, and, of course, the Rostens. It would be interesting to know for sure whether her gaiety at such times was manufactured or real. Nobody can say. Not even Miller. What can be stated as a certainty is that the ingredients for contentment were there. Marilyn knew they were there. And she was building a life quite outside her fame.

CHAPTER SIX

Marilyn's inactivity in films was not for lack of offers. Scripts arrived daily at the East 57th Street apartment and Marilyn had hired May Reis, who had worked for Miller, to handle the correspondence attendant to them.

May, a quietly efficient matronly woman, became increasingly drawn to Marilyn's problems. Of all those moved to protect Marilyn, she went further than anyone. Years after Marilyn's death, she still protected her memory and has been nearly unapproachable where Marilyn was concerned.

When Billy Wilder first discussed with Marilyn the possibility of her doing Sugar Kane in *Some Like It Hot*, she wanted to know briefly what it was about. Wilder jotted down a two-page synopsis and sent it to her. She loved the idea: the spoof of the gangster era of Chicago, the all-girl band infiltrated by men on the run. But some months later when she got the final script, she was so troubled she rushed to Lee Strasberg for reassurance.

"I've got a real problem, Lee," she told him. "I just can't believe in the central situation. I'm supposed to be real cosy with these two newcomers, who are really men in drag. Now how can I possibly feel a thing like that?" she wailed. "After all," she added with just a trace of irrelevance, "I know the two men."

Strasberg recalls that he considered the problem for several moments. "Well," he told her finally, "that shouldn't be too difficult. You know, Marilyn, it's very difficult for you to have a relationship with other women. They're always jealous of you. When you come into a room, all the men flock around, but women kind of keep their distance. So you've never really had a girl-friend."

"That's almost true," Marilyn said.

"A lot of men have wanted to be your friend," Strasberg persisted. "But you haven't had a girl-friend."

Even if once Marilyn did have a girl-friend, she nodded now as Strasberg expected, for he was getting to something she felt she could use.

"Now here suddenly are two women, and *they want to be your friend!* They like you. For the first time in your life, you have two girl-friends."

Marilyn's eyes glowed in appreciation. From that moment on, the movie would work for her.

Miller finally finished his first draft of *The Misfits*. He was excited by what he had done and hurried to the phone at their country place to inform Frank Taylor, who had been more concerned than anyone about Miller's writing career. "Can you come up?" Miller wanted to know, and when Taylor asked what day he had in mind, Miller said, "Now. This afternoon."

Within a few hours, Taylor, his wife and two of their sons arrived at the Miller farm. Miller did not seem to mind the inclusion of the family in this rather special visit, and soon he was reading aloud to the four of them while Marilyn house-cleaned upstairs. She may have felt that the heroine, Roslyn, was far too close to her own private self to sit in on the script's first reading.

Miller took all of the parts, adding what he believed to be a western twang to the cowboy roles. At the conclusion, Taylor suggested that a copy be sent at once to John Huston, then in Paris concluding his latest film, *The Roots of Heaven*.

The following day the film play was dispatched by air mail. Huston read it quickly and wired back that it was magnificent and that he would be pleased to be associated with it.

During that week, Taylor discussed possible casting of the film with Miller and a copy of the script was sent to Clark Gable on the coast to see if he would be interested in playing

Gaylord Langland, the misfit cowboy. Gable was very excited after reading it and wondered when production might commence.

Now Miller had a director, a leading man, and, of course, his own leading lady, but no producer. When Taylor went again to the Miller farm near the end of the week, Marilyn told him, "This movie doesn't have a producer and I want you to do it. Will you? You're an old friend of Arthur's. We trust you."

Taylor protested, saying he wouldn't impose himself on John Huston, but Marilyn persisted, saying, "All films need the independent eye of a producer."

"If John will accept me," Taylor finally conceded, "I'd be interested, provided UA (United Artists, the distributing firm that had expressed an interest in financing the movie) finds this acceptable and provided I get paid enough, because this means stepping out of my career and taking a leave."

Marilyn quickly said, "We'll pay you", but Taylor told her in a friendly way, "I'm not going to be captive to you. Either I'm paid by UA or not at all. I have to be free to state my opinion." The Millers then agreed that this was a laudable attitude.

Taylor was acceptable to United Artists on several grounds. His four years as a producer in Hollywood from 1948 to 1952 qualified him as experienced and he was someone Marilyn herself had recommended. Everyone who knew him felt he had the sensitivity to handle the delicate chore of being Marilyn's boss as well as the integrity to guide the production of Miller's unorthodox script to completion. Marilyn, Miller, and Taylor formed their own production company. Before production began nearly a year later, just under two million dollars had been paid out in preproduction salaries, including advance payments to the cast, director, Huston, Miller, and Taylor, and United Artists was becoming somewhat apprehensive about costs.

At the time, all parties believed *The Misfits* would begin shooting just as soon as Marilyn's present commitment to Billy Wilder was out of the way. Later, a commitment to Fox would intervene.

They were shooting *Some Like It Hot* at the old Sam Goldwyn Studios, which was Wilder's headquarters. Marilyn came to the sound stage with an entourage that included her husband for the first day's shooting on August 4, 1958. She also brought her own hairdresser, make-up man, press representative, a maternal dramatic coach confidante, and untitled others.

Miller was present for reassurance, and as it became apparent during the course of the shooting that Wilder could not be entrusted with this function, Miller would appear on the set, with increasing frequency. This was all right with Wilder as Miller behaved with all the decorum of a banker.

By the time Marilyn and Miller had settled back in Hollywood in the Beverly Hills Hotel for her assignment in *Some Like It Hot*, Marilyn had discovered Eleanora Duse. Paula had often referred to the Italian actress, and Strasberg possessed a considerable collection of Duse memorabilia and books in a corner of his massive private library. And then, quite on her own, Marilyn had asked her bookseller to send her the best biography she could find. She read it, and found that La Duse in mid-career had taken as her lover one Martino Cafiero, a well-known Italian writer. Martino's reputation as a critic and scholar perhaps eclipsed his fame as an author. Eva La Gallienne, who knew Duse as an actress and friend, once wrote of Martino that "his knowledge of art and literature was inexhaustible: he opened innumerable doors for the 'little Duse', fed her innate craving for beauty in all its forms: poetry, drama, painting, sculpture, music.... She looked up to him as some godlike creature, and worshipped him." Marilyn identified with Duse, and often carried the volume with her to her dressing-room.

It was a disturbing identification, and certainly not a healthy one. Duse's affair with Martino had terminated abruptly when their love was soured by charges of betrayal on both sides, and he fled from her.

It would be perhaps too easy to trace Marilyn's development through her own analogies: her early identification with Lana Turner, Ginger Rogers, and Jean Harlow when she was a novice; when her own legend began, with Garbo; and finally, this sense of being at one with Duse. But those who knew her well claimed it happened. And on a deeper level, these associations charted her own solitary passage.

The opening scene of *Some Like It Hot*, showing the lady

band leader and her girls crowded into a Pullman sleeper, required Marilyn to appear just as one of the girls. The cameraman, through close-ups of Marilyn with her ukelele, was to indicate she was the heroine of the film.

To Marilyn, this was not enough. Marilyn and Miller had already become aware through careful study of the script that the role of Sugar Kane was essentially that of a straight man for the antics of the two leading men. She was so acute about such things that a man as canny as Wilder soon realized he had hired more than an actress in Marilyn.

After she had seen the first day's rushes, Marilyn was aware that Sugar Kane's kooky character had to be established at once, in the very first glimpse of her in fact. She called Wilder that evening and told him what was needed.

Wilder phoned his owlish collaborator, I. A. L. Diamond, and they agreed to meet very early the next day to rewrite the opening. They decided to show Sugar rushing down late to the train, wobbling dizzily on her high heels, just as it is about to pull out. As she hurries up to the other girls, she is frightened by a great and visible puff of steam that strikes her in the rear. Marilyn was enchanted and so was everyone else.

But Marilyn's troubles began early in the shooting. On a swaying coach jammed with girl musicians (among them bewigged Tony Curtis and Jack Lemmon), Sugar drops a concealed whisky bottle in front of the lady band leader. She is supposed to act surprised, then cover her embarrassment with a giggle.

"You aren't surprised enough, Marilyn," Wilder said.

Marilyn wasn't sure she should be surprised at all. Under the circumstances she would have been frightened, not surprised. But she repeated the action with a cautious increase in her surprise.

"*Cut!* You still haven't got it, dear." And Wilder saw that Marilyn was trembling in a fit of insecurity. He moderated his tone. "Don't strain for it. It's a very simple reaction."

Marilyn shook her head and hurried over to an area back of the lighting equipment where Paula was standing. Marilyn whispered something to Paula, and Wilder and his script girl exchanged glances.

During the ensuing fifteen minutes, Wilder made an effort to seem busy. He conferred with the script girl, checked and rechecked the camera angle. But as the wait approached twenty minutes he had run out of make-work and was nearly beside himself with frustration, anger, and finally humiliation.

The incident is still vivid in the memory of both Miller and Wilder. Miller recalls, "Wilder's embarrassment was tremendous at the time. Wilder on the set, as it is with any director, is the final authority, the law, and when a man is kept standing and waiting for five, ten, fifteen minutes, half an hour, it's a great humiliation."

Wilder did not blame Paula Strasberg in any way for this indignity. "Paula was no problem whatsoever," he said. "She sympathized with Marilyn, but by the same token, she sympathized with me. She was most co-operative in trying to pull the girl together. I didn't experience her [Marilyn] waiting for the big O.K. from Strasberg. Paula never made any signal like that on the set. I regarded them [the coaches] as my co-workers, and they suffered with me when she would go as much as forty takes. She had one line, four words: 'Where is that bourbon?' She is going through a drawer looking for it and we finally pasted the line inside the drawer. Another time, Mr. Curtis and Mr. Lemmon, dressed as women, were in the hotel bedroom. One of them says 'Yes' after Marilyn says, 'It's me, Sugar.' Then one of them says, 'Come in.' There were forty-seven takes. She stumbled on 'It's me, Sugar.' After take thirty, I had the line put on a blackboard. She would say things like 'It's Sugar, me,' etc. The two leading men had to stand around in high heels for two-thirds of the day. Their business had to be repeated again and again. They might not be as good on take thirty as they were earlier. I'll say they were both patient men, and it's a strain wearing high heels when you're not used to them."

Miller and others, thinking back on Paula's actions at the time, are less charitable than Wilder. When a spoiled child runs to her mother and the mother comforts her for half an hour, perhaps the mother's attitude should be examined. Paula was apparently becoming a kind of broker between director and star. After one of those lengthy conferences that would hold up production endlessly, Paula would tell Wilder, "I've asked Marilyn not to talk to me on the set. I'm only here because she feels insecure." And then she would turn around and take Marilyn's side and agree with her that perhaps Wilder didn't fully understand all the nuances of a certain scene, that he didn't begin to delve into the psychological motivations underlying it. "But he's an excellent slick director," she would add. "He can do a film like this blindfolded."

By this time Marilyn had been involved in Strasberg's teachings for nearly three years. The so-called Method was working for her. She was giving the role of Sugar Kane far more humanness than Wilder could expect, but those around her had to pay a high price for her emotional articulation of the part. In a sense she was emotionally bankrupt – part of her difficulty in remembering her lines and in getting to the set on time was due to her conscious or unconscious refusal to respond to any emotional appeal. Miller bore the brunt of much of this anguish. Wilder received much less abuse. However she may have treated him at times, she was afraid of him. When she would notice that he was on the brink of losing his patience (after nearly fifty takes to get one line right), Marilyn would be reduced to a state of absolute terror.

"What about my own patience?" she asked Miller, who usually waited for her in her dressing-room. "She tried to be real," Miller later said. "To face enemies as enemies – Wilder was at the time an enemy – and it simply was tearing her to pieces."

She wouldn't trust anyone on the set except make-up man Whitey Snyder, Paula, and a handful of others who worked for her. She needed them as a protective ring about her. She felt that Wilder was mocking her own complaints by feigning some strange back ailment and bursitis in his arms. This was clever of him, she believed, because she had a percentage in the film and a stake in getting it completed more or less on schedule. If both of them were ill at the same time, the consequences would have been disastrous. Wilder's pain at the time was so acute, he was forced to rest sitting up in a chair at night. In truth, he said little of his problem to Marilyn, although she knew of its existence and further alienated him by never inquiring how he felt. Pain-killers kept him going much of the time, for he was determined not to give in to his ailment. "We were in mid-flight," he later said. "And there was a nut on the plane."

Marilyn knew without being told that Tony Curtis, one of her co-stars, was down on her. Miller tried to explain to her why Curtis was offended or at least annoyed when Wilder insisted on shooting a tiny scene over and over again until he was satisfied with Marilyn, while Curtis's own performance began to deteriorate.

During one scene Curtis was required to gnaw a chicken leg to indicate his imperviousness to Marilyn's sexuality. There were forty-two takes because Marilyn got rattled in her lines, and Curtis was incensed because she didn't apologize to him. He lost his appetite for chicken for months afterwards.

In an excess of patience Wilder would occasionally go up to her and say, "Now look, Marilyn. Don't worry. We'll piece it together." And Marilyn would look at him as though he had lost his wits. "Who's worried?" she would ask.

On one morning, "mid-flight", Marilyn came along to her dressing-room carrying, of all things, Tom Paine's *The Rights of Man*, which she was reading with some care. The book was open in her hand when the second assistant director, a young man of twenty-nine, rapped softly on the door. He got no answer at first so he knocked a little harder. Marilyn opened the door, and the man explained that Mr. Wilder was ready on the set. Then he added, "It's eleven-thirty and the other actors are waiting."

This last more urgent appeal was unfortunate for it triggered an immediate reaction in Marilyn. "Go screw!" she told him, slamming the door in his face. This is what Marilyn *told* Miller she had said, although Wilder insisted later she had been even more graphic in telling off the director's aide. Miller shared Marilyn's view that there were certain prerogatives of a Garbo or a Monroe that could not be abrogated by an officious underling or by a director either, for that matter. Marilyn adamantly refused to be caught up in the studio pressure surrounding any film production. "People let others make them frantic by watching clocks too much," she said.

After what she considered to be a proper interval, she made her way to the set and was fine the rest of the day.

She was even better the second week in September when the entire company moved to an exterior location by the seaside at the Coronado Hotel, an old verandahed Victorian structure which was being used as a substitute for Miami (in the twenties).

Marilyn had learned before leaving New York that she was pregnant again. Determined that nothing was going to terminate this pregnancy before its time, she retired early each evening in their Beverly Hills Hotel suite, after studying the next day's scenes. Some of this work was even done in bed to spare herself further.

Pleased to be working in the sunshine and fresh air on the beach, she told Miller, "This will be great for the baby." Between takes she would stand on the verandah and take long breaths of sea air. The company remained at Coronado for seven days and Wilder recalls that the weather was perfect.

Wilder, whose temper was wearing thin from pain and frustration, had feared disaster. He knew they would be fighting the blinding sun on the beach, and the hotel was adjacent to a Navy jet port with planes zooming overhead about every twenty minutes. But much to his amazement, Marilyn seemed on her mettle. She went through two or three pages of dialogue without hesitation or need for numerous retakes. The whole scene of recognition between Curtis, impersonating a wealthy yacht owner, and Marilyn, as a girl he meets on the beach but whom he had already coveted as a fellow member of the all "girl" band, was done without a hitch.

To Wilder, working with Marilyn was like setting out to conquer one of the Himalayan peaks. He considered her sense of humour, her timing, every bit as fine as Judy Holliday's. And years after Marilyn and Judy were both in their graves, his eyes became moist upon remembering Marilyn. "We just happen to miss her like hell!" he said. "A whole category of films has been lost with her gone. And people fool themselves. They say, 'I have just bought myself a car and it looks like a Cadillac,' but it turns out they've bought a Pontiac. The luminosity of that face! There has never been a woman with such voltage on the screen with the exception of Garbo."

But in the immediate aftermath of the filming, which had gone several hundred thousand dollars over the budget because of Marilyn's absenteeism, Wilder had been less mellow and chivalrous. When asked if he would make another film with her he told reporters that his analyst had suggested he was too old and too rich to go through such an ordeal again. "My back doesn't ache any more."

At a celebration dinner at Wilder's apartment on November 6, he invited co-stars Jack Lemmon and Tony Curtis, his director-colleague Charles Vidor, and their wives, and failed to include Marilyn.

When Miller read the interview with Wilder the following

week he sent the director a steaming telegram describing Marilyn as "the salt of the earth", his usual defence of his wife, and was shocked to receive an immediate reply stating "the salt of the earth told an assistant director to go fuck himself".

Two years later, Wilder was to meet Marilyn socially, a circumstance unavoidable in the tightly knit Hollywood society. The original invitation to a sneak preview of *The Apartment* had gone to Doris Vidor with a suggestion that she bring her close friend Yves Montand. Montand was Marilyn's constant companion at the time, and he had told Doris that he would be happy to attend the preview if he could bring Marilyn. When Doris got back to Wilder, she recalls that he hesitated a moment, then said, "All right. He can bring her, but under one condition, that you're all here on time and there's going to be none of that business of Marilyn making a grand entrance and people lined up to gape at her and Yves and thereby putting the whole preview audience in a frame of mind that has nothing to do with seeing *The Apartment*." Montand immediately reassured Doris, "She'll be anywhere I say on time. You needn't worry about that for one second."

After the preview, the party was invited to meet with Wilder and his friends at Romanoff's. Marilyn came into the large dining-room, flung her arms around Wilder, whispered to him how great his movie was, how much she wanted to work with him again. They were like children after a scrap, according to one witness.

During that evening, the two former combatants were getting on so well that Wilder was heard to ask Marilyn if she would like to play *Irma La Douce*. The follow-up to this is in some dispute. It was reliably reported that the Mirisch Brothers, who were to produce the film, wanted Marilyn and pursued her all the way to Nevada, where she was about to make *The Misfits*. They discussed a multipicture deal. Wilder subsequently denied this, saying that Marilyn had brought up the possibility of playing Irma, but that he had already signed Shirley MacLaine for the role, and "You don't ever tell a star of Marilyn's magnitude that she cannot do a film because you've chosen someone else. You go along with it. You sugar-coat it. Besides, she had a commitment to Fox."

Somehow Billy Wilder and so many others could only communicate with the insecure woman, and never the artist. And on that level there were only snarls and recriminations, shallow coaxings, the pats on the head usually tendered a petulant child, and festering resentments that would live beyond Marilyn's burial. As late as 1966, Wilder stated in an interview that Marilyn was the meanest woman he had ever encountered in Hollywood. He meant this remark to undercut a growing cult that was canonizing Marilyn in death.

Arthur Miller had sustained Marilyn now through two films. While his intervention was sometimes foolish and ill-advised, it had become as necessary to her as Paula's presence near the camera. On one occasion during the filming of the Wilder comedy, Miller came by the Goldwyn studios in the late afternoon and whispered to Wilder, "Marilyn is pregnant. Can't you let her go home? It's nearly four o'clock." And Wilder told him, "Arthur, it is now a quarter to four and I haven't got a shot."

Miller's protectiveness did not stem only from love. He saw in her an immense feeling for life. "That degree of suffering," he explained, "would normally incapacitate anyone in any other field. In an office, for example, her employers would tell her frankly that she would have to leave her problems at home. But her role in life as a film star was the one thing she could sustain because a star can get away with this kind of behaviour." When it was suggested to Miller that this did not explain the final showdown with Fox when she was fired, he seemed to withdraw and said that this occurred long after he had lost touch with her.

CHAPTER SEVEN

The sprawling Strasberg apartment was a warm and friendly oasis for other actors and people in the theatre besides Marilyn. Often there were half a dozen friends and friends of friends in the kitchen alone, seated about the table drinking tea, having a beer. They might be Suzy's friends or Johnny's or family acquaintances such as Ralph Roberts.

Roberts was a muscular actor with the stern manner of a constable and the soft drawl of a Southern aesthete. Friends called him "Big Ralph" and he was perhaps better known to other performers than he was to the public, much to his chagrin. Apart from the theatre Roberts had another profession, that of a masseur, and his growing clientele was beginning to interfere with his acting career. He had little time in the morning to make the rounds of producer's offices since from ten o'clock on he was rushing about Manhattan from one aching back to another.

Knowing the Strasbergs had helped more than a little. Paula recommended Roberts's services to more friends than he could squeeze into his busy schedule. Soon, despairing of ever getting back into acting, he fled New York and moved to Hollywood.

One evening when he was still trapped in New York, he was seated at the Strasberg kitchen table having some hot tea when Suzy came in with an actress friend, a blonde with little or no make-up, her bleached hair needing attention. Preoccupied with his plans, Roberts didn't catch the blonde's name but he observed that she was frightened and he wondered why. He asked himself if such a young woman could be an actress.

Soon, with apologies, the blonde skittered away. Roberts grinned at Suzy and shook his head in disbelief. "Who was that?" he wanted to know. "I didn't catch the name, but I heard someone say she was an actress."

"That was Marilyn," Suzy told him.

Marilyn had lost her second baby in November 1958, this one almost in its third month, making the loss harder to bear than the first. She had been very careful even to the extent of having an ambulance take her to the plane when she flew back to New York from Hollywood. Just before Marilyn left the West Coast, Anne Karger had visited the Miller suite at the Beverly Hills Hotel, where Marilyn was lying in bed "so as not to jar the baby". But she got up to embrace Anne. "It's the least I can do when someone I love comes to see me," she said.

The loss had made her fretful in private and more diffident than usual among strangers. She felt some deep inadequacy.

A few nights after that kitchen meeting, the Strasbergs were having an informal get-together on a Saturday night. Marilyn had left Miller working on a final draft of *The Misfits* and

appeared at the party around 11 P.M. Roberts was again introduced, and he said, "We met the other evening in the kitchen.
But I fear I didn't know who you were. I'm sorry."

"Don't be sorry," she said. "It's good to know I'm not all
that recognizable."

The next time Marilyn was with Paula she told her that she
was much impressed with her friend, Ralph, but that she was
ruining his acting career by recommending too many clients
to him. "He says he's going to have to move to the coast and
go into the movies to break up his practice."

The première of *Some Like It Hot* was held at Loew's Capitol
Theatre on Broadway on March 29, 1959. Marilyn attended
with Miller and was interviewed in the lobby, where she reverted to her childhood stammer. She *looked* magnificent in a
sequined gown, but a keen observer could detect a subtle loss
of control in her public stance. Miller was sober as always, so
it would have been difficult to analyse his look of concern.

It was to be Marilyn's most successful film financially. A. H.
Weiler, reviewing the film in *The New York Times*, wrote
that she "contributes more assets than the obvious ones to this
madcap romp. As a pushover for gin and the tonic effect of
saxophone players, she sings a couple of whispery numbers
("Running Wild" and "I Wanna Be Loved By You") and also
proves to be the epitome of a dumb blonde and a talented
comedienne." Years after her death, the film was still making
money for her estate and enabled it to pay off its obligations,
including all of the bequests.

Two months later, Marilyn received her only acting award
of any consequence, the David Di Donatello statuette from
Italy for her portrayal of Elsie Marina, the Showgirl in *The
Prince and the Showgirl*, which had been released two years
earlier. Belated though it was, Marilyn didn't seem to mind.
She managed to talk Miller into accompanying her to the
Italian Cultural Institute, where Italian officials made the
award and Anna Magnani embraced her and made her feel a
part of the world film community.

The award provoked a positive response in Marilyn that
pulled her together for a time. She made a valiant effort to
wrest herself free from the dark grip of her melancholia and
entered Lenox Hill Hospital in June for corrective surgery so
that she might have the child she so desperately wanted.

Whether or not the operation was a success was to remain in doubt, for a permanent strain had come between her and Miller before the summer had advanced very far.

When, in the middle of September, Premier Nikita Khrushchev announced he was coming to the United States and was planning a visit to Hollywood, Marilyn expressed interest in meeting him and discussed with Miller the possibility of their attending a luncheon at the Fox Studios for the Russian leader.

After some days of soul-searching, Miller decided that it would be best if he did not accompany her. Perhaps he felt he was in enough trouble with the reactionaries of America without flying across the continent to greet the Communist leader.

They called Frank Taylor and asked him if he would mind accompanying Marilyn to the luncheon. He said he would be delighted. Taylor and Marilyn flew out the day before the Khrushchev luncheon. When the plane landed, it was surrounded by reporters and photographers. Marilyn was sitting in the forward lounge surrounded by cosmetic kits and beginning the familiar ritual with her face. Taylor remembers telling her he would run off ahead as a discretionary measure so no one would wonder who her unfamiliar travelling companion might be. "She agreed," Taylor recalls, "and might have suggested it, if I hadn't. Then after I got off and had found the waiting limousine, I looked back and saw Marilyn descending the ramp. She ambled down the steps slowly, her pelvis thrown back, her chest thrust forward, her hips swinging rhythmically from right to left and back again. It took all of three minutes for her to reach the bottom." One reporter asked her if she had come out just to see Khrushchev and Marilyn said, "Yes. I think it's a very wonderful thing and I'm happy to be here." Then the reporter asked, "Do you think Khrushchev wants to see you?" "I hope he does," she said, and she looked carefully at her questioner for a moment. Apparently, Marilyn wanted to know and remember her enemies.

Early the next day, a regiment began to get her ready and on to the Fox lot on time. Taylor phoned Ralph Roberts, at Marilyn's request and asked him to come at 7 A.M. to her bungalow at the Beverly Hills Hotel and give her a massage.

At nine, Agnes Flanagan arrived to do her body make-up, followed shortly afterwards by Whitey Snyder, who did her face. As Snyder was leaving, hair stylist Sydney Guilaroff arrived to style her hair.

While this was going on, Spyros Skouras, the head of Fox Studios and the man who had masterminded the entire affair, came into the bungalow unexpectedly. He apparently wanted to make sure Marilyn was going to attend. "She *has* to be there," he said. He apparently thought it quite normal for Frank Taylor to be accompanying her instead of Miller and made no comment about it.

All of these preparations took more than two hours, including getting her into a black-net dress. This dress was rather transparent in the bosom but no one at the luncheon, including Khrushchev himself, would question its propriety with Marilyn encased in it.

At a little before twelve, Rudi, Marilyn's chauffeur, pulled up near the bungalow and they began the five-minute drive to the studio lot. They arrived there at 12.05, and Marilyn, forgetting the time, plunged into despair. "Oh!" she groaned. "We must be late. It must be all over." There were few other cars in the parking area.

But for once, Marilyn was very early, so early in fact that the reporters, gathered in the studio building converted for the occasion into a banquet room, had her to themselves for a few minutes.

When the Russian leader was escorted by Skouras into the room and taken around to meet the guests, he stopped for a moment and took Marilyn's hand. "You are a very lovely young lady," he told her. "My husband, Arthur Miller, sends you his greetings. There should be more of this kind of thing. It would help both our countries understand each other." Khrushchev beamed as the translation came through to him, and he gave her hand another squeeze.

The winter of 1959–60 was the last season Marilyn and Miller spent together amicably. Miller attempted to analyse what was happening to them, but the closest he could come to any truth was that he, along with nearly everyone who had come into her life with the exception of the Strasbergs, represented a long series of betrayals. She would retaliate by sending him on demanding errands.

In rational moments, her behaviour made little sense even to her. Miller was still very much at the centre of her life. All that was decent in that life was there. What stability she had was there. It almost seemed as though she were following some dimly recalled pattern set by her grandmother years earlier.

At first Miller responded by compliance and stoicism, but there were times later on when he could not regress his anger and frustration. One of his killing glances was observed by Billy Wilder during the filming of *Some Like It Hot*, and the director wondered if perhaps Arthur didn't dislike Marilyn more than he did.

By February 1960, when Marilyn was due in Hollywood to fulfil yet another commitment to Fox on her four-picture deal – her most unsuccessful starring vehicle, *Let's Make Love* – their relationship had disintegrated to such an extent that Marilyn no longer confided anything of importance to her husband.

And yet there was no question in Miller's mind of allowing her to go alone to the coast. If they could not talk together, at least he could keep her pulled enough into shape to do the film. This had become his role in life, a guardian who slept with her and counted her pills.

By now she was seeking confidantes outside her marriage. Very soon after they had settled in Hollywood she phoned Ralph Roberts and enlisted him in her entourage.

Roberts was playing a small role in a musical film. With Marilyn wanting a massage several times a week, Roberts well might have become annoyed at the demands upon his time. His film work was again beginning to take second place just as his theatre activities had. But gradually he realized he was looking forward to the sessions with Marilyn. She told him things she had never told before "to a living, breathing soul". He became a depository of all her complaints, intimate and otherwise. It was a sacred trust and it made him reappraise his situation as an actor. Marilyn needed him more than the public seemed to.

In that casual way, Ralph Roberts became the advance guard of a small platoon of trusted servitors with whom Marilyn surrounded herself. Most of them would survive the break-up of her marriage, and take the place of nearly all the friends she had made as Mrs. Arthur Miller.

She and Miller had taken a suite in the big bungalow at the Beverly Hills Hotel. Her leading man, Yves Montand, and his wife were just across the hall. It was a friendly arrangement, and at the beginning both Miller and Montand's wife, actress Simone Signoret, were parties to it.

The Montands' admiration for Miller dated from their having co-starred in a French adaptation by Jean-Paul Sartre of Miller's play about the Salem witch hunt, *The Crucible*. They were as liberal politically as the Millers and had been barred from the United States until late 1959 for refusing to answer the question, "Are you a member of the Communist Party?" on their visa application – a holdover from the McCarthy era.

In 1959, Montand was permitted to bring to Broadway his one-man show of songs, dances, and monologues. Simone accompanied him on the journey. Marilyn had attended a performance with Montgomery Clift. She was very excited about it. Montand projected almost pure sexuality, something that had long been her speciality, but in his case it was suffused with cynicism instead of innocence.

Simone Signoret had no reputation for naïveté herself. Like many French women, she was sure of her sex, her role in life, and her husband. She had to be tolerant of Montand's appeal to women in much the same way Miller had to become inured to the heady attraction Marilyn was to men. She immediately liked Marilyn, and like so many new friends was moved to regard her affectionately as a child who needed reassurance.

There was something waif-like in Marilyn that appealed to Simone. Perhaps it was of what had attracted her to Montand in the first place. The two women went shopping together, sunned themselves near the pool for hours, talking, giggling, miming. Simone's English was excellent (she had once taught the language) and, unconscious of any possible entanglement, she spoke to Marilyn about her husband, about the gruelling years before success had come to him.

There were several striking similarities between Marilyn's and Montand's backgrounds. Both had emerged from the working classes, changed their names at about the same age and gone into show business. Montand was born Ivo Livi in the Italian village of Monsummano. His father was a Tuscan peasant who chose to live in town rather than in the hilly country, but he was unskilled and life was a hard business. Ivo's mother like his father was poorly educated, but both parents had a resilience and cunning that kept Ivo and the two other younger Livis ignorant of their grinding poverty.

The elder Livi was a political activist. He deplored the rise of Mussolini and the Black Shirts in the early twenties soon after Ivo's birth, and tried unsuccessfully to enter the United States. Failing that, Signor Livi made his way to Marseilles, where he found steady employment on the docks and was able to send for his family.

Ivo had all of the schooling he was ever to get in France, but life was not much better for the Livis there than it had been in Italy, and it was decided that Ivo must leave school when he was in the sixth grade. When he related this detail to the Millers, Marilyn felt very close to him.

His working background from the age of eleven on had embraced bartending, hairdressing, factory work, and waiting on tables, but within seven years he had sharpened his theatrical talents – which appeared to be innate, especially his mimicry and dancing – to the point of professionalism. He made his bow at eighteen at the Alcazar Revue Theatre in Marseilles.

Soon he was in Paris, where the sparrow of the streets, Edith Piaf, took him under her wing. She made him abandon his pseudo-American ballads for French street songs. He had found himself.

When Gregory Peck bowed out of the film, *Let's Make Love*, because revisions had displeased him, Miller recommended Montand for the role unhesitatingly. Not only had he followed Montand's recent career with some interest, but both his own *The Crucible* and the earlier *Wages of Fear* had impressed him, and he admired any artist with the integrity to stick to his principles at grave risk to his reputation. He felt that Montand was a man cut from the same cloth as himself.

Basically, and aside from his acting ability which was considerable, Montand's appeal was a projection of a primitive sexiness. Despite the disadvantages of a broad mouth, gaunt cheeks, and a weak chin, he had smouldering eyes sunk deep in their sockets, a natural grace of movement, a tremulous voice as forlorn and as tinged with Parisian back alleys as Piaf's, and a Gallic charm that appealed to men as well as to women.

It is likely that casting Marilyn in a film with her male counterpart was a mistake. There was no foil for either one, nothing but sex to play against. Marilyn's innocence was slightly dimmed by her falling for such a man, and Montand appeared to be out of his element with the vague but sensual American girl-next-door, despite her aspirations (in the film) to be a musical comedy queen. What read humorously appeared on the screen as artificial beyond redemption. The film only came to life during its musical numbers, in which Marilyn was vigorously coached by Jack Cole.

But these deficiencies only began to emerge as the film was being put together. The auguries at the outset were all hopeful. Miller even took Montand in hand and worried over his English, which was dreadful, and Montand gave Miller a refresher course in gin rummy, which he played almost constantly.

So all was apparent bliss when the film was put into production in mid-February by Jerry Wald, with trustworthy George Cukor at the helm. Marilyn's only peeves were about the script. She had an extraordinary ability to sense whether a particular scene would play well or not upon the screen. But it was almost impossible for her to convey this grasp to a screen writer since she phrased her critique in such a way that unless one was familiar with her argot, what emerged seemed illogical and senseless. Her scriptual opinions were always couched in similes, in articulations of her own experiences. "Isn't this like . . .?" Or "Isn't *that* what she's doing? *Burning*? Like sitting on a hot stove?" Her language was nearly always concrete, almost never conceptual. She might say, "Yeah, she's saying that, but at the same time, she's doing *this*. So she's not *really* saying that. So what do you want her to do?" and she would stare wide-eyed, waiting for an answer from the latest screen writer assigned to the script.

As soon as shooting began, Marilyn had much less time for Simone, although Montand, as her leading man, was with her a good part of every day. In the evening, she would closet herself for an hour or two with Paula to study the script for the next day. Paula had asked the studio to give Marilyn "sides" instead of the whole script, so every few days a sheaf of papers containing the upcoming scenes was delivered by courier to Marilyn's dressing-room.

Marilyn knew the film was going badly when she saw the first rushes. She asked her husband if he would rewrite some of the scenes, and he complied at once. But Miller, who in private had a dry and inventive wit, was not a notable writer of comedy. He believed the script needed humour of character; the two essentially bland central roles badly needed motivation, which he hastened to instil. But he was beating a dead horse. Both he and Marilyn knew it.

Marilyn's shifting moods were deeply disturbing to him. She seemed to be accepting the disasters of her personal life – her second miscarriage, the unpredictable rages – with some stoicism, but the central tragedy of her life as she saw it, her marriage with Miller, she reacted to with such active venom and contempt that she repelled forever people who were once close to her. Her doctor was among these. He was to say, "I couldn't take it. All that bile. That recrimination."

Miller noted that once the Montands were adopted into her inner circle her habit of sedating herself during the day to level out her moods was forgotten part of the time. He could only assume that his presence alone was an irritant, but as part of a more harmonious quartet, he was acceptable. "Anyone who could make her smile came as a blessing to me," Miller said later about the close liaison that was being forged between Marilyn and Montand.

About six weeks into production, an actors' strike was called. After fretting about the hotel for a day or two, Miller decided to use the time to go over some of the Nevada locations for The Misfits, which was to follow immediately after the Fox musical. Frank Taylor, anxious to get the preliminaries out of the way, flew out from New York to join him on his safari, and together with art director Steve Grimes, took off for Reno.

Simone had to make a television appearance in Canada, which was to be shown a day or two later in the United States. While away, Simone called Marilyn to ask if she had seen the show and what she thought of it. Marilyn, recalling her own frightened face on the kinescope of her Person-to-Person interview, was much impressed by Simone's composure and intelligence, and told her so.

Soon after Simone returned from Canada she received a cable that her next film, to which she was contractually committed, would begin shooting within ten days, and she was needed for fittings and other matters in Europe.

Simone must have felt terribly alone with that telegram in

her hand. She later told a friend that she had had herself a
good cry. But before her tears were dried, she was thinking
desperately of something to do. Marilyn needed looking after,
if not watching. She needed a lover and father all in one, and
Arthur Miller, it seemed clear, was abdicating.

Montand made no effort to hide the truth from his wife.
His assurances that everything was all right were not reassuring to Simone and finally she thought of someone who might
help her through this crisis. He was open about his affairs with
others and Marilyn was aware of it. She told Ralph Roberts
during a massage session that she was certain that Montand
was boasting to friends about her "case" on him.

Doris Vidor, wife of the late director Charles and daughter
of Harry Warner, spent a great part of her time in France.
Some years earlier she had met Simone on the Riviera, and
they had become fast friends. Later, Simone introduced Mrs.
Vidor to Montand, and they became a threesome around
Paris. Mrs. Vidor was thin and angular, with a great shock of
dark blonde hair streaked with grey. Her eyes were large and
sensitive and often hidden behind smoked glasses, her voice
deep and rather intimidating at first meeting. Conveniently
for Simone, her friend lived only a block away from the Beverly Hills Hotel. When Simone wasn't with Montand and
Marilyn, she ran up to the Vidor residence. Now she decided
to run up the block and her purpose was anything but casual.

"I've been called back to France to do a movie," Simone
told Doris in her liquid, husky voice. "And Yves takes a lot
of looking after. Will you do it for me?"

Doris assured her that she would, and the following evening, Simone flew off with profound misgivings to her appointment in Paris.

On an evening in early June when the shooting of *Let's
Make Love* was about halfway along, Miller invited Montand
to join them for dinner around nine. Montand later told Doris
that he felt very uncomfortable during the meal. Miller
seemed to have come to a decision, Montand sensed, and he
announced to the two of them that he was going to fly back
East because "Jane and Bobby are getting out of school, and
I haven't seen them for too long".

Marilyn took the news calmly as though it was expected
and looked to see Montand's reaction. He was shaken by the

prospect of being alone with Marilyn. He fled the dinner as early as he could and rushed over to Mrs. Vidor's. "What am I going to do?" he asked. "He's leaving me with Marilyn. Do you think he doesn't know that she is beginning to throw herself at me?"

Mrs. Vidor told him that no one could know that better than Miller, having been around the two of them for weeks.

"Well after all," he continued plaintively, "I'm a vulnerable man. We're going to go on working together, thrown together on the set every day, and I don't want the responsibility. She's not well. Anyone can see that. I'm really in a spot." He was pacing about her living-room now and beads of perspiration were trickling down his forehead. "I can't alienate her because I'm dependent upon her good will, and I want to work with her. I can't deny it. It's very exciting working with her."

But Montand did nothing to alter the situation. Indeed, from then on both his vanity and his manhood appeared to have been flattered. Gossip columnists were publicly aghast at their behaviour, especially Hedda Hopper, never a friend to Marilyn.

If the legend of Marilyn had not already grown to such dimensions, the affair might have seriously damaged her. As it was, it was just new gossip to help keep the legend alive and glowing during the long wait between released films. A few columnists, friendly to Marilyn, took Montand to task for exploiting her vulnerability when everyone knew she was more or less under the care of an analyst much of the time. There was a small grain of truth in this. But it should be remembered that the aggressor was not Montand, but Marilyn.

So far as the director and crew on *Let's Make Love* were concerned, it was all to their benefit. Marilyn became more tractable with Cukor, although in private she would ask Montand if what Cukor was telling her made sense. She thought Montand had a professionalism that exceeded anything to be found in Hollywood, and she was very nearly correct in this, although it was never to work successfully for him in American films. He told some of his friends that "She's got so she'll do whatever I ask her to do on the set. Everyone is amazed at her co-operation, and she's constantly looking at me for approval."

Marilyn, it should be pointed out, was not doing anything she hadn't done since she was sixteen years old. Never having

known a father and being a deeply mistrustful human being
as well, she usually sought to have a man around who could
fulfil several functions: reassure her, satisfy her sexual needs,
and take the place of her missing father. Miller was walking
away from her, possibly in despair, certainly with the knowledge that she would not permit him to do any more for her.
In essence, what he now represented was a long series of betrayals, beginning in England and leading up to his final disavowal. Once Marilyn felt betrayed there was no redemption,
and difficult as it was to believe, knowing what Miller had
meant to her, she was ready to dismiss him now from her life
despite the clear risk that it might precipitate much trouble
for herself.

Through their four years of marriage, Miller always hoped
Marilyn would realize that he was not The Grantor of all her
needs, a sort of household deity by day and a lover by night.
It would not be easy to bow out. The nightly vigil was very
much in his mind.

But leaving Marilyn was not as simple as taking a plane
East. There was *The Misfits* looming before both of them,
and not only were they legally committed to it, they had no
way of abandoning it. It was crucial to both their careers.
Let's Make Love was supposed to be pure entertainment,
but it was a clear failure in this area. It would do little more
for Marilyn than satisfy a public titillated by the gossip of
her romance with Montand, and it was to be a serious setback to Montand's American film career. His future, even
more brilliant than his past, was to be in European films where
he was at ease and doing things that mattered to him.

The Misfits would be the first major Miller work since *A
View from the Bridge*. In Roslyn, Marilyn had the most original and most off-beat role of her career. It could be played
only by her because essentially it *was* Marilyn – her loser
philosophy, her speech patterns, her inborn innocence. Only
Marilyn could do it if it was to be done at all.

There was the definite possibility, too, that something would
happen to Marilyn's relationship with Montand – nearly
everything was against permanence. And perhaps Miller believed that his trip to New York might bring about a sudden
rupture between his wife and her leading man and precipitate
a crisis in her life. That she would need him in that event there

was no doubt. But if this was in his mind, Miller confided in no one about the matter.

Some of Marilyn's friends warned her not to commit herself altogether, since "European men have different standards", but she felt if she didn't try she was to regret it always. Montand was tender and sympathetic. If he never once declared himself, she could understand that.

She was not forgetting Simone. If she and Montand were to marry, she wanted desperately to keep Simone's friendship. This was not an uncommon possibility in the film world, but she wasn't too sanguine about it. Its unlikelihood was one of her sorrows at the moment, and she was absolutely sincere when she told Montand that she would do almost anything rather than hurt Simone.

Like many Americans, she believed implicitly in actions, in observable behaviour and reactions. Who needs a declaration when every gesture reveals your lover's true regard? Who asks about intentions when there are so many quagmires in just living from day to day? She felt she had been set adrift by Miller, and that only a close emotional attachment could keep her from foundering.

CHAPTER EIGHT

Early in the summer of 1960 Joe Schenck became gravely ill. He had suffered a heart attack, one of several that afflicted him until a final thrombosis killed him over a year later. For more than a year he had been in failing health and telling his friends, "I wish that little blonde would give old Joe a call." He had heard that the Marilyn he had known so well ten years earlier had changed drastically and he was concerned.

The message was conveyed to her, and she was conscience-stricken for a time and promised herself to drop by his house, but then her activities and problems enveloped her again and she did not. Her circle of friends was never wide in Hollywood, and it was to narrow even further. Away from the film world grapevine, she was unlikely to hear of a very critical turn Schenck's health had taken.

One Sunday, David Selznick and his wife, Jennifer Jones, were having a buffet supper. They had invited Montand and Marilyn, who were socially accepted as a couple, a permissiveness that was more a comment on the times than on Hollywood proper. Montand had telephoned Doris Vidor and invited her to come along.

The three of them drove in a rented limousine to the hilltop house of the Selznicks'. Mrs. Vidor remembers that conversation stopped entirely as they entered the living-room, or if it continued it did so in a flat distracted way. Marilyn had always caused ripples of excitement around her. Now, with Montand as her escort, even the veterans of Hollywood society could not resist gawking.

Mrs. Vidor realized while they were driving over that she had little in common with Marilyn. Hardly a word was exchanged by the two women, although Montand made an effort to banter with each of them in turn. At the party, Mrs. Vidor soon left her companions' side and circulated among the guests, most of whom were her old friends.

Marilyn began drinking champagne almost at once. It was a drink she could consume in fairly large quantity without becoming incapacitated. Montand was not as attentive as usual. He kept drifting away from her, seeking out Doris Vidor to see if she was enjoying herself.

But as Marilyn became a little less sure on her feet, she remained in the drawing-room where she overheard Gregory Bautzer, a perennial Hollywood man-about-town, say something about the grave illness of Joe Schenck.

"What did you say about Joe?" Marilyn asked, suddenly sober.

"He's in a coma," Bautzer answered, in a tone that suggested "Why should you care?"

"But he can't be!" Marilyn wailed "Someone would have called me."

"Save your tears for someone who doesn't know you so well," Bautzer rebutted. "Joe Schenck is dying. He's unconscious. And he'd better go fast so he won't suffer any more."

Marilyn's eyes widened in terror and fury. "I've got to go to him. I'd never forgive myself if I didn't go."

Bautzer looked at her in disgust. "Aren't you a little late with all that?"

"But I *have* to see him! I've got to see him while he's still alive," Marilyn repeated, forgetting Montand, forgetting the party.

"You're a fine one!" Bautzer almost shouted at Marilyn. "Now you want to see him when he's dying. He's been sick for a couple of years and he wanted so much to see you, for you to come by. I heard him say it a hundred times. Then it would have done him some good. Now he won't even know you and *you have to see him*. Well, it's too damned late!"

Marilyn was trembling in a corner. There were no friends of hers in the room to comfort her. A few of those present were apparently shocked by Bautzer's outburst but seemed to accept his judgement. They were as misguided as Bautzer. Joe Schenck would have understood why Marilyn had not visited him during the months of his illness, for he knew that she should not be judged by ordinary rules. He would have known that her present determination to see him was due neither to drunkenness nor to hypocrisy, but that it was motivated by sincere affection. Marilyn – and Schenck was aware of this – was unable to blend the old with the new. Since her marriage to Miller she seemed to have immersed herself completely in his world and have shed or turned her back on the past.

It is unlikely that when she learned that Schenck was no longer in a critical condition, the urgency to see him disappeared. With the collapse of her marriage, Marilyn seemed to disengage herself from active participation in life. But for very brief spells, she was to remain apathetic until her death. Her emotional and sensual responses hid from those not so close to her, her deep detachment. However, Miller and those intimate with her in those days realized fully well that she neither looked forward to the film she was about to make (*The Misfits*) nor did she appear to care whether her affair with Montand ripened into a permanent relationship. She existed in a state of suspension, seemingly, waiting to turn some corner that would change her life.

Meanwhile at the Selznick party, Montand decided that it was getting late. He found Mrs. Vidor and told her that he had an early call at the studio and wanted to go home.

"You'd better tell Marilyn," she suggested.

Mrs. Vidor recalls that Montand's tone was a little petulant when he reached Marilyn's corner of the drawing-room. He told her that it was time to leave. Marilyn, immersed in her own thoughts, seemed not to hear him. She said that she had to settle something. Montand then wheeled about, saying, "I'm going to the car."

Unaware that she had not heard him, Montand, angry, left the party. He went to the limousine and told the chauffeur that Marilyn would be along later and he could come back and pick her up. He went off alone.

Marilyn realized finally it was no use talking to Greg Bautzer. She got up from the sofa and began looking for Montand. When she couldn't find him, she sought Mrs. Vidor.

"I'm ready," Marilyn told Mrs. Vidor. "Where's Yves?"

"He took the car and left. He's going to . . ."

Before Mrs. Vidor could finish, Marilyn mumbled something like "No, he couldn't!" Then she ran out of the house, apparently terrified of being abandoned. The startled guests on the outside steps waiting for their cars pressed back a little as she continued running down the slope toward the street, crying, "I'll catch the car! I'll catch up with it!"

Marilyn's driver was already on his way back when he saw her running down the steep incline of the road from the Selznicks'. He drove her back to the bungalow. Marilyn suddenly remembered their companion. "Go back for Mrs. Vidor," she instructed the driver. "I forgot about her."

Early the next day, Montand called to ask Doris Vidor, "Why was Greg Bautzer so vulgar to Marilyn last night?" He seemed nearly ready to challenge the man. Mrs. Vidor explained that he had been drinking and lost his temper, but Montand would have none of it. "I know what happened," he said. "He tried to make her and she wouldn't have him."

Mrs. Vidor said, "I don't believe that's the case," and the conversation died. It is likely that it was Marilyn who put this notion in Montand's head. Quite often when a man crossed her, she would fall back on this kind of explanation.

PART SIX

The Misfit

CHAPTER ONE

It was characteristic of Marilyn until the filming of *The Prince and the Showgirl* to be totally immersed in her own role, while remaining basically uninvolved with the production as a whole. But this film was to be the turning point, for from then on each picture became a cause for Marilyn.

Misfits producer Frank Taylor, fearing that the nuances of Miller's drama would be missed if the film was shot in the customary fashion, that is, episode by episode, suggested that it be filmed following the sequence of the script. Since Miller was a writer for the theatre, Taylor thought it best, and Miller and Huston agreed, that *The Misfits* be treated as a play. When shooting began on the disconnected scenes, the actors had constantly to refer to their script in order to recapture the momentum of the previous scenes which often had been shot either days or weeks earlier or had yet to be touched on. By the sequential method not only the director but the actors themselves were in greater control of their performances.

Marilyn began living two lives simultaneously: that of the cautious and fragile Roslyn, whose inner being was explored each day before the cameras; and her own life which was lived in what might be termed a potentially explosive state of suspension – insulated from feeling too keenly by the pills and protected by her well-intentioned staff who carefully hid any expression of annoyance with Marilyn over her control of the film's production. This protective attitude originated with Miller who, aware of Marilyn's precarious emotional balance, was afraid she might suffer a dangerous breakdown.

There was something weirdly apt about the setting chosen for the film. Enormous flat vistas of lunar landscape guarded at their perimeters by the dark humps of the Washoe mountains; a land of shadows, a graveyard for prehistoric mammoths, a dead place of played-out mines.

John Huston was a member of a dying species, an unmitigated individualist, at once insular and sophisticated. Out of touch with Hollywood's headaches, his personal and tactical problems were confined within the boundaries of his current film's location or the acres of Saint Clerans in County Galway, Ireland, his home base.

He came to Nevada in the summer of 1960 nearly entirely innocent of any knowledge of Marilyn's multiplying difficulties. Miller had spent over a week with him at Saint Clerans revising the script of *The Misfits*, had shared several bottles of the best Irish whiskey before a roaring fire with his host, but had said nothing about Marilyn.

Perhaps he felt that a director of Huston's sensitivity and basic humanness could bring Marilyn through. He would not risk losing him by suggesting that she was not in condition to do the film. And there was always the possibility, however remote, that the involvement amounting to nearly total engagement that goes into making a picture might work a miracle.

Shortly after the middle of July 1960, the complete production company assembled in Reno. Marilyn and her entourage were the last to reach the location, and a ceremony was made of her arrival at the Reno airport. There was a bouquet from the governor's family, and she rode into town and up to the Mapes Hotel in Frank Taylor's open red convertible. There had been only about a twenty-minute delay at the airport after Marilyn peered out of the plane window and saw the crowd, and then began redoing her make-up and changing her dress.

Every provision was made for her comfort and reassurance. Ralph Roberts was put on a salary as company masseur. He had already been asked to appear in a small role as an ambulance attendant at the rodeo. Whitey Snyder was on hand to do Marilyn's make-up, Agnes Flanagan was there to dress her hair, and Sydney Guilaroff would style it, all trusted friends.

She would be surrounded by old colleagues. Kevin McCarthy, brother of Mary McCarthy, the novelist and caustic critic, and an actor from Marilyn's Actors Studio days, would play a camera role as Roslyn's husband whom she has come to Reno to divorce. And her old friend from New York, Mont-

gomery Clift, was to play the sensitive cowboy. He was a performer of a temperament even less predictable than Marilyn's.
In fact, she confided to a friend that he was the only person
she knew who was in greater trouble than she was. He was
described by some who knew him well as often behaving like
a child, more tormented by self-doubt than Marilyn. Marilyn
embraced him when they met at the hotel. In the weeks ahead,
he would keep to himself, seeing only Marilyn occasionally
and confiding in no one but his make-up man.

Finally, and not least, there was the King himself. Gable
was more excited by Miller's script than by anything he had
read in over a decade. In some respects, he seemed to understand the nuances of the script better than the author, for he
was a man not unlike Gay Langland, the hero of *The Misfits*.
Marilyn worshipped him. When in the mid-fifties she had met
Gable at a Hollywood party and had danced with him, she
told him that as a child he represented the kind of father she
wished she had. A man without any perceptible vanity, Gable
laughed and loved her for it. Throughout the film he retained
a paternal interest in Marilyn, at least when she was in his
presence.

Gable, through his agent George Chasin of MCA – who by
the way also represented Marilyn and Clift – made stiffer demands on the management of *The Misfits* than he had sought
on any of his recent films, his last two having been failures. In
addition to his salary of $750,000, he was to receive 10 per
cent of the box-office receipts, and as the film moved beyond
its completion date, he would be paid nearly $58,000 in over-
time.

Unlike Huston, Gable had heard rumours of Marilyn's
problems, and had braced himself for a trying time. As the
precise nature of her difficulty revealed itself during the first
days of shooting, he felt an enormous compassion for her, and
remained patient like the others, a slightly bemused smile
on his lips.

The marriage with Miller was not dying; it was dead. Marilyn had realized that before she flew to Reno. None the less,
she had reached an understanding with Miller that nothing
was to be said about a possible divorce until the film was completed as it was a joint venture and their careers were seriously involved. They shared an attractive suite on a high floor
of the Mapes Hotel, an arrangement that brought Miller to

the verge of a breakdown. In the early stages of the film's production, they made an occasional public appearance together. Later, this concession to face-saving ceased almost entirely.

When she arrived, Marilyn appeared to be in a fretful state which lasted for a day or more. Although some guessed that Miller had something to do with it, they were wrong. She was angry about the way she had been rushed into costume fittings for the film almost the minute she completed *Let's Make Love*. She told anyone who would listen that it was grossly unfair of her employers not to have given her a week or two of rest between films. She failed to note that she, along with her husband and Taylor, were considered by others as part of the management because it was primarily their film and not a studio project. She chose to forget that she had contributed to the delays on her last film and said she was not to be penalized for the actors' strike that had stopped the production of the film for so long.

Miller was upset by Marilyn's complaints. Unlike her, he could not turn off his feelings towards a person when something went wrong with the relationship. As the film progressed, a schism split the company into two camps, a division initiated and encouraged by Marilyn. The Miller faction included Frank Taylor, Angela Allen, Huston's script supervisor since *African Queen* days and the only woman included in this inner circle; Edward Parone, Taylor's assistant; and eventually and quite innocently, Huston himself.

John Huston had made it an operating policy never to get involved in the off-the-set tensions of the actors. He was fond of Marilyn and often had wondered how she had got along during the two-year interval between their meetings. He last had seen her in 1958 when he flew into New York for a business meeting and took her to see *Separate Tables*. And Marilyn was fond of Huston and told him he was "lucky" for her.

The Marilyn camp included all her entourage, two of whom, May Reis, her secretary, and Paula Strasberg, would appear most of the time in black, quietly watching the struggle between Marilyn and Miller. Despite his detachment from the company as a whole, Marilyn's group would claim Clift as a member, and later, even Gable.

Paula was to remember her months in Nevada as a nightmare. Without her knowledge, production executives on the film had elected to treat her as a pariah, but with courtesy.

Huston, who frankly liked Paula (perhaps out of admiration for her nonconformist zeal) glossed over this decision when they were in a huddle together and he set down some guide lines for her to follow in coaching Marilyn. Marilyn, during the first weeks of production, saw what was happening and flew to Paula's defence. She quarrelled briefly with Miller over it, but he answered, quite truthfully, that the decision was not his. She surprised nearly everyone including Paula by backing down. There was something of the campaign general in Paula's nature, and when she was not involved in an actual battle she would stir up at least a skirmish.

In this explosive atmosphere the filming of *The Misfits* began.

On the morning of Marilyn's first call for shooting, Huston had everything set up. They were shooting in the old Reno USO building, a nondescript frame house. The first set-up was in the driveway. Marilyn was to be caught at a window, looking down at Thelma Ritter playing the role of Isabel. Huston had his cameras and lights all ready for a ten o'clock call. He would have preferred nine, but out of deference to Marilyn he had settled on the later hour.

She had few lines in this opening sequence. Isabel, her newly found friend and "witness" for her divorce, is in the driveway talking with Guido, played by Eli Wallach, who has come to give Roslyn an estimate on her wrecked Cadillac. Roslyn learns that the hour is approaching for her appearance in court, but she is in such a state of near panic, she feels far from ready. The scene parallels almost exactly the mood of Marilyn's dressing-room when she had an appointment with a director and cameraman. "Five minutes!" she cries. "What about you?" And then, "Will you come up here, Iz?"

That was substantially all Marilyn had to do in the first set-up, and with the recognition of the scene's origins very much in everyone's mind, there was a touch of irony in the delay as the minutes ticked away, the hour of eleven was tolled audibly by the crew, and no leading lady was in sight.

Miller conferred with Huston, perhaps hoping that earnest conversation about the script might deflect the director's attention from his watch. Miller and his friends on the set were all praying that this first small crisis would not lead to a breakdown in his good relations with Huston.

From that first morning on, the truth began to seep through the company that Marilyn was terribly ill with insomnia and emotional problems. Her intake of Nembutal had risen from six or eight a night to what would be a lethal dose for the average person. She required the attentions of several persons to get her in walking condition in the morning.

There is considerable evidence that beginning with that first embarrassment and continuing through numerous others, Huston had to fight to keep alive his vision of the film. This ordeal, of which nearly everyone but Marilyn was aware, caused some in the company to speculate that Huston had lost interest when the time arrived to stage the climax of the film (the fight with and subjugation of the stallion), but what had happened in that instance was simply that Miller had not thought the scene through clearly. To remedy the situation producer Taylor suggested that story boards be used (drawing delineating camera angles with all the action sketched out). The scene was actually directed by assistant director Tom Shaw.

On an average day, Marilyn was awakened between six-thirty and seven. This hour would be advanced to eight-thirty or nine if she had undergone a particularly sleepless night as happened on the morning she was to do her first scene with Gable.

Coffee was poured into her, and then Ralph Roberts entered her bedroom to give her a massage. She readily responded to the massage, perhaps because of her anticipation of working with a man she had admired nearly all of her life. Whitey Snyder then was able to apply her make-up before an improvised studio mirror above her dressing-table. Agnes Flanagan followed to do her hair.

The scene was set in Harrah's Reno Club, a city block of slot machines, crap tables, and roulette wheels, in Miller's words, "a sea of cold chrome". The Club was usually open twenty-four hours a day, but three morning hours had been set aside for shooting and Bill Harrah hoped that the publicity connected with the world-wide showing of the film would compensate him for what he was losing in the gambling take each morning he was closed.

Marilyn's trailer was pulled up in front of the Club just behind Huston's. Company patrolmen kept the curious behind a line across the street. She arrived ready for the cameras at 11.45. She came in her white Cadillac with Rupert Allan, her press agent, driven by her long-time chauffeur Rudi Kautzky. Waiting for her at the trailer were Paula and May Reis, and inside the mobile dressing-room were Hazel Washington, her personal maid, and Shirlee Straham of wardrobe. Evelyn Moriarty, her stand-in, had already been standing under the big lights installed inside the Club.

While Marilyn was nervous as shooting began, there was a calming influence about Gable that began working almost immediately. It is a bar scene in which Roslyn is seen sitting with her friend, Isabel. She's then asked to join Gay Langland and Guido's table after Gay's dog, Tom Dooley, has run over at Roslyn's call. Additional takes were required due more to the difficult behaviour of the dog than by any fluff on Marilyn's part. Despite Tom Dooley, Huston was able to complete the work at Harrah's in less than two days.

When Marilyn was able to work, it nearly made up for the frustrations surrounding that achievement. Her reactions to Gable were like quicksilver, but her presence caught by the camera was gauze-like. She seemed an exhausted angel trapped among earthlings. Huston observed that between *The Asphalt Jungle* and *The Misfits*, something disturbing had happened to Marilyn, but that, whatever it was, it had deepened her responses. Her acting came from her insides. The veil over reality she demanded off camera was entirely missing during her scenes.

Angela Allen, who was constantly at Huston's side, was a handsome Englishwoman, ruddy-cheeked from working outdoors much of the time, her nose slightly upturned so that her good upper teeth were often visible. She disliked Marilyn almost upon contact, and was repelled by her entourage. "They're around her all of the time, devouring her," she remarked. "And some of her lateness is deliberate. She's getting back at the world for all the deprivation of her early life."

After a few days of working closely with the star, prompting her numerous times from the master script, Angela became even more critical. "I think she's rather vulgar. Not in language. I never heard her swear in my presence, although I'm sure she knows how, but there's vulgarity in the way she dresses and behaves off camera. No one around her dares criticize her in any way. She's a queen surrounded by courtiers."

Then Angela Allen saw the rushes. "When I saw her up there," she said, "it was nearly incredible. The legend, which I thought a kind of joke in questionable taste, suddenly made sense. I could understand why all the fuss had been made, why the crowds went out of their minds whenever they caught a glimpse of her. It's a kind of magic." After that, Angela didn't resent Marilyn's lateness nearly so much. Years later she was to say, "I never came to really like her, but I realized her worth as an actress, her value to any production. "

Gradually, Huston began shooting around Marilyn whenever she was indisposed, his production schedule adjusting itself to this singular situation. It had happened before with other directors, and now it was his turn. But what really mattered was that he was getting something very worthwhile on film.

On the numerous occasions when Marilyn could not get out of bed, Snyder made her up horizontally, turning her when necessary. The ten or more pills taken at intervals through the evening and into the night enveloped her eventually in a sodden slumber. To get her on her feet, a few hours later, was virtually impossible.

And it was a self-cancelling cycle. Her body was becoming immune to the pills, and the nature of the drug was such that it sank her into profound depression. She sought oblivion at such times, and these occasions were becoming alarmingly frequent.

"I'm caught," Huston decided. "I'm too far into this thing to back out." He said nothing to Miller to indicate he had been in any way deceived. Rather, his protective instincts were aroused for both of them, for Miller in his misery and for Marilyn in her addiction.

To an outsider, it appeared that Miller was the victim. This was only half true. Trapped at his own suggestion in three rooms with Marilyn, Miller spent as much time out of the suite as possible. But he was usually there when Marilyn was ready to begin her nightly ritual of the pills. If she were beside herself with wakefulness in the middle of the night he would talk to her, carefully avoiding anything that might irritate her. Often during these small hours, Marilyn would cheat at the game and lash out suddenly, her voice carrying far down the hall.

Whenever it was suggested that perhaps it was time for the tortured couple to call a halt to their act of staying together for the sake of the picture, Miller would withdraw, unwilling to take the step that might save himself but destroy Marilyn. Their relationship had deteriorated, but as long as Miller was on the scene, Marilyn, aware that his feelings had remained constant, found in him an irresistible target for her indignant and imperious protests.

After one such all-night vigil, with Marilyn finally asleep while others were getting ready for the day, May Reis arrived in the living-room of their suite. Miller was slumped in a heap on the sofa, lapsing at moments into fits of trembling from nervous exhaustion. Nan Taylor joined them in the suite. She had heard that Marilyn had spent an especially bad night, but she was even more distressed to see what it had done to Miller.

His hands half covering his face, Miller agonized over his situation. He confessed that he obviously was no help to Marilyn in seeing her through these terrible nights. He wondered if he shouldn't take a room in another hotel. "She needs care at night," he said, and then he seemed to defeat any hope of salvation by crying out, "But I care for her so much!"

With Miller's reluctance to abandon Marilyn so obvious, the possibility of someone else volunteering to take over at night – someone slightly less involved such as May Reis – hung in the air, though it is doubtful that any such proposal was made explicit. Possibly sensing this, May said, "What I do for Marilyn is out of pure love," but she could not bring herself to stay up all night.

The conversation was leading into the same impasse as earlier well-intentioned efforts to find some way to keep Marilyn functioning. "Perhaps we can't solve Marilyn's problem this morning," Nan Taylor said, "but we can do something about you." Then she turned towards the door. "I'll be right back," she told them.

Nan went down to the lobby and sought out the manager. In a matter of minutes a room was secured down the hall from the suite. She hurried back upstairs with the key and handed it to Miller, with the comment, "Now you get some sleep."

That spare room was Miller's escape valve during the next few weeks. When things became too strained in the suite, he excused himself and went down the hall. Marilyn appeared to accept this arrangement without complaint. She was now lapsing into silence when with Miller. This had the side benefit of enabling him to spend more hours working over the script. Somehow the film was progressing.

CHAPTER TWO

"I don't remember a picture that depends quite so much on oddity. If anyone (of the actors) were average, it wouldn't work. You've read this script. What would it be like if it were cast out of an agent's office?" This comment was made by Thelma Ritter to James Goode, a writer who had joined the company in the hope, later to be realized, of publishing a log of the movie's rather unorthodox making. She had struck at the heart of the strength and of the problems of this production. It took all the ingenuity and presence of mind that John Huston and Frank Taylor could summon to pull together such a clutch of eccentrics and to keep them not only from upstaging the others but from exploding precipitously like so many malfunctioning nuclear devices.

There were numerous compensations for both men, of course. One of them was Marilyn's wit, which seemed to revive each day right after her last cup of black coffee. On one occasion, Taylor brought a man who was to produce a movie trailer, or "coming attractions", on The Misfits, to Marilyn's dressing-room, "Marilyn, here is the gentleman I was telling you about who's going to handle the trailer." Marilyn took the man's hand and breathed a great sigh of relief. "Am I glad to see you!" she told him. "The air conditioning doesn't work."

Montgomery Clift kept himself so much apart from the others that he would have been thought a snob by a less sensitive group. It was his way of coping with the exposure required by his approach to the screen. Between films, his life was a series of disasters. Like Marilyn, he was cushioned to a degree by protective friends, but in addition he attempted to insulate himself through alcohol. Often liquor, instead of muffling his pain and rage against life, would aggravate his angry despair.

His drinking was moderate on the set. There he confined

himself to a sort of whisky sour made with grapefruit juice he carried in a Thermos. He was very high on both Marilyn and Miller. "My feeling about Miller is that I sort of face East every time I see him," he said. He also confided to James Goode that his problem was "how to remain thin-skinned and yet survive. One can uncallous one's self, you know. . . . I think Taylor's tremendously talented to put together this network of people. Nothing of him is the norm. There is the whole terrible problem of remaining vulnerable, and Taylor has the small, intimate means of making you feel wanted. . . . I wish I were even more thin-skinned. The problem is to remain sensitive to all kinds of things without letting them pull you down. . . . The only line I know of that's wrong in Shakespeare is 'Holding a mirror up to nature.' You hold the magnifying glass up to nature. As an actor you just enlarge it enough so that your audience can identify with a situation. If it were a mirror we would have no art."

Clift was to die of a heart attack in 1966, and as with Marilyn, his approach to his craft was, in part, a reason for his death. He was simply too exposed to survive for very long.

The smoke from the brush fires that ringed Reno on an evening in late August had brought an early nightfall. Dramatically, the fires had burned the power lines supplying the town so that the buildings were in total darkness.

Marilyn found the situation exciting enough to want to join others and talk about it. She left her suite and walked along the darkened corridor to the farther end, where wardrobe had set up headquarters. A worktable had been converted into a bar, and candles glowed on each end of it. Agnes Flanagan and Ralph Roberts were splitting a bottle of Scotch.

"Mind if I join the party?" Marilyn asked. Roberts, always shy and reserved in Marilyn's presence despite the trust she had placed in him, stood up and offered her his chair. Then he wandered off to find himself another one.

Marilyn walked over to the window. Dimly through the pall of smoke she could see the burning scrub pine a few miles away. She contracted her shoulders, quivering a little. "It's scarey," she said.

Marilyn returned to the table and sat opposite Agnes as Roberts poured. She rattled her drink over the rocks. "There *are* a few combustible people inside," she said and then took a long drink, holding some of it in her mouth for a moment, her head arched back, her eyes closed. Then she swallowed and sighed in relief. "I've missed you both. Being together like this. We should have thought of it sooner."

Agnes nodded, feeling deeply sad. Agnes sensed that Marilyn could not manage life alone; like Paula, Roberts, Whitey Snyder, and Rupert Allan, she cared about Marilyn. Each of them appeared to have a function in her life aside from their professional duties. Roberts and Agnes were confidantes and Allan was often her escort to and from locations. Miller made no effort to ride with her since the time she had become annoyed with him at a desert location and had shut the door of the limousine in his face, ordering Rudi to drive on. Snyder was now handling the approval on all of Marilyn's still photography for her. She felt that he knew her preferences in the stills well enough to act as her proxy and she didn't have the energy after half a day before the camera to do it herself.

"Anyway," Marilyn told her two drinking companions. "It's cosy. *The big Reno blackout.* It's fun."

They drank quietly for a few moments. Then Marilyn glanced at Roberts. "Tell us about the time I called you on the set of *The Bells are Ringing*." Then to Agnes: "This is a howl!" Marilyn laughed, the notes rising to a squeak.

Roberts became aware of the smaller amenities. "There's no ice, Marilyn," he confessed.

"The refrigerator in the suite!" she said. "It couldn't have melted yet. I knew it would come in handy some day."

Roberts got up once again to fetch the ice, but then turned and said in his soft, deep voice: "Is anyone home down there?"

"Arthur's there," she said. "He called downstairs for help. He can't work by candlelight." Miller was working on revisions until midnight nearly every evening. The chief electrician had ordered a huge generator brought into the Mapes from one of the outdoor locations and it was supplying lights for the street-level bar, the lobby, and now the Miller suite.

"He's such a sweet man," Marilyn said to Agnes as their friend went off into the darkness. "I'd really be lost without him." She was gradually working up to a very gay mood.

Roberts returned with a bowl of ice cubes. "I can tell by your face," Marilyn remarked. "You saw old Grouchy Grumps. Did you speak to him? I mean, did he say *hello*?"

"He was lying on the sofa," Roberts explained.

"He'll go that way until he's too exhausted to move. From the desk to the sofa and then back again." Marilyn picked up a cube and dropped it into her glass. "Klunk! At least we got a little ice out of that room."

Marilyn's collapse did not happen overnight. A week before it occurred Huston conferred with Miller. "This has to stop," Huston told him. "Marilyn has only had two afternoons before the cameras in a week." Miller agreed that something drastic had to be done.

A few days later, Marilyn was driven to the set by Rudi Kautzky. It was almost noon and the temperature had soared to 110 degrees. She was helped out of the car. Huston saw that someone was leading her over to the camera location, and he sighed. "This is it," he thought.

Marilyn looked blankly at Russell Metty, the cameraman. At other times she used to joke with him even when not feeling her best. Now, she looked around dazedly. She clearly was not sure where she was. Someone helped her to the spot Huston had indicated beforehand, and she turned instinctively towards the camera.

Metty trollied in for a closer look in the viewfinder. Then he ran the camera away from her, shaking his head. Huston came over to him. "It's hopeless," Metty whispered. "I can't do a thing with her today. Her eyes won't focus."

"We must shut down for a week or so," Huston told producer Taylor. This was not an opinion; it was a decision, and it would prove to be a costly one, but there was never any thought of replacing Marilyn. She had to be rehabilitated, at least temporarily.

It was the end of August. Marilyn was flown to Los Angeles to be admitted to a clinic. Yves Montand later said that Marilyn made an effort to see him at the Beverly Hills Hotel, but that he was not in his bungalow when she had called. She left a note, he said, with a number where she could be reached, but he chose not to get in touch with her.

On Saturday, August 27, Rupert Allan announced that she was a patient in Westside Hospital in Los Angeles and was suffering from exhaustion.

Dr. Ralph Greenson, psychiatrist to a number of Hollywood personalities, took care of her during this trying period. She had sought his help several times before her Nevada breakdown. It was not his fame that had drawn Marilyn to him at first. He was the brother-in-law of Mickey Rudin, Marilyn's Hollywood attorney, a fact which predisposed her favourably towards him. In the months to come she became even closer to Greenson and, in fact, to his entire family.

Huston took advantage of the lull to fly to Hollywood for conferences with the studio management. He also met with Greenson and inquired about the state of Marilyn's health and asked the doctor when he might expect her back on the set, "Can she finish the picture?" he wanted to know.

Greenson believed that she could, after about ten days of rest and medication. But the psychiatrist was upset by Marilyn's having got hold of such large amounts of Nembutal in the first place. "How did she get them?" he asked.

Huston, equally distressed, told how his company doctor had given her one night's supply after she had begged him for them. Then he had balked when she came back the next evening. "He came to me, believing he would be fired for refusing her a new dose. I backed him up a hundred per cent," Huston told Greenson. "Everyone in the company applauded him. But then," and Huston's face clouded over, "then she went out in Reno and scouted up a doctor on her own. She told him of her woes and he gave her a prescription. The doctor who gave Marilyn the pills should be charged with criminal action."

Greenson was silent. Huston felt that they were in agreement about her condition and the course of treatment needed. Huston left the doctor's office a little amazed that he had become so involved in such a strange business. It was the first and only time in his film-making career that he would have to place his star in the hands of a psychiatrist in order to complete his picture.

Over a period of seven or eight days, Marilyn was withdrawn from Nembutal and put on Dexamyl. She received a steady procession of visitors. Lee Strasberg had flown out for a month and later went back with the company to Nevada for a week or so. He and Paula came twice, their actress daughter Susan accompanying them.

Rupert Allan and May Reis met in the hospital waiting room with a copy of a Los Angeles newspaper that had disturbed them. A columnist had reported that Yves Montand had told her that Marilyn had "a schoolgirl crush on him".

Since the French actor-singer had been out of Marilyn's life for two months, the statement seemed gratuitous and exploitive. In fairness to Montand, it should be stated that the lady columnist could have put words into his mouth and he may have parroted them back not knowing what he was saying. His English remained poor to the end of his stay in Hollywood. He later denied making such a statement and admitted that "I was too tender and thought that maybe she was sophisticated as some of the other ladies I have known.... Had Marilyn been sophisticated, none of this would have happened." Still later, Simone Signoret would take herself and Montand permanently out of Marilyn's life by telling a reporter, "A man doesn't feel he has to confuse an affair with eternal love and make it a crisis in marriage." In early November, when Marilyn returned to New York after completing the final scenes of *The Misfits* at Paramount Studios, she spent several hours with Montand in the back seat of her limousine as he waited for his flight back to Paris. They drank champagne, while Montand bid her farewell and told her of his decision to remain with his wife. It was the last known contact between them.

Miller came once to the hospital to see how Marilyn was doing. It was a curious reunion. She made it clear to him that she would be going back to Nevada to finish the picture. Following that encounter, she seemed to have resigned herself to a life without him.

Even Joe DiMaggio visited her and never again lost touch with Marilyn. He found her completely surrounded by flowers. Everyone had accepted the story of her "exhaustion", although she would not be so fortunate on the occasion of her next collapse. With DiMaggio, it is said, she was candid and told him of the real reason behind her physical crisis.

Marilyn returned to Nevada on September 5. She stopped off to see DiMaggio in San Francisco, and in a light-hearted mood while waiting for her plane for Reno, she bought a strange souvenir hat for a dollar, patterned after those worn by Peruvian Indian women in the Andes. She reached Reno late that night, wearing her Indian hat, smiling. She seemed happy to be back. Frank and Nan Taylor met the plane, accompanied by a taciturn and distracted Miller. He appeared to be in need of similar rehabilitation for he had spent most of the time the company was shut down working on revisions. His eyes were sunken with dark rings, his cheeks gaunt. He did not embrace Marilyn, nor join the Taylors' joy at having Marilyn back among them.

The next day there was a festive air about the movie company that infected even Miller. No one really believed that Marilyn was off the pills. The most reliable word was that the doctors had switched the chemical combinations in such a way that she could manage with smaller, less debilitating doses. But whatever happened, it was a minor miracle, and there was every expectation that the film would now be completed.

Shooting resumed at once in the Odeon Bar in Dayton, where Roslyn, Gay, Guido, and Perce (Clift) have adjourned, following the rodeo and Perce's head injury. Perce asks to dance with Roslyn, and Miller won a light round of applause from the cast crew by dancing with Marilyn, his head thrown back and his arms thrust out like semaphores, to demonstrate to Clift what sort of provincial polka was required of him. That evening, possibly moved by Miller's amusing gesture on the set, she joined her husband for a walk near the hotel. When stopped by an amazed reporter, she said, "We're only going for a walk, just like everyday people."

Enthusiasm was still high a couple of days later when the principals saw the rushes of the Dayton bar scene. Gable was enormously impressed with Clift and said, "In that scene at the table when he said 'What was that they put in my arm,' he had a wild look in his eye that could only have come from morphine ... and booze ... and the steers ..." Huston commented that you could believe that Perce has had it all.

Gable himself would win wild applause from the company that afternoon when he, as Gay, has become very drunk in the bar, sees his children from whom he has been separated for years outside in the crowd, and hurries back in to fetch Roslyn to meet them.

Huston: "Action."

Gable: "Roslyn ... Roslyn..."

Monroe: "We're here!"

Huston: "Cut. Not till after he says 'Roslyn' three times, dear. Action."

Gable: "Roslyn ... Roslyn ... Roslyn ..."

Monroe: "We're here!"
Huston: "Cut. The line is "Here we are!' dear. Action."
Gable: "Roslyn ... Roslyn ..."
Monroe: "Here we are!"
Huston: "Cut. After the third Roslyn, dear. Action."
Gable: "Roslyn ... Roslyn ... Roslyn ..."
Monroe: "Here we are!"
Huston: "Fine."

Marilyn tried to explain to Miller earlier in the production that it didn't make any difference whether she scrambled a line or not as long as the meaning was there. "The life in the scene is to be considered too," she said. "The writer has done the words, then it's up to the actor. It's like Jack Cole (choreographer); he'll teach me the steps and then he'll say, 'forget the steps, do it.' I can't work unprepared. I'd sooner shoot myself. But I can't memorize the words by themselves. I have to memorize the feeling.... Lee has told me you can have conscious preparation, but you must have unconscious results. He always said two and two don't necessarily make four...."

The scene then called for Gable to climb to the top of a car just outside the bar and call his children, who have disappeared in the crowd. Then he falls drunkenly, with Marilyn gasping, her hand to her mouth, from the car to the pavement. His persuasive drunkenness, his naïve eagerness to show Roslyn his children, and his forlorn distress when he cannot, were possibly the finest moments in Gable's acting career. His pregnant wife, Kay, sat near Huston, radiant to see him at the top of his form. The entire company applauded as Gable picked himself up from the crowded pavement. The actor was visibly pleased by the reaction and probably surprised. A few years had passed since he last had a role that made any demands upon his acting talents.

On September 14, the company passed what had been the original completion date for the film. They now hoped to finish by October 15, although shooting would not be completed until November 4. The filming took ninety days. The production was half a million dollars over budget; the most expensive black and white movie ever made.

Three days later, they were filming an exterior scene during which Gay discovers in the morning that someone has trampled the heliotropes that he and Roslyn have planted during their weeks as lovers in Guido's house. Marilyn arrived at least an hour earlier than usual that morning, saying she had enjoyed six consecutive hours of sleep, but after the lunch break, she failed to reappear for hours and the company was scattered over the front lawn, attempting to relax. In a Magnum photo, Huston is seen asleep on the grass, his right hand clasped about the dog Tom Dooley's head; Montgomery Clift dozing a few feet away; and Miller, in a valiant effort to seem composed, in a recumbent position in the background.

Gable had ambivalent feelings about Marilyn. He said later that she was "completely feminine, without guile ... with a million sides to her". He also told a writer that in the old days of Jean Harlow, a star would be fired for being late all the time. Apparently, he never showed Marilyn his very real impatience with her lateness and only his wife knew how he really felt.

First assistant director Tom Shaw several weeks later was so overwrought by her failure to appear that he resorted to a dramatic gesture. This is how he described it to his superiors in the company, "I got down on my hands and knees and begged in back of the saloon." When Huston and Frank Taylor suggested that Miller was as concerned as they about the overtime and that he would get Marilyn before the cameras, Shaw replied, "She'll say that she'll be there, but you have to follow past history."

Production manager Doc Erickson expressed his fears concerning Gable, "He told me, 'I don't care what call you give me after this, I'll be here at 10.30.' "

The simple truth was that while Marilyn was now able to finish the film, it would still have to be done on her terms, shooting around her when she felt indisposed.

Occasionally, it was not her failure to show that was disruptive. Her resentment of Miller made nearly everyone in his "camp" on the alert to any slight or hostility from Marilyn. When Marilyn became convinced that script supervisor Angela Allen was having an affair with Miller because he was increasingly in conference with her (as revisions of work shot earlier were required), one of Miller's friends heard about it and kidded Angela, "I hear you're Arthur's girl-friend now. Are you enjoying it?" Angela suggested that a message be relayed to Marilyn informing her that if she knew that much, then Marilyn must surely also know how much she was enjoying it. A week before they left the Nevada location and shortly after this incident, Angela tossed her script into the air and declared she was quitting. "I try to be sweet, calm, and gentle," she complained, "but it never lasts very long. It all depends on the people you're with." Two days later she was back at work following a long, conciliatory talk with Huston.

Marilyn had lost some weight in the hospital; it was discovered that she looked more beautiful thinner. When Marilyn saw the first rushes, she was delighted. She told Paula, "Someone ought to shoot me if I ever put on weight again."

Marilyn *did* seem renewed in some indefinable way. Although she treated Miller and Eli Wallach with almost total disregard, with others she was sportive, laughing a great deal. She seemed alive to her surroundings.

She rediscovered nearby Virginia City, where she had once gone with Fred Karger and which was now a bustling tourist-crowded "ghost town". As September moved on towards October, the tourists thinned out, and Marilyn loved the place. She spent part of the day visiting the Chollar Mansion with its Victorian antiques and was impressed by the obvious wealth enjoyed by the Comstock miners. "And here I thought they were hard-off pioneers," she remarked to her companion, Ralph Roberts.

In Virginia City, Roberts took Marilyn to the Country Inn, Edith Palmer's exclusive dining-room on the topmost ridge of the town. Marilyn found its monastic quality appealing. The main dining-room was womb-like and windowless, sunken one or two steps from street level, its high rough stone walls having once contained a wine-cellar. "This is my oasis in the desert," Marilyn said, much to Edith Palmer's joy. From then on, she managed to come up Sun Mountain to the Inn at least twice a week for dinner. In between times, Edith prepared hampers of food to be sent out to Pyramid Lake or over to Dayton, wherever Marilyn was shooting that day.

The breakfast scene with Gable and Marilyn came off so well that those who had begun to feel that *The Misfits* might bring Gable another Academy Award began seriously discussing Marilyn as a contender. "You like me Hunh?" was said with such simplicity and yet with an implication of so much more that Huston embraced Marilyn after the shot. A photographer recorded the embrace when they repeated it for him. When Marilyn was shown this friendly pose with Huston a few days later, some of her old mistrust asserted itself. "Save this picture," she told one of her staff. "I want to have it to show around when he begins saying things about me." Her ego and feelings bruised by Preminger and Wilder, she couldn't believe that a director might carry away a warm feeling for her.

Just prior to this scene, Huston had shot a bedroom scene with Roslyn waking in the morning to find Gay looking down on her with awe and great tenderness. She raises slightly and we see that she is nude. In the best take, Marilyn's breasts were exposed for a moment and Frank Taylor felt strongly that it should be retained. They had already lost hope of getting a seal from the Motion Picture Association, which had insisted upon having the script rewritten so that the illicit love relationships shown would be made to seem wrong and not permissible, that the ending would no longer "glorify" such illicit sex, that Roslyn's somewhat light treatment of marriage when divorced should be eliminated as well as the excessive swearing – words such as "hell", "damn", "bastard", and "sumbitches" – which bothered Geoffrey Sherlock of the Association particularly. Marilyn told Miller and Taylor, "Let's get the people away from the television sets. I love to do things the censors won't pass. After all, what are we all here for, just to stand around and let it pass us by? Gradually they'll let down the censorship – sadly probably not in my lifetime."

Huston opposed this viewpoint. "Fine," he said. "I've always known that girls have breasts." Huston's view prevailed, except in the European cut of the film where the shot was retained.

Marilyn's evenings and Sundays off were now spent in the company of those she trusted. Much of the time she would retire early, often just after dinner. Except for her work on the film, her public appearances with Miller were practically eliminated, although she induced him to move with her from the Mapes Hotel to the Holiday Inn Motel. She said she wanted a change, but it is likely that some company criticism of her treatment of Miller, which ranged from silent, bare tolerance to naked hostility, had got through to her and she was sensitive about it.

One of her inner circle, perhaps concerned that Marilyn's tensions might incapacitate her again, proposed that they run down to San Francisco or over to Lake Tahoe on the weekend. Marilyn thought it was a fine idea, and a group of them drove down to the Bay city in two cars, including her white Cadillac. Monty Clift came along with his make-up man and companion, Frank LaRue. There was also Agnes Flanagan and her husband, Ralph Roberts, and Whitey Snyder. It was about the most congenial group imaginable to Marilyn.

On the way down, Marilyn asked to stop at Lake Tahoe away from its gambling area and a few miles shy of the crowds. While the others waited, she ran several hundred feet into a resort area on the lake shore. Apparently she had been there before, probably with DiMaggio.

It seemed evident that she had known some happiness there, for she lingered in front of the largest of the guest cottages. Smoke curled from its huge chimney. There was someone inside. As she began moving back towards her car, a youth appeared on the porch deck and then called to his family. Marilyn had nearly reached her Cadillac by the time several other surprised vacationers had joined the boy on the porch.

Finocchio's in San Francisco is one of the few tourist attractions of that city of special interest to show folk. It features some of the best female impersonators in the business. Marilyn had expressed an interest in seeing the show when others of *The Misfits* company came back talking about the place. Now it had been rumoured that one of the boys was impersonating her. She had seen and laughed at Edie Adams, a good friend, in her celebrated parody of Marilyn, but the *Finocchio* act was something special she would go out of her way to see.

Everyone in her party was a little tense as they took their ringside table at the nightclub. Snyder was frankly apprehensive and kept reminding Marilyn that she should keep in mind that it was all in fun. And then the breathless moment arrived. The man was gussetted in a skin-tight sequined gown, a wind-blown platinum wig on his head. The resemblance was uncanny. Roberts observed Marilyn's eyes widening in recognition, and then she grinned. Her mimic was undulating his lips in the familiar insecure smile and cupping his breasts, taking little steps around the floor, wriggling his rear.

"You're all terribly sweet," the mimic said in a little-girl voice. Marilyn put her hand to her mouth. "I love you all!" the man was saying as he began to point at the men in the audience in turn. "You . . . and you . . ."

While Marilyn might have worn her black wig and tried to control the fits of girlish laughter that would give her away, this night she had not wanted anonymity. She had told the others she might leave them later on and wander down to Fisherman's Wharf to visit DiMaggio's Restaurant and then perhaps Lefty O'Doul's. Neither establishment would find a Marilyn incognito especially amusing.

The mimic, discovering his model, could not avoid playing to her. There was a rising buzz of whispers around them as the audience saw the rapt and smiling original. Regretfully, Marilyn suggested they leave. The impersonator rushed to finish his turn. It was a short one anyway. No one could sustain such a parody for very long. As Marilyn and her friends were leaving, the man, blowing kisses to the audience and then to Marilyn, removed his silvery wig.

CHAPTER THREE

In October, near the windup of *The Misfits* at its Nevada location, a celebration was planned. Originally it was to have been a birthday party for Frank LaRue, Montogomery Clift's make-up man, but that was nearly forgotten in the need for some release from the tensions that had reached almost unendurable levels during the past weeks.

Paula Strasberg planned the party. She went up to Edith Palmer's Country Inn and conferred with the owner about details. Miller was specifically not invited. This decision did not disturb Paula at all, nor did it cause any comment from anyone else. It was understood by everyone in the company that the Millers were barely on speaking terms. The two camps were clearly defined now, and Paula obviously relished the conspiratorial air about it all. None of her enemies was present, and she was very gay that evening.

It is possible that Paula had invited Huston, but if so, he made his excuses, sensing he was squarely in the middle of the schism that divided his company. According to some of the company, the final rupture grew out of Miller's wish to revise the script, developing the secondary relationship of Roslyn and Guido into something of an affair. This *conspiracy*, as Marilyn and Paula branded it, had already destroyed a five-year friendship between Marilyn and Wallach. Although some of the company attributed this break to an alleged attempt on Wallach's part to upstage Marilyn in a Lindy dance sequence by keeping her face turned from the camera, this appears to be questionable in the light of Marilyn's own words on the matter. "The audience is going to find my rear more interesting than Eli's face anyhow."

The most probable reason for Marilyn's coolness to Wallach was his closeness to Miller, Huston, and Taylor. Two months earlier, Marilyn and Wallach exchanged smiles and Marilyn told him, "Eli, you're going to be working all your life." She spoke with a sweet tenderness as though she knew that was both inevitable and what he wanted. Now, unless they were on the set involved in a scene together, she didn't speak at all.

On this October night, an autumn thunderstorm had made the drive over to Virginia City a trial instead of a pleasure, but all the guests had made it. Gable dropped by in the early part of the evening to pay his respects to Paula and Marilyn. He had one drink with the group to make his visit official. "I hope," he said jokingly, "I'm welcome in this den of undercover agents." Then he kissed Marilyn and left in his silver Mercedes special.

The seating arrangements were such that an outsider might think that Paula was a dowager giving a banquet for her débutante daughter. They were seated in the middle of the longest communal table. Paula sat between the guest of honour, Frank LaRue, and Clift. Marilyn sat on the other side of Clift, who was quietly getting very drunk on vodka. He and Marilyn were in frequent huddles from which squeaks of Marilyn's muffled laughter could be heard.

The banquet room looked terribly autumnal, in tune with the personalities of most of those in the room. An exception might have been Whitey Snyder, whose Irish insouciance and stability created at least the illusion of verdant health. He lifted his tumbler of vodka and drank more than half of it. Marilyn watched, impressed. "I'm beginning to understand why the old-timers drank so much," Whitey said, and then laughed. "There wasn't anything else to do, stuck up here in the hills."

Everyone was getting a little high, but it was a happy high.

The causes of their tensions were outside, about twenty miles away in Reno.

When the party broke up around two-thirty in the morning, the rain had stopped, but fog had rolled into the hills, obscuring even the cars parked along the high, narrow street. Virginia City below them seemed to have vanished.

On October 17, a few days after the Country Inn festivities, the more democratic opposite camp threw a surprise birthday party for both Miller and Clift to which Marilyn and her chauffeur, Rudi Kautzky, at least were invited. Marilyn surprisingly accepted, the last social occasion of her life with Miller.

Chief cameraman Russell Metty primed himself with a few drinks and then addressed the assembly over the dining table: "Arthur writes scripts," he told them, "and John shoots ducks. First Arthur screwed up the script and now his wife is screwing it up. Why don't you wish him a happy birthday, Marilyn? . . . This is truly the biggest bunch of misfits I ever saw."

The party was held at the Christmas Tree Inn outside Reno, which had an adjoining casino. When the dinner group broke, they all went into the casino to shoot craps. Marilyn picked up the dice and asked Huston, "What should I ask the dice for, John?" Huston told her, "Don't think, honey, just throw. That's the story of your life. Don't think, do it."

On October 24, the company reassembled on Stage 2 at the old Paramount Studios in Hollywood. Because of Marilyn, a twelve-to-six shooting schedule was approved by the craft unions and shooting began in the afternoon. Marilyn lost her trusted friend and make-up man, Whitey Snyder, to a new film, but the rest of her court was intact.

At this time, a rough cut of the film was assembled for Huston, Taylor, and selected friends, including Huston's mother, Nan. She thought it was beautiful. "She [Marilyn] understands it," she told them, and Frank Taylor attempted to explain Marilyn's grasp of the film by saying, "It's a spiritual autobiography. This is who she is. This is why life is so painful for her and always will be . . ."

Considerable credit was due and given Paula Strasberg for her help to Marilyn. Huston was to say that without Paula, the picture would have simply fallen apart. Paula herself said,

"I feel that I have contributed to every frame of *The Misfits*. If it doesn't work out, that's something I must share with her. My work is not a mystery. This is my twenty-fourth picture. My work is evident on the screen."

But when the final process scenes had been intercut into the film and it was shown to Max Youngstein, head production man with United Artists, who was financing and distributing the picture, he told Frank Taylor he was disappointed, that somehow the conflict among the people in the drama had disappeared. He said that he didn't see the fine hand of John Huston in any of it. Miller, shaken by two seasons of hard work under the most trying conditions, at first agreed with Youngstein.

Taylor explained to Youngstein that his role as producer had always been indirect and that Huston and Miller had spent long days working together without interference. He had stayed in the background, listening to each in turn, and acting as arbiter. He said that having been a book publisher for over twenty years, he had a respect for creative genius and there was a lot of it in *The Misfits* company. He stated as his principle that while not tolerating any technical inadequacy, with creative artists he would go to the wall in order to ensure their free expression.

In recoiling from the shock, Huston was to blame Miller. "These things are not in the script," he complained. Miller, sorely tried, sat down alone in his new suite of rooms at the Sunset Towers West where he had fled after his final argument with Marilyn. He began rewriting the scenes that had seemed thematically confusing.

Ralph Roberts has said he was with Marilyn at the time of her showdown with Miller. It was the culmination of months of recrimination, suspicion, and mistrust. The film was nearly completed. There was no longer any need, as she saw it, for any face-saving, and she told him to get out.

Frank Taylor and his aide, Edward Parone, came to the Millers' Beverly Hills Hotel suite to help Miller move out. When they got there, secretary May Reis was already far along in getting his things together. They carted them down the hall and out to a waiting station wagon as inconspicuously as thieves. They were on their guard to avoid being seen by any bellboys since these staff members were often paid outrageous sums by the Hollywood columnists for exclusive news items.

Marilyn used the delay while revisions were mulled over to pose for a day for photographer Eve Arnold of Magnum. The two women had enjoyed some rapport during the shooting of the movie and it was a memorable session. The draped and undraped (a sheet covered her censorable parts) shots were a close, collaborative effort, and Marilyn's figure was yet magnificent. A year and a half later, shortly before Marilyn's thirty-sixth birthday, they had another session, and Marilyn declined to wear some well-designed garments especially selected for the photography, but wore instead a filmy, revealing black negligée. "She had lost the contours of a young woman by then," Miss Arnold recalled. "But she refused to acknowledge her body was becoming mature. She insisted that she could measure up to the kind of nudity or semi-nudity that was being printed in *Playboy* and similar magazines. Her blindness to her physical change was almost tragic."

Four of her inner circle accompanied Marilyn to the last *Misfits* photographic session: a make-up man, a body make-up lady, May Reis, and the press agent she had disliked on *Bus Stop*, Patricia Newcomb. Rupert Allan, who had handled her press relations throughout the location, had been offered a lucrative assignment elsewhere and had asked Marilyn to be relieved. "I'll stay though, if it matters that much to you," he told her. But it hadn't mattered. In fact, little did matter to Marilyn at that time. Allan recommended Pat Newcomb, and the question seemed to be settled.

It would be interesting to know exactly how Marilyn had changed in the four and a half years following *Bus Stop* to enable her to accept Miss Newcomb. In her, Marilyn would find not only a trusted press agent, but more important, a close friend.

Pat Newcomb had lived alone most of her adult life except for a brief interlude during an unsuccessful marriage. In a different way, she was as complex as Marilyn, and yet she had learned to cope. With a disarming diffidence that masked a toughness which would always see her through a crisis, she went out to meet people. She was convinced that through osmosis or persuasion, Marilyn likewise could begin to live non-combatively with herself. In time she would build a rather secure protective screening around her client that was almost impenetrable.

The crucial scene Miller felt was necessary after the agonizing reappraisal of the rough cut of the film was to be shot in Isabel's Reno home (for which the Reno USO building had been used). Steven Grimes scouted the entire Hollywood area searching for a replica, but before any work could be done at reconstruction, the scene was cancelled. Clark Gable had read the additional scene and turned it down cold. He was the only member of the cast to have script approval and he said he liked the film as it stood. He would not appear for another ten seconds of new shooting.

There was considerable rejoicing in Marilyn's camp the day word reached them that Gable had rebelled. Paula apparently had delayed giving Marilyn the revision for some hours in fear she would be upset, and when she did read the scene, she became hysterical. The scene, in which Guido clearly demonstrated he was an ex-lover of Roslyn's, made her out as a kind of tramp, she believed. This threw the entire film out of key, she told Paula.

Miller had to agree with her. He said he was grateful to Gable for rejecting the scene. "Why should we suddenly become literal?" he asked. "I remember a man saying after *Death of a Salesman*, 'Why didn't Willy Loman go to the Household Finance Corporation and solve all of his problems?' "

When Gable and Marilyn did a retake of the fadeout scene in the station wagon as it moves through the Nevada wasteland, Huston said "Print it" on the first take. The film was over, and so in a very real sense was Marilyn's career. *The Misfits* had been produced in an atmosphere of some affection. When the affection ran out, there still remained a tolerance for Marilyn's difficulties. She would never again find such a measure of forbearance among professional movie people.

CHAPTER FOUR

On November 16, the King was dead. Although Gable had been gravely ill from a massive heart attack he had suffered the day after the picture was completed, everyone thought he would improve. But after a day of cheerful banter with his wife, Kay, the end had come.

Marilyn had flown to New York a week earlier with May

Reis and Pat Newcomb. Reporters got through to her at her
57th Street apartment around two in the morning. She was
finding sleep as elusive as ever and was awake when the first
call came. The reporter said she became hysterical and was
incoherent. After several other calls she found it more and
more difficult either to accept the grim news or to make any
intelligent comment. She phoned Rupert Allan. "What can I
tell them?" she wanted to know.

"Tell them the simple truth," Allan suggested. "*You're sorry*.
Nothing you can say will alter the fact of Clark's death."

"But Kay and the baby!" she said, and began sobbing.

After she had finished talking with Allan, Marilyn took the
phone off the hook and muffled it in a towel. It was a long
night. She was to say later that living alone was "like being
stag at a party". She had needed someone that night.

The morning after Gable's death, she decided to call the
Associated Press. "This is Marilyn," she told the man on the
line. "I'm sorry I couldn't talk last night. All I can say about
Clark is *I'm very sorry*."

The day of Gable's funeral, Marilyn tried courageously not
to think about it. She had realized from the beginning that it
would be unwise to attend. If few in the company of *The Misfits* could understand the rare and precious rapport between
Gable and herself, she knew that the public's failure to understand would be even greater once she appeared in the funeral
chapel. She might not even be able to bear the strain, and collapse. How to explain a misadventure like that? It would be
unfair to Gable and to herself as well.

A week earlier, on Armistice Day, she had officially broken
with Miller. Pat Newcomb met with reporters gathered in
the lobby of Marilyn's apartment building and announced the
news, but said the matter was not yet in a lawyer's hands.
Miller, when reached at the Chelsea Hotel, was more candid
with the press, saying there was little chance of a reconciliation. One of his closest friends, Jim Procter, a public-relations
man, was more specific, "Marilyn is not just a star, she is an
institution and must constantly be in the centre of excitement
and activity. The nature of Miller's work requires him to be
frequently alone and away from the stresses of show business."
This was only a surface truth. Marilyn had by now withdrawn
much further from public exposure than Miller. Her all-

pervading insecurity, which affected most of her personal relationships, now caused the end of many of those even remotely connected with Miller. Once a relationship ended she
almost never reversed her decision. From this time onwards,
when she could no longer draw on Miller's energies and
strength, her own seemed to sag. And she was close to being
physically ill.

Partially through her reliance upon Pat Newcomb to keep
reporters at a safe distance, and partially through the help of
sedatives, Marilyn retained enough control to enable her to
function. Sometimes during that week she had had the courage to open the door to Miller's study to see if he had been
there or had sent anyone to pick up his manuscripts and
books. The room had been cleaned of everything portable, his
typewriter, his papers. But he had left her portrait on the wall,
an 18 x 24 enlargement of a studio photo taken by Milton
Greene when they were in London. She felt the empty room
was an outrage, for this room had simply meant her faith in
Miller as a writer. It had been a gift of love and now her image
stared back at her, perhaps mocking her intention.

She confided to a friend later in the day that she was certain
this was an act of vengeance on Miller's part. But following
her divorce some weeks later, she had modified her stand
about this act of Miller's. She drove up to Roxbury in a station
wagon with Ralph Roberts and her half-sister Berneice, who
had come to New York for a brief visit. In Miller's words:
"She came up to the farm to get some things. It was a difficult
meeting. She was obviously so lost and yet she was trying to
put a new face on things and make me believe that she was
happy, carefree, the way she wanted to be. I think she was
trying to go back to her girlhood and yet she couldn't. She
was trying to surround herself with gaiety but it wasn't working."

She loaded up the wagon with only her choicest possessions,
the books she had collected, several pieces of sculpture, the
set of bone china, the colourful cocktail glasses. She left behind a dozen jelly glasses for Miller, saying, "They're good
enough to drink out of," although she later regretted having
left Hugo, their basset-hound, behind. She had been tempted
to take him, but she was afraid that Miller might miss him
and call her up about him – she wanted the break to be final
– and she knew the dog was happier in the country.

Marilyn's brief visits with DiMaggio on the West Coast and their meetings in New York must have been unsettling for him. Her fearful weariness must have touched him. But Di-Maggio was not a husband, and he clearly wanted to remain her friend, perhaps the only one besides May Reis in whom she had complete faith. They were now the reliables, the constants, in a world of shifting ground, and neither of them ever challenged what she was doing with her life or her dependency upon hangers-on of the moment. Still, DiMaggio was *there*, available at the other end of the telephone line, and this was surely one of the sturdiest props for Marilyn during that difficult week.

CHAPTER FIVE

At this time, Marilyn had a new will drawn up – the last of a long and revealing series. For the first time since she had left the family intimacy she had known at the Goddards' and Aunt Ana Lower's she began thinking of her own family ties, distant though they had become. Her half-sister, Berneice, in Florida, was first in the line of heirs. Marilyn had only seen Berneice herself a dozen times but these occasions included one reunion on the farm in Connecticut that had been especially congenial and "family like", and when she had gone to visit DiMaggio at Fort Lauderdale they had seen one another briefly. Putting Berneice ahead of all others took some of the edge off her acute sense of having no real family to remember.

And May Reis was equally remembered. She was the only one on this earth who left her alone, never was overly solicitous, never asked questions. Marilyn no longer thought of May as just her secretary, although she performed this task with energy and dispatch. She was the kind of mother Marilyn had always sought. *There*, but not involving herself in Marilyn's problems and affairs; her opinion, at those times when it was sought, carried far more weight than that of others.

Finally, after other bequests had been taken care of, she wanted Lee Strasberg to have whatever remained. She found in him the father she had pursued as a phantom. But in Strasberg he was embodied as solid, reachable. Perhaps most importantly, he believed, *as she never dared*, that her talent was something rare.

During the Christmas holidays she called Aaron Frosch, the attorney who would act as her executor, to add as a further bequest to Strasberg all of her personal belongings, and as January progressed, she called Frosch from time to time to add or delete a bequest. She decided not to mention Paula. Her feelings about her were now ambivalent. She felt she had given Paula a great deal in a material sense. There had been a considerable amount of A. T. & T. stock, extensive loans whenever Paula needed extra money, and, of course, Marilyn was responsible for Paula's $3,000-a-week salary whenever a film was in production.

To those closest to Marilyn, it seemed she had become more preoccupied with her will than with the everyday business of living. She became fretful, even irritable, over trivial incidents.

In mid-January 1961, Marilyn spent an hour with her attorneys to have the finished document read to her. Some of the legal language was translated by Frosch at her request. They discussed the income expected from *The Misfits*, which had just opened in general release across the country. Marilyn had been paid $300,000 for the picture. Owning a 10 per cent in it, she was now counting heavily on its success. What critical word had come in by that time was generally good. The quality of the script was being praised, as well as that of the performances.

As winter deepened, Marilyn became increasingly reliant upon Pat Newcomb. It was at Paula Strasberg's suggestion that Pat had accompanied Marilyn back to New York to announce her separation from Miller, but it was becoming evident to Pat that her job was not to end there. An uneasy relationship had developed between the two women – uneasy because they shared an ability to antagonize others, often without meaning to. Part of Pat's difficulties with long-time friends of Marilyn's arose from her over-protectiveness. Even Rupert Allan, who had recommended her for the job, attempted during this period to get hold of Marilyn, and Pat asked him what it was he wished to discuss with her. Rather angrily he told Pat, "That's a private matter between Marilyn and myself."

There were others equally protective, but not on a day-in-day-out basis. Frank Sinatra, who dated Marilyn occasionally, was always kept informed of her well-being, both physical and emotional. He saw Marilyn over a period of several days and commiserated with her over the loss of Hugo's custody. Before he left New York, he sent around a small white poodle to her apartment. There had been a running gag between Sinatra and Marilyn about his alleged friends in the Mafia, so the poodle was promptly dubbed by her a member of this underworld syndicate with mock gravity and known from then on as "Maf".

None of the old props seemed to be working. Paula's ministrations no longer helped, and Marilyn now seldom crossed the park to that book-lined sanctuary where she once had felt so comfortable, surrounded by intelligent, sensitive people. Instead, she was gradually slipping into a narcotic haze – a world without pain, but also without meaning.

She made no effort to conceal her pill ritual from those around her. Mornings, she quite deliberately and with a practised gesture pricked the pain-killing capsule with a straight pin to speed the pill's effect. Later in the day, as she became more withdrawn and her faculties slowed, she dispensed with this step. Perhaps she sensed that by then endurance was more vital than speed.

Pat made an effort to shake her free from this cycle. She took Marilyn for rides on the Staten Island ferry and shared hot dogs, which Marilyn loved. When Marilyn seemed overly fascinated by the murky depths of the New York Harbour, Pat would move close enough to reach out in case of emergency.

Pat took a great many of Marilyn's calls but she also insisted that they be returned when Marilyn was able to do so. José Ferrer phoned on one occasion, and when Marilyn did not seem in any hurry to return the call Pat pointed out that Ferrer might be a little despondent about his own career, which had entered a temporary decline. Marilyn hastened to get in touch.

Pat was undeniably a skilful press representative in film work. She had got her start with Arthur Jacobs six years earlier in Hollywood after her graduation from Mills College. Although there was some shyness in her manner, she seemed to enjoy being with groups of people she liked – small dinner parties were her element. She had lived in Los Angeles during World War II when her father was appointed a Judge Advocate General for the Pacific area.

On January 20, 1961, Marilyn and her lawyer Aaron Frosch, with Pat Newcomb, flew to Juarez, Mexico. The plane made one stop at Dallas. It was Kennedy's Inauguration Day, a date selected in advance for Marilyn's divorce from Miller by Pat and John Springer. The headlines, they were confident, would all be the President's the next day.

During the two-hour layover in Dallas, Marilyn, who had been the new President's admirer ever since the Stevenson boom had collapsed during the 1960 convention, and her party adjourned to a cocktail lounge in the terminal building to follow the ceremonies on television.

It was not easy for Marilyn to keep even a semblance of good humour at the Mexican airport where she and her companions were cornered by several dozen reporters, some representing magazines or newspapers as far away as Paris and Rome. The press was convinced there was another man in Marilyn's life, probably Yves Montand, and was determined to get some confirmation from her. Finally she broke free to a waiting limousine while Pat, stonily replying to the frantic newspapermen with little or nothing they could use, acted as buffer.

The divorce was painless. It was a time of rejection. But the loneliness of the life suddenly stretching before her must have been terrifying. Given Marilyn's acute mistrust of people and her near total dependency upon those for whom she was a meal ticket, this isolation was disastrous.

Marilyn knew not to be aware that it was important to her staff that she continue to work in films. She might confide in her hirelings, but it was difficult to lean upon them. Nevertheless, she was surrounded by them and at least one volunteered to help sustain her through this crisis. Pat Newcomb, who was handiest, realized that backing up Marilyn would be a full-time job, so she arranged for her press work to be largely taken over by soft-spoken, diminutive John Springer, the New York partner of Jacobs and Springer. In the main his assignment was to keep publicity to a minimum, and he was a man of tact and patience, with an innate sense of how much the world should know about any client of his.

As Marilyn's ability to function collapsed further under the weight of the sedatives she was taking, Dr. Marianne Kris suggested that she enter the Payne-Whitney Clinic, a New York institution concerned mainly with mental and nervous disorders.

Marilyn was not told that she was being taken to a section of the Clinic that housed the mentally ill. She agreed that she needed hospital care, however, and went inside with Dr. Kris. As they proceeded through the hospital, iron doors slid open and then slammed shut behind them. Marilyn was frightened by the security arrangements. Before she was even taken to her room, she looked around a little wild-eyed. *"What are you doing to me?"* she asked. *"What kind of a place is this?"*

Admission was completed and Marilyn, under the name of Faye Miller, found herself in a room barren of any of the comforts which had made her previous hospital stays something of a respite from the limelight. The windows were barred, the door opening on to the corridor had a transparent glass pane so that the patrolling nurses could glance inside as a precautionary measure. Marilyn was convinced that the aides, doctors, and nurses never failed to stare at her as they went by, a sort of caged celebrity and an interesting distraction from their routine. There is some talk about the form of Marilyn's rebelliousness in the Clinic. One persistent rumour was that once she tore off her hospital gown to give the curious attendants something *really* to stare at. Whatever she did, she told Pat Newcomb that if they were going to treat her like a nut, she would behave like one.

Within two days, Marilyn degenerated from a state of high nervous tension to hysteria. What she had hoped might be her salvation had turned into a nightmare.

John Springer was besieged by reporters from everywhere demanding to know the precise nature of her "mental illness". He first professed ignorance that Payne-Whitney specialized in psychiatric problems, but few accepted his prepared story which insisted Marilyn had been troubled only by a persistent cough. Later that same day he decided that only a fairly straightforward account could scuttle the bizarre rumours appearing in the press. His new statement informed newsmen that "Marilyn was admitted for a period of rest and recuperation following a very arduous year in which she completed two films and had to face marital problems. . . . It is expected her stay will not be prolonged."

Reporters kept a constant vigil in front of the Payne-Whitney Clinic. At least once they were able to corner one of the doctors in charge. "Is is true she's under restraint?" one of them asked. And another: "What happened in her apartment? Is she coherent?"

The doctor anticipated this insensitive bombardment and was prepared with answers. He told them she was not under restraint. "Nothing happened in her apartment," he told them, "except that she decided to enter the hospital. And she is completely rational, here of her own free choice." But the speculation, much of it absurd, continued in the world press.

Miller, who had tried to persuade himself that Marilyn was a closed chapter in his life, heard and read the many stories about her condition and phoned Nan Taylor late one night. "I've thought a lot about it," he told her, "and she doesn't seem to have anyone around who means anything to her. I feel I should make contact and see what I can do."

Mrs. Taylor suggested to Miller as kindly as she could that he stay out of it, that he was no longer a part of her life and must accept it.

John Springer's prediction that her stay at Payne-Whitney would be brief proved to be accurate. After three days of alternating fits of hysteria and despondency as she gazed through the glass pane towards the busy corridor and then back to the dismal barred room with its doorless toilet (another precaution), Marilyn finally was able to make one call, the first allowed her in three days. She called DiMaggio for help.

DiMaggio, already settled at his Yankee Clipper Motel in Fort Lauderdale, assured Marilyn that he would fly to New York that evening and do all he could. It would not be easy.

But Joe DiMaggio was still a power of considerable force in New York. He made a number of calls bringing influence and pressure to bear on the hospital. Early the next morning, Marilyn emerged secretly from the Clinic, clutching tenaciously to DiMaggio.

The arrangement for the change of hospitals had been made swiftly through DiMaggio's intervention. She went at once to a private room in the Neurological Institute, a unit of Columbia-Presbyterian Hospital. There was so little advance word that reporters overran the Payne-Whitney Clinic in confusion. Some were convinced she was being concealed on the premises. Others were equally certain she had gone, but did not know where.

After less than three weeks of rest and withdrawal from the pills, Marilyn felt well enough to ask to be discharged. Pat Newcomb accompanied her back to her apartment – where there was relative peace following the madness of the reporters who surrounded their limousine when she left the hospital – and it seemed for a brief time that she was almost as keen about her life in the city as when she had first arrived to stay back in 1955.

She slowly attempted to pick up the pieces. There were a few interviews when Pat Newcomb felt the writers were sympathetic. Margaret Parton, on the staff of the *Ladies Home Journal*, who had never met Marilyn before, arrived on a Saturday afternoon in mid-March, carrying some knitting in a bag in case Marilyn was true to form, but Pat Newcomb entertained and briefed the lady for an hour before Marilyn appeared. There were to be no questions about the past – "That's all been written to death," Pat told Mrs. Parton. "She's looking forward, not back."

Marilyn was very co-operative with her interviewer when the questions were confined to the limits prescribed. She spoke anew of her plans to do *Rain* on television. "You know," she said, "I had a letter from Somerset Maugham the other day, saying how happy he was that I was going to play the part, and telling me something about the real woman on whom he based the character. I'm really excited about doing the part – she's so interesting. She was a girl who knew how to be gay, even when she was sad. And that's important – you know?"

Mrs. Parton came away with a sense of having met a sick little canary instead of a peacock. "Only when you pick it up in your hand to comfort it . . . beneath the sickness, the weakness and the innocence, you find a strong bone structure, and a heart beating. You *recognize* sickness, and you *find* strength." The lady journalist wrote a most sensitive study of Marilyn at that tremulous moment before Marilyn plunged again into life and commitments, certainly more perceptive than many of the personality profiles Mrs. Parton's magazine had done in the past. When it was submitted to her editors, the Goulds – husband and wife – who ran the magazine for many years, she was informed that it could not be published. Marilyn, they said, emerged as far too sympathetic. Mrs. Parton had obviously been "mesmerized". "If you were a man,"

Mr. Gould told her, "I'd wonder what went on that afternoon in Marilyn's apartment." The sickening reaction, the cynical disbelief, shrouded the article and it remains unpublished to this day.

Marilyn's problems in getting a good press had begun as far back as her alliance with Yves Montand. The situation was perhaps aggravated by a defensive stance on the part of her publicists, who had begun a policy of keeping away all journalists who did not declare their affection and sympathy for Marilyn in advance. The screening process resulted in only a handful of the kind of sensitive articles her publicists were seeking – notably in *Life* and *Redbook* magazines. In this vacuum, numerous accounts were published based upon rumour and hearsay, which unfortunately created an image of a woman incapable of controlling her moods or impulses. With her death, an opposite attitude would occur – first a wringing of journalistic hands, and then the kind of documentation that leads to canonization – carrying with it the same hypocrisy that accompanied the film community's solid support of Joe Schenck when he was sent to prison.

Jeanne Eagels was, for a period of four or five years in the twenties, a major star of the American theatre. A delicate blonde beauty, she had an equally delicate spirit, and she coped with her terrorists by using heroin, an addiction which eventually killed her while still a young woman.

Among her greatest successes was an adaptation of Somerset Maugham's short story, *Rain*, in which she starred as Miss Sadie Thompson. Lee Strasberg had been among the many thousands enthralled by Miss Eagels's masterful portrayal of "Sadie". He had remembered that performance for nearly forty years and pointed out to Marilyn that she shared some of Jeanne Eagels's gossamer qualities.

Certainly Marilyn had become, through successive peelings of protective layers, as exposed as Jeanne Eagels. The possibility that Marilyn was moving towards an identical finale did not seem to occur to Strasberg at the time.

He told Marilyn he felt she would make a fine "Sadie", and recalled for her what he could of that performance in 1922. She became very excited and it was decided this would be an ideal vehicle for her introduction to television.

The National Broadcasting Company had been in touch

with her about doing a special, a ninety-minute programme that would showcase her talents. Negotiations were begun at once with *Rain* as the property, and no one at NBC disagreed with her about Strasberg's "marvellous concept of the whole thing".

Strasberg had never attempted the direction of a television drama, and word came back very soon to Marilyn that he would be unacceptable as director. She balked at this, her first reaction being to withdraw altogether, although she had already signed the contract.

Then a compromise was worked out and the programme was re-scheduled for the Fall of 1961, with taping to be done in the spring, and announcements published. The network was offering the package of Marilyn and *Rain* to a top-echelon director and Lee Strasberg would remain "in artistic control". This, however, was not sufficient.

She had a final conference with a production executive from the National Broadcasting Company about *Rain*. They were having trouble finding a first-class director who would touch the project with Lee Strasberg in artistic control. Every director they contacted wanted complete command of the production. Strasberg, himself a stage director on occasion, understood this and was inclined to give in.

But Marilyn was adamant. Strasberg's vision of the whole thing had intrigued her in the first place. She told the executive she wanted to be released if the impasse remained. "I wanted to do it because of Lee's concept," she said. "If I can't, then there's no point in going into it. It's not that I have any concern about the director or any criticism of the director, but I don't know what his ideas are or will be. I only know what Lee's ideas are, and those are the ideas I want to put into the thing. I don't again want to go into something and then find myself in something totally different from what I expected or what I hoped for."

She asked the man at the network if they could come up with something else. She *did* want to get back to work. What was the point of life now, she reasoned, if she didn't go on working.

Her artistic dependency upon Lee Strasberg was no small sacrifice to her. Not only had she just turned down a six-figure contract to do an evening of television for his sake, but earlier in the year she had advanced Strasberg beween seven and eight thousand dollars for an extensive trip to Japan to study the Japanese theatre.

With the *Rain* production shelved, she felt restless. She accepted an invitation from DiMaggio and went to Fort Lauderdale where the Yankees were in pre-spring training. Skies were sunny, and the change did her more good than she had thought possible. She again made contact with her half-sister Berneice in nearby Gainesville. She and DiMaggio went surf-fishing along the beach. When she grew impatient she flew back to New York.

Back in New York, before she could get deeply involved with her career again, Marilyn read in a newspaper column that Kay Gable purportedly believed that Marilyn had caused her husband's death – that prolonging the picture for weeks had brought on Gable's fatal heart attack from tension and exhaustion.

It was always easy for Marilyn to accept guilt because she had been oddly insensitive to it, but this was more than she could handle. She dropped the newspaper and opened her living-room window as wide as she could and leaned out. Desperation moved her, and it must have been difficult for her to think clearly, but she knew that she had to make up her mind inside the room. If she climbed out on to the ledge, someone below would be certain to recognize her and a spectacle would be made of her efforts to end her life. Possibly death was easier to face than life at that moment. She had told one of her inner group in Hollywood many months earlier, "There is too much pain in living. When they brought me back to life after my suicide attempt, I was very angry. People have no right to make you live when you don't want to."

Marilyn repeated in detail the account of her attempt to leap to death to one of her staff later the same day. She said that she had squeezed her eyes shut at the open window, her fists clenched, trying to summon her courage. She recalled reading somewhere that suicides from heights lose consciousness before they hit the ground. She prayed that it was so. When she looked down, she saw a woman walking along the sidewalk near the building awning. The woman was wearing a brown dress and Marilyn was certain she knew her. She turned away from the window, shaking with frustration.

Word of Marilyn's attempt flew from one friend to the other, and they decided that she should be persuaded to leave the apartment and Marilyn agreed with them. She closed down the apartment temporarily and flew back to Hollywood. The reality of New York – now that Miller was no longer at her side – was more than she could take. She would sooner lose herself in the unreality of Hollywood.

CHAPTER SIX

Hollywood has been called a state of mind or, rather, a mindless state, light on intellectual exercise and long on complacency. But there *is* a colony of thinkers there. Isherwood seems to thrive in it and Huxley died there. There is an even smaller colony of film men of some genius who appear to enjoy the challenge of an industry totally geared to producing films for television or "hard-ticket" spectaculars. This view of the western film capital is not meant to be denigrating. A creative artist can as easily become a panderer in New York as in Hollywood and panderers rarely have a hand in the great films which occasionally come out of Hollywood. Marilyn's decision to return to Hollywood in 1961 must have been prompted by her realization that she had failed in all but one of her efforts in New York – the exception being her close association with the Strasbergs. This relationship was the reason for her retaining the East 57th Street apartment for future trips back East.

Her first weeks back in California were spent as a guest at the Beverly Hills home of Frank Sinatra, who was away at the time. She then moved once again into the Doheny Drive building at the corner of Cynthia and had many of her books shipped West, along with a bust of her poet friend, Carl Sandburg.

To Marilyn, Hollywood was now a vast area of gleaming white doctors' offices, pharmacies, and hamburger palaces. Food was no longer something planned in advance for friends at her apartment or country house: it was caught on the run between visits to her doctor, her analyst, or her drug store.

It would have been helpful if she had returned on a wave of renewed popularity at the box office, but *The Misfits* was now receiving mixed reviews and middling business. Although Marilyn's most adventurous and mature film, it puzzled many. Its reception disappointed her. She could not have known then that it was destined to survive along with her classic *Some Like It Hot* and a handful of other American films to be seen in frequent revival around the world, especially in Europe. Paul V. Beckley, writing in the New York *Herald Tribune,* cheered it as it deserved, for it had emerged as vital and exciting cinema despite its neglect, abuse, and combustibility during production. With considerable insight, Beckley wrote: "There are lines one feels Miss Monroe must have said on her own. ... In this era when sex and violence are so exploited that our sensibilities are in danger of being dulled, here is a film in which both elements are as forceful as in life but never exploited for themselves. Here Miss Monroe is magic but not a living pin-up dangled in skin-tight satin before our eyes. ... And can anyone deny that in this film these performers are at their best? You forget they are performing and feel that they 'are'."

The ghosts of Marilyn's past were not long in making their reappearance. Pat Newcomb had returned with her and settled into a comfortable apartment about ten minutes away from Marilyn's place on Doheny Drive. When she was not by Marilyn's side as her most constant companion, she stayed close to her telephone, alert to any call from her employer. In late summer that year, a call had come in the morning.

"Please, Pat! Come over right away. I've just heard from my father!" Marilyn sounded panicky, gasping between words.

Pat hurried out of her apartment building in Beverly Hills and drove more riskily than she would have preferred along Sunset Boulevard to Doheny Drive. When she entered the first-floor terrace apartment, Marilyn had an envelope in her hand. Inside was an expensive greeting card made of embossed silk. It read: "Best wishes for your early recovery." It was signed: "From the man you tried to see nearly ten years ago. God forgive me."

Marilyn quickly explained to Pat how she had driven to Hemet years ago and wasn't able to get through to her father. "What does it mean?" she asked. "It's all too late."

Pat saw Marilyn was greatly upset so she stayed with her all that day and night. The next morning, nothing was said about the greeting card, which apparently had been sent to Marilyn's hospital in New York and then forwarded.

During the next three weeks, Dr. Hyman Engelberg, Marilyn's Hollywood doctor, supervised a regimen of rest and diet to prepare her for a gall-bladder operation. The operation was scheduled for the end of June in New York.

Perhaps that physical ordeal was helpful. Recovery gave her time to think, to make some plans. She wanted most of all to put some order into her life, to end the drifting course she was following. She decided to enter intensive analysis under Dr. Ralph Greenson. Whatever the consequences, she would begin a new life, and Greenson would help her establish it.

In February of the following year, 1962, Marilyn began searching for a house to buy. She seemed to be making some progress in her analysis and Dr. Greenson had urged her to put down roots somewhere and she had elected Los Angeles County. She found a small but luxurious one-storey "hacienda" in Brentwood. The house was one of two built over thirty years earlier at the end of Fifth Helena Drive. Both houses had ten-foot brick walls surrounding their fronts and, because they were on a dead-end, maximum privacy.

While Marilyn kept her New York apartment, she also kept her New York self and her California self neatly compartmented. There was little crossing over of friends or activities.

In Brentwood, she was seeing DiMaggio regularly. Through an accretion of bravely met but ill adventures she was becoming as solitary as he. Her garden and her home were two of her joys.

The problems of her everyday life were her primary concern now; making movies had taken second place. But scripts piled up in corners of her living-room and study; most of them were read and sometimes deals were discussed.

Not long after she was settled into the new house, Dr. Greenson urged her to take a companion-housekeeper by the name of Eunice Murray. Mrs. Murray was a family friend of the Greensons, had retired from part-time interior decorating work, and though she had never been a housekeeper before, she was available. Mrs. Murray, who spoke in careful accents, was to keep in constant touch with Dr. Greenson. Marilyn knew of this arrangement, but she was so deeply involved with her analysis she did not protest.

As the house was Spanish Colonial, Mrs. Murray suggested that the best way to furnish it was to go to the source. Marilyn agreed, and the first of several buying trips to Mexico was planned.

When they reached Mexico City, Pat Newcomb decided to stay in town and visit with friends there, while Marilyn and Mrs. Murray went to Cuernavaca and nearby towns on the prowl for furniture and decorative pieces. The women made an odd pair. Eunice Murray was tall and matronly. Marilyn was in slacks and a kerchief much of the time, with wrap-around glasses. She wore little make-up and was pleased that most Mexicans did not recognize her.

They found some stiff, heavy, red hand-loomed material. "This would make fine sofa upholstery," Mrs. Murray told Marilyn. The colour appealed to Marilyn, and she bought fifteen yards on her friend's advice. Then tables of a rough trestle variety were purchased and tagged for shipment. Mexican Indian masks of tin were cheap enough to give Marilyn the satisfaction she had found at least one bargain.

When they returned with their receipts and trinkets to the hotel in Mexico City, Marilyn was feted by the movie people of Mexico. She had met Cantinflas in Hollywood, and she was delighted to see him again. At one of these evenings she was introduced to a film writer, José Bolanos. The following day, he called and they had half a dozen dates.

When visiting a Catholic orphanage for Mexican-Indian children, Marilyn decided to begin application at once to adopt one or more of the orphans. The sisters did not appear to take her enthusiasm too seriously, although they humoured her in this good intention.

There was a flurry of activity, decorating the house, when they got back. During this period, Marilyn heard yet another time from her father. She was with Ralph Roberts when the call came through. Roberts had come to give her a message and she had asked him to stay for dinner. Roberts says that while he was broiling steaks on the outdoor grill the phone rang. It was a nurse in Palm Springs Hospital asking to speak to Marilyn. When Marilyn got on, the woman said she was calling for "your father". The nurse spoke in hushed tones, Marilyn told Roberts afterward, and said it seemed likely that her patient, Mr. Gifford, would not survive his heart attack. His condition was grave. One of his strongest desires was to see her. "He keeps talking about it all the time," the woman told Marilyn.

Roberts remembers that Marilyn looked uncertain only for a moment. Then she spoke clearly into the phone: "Tell the gentleman I have never met him. But if he has anything specific to tell me, he can contact my lawyer. Would you like his number?"

The nurse must have been shocked into silence for she declined to take the lawyer's number. Then Marilyn glanced at Roberts as though to say: "You see? I can be tough too, sometimes."

But the call may have upset her more than she let on. She had begun seeing Greenson several times a week and, while it cannot be corroborated, she probably discussed the phone call with her psychiatrist. Roberts and others observed some contrition in her over her rejection of a man she was told was dying – the man she was certain was her real father. She later took the trouble to discover that he had recovered from the attack.

A shooting date in early April had been assigned to her film commitment at Fox, *Something's Got to Give*, and she realized she would have to face her public again. When she was withdrawn, as she had been for sixteen months, she would neglect her hair and seldom even wash her face. But when she was in contact with the public that had made her a star for good or ill, she attempted to revive the image she had kept in obscurity for so long.

Pat Newcomb took a look at Marilyn's wardrobe and told her that there wouldn't be much to choose from when she received a call to go to the studio – or anywhere else. They decided to fly to New York and get Marilyn outfitted.

Marilyn came back to her partially furnished house, after less than a week in her comfortable New York apartment, and rebelled. She wanted the place pulled together. She wouldn't be able to touch it during the twelve weeks or so it would take to do the movie, and "It has to be finished up some way", she said. She knew she would be missing a living-room sofa for some time, as she had taken the Mexican design for it along with her red upholstery material to a New York furniture maker on her trip East.

Mrs. Murray called in her son to help complete things. He

hung the tin masks and helped the electrician put the Mexican lighting fixtures where they would look best. There were practically no closets in the house, all of her extra books, magazines, scripts, records, souvenirs, oddments, had to be piled in corners, mostly in the dressing-room, which was dominated by a floor-to-ceiling mirror she had moved over from the Doheny place. The house finally began to take on a look of comfort, but it never lost its cluttered look.

She was beginning to take great pride in her home, and called friends to ask them when they were coming to see her house. Nearly everyone she knew and was still in touch with was invited to her snug sanctuary at least once; it was the most successful enterprise of her last year of life.

Marilyn had at first shown scant interest in the script of her new film, *Something's Got to Give*. She felt that it was very funny the first time around (some two decades earlier). It told a slightly risqué story about a woman who returns from the "dead" (supposedly drowned in a yachting accident) to discommode her husband, who has remarried. She has spent the intervening five years on a desert island with another man. Nunnally Johnson had attempted to resuscitate the script and Marilyn, with considerable reluctance, consented to do the film to help get her four-picture commitment to the studio out of the way. It would be her third film under the agreement signed in 1956.

Privately she told Whitey Snyder and costumer Margie Plecher, among others, that she had no faith in the script at all. Some news of her off-screen opinion must have reached Nunnally Johnson, for his relations with her cooled before the last-minute revisions in the script were done. She may have remembered, too, what Johnson had said about her sometime after the completion of *How to Marry a Millionaire* (1953): "Marilyn made me lose all sympathy for actresses. In most of her takes she was either fluffing lines or freezing. She didn't bother to learn her lines. I don't think she could act her way out of a paper script. She has no charm, delicacy, or taste. She's just an arrogant little tail switcher who's learned to throw sex in your face." Even Johnson had come to realize the inaccuracy of this remark by 1962, but probably Marilyn had never been able to forget it. It was an unforgettable comment, and barely forgivable.

Marilyn was also uneasy about the new studio head at Fox,

Peter Levathis. Levathis had taken control of Fox production while she was involved with *The Misfits*. She had never heard of him, but it was rumoured that he was hostile to most film stars, a hostility fed by monumental problems at the *Cleopatra* location in Italy. It would be difficult for Marilyn to make her own crises sound meaningful to a man who was fighting an inflationary budget that might well destroy the studio.

When the first call for the film came, Dr. Engelberg was treating her for a virus infection. At the same time, Dr. Greenson was still seeing her several times a week. It would seem clear that he considered her *detachment* from the swirl of activities about her a deepening case of melancholia. She was very much in her doctors' hands and neither believed she would be able to perform for the studio.

But studio pressures mounted, and in mid-April Marilyn appeared, wan and remote, for hair and make-up tests. The following week she came on to the set for her first scenes. Whitey Snyder and Agnes Flanagan saw at once that she was ill. Word reached George Cukor, whom Marilyn had approved as her director.

Cukor is known as a ladies' director. He is gentle and resilient. With Marilyn, he was something more. He was sensitive to her moods and states of health. But as Levathis stormed about making threats (out of earshot of Marilyn, of course) and the film's producer, Henry Weinstein, began to lose his temper, Cukor knew that something had to be done. He could not state this to her baldly, for this would ruin any chance of bringing her through.

Marilyn's co-star, Dean Martin, whom she had personally selected, agreed with Cukor that they should attempt to run on Marilyn's erratic schedule, shooting around her when she was unable to be on the set, and praying that somehow they could get most of the necessary footage on her.

Marilyn knew she was in bad health while on the Fox lot and took her temperature several times a day. An agreement was reached with a studio official that she could go home if it climbed to 103 degrees. It hovered between 100 and 101 degrees.

Well into May, they were still shooting mostly around her; she had been on the set less than six days.

On the weekend of May 18, Marilyn flew to New York. There was no doubt about the risk she was running with her studio after running up approximately a million dollars in excessive costs because of her illness. In New York, Marilyn came out from the lobby of her apartment building to greet May Reis who had come East several days earlier. There was no hint of poor health and Marilyn didn't refer to it. She had been invited by Peter Lawford to sing "Happy Birthday" to President Kennedy at a massive birthday celebration to be held in Madison Square Garden. Aware of her film commitment, no one on the planning committee was sure she would make it. But Marilyn seemed to look upon the honour as equivalent to a Command Performance. She plainly felt that it took precedence over her obligation to Fox.

Producer Henry Weinstein learned of her departure on Friday afternoon. Departure was not the term he would have used: *defection* was more to the point. Although his production of *Something's Got to Give* had been rewritten by Nunnally Johnson as a vehicle for Marilyn, he now began to take definite steps towards discharging her from the film.

Later that afternoon Marilyn was picked up at her apartment by her New York press aide, John Springer, and taken to the Savoy-Plaza. A *Life* writer, Richard Meryman, was waiting at the bar with a lady assistant named Barbara Villet. The quartet sat at a table near the bar, Marilyn sipping absently at a glass of champagne. Meryman explained that they wished to interview Marilyn in depth – how she felt about her marriages, her studio bosses, fame, and life as a legend.

"The legend may become extinct before publication day," Marilyn suggested. "Not the girl, but the legend."

She was instantly reassured, and Mrs. Villet began a rundown on the technical handling of the planned session. Someone said that basing the interview on Marilyn's verbatim answers should shut up the critics who asserted that Marilyn didn't create her own best lines. Marilyn smiled remotely from behind her glass.

They decided on a date for the taping agreeable to all parties to be done at Marilyn's Brentwood home. Interrupting the small talk which concerned the arrangements, Marilyn interposed, "Peter Lawford is upstairs. Why don't we drop in on him? He told me to look him up soon as I got in town."

Having had four or five rounds of drinks, her three companions were immediately agreeable, and the foursome emerged from the elevator on the tenth floor. There was some hesitation as Marilyn wondered in which direction to walk. They followed her to the right down the long corridor. She knocked on the door.

A young man, tanned and athletic, and, as Springer remembers, wearing a hotel towel and little else, opened the door. Marilyn flushed slightly, then smiled in a puzzled way. "We're looking for Mr. Lawford."

This drew a blank and the man kept staring incredulously at Marilyn, saying nothing. "He must be in another room," Marilyn said.

"Ye-s-s," the young man stammered. "He's not here. Not here." His eyes remained fixed on her as she spoke. Marilyn thanked him and he nodded in wonder, closing the door slowly, dazedly. As they turned to go down the hall, Marilyn erupted in a fit of giggles. "He probably thinks he's drunk. He's seeing pink Marilyns."

After they had determined at the desk that Lawford was registered, but out for the evening, Springer suggested that Marilyn join him and his wife for dinner. He knew she had no plans, but Marilyn demurred, saying that she'd had a fairly exhausting day. Often she felt that friends invited her at the last moment out of misplaced kindness, a sort of pity she couldn't abide. And she ate a cold dinner from her refrigerator that night as she had done several thousand other nights since she had become a star.

On the night of Kennedy's birthday celebration, Peter Lawford made an insider's joke about Marilyn's reputation for tardiness and, after having the lighting crew throw a spot on empty space two or three times, he finally introduced her as "the *late* Marilyn Monroe". She was breathy and a little giddy from several glasses of champagne when she began singing as sultrily as she could manage, giving the birthday song a measure of control and professionalism. The rapt audience loved it, and John F. Kennedy, grinning broadly, acknowledged the tribute from Marilyn before making his address to the 17,000 Democrats in the crowded Garden.

Just before the President went on stage, he spoke for a few minutes with Marilyn and her ex-father-in-law, Isidore Miller. Kennedy and Marilyn had met socially some months earlier in New York. The elder Miller, alone of all the family and close friends of Arthur Miller, had kept in close, regular contact with Marilyn. "Marilyn is like my own daughter," he often told anyone who might remotely challenge his attitude, and Marilyn returned his affection by calling him at least once a week and always seeing him whenever she could manage it when in the East.

When Marilyn returned to the coast, she did not report at once to the studio but called attorney Rudin to learn what had happened in her absence. Now her behaviour began to seem more defiant and less dependent upon the state of her physical health, which had considerably improved. Her salary of $100,000 especially galled her, knowing as she did that she was worth many times this and that the studio was taking gross advantage of an old contract. Rudin advised her to continue the picture.

Within the next two weeks, Marilyn managed to appear on the set at least six more days. She even felt well enough to do a nude swimming scene, although actual nudity was not called for in the script and she began the scene wearing a flesh-coloured swimsuit.

Possibly because she was only to simulate nudity, several photographers were given access to the closed set – a swimming-pool (a studio tank) next to a two-storey house from which Dean Martin was supposed to look down upon her with considerable surprise. One of these freelance photographers was Lawrence Schiller, who had been asked by *Paris-Match* to take some shots of Marilyn at work on *Something's Got to Give*. What later became known as "The Nude Session" occurred three days before Marilyn's final appearance on the lot. In exchange for permitting Schiller to shoot freely, he had agreed that Marilyn would have approval of the pictures.

Another photographer, Don Ornitz, was supposed to shoot a series of similar photos for Globe Photos, Inc., but he was ill and Fox had supplied their own stills man, Jimmy Mitchell, to handle the assignment. A colleague of Schiller's, William Reed Woodfield, was going to shoot the same sequence from a different angle.

Director Cukor was using several cameras, a routine arrangement to enable him to choose a cut that would suggest nudity without showing either nipples or the pelvic area. Almost as soon as Marilyn got in the water she complained that she couldn't do the scene in the skin-tight swimsuit. She took off the suit and tossed it out of sight. Then she began doing the dog paddle, the only stroke she knew, she insisted, although she had managed the Australian crawl rather well when she was married to Jim Dougherty.

The photographers were using motorized cameras, Mitchell shooting black and white and Schiller and Woodfield shooting colour. Marilyn seemed to be enjoying herself, Schiller recalls, as if her nudity had no significance. Probably it had none for her. She stood up, enabling the three men to get front exposures. Schiller and Woodfield realized immediately the excitement of what was happening – the first absolutely nude shots of Marilyn Monroe in fourteen years. All three men were crouched low so the splashing water about Marilyn would not obscure what they were after. Excited by what was happening, Schiller told Woodfield, "Look, Billy, you go your way and I'll go mine."

During the lunch break, only the still photographers seemed to know how important the photographs were. Schiller was wound tight as a spring. He knew he could decide where his pictures were to be processed. He felt this was important because Paul Ullmer of the Life Laboratory on Wilshire Boulevard was a man to be relied on. He didn't want to run the risk of a processing lab snipping out transparencies.

What had begun by Marilyn's peeling off a tight swimming costume was beginning to shape up into an event of international interest. No other actress would have discarded her costume before the cameras without prior consultation with her director and possibly her producer, but by this point it was clear to nearly everyone that she simply didn't give a damn about the film. Even Marilyn's first press agent and old friend, Rupert Allan, believed that what motivated her was the desire to get out of the production. Having become a good judge of scripts she knew this one was a loser and proceeded to disrupt its filming as best she could. It is wrong to assume, as several executives at Fox have, that she was very mentally disturbed at the time. No one will deny that she was having problems – and major ones – but in this instance she was reacting in fairly typical fashion to what she considered an outrageous situation.

Schiller and Woodfield knew they had something remarkable on film and they put it squarely to Marilyn. They wanted to cash in on it. Marilyn was receptive and began scheming a little herself, although money was not on her mind.

Schiller took charge of the delicate negotiations. Somehow he persuaded Globe Photos to relinquish their rights to the Mitchell photos and through Pat Newcomb, Schiller formed a partnership with William Reed Woodfield. The men were far too shrewd to repeat Tom Kelley's error when he sold his rights to Marilyn's calendar shots for next to nothing. These gentlemen planned to saturate the world with Marilyn's latest – and final – image in the raw.

"The Nude Session" happened on a Monday morning. It was a spontaneous development; nothing had been planned. By midday Tuesday, Marilyn had the developed photos to approve. The two photographers approached movie reporter Joe Hyams, who agreed to handle the story about how the pictures came about.

Sobered to a degree by the nude photographs in her hand, Marilyn at first insisted that none of the pictures be sold to *Playboy* magazine. (This decision would be withdrawn later.) She saw immediately that the shots were excellent. Her body had trimmed down considerably since her earlier session in 1962 with Eve Arnold. She was naïvely pleased with her contours.

The photos taken by Jimmy Mitchell worried Schiller and Woodfield. Schiller approached Perry Lieber of the Fox publicity staff and convinced him to destroy the shots taken by Mitchell and promised that he would reimburse Mitchell for his considerable loss. Later, it was reliably reported that the Fox stills man received $10,000 of the proceeds from the photographs' sale. Fox, like Globe, had agreed to relinquish all of their rights.

On Wednesday, the Hyams story broke in the world press. In most instances, it made the front pages. Interest in the films was enormous and offers began coming in to Tom Blough, who was Schiller's London agent and in Los Angeles at the time. The pictures appeared in thirty-two countries. There were forty black and whites and twelve colour transparencies to choose from. *Life* magazine, the first to be approached, paid $10,000 for U.S. Rights alone, and more for their foreign editions and subsidiary rights. They were eager to rush into print, but Blough informed them they would have to wait.

Every magazine would have to release their issue on the same day, a date set thirty days ahead.

What Marilyn wanted – and her wish was splendidly child-like and innocent – was her naked and magnificent body on the covers of these magazines throughout the world at the same time.

On the first of June, Marilyn's thirty-sixth birthday, she made her final appearance on Stage 14 at Fox. The day's shooting seemed to go well, except that Marilyn was more nervous than usual, her laughter a little shrill. Surrounded by friends, Whitey Snyder, Agnes Flanagan, Dean Martin, and the grips and soundmen who always loved and protected her, a huge birthday cake glittering with several dozen sparklers was dollied in. Marilyn wept.

Lawrence Schiller was present at the impromptu celebration and took several photographs of Marilyn standing near the cake. Shortly afterwards, he asked her, "What would you like in exchange for the photos we took on Monday?" She thought a moment, then grinned and said she wanted a slide projector to show the pictures. Schiller says that the remark nearly moved him to tears, but instead of weeping in her presence, which might have alarmed her, he said, "This will probably make Billy and me a lot of money. It will go a long way towards buying a new house."

Marilyn looked pleased by this and said, "At least I'll be helping to make your wife happy. I'll be happy, too, to see all those covers with me on them and no Liz [Taylor]." That seemed to delight her more than any other aspect of the situation – pushing Elizabeth Taylor from the world's magazine covers. Then she became thoughtful and asked him, "Do you think I should really send those pictures out?" Schiller told her. "You're already famous, Marilyn. Now you can make me famous."

Most of the following week, Marilyn was busy talking with her lawyer and seeing her two doctors. All three were concerned about the strain she was under.

On the second Friday in June, by ten-thirty in the morning, Marilyn had not yet appeared on the set. Dean Martin walked straight to Whitey Snyder, "Where's the woman?" he asked.

"I hear she's off the picture," Whitey told him; his voice revealed his anxiety.

Martin hurried into his dressing-room and, leaving the door ajar, he phoned first his agent, then his lawyers. No one within earshot could have failed to learn that he was furious and that he simply would not complete the film without Marilyn.

Marilyn had been fired from the picture late Thursday night and had gone into seclusion. Only in the evening, she came out to the living-room and sat in a chair, listening to Pat Newcomb intercepting the numerous calls. Maf lay next to her bare feet. She had been crying and now, emotionally drained, sat seemingly in a stupor.

Pat looked in Marilyn's direction. She needed a statement from her for a news-wire service.

"Tell them I have nothing to say." But then Marilyn swung forward angrily in her chair, "Wait! Tell them I said it's time some of the studio heads realized what they're doing. If there's anything wrong with Hollywood, it starts at the top."

Pat, relieved to find that Marilyn was feeling well enough to be angry, began to relay the message.

"And something else. It seems to me it's time they stopped knocking their assets around."

Peter Levathis called a press conference on Saturday morning. As he walked determinedly into the crowd of reporters, he behaved as though it were a historical moment. An advertising man before inheriting his present assignment, he was looked upon by most in the industry as an outsider. But today he was very much *in*. He had done what no one else had dared. He had fired Monroe.

"Gentlemen," he told them, "there isn't much I can say. We can't afford to risk millions on unreliable stars. This was behind my decision this week to sue Miss Monroe and her corporation for half a million dollars. We may have to increase that figure to a million."

The publicity files at the Fox studio revealed some of the background to Marilyn's firing. The studio's Hollywood management, according to a memo, attributed Marilyn's misbehaviour to the same emotional problems which they knew had plagued her during the filming of *The Misfits*. It is clear that they had failed to realize that they had compounded those problems by further irritating her in their total disregard for her as a serious performer. They had treated her as a mere commodity and she had rebelled in ways open to her.

"At 5.30, Friday evening, June 1, her 36th birthday, Marilyn Monroe cut a birthday cake on the *Something's Got to Give* set. . . . then walked out to her chauffeur-driven limousine and rolled away. That same night she made an appearance on behalf of the Muscular Dystrophy Fund at Chaves Ravine baseball park, but the studio was not to see her again.

"Although called to work on Monday, June 4, she reported ill and unable to perform. The same thing happened Tuesday, and that night the production was suspended.

"On Wednesday, June 6, Harrison Carroll, *Herald-Examiner* columnist, quoted Producer Weinstein in part as follows: 'There had had to be an agonizing reappraisal of the situation. We have to decide whether Marilyn can recover in time to continue with the production, and if the studio can stand further delays.'

"On Friday morning, June 8, *Variety* reported that the star's press agent had issued this statement: 'Miss Monroe is ready and eager to go back to work on Monday.' Later that same day, Peter G. Levathis, vice-president in charge of production at 20th-Century Fox, announced that Miss Monroe had been discharged for 'wilful violation of contract'."

There were charges and countercharges. Actress Lee Remick was offered Marilyn's role. She signed, and went for costume fittings. Mr. Levathis was happy to learn that Miss Remick and Marilyn had nearly identical figures and the costume would need little alteration. But Dean Martin refused to do the film without Marilyn and told reporters on June 18, "The studio last week offered to reinstate Marilyn (at Martin's insistence), but it was with the understanding that if she failed to show up for work, then I would have to work with Lee. I signed to do the picture at less than my usual fee, because I wanted to work with Marilyn . . . because she is good box-office. . . . People are painting me as the heavy in this whole thing because production stopped. But I'm only living up to my contract." That afternoon, the Fox studios filed a suit against Martin and his independent production company asking $2,339,000 actual damages and $1,000,000 "exemplary" damages. Martin replied by filing a countersuit for $6,850,500, alleging damage by the company and loss of expected profits.

All suits were dropped soon after Marilyn's death, but a sense of guilt hung over the executive offices at the studio for a very long time and their embarrassment would revive at the mere mention of her name.

At first Marilyn tried not to think about the film. She busied herself with other matters, including the nude photographs soon to be published around the world. Photographer Schiller either dropped by her house or phoned her every day or so. He approached her again about *Playboy*. He and Woodfield had three fine shots showing nipples. There was even a funny shot of her with her knees up where her breasts should have been. Schiller was inclined to kill this shot but Marilyn laughed and said, "No, please! The Japanese will go for it." And she was right.

Schiller had come up with a plan for a simultaneous front and back cover for *Playboy*. The front would show her draped in mink, while on the back cover she would be nude. The idea excited her and she told him to go ahead and get the contracts ready. A special sitting would be required for the cover shots.

All this flurry over a matter that was essentially a charitable act on Marilyn's part served to keep her occupied part of the time.

Despite her efforts to distract herself, Marilyn felt alone and especially desperate at the realization that her will to go on had collapsed. She phoned her friends, cabled them. Frank Sinatra was reached in Monte Carlo where he had gone to do a benefit for Princess Grace. He was appalled by what Fox had done. "A girl as sick as that! A girl who needs help as much as she does!"

To the Strasbergs sitting stunned in their New York apartment, Marilyn was the most valuable talent they had encountered in more than three decades of intimate association with actors, as well as a gravely troubled human being whom they loved. Marilyn had kept them fully informed of her mounting crisis with the studio and when she was fired on June 8, Lee and Paula were wildly indignant over Hollywood's abuse of this oversensitive creature, whom they considered now as part of their family and who they felt should never have been trapped in films in the first place.

What was most cruel and difficult for Marilyn to accept was the knowledge that she was still so vulnerable to people such as Levathis. Her addiction to the pills had been no secret during the last eighteen months of her life. The barbiturates were a crutch that somehow made her nights tolerable while destroying her health and ability to work. Executives at Fox had known about her habit long before they began production on *Something's Got to Give*, and her disturbed state had surprised no one. They were inured to actresses muffled from the ordinary abrasions of life. What these men had not foreseen was that Marilyn's protectors through a decade of fame had multiplied to include a large portion of the public and many of these anonymous fans knew of her emotional difficulties as well as her pill problem through not always veiled references in gossip columns and magazines. The Fox studio had committed a major blunder from a public-relations point of view. This soon became apparent, and harassed officials at the company were as yet untouched by the obloquy that would ensue after Marilyn's sudden death two months later.

When several days passed and nothing seemed to be happening to reverse the studio's decision, she again phoned the Strasbergs and told Lee, "I've got to start thinking about the stage." Early in the week after her dismissal, she was back in New York where she joined a small group of actors in one of Strasberg's classes. They were already well along in the staging of a one-act play adapted from a short story by Colette. Everyone knew, and it was unanimously agreed that she should have the leading role in the play as a tender get-well present.

Her tremulousness once more enhanced her acting. Her emotional rawness made her reading of the part as exciting as her years-earlier portrayal of "Anna Christie". The Strasbergs and their friends spread the word that Marilyn was now seriously preparing herself for a career in the theatre. Avid producers inundated her East 57th Street apartment with scripts: dramas, comedies, and musicals.

But her brief experiment in this new direction was to end abruptly. She became unsettled once more and she needed to know why. She felt only Ralph Greenson, her analyst and friend, could help her to regain some peace and back she went to the coast.

CHAPTER SEVEN

Early that summer many were quick to say that Marilyn was through, that her career was in a steep decline. They were wrong. As it turned out in July, she wasn't even through with the film from which she had been discharged. In fact, after the initial shock that reverberated from Hollywood to New York, a reappraisal was made that was favourable to her. When Marilyn had said it was not her fault, she was partially right. Even the New York *Times* in an editorial attributed some of the blame to the Fox studio for giving her too much power for many years and then suddenly depriving her of it. The fault really lay buried in the past.

Marilyn did not remain completely in seclusion as she had during her similar break with Hollywood and the studio in 1955. Then she had not only withdrawn from the public eye, but socially as well. She had chosen to be alone to reassess her life and to recover her strength. This time she preferred privacy because she was involved with a married man. He was not in the industry; he was an Easterner with few ties on the coast. He had come West mainly to work out the details of a film production of a literary property in which he had had a hand and to escape the pressures of his work as a lawyer and public servant.

If anyone was to blame for the relationship that developed during his California stay, it was his host who was connected with films and knew Marilyn well enough to realize how vulnerable and exposed she was that summer. He knew her doctors and was aware that her hold on reality was tenuous. For the attorney, his holiday on the West Coast was a lark, a vacation from his wife and children. He and Marilyn were discreet, almost never venturing beyond the stuccoed wall surrounding his friend's beachhouse.

The alliance was surprising, even shocking, to those who were in daily contact with Marilyn. Marilyn seemed only alert to distraction, killing the long days and quite a few of the nights. Was that the reason for the affair? Most of her close friends wondered and all of them worried.

Their relationship had nowhere to go. Publicity about the

affair might destroy all his chances for an important political career. How sensitive he was to Marilyn's precarious emotional state is difficult to assess. Within days of their meeting he and Marilyn became nearly constant companions, a relationship interrupted only by his flights to New York or Washington when called on some business that could not be resolved over the telephone.

It is doubtful that Marilyn at first informed her psychiatrist of her growing intimacy with the man. But the complications caused by her increasing dependency upon the relationship must have impelled her to confide something to Greenson – in a plea for help and reassurance.

During the final summer, Marilyn confided to a friend that Dr. Greenson was attempting to make her more independent and less insecure in her opinions. She volunteered this information when asked why she was cutting herself off from several old and trusted friends. Clearly Dr. Greenson was concerned by her reliance upon the judgement of her hirelings. During that summer, the regulars who had been in her employ, along with a few others, found themselves outside Marilyn's inner circle. Each of them felt that neither word nor deed of theirs was responsible for this change in her attitude towards them. A few felt that Mrs. Murray was an ally to Dr. Greenson in trying to keep them away. Ralph Roberts was to feel Mrs. Murray's role in this very keenly, for when he came in the evening to give Marilyn her massage, he found after his services were over that his presence was no longer appreciated. Once, as he was lingering by Marilyn's bedroom door exchanging a word or two as in the old days, Mrs. Murray gave him a look that clearly implied, "I thought we'd gotten rid of them."

If Marilyn's new friend had been free of family obligations, he might have filled admirably the void in her personal life. But he only served to deepen her anxieties while temporarily relieving her sense of feeling unwanted.

The entire Greenson family attempted to help fill this void. Daughter Judy, then emerging from adolescence, attracted Marilyn's attention briefly. They discussed ways Judy might enhance her appearance, an art at which Marilyn had become an expert. As the end of June approached, both the Strasbergs and the Greensons, at opposite ends of America, were attempting to save Marilyn from disaster. The Strasbergs, although far away, nevertheless sensed that Marilyn was in serious difficulty. It was almost as though the past fourteen years of growth had been destroyed overnight and that the same guileless gift for attracting trouble – her principal demon when Lucille Ryman and her husband had taken her by the hand – had surfaced again. Her stubborn innocence through all temptations, both resisted and indulged, had inspired Arthur Miller to write about "her spirit shining through everything she does". Now her spirit was not so visibly radiant and it worried her few friends in the film colony. Clifton Webb was one, and the Dean Martins, singer Connie Francis, and Frank Sinatra. They knew how close to defeat she was and saw how rather than fighting back she seemed to be courting annihilation.

In late June, Marilyn's lawyers were having daily conferences with Fox studio executives to resolve the dispute and get *Something's Got to Give* rolling again. Her distaste for the script was pushed to the background. She had been moved by Dean Martin's defence of her and felt an obligation not to let him down. Her attorneys, Rudin and Frosch, had advised her to complete the film to reinstate herself as an insurable property for future films. Producer Weinstein and studio boss Levathis were overruled by the Board at Fox, which was sitting in New York away from the heat of the argument but close to the heart of public opinion. Popular sentiment was nearly all in Marilyn's favour, and the Board in part believed her declaration by telegram to the crew that the problems were not her fault.

Marilyn continued to see her summer friend. She was living the sort of double life she had lived several times before – in the Dougherty family home when she was attempting to be at once a dutiful daughter-in-law and launch her modelling career; with the company of *The Misfits* when she and Miller had decided to part but remained together in the same hotel suite; the Marilyn who was the friend of Yves Montand as well as of Simone Signoret. This was not duplicity but a neat splitting of self, possibly because of her quick and unconscious shifts in attitude and behaviour.

Now she was the same Marilyn her friends remembered when she opened her door in Brentwood, only thinner, perhaps, than she had ever been. Often with these friends, she

became very animated in discussing her career and the
possibilities of advancing it after her bondage at Fox had
ended. It seemed evident to all that she wanted to succeed as
a dramatic film actress. There was little, if any, further discussion of the stage. In his eulogy at her funeral, Lee Strasberg
said, "I am truly sorry that the public who loved her did not
have the opportunity to see her as we did, in many of the roles
that foreshadowed what she would have become. Without
doubt, she would have been one of the really great actresses of
the stage. Despite the heights and brilliance she had attained
on the screen, she was planning for the future. In her eyes and
in mine, her career was just beginning. . . ." Marilyn had been
innocently playing another role for Strasberg out of respect
for him. With no one in Hollywood did she ever discuss the
possibility of her becoming a stage actress, reserving such
speculation for her easy conversations with the Strasberg
family and their Studio associates. Lee and Paula Strasberg
had lost their battle to save Marilyn through the inauguration
of a new career on the stage, but her days were spent in con-
structive work towards salvaging her film career. New scripts
arrived daily, and Marilyn read some of them. Arthur Jacobs
– whose office was then in a state of transition from a publicity firm to full-time film production and who had supplied
press aides to Marilyn for years – was doing all he could to
help in that delicate area. He sent her a screenplay, *What a
Way to Go*, a farce about a woman who is a fatal jinx to her
husbands. The comedy impressed her enough so that she was
discussing possible directors for the production, which would
presumably follow the completion of *Something's Got to
Give* by no more than a week or two. Marilyn tentatively
accepted J. Lee Thompson as its director, and it was to be
filmed and distributed by Fox in conclusion of her four-picture
commitment that had begun with *Bus Stop*. She would then be
a free agent, probably able to command anywhere from
$500,000 to a million dollars per film.

But the future as a viable proposition was beginning to seem
·uriously remote to Marilyn. She had no peace of mind. With
the exception of seven days in July she was seeing Dr. Greenson at his office or at her house every single day. Her ego was
badly bruised, her belief in herself was profoundly shaken and
sleep eluded her. And there was the man, his cultivated voice
on the telephone telling Marilyn that he was back in town

and asking if she could come by for a drink and maybe dinner. She was apparently beginning to see the hopelessness of her alliance; still, a phone call from him would alter whatever else she had planned for the evening and she would go to him.

She made brave attempts to face adversity. Reporters and photographers came to the Brentwood house expecting to find her crushed, and were surprised to see what they believed to be the old Marilyn coming to greet them. In the remarkably candid photos published by *Life* – entirely by chance the week of her death – she was dressed casually, wearing a dark pull-over sweater, and appeared to be mistress of herself. On July 12 she went to another meeting with studio executives, her second since she was fired. Agnes Flanagan dropped by the house to dress her hair and Whitey Snyder to give the finishing touches to her make-up. The word at Fox that day was brief and comforting. *Something's Got to Give* would resume in early September or later in the Fall when Dean Martin had concluded an interim booking on the night-club circuit.

Joe DiMaggio was on the phone to her almost every day. In late July when word reached him of her interest in the Easterner they had a bad row. DiMaggio had reason to be alarmed and angry. What had begun as nothing more than a diversion for the man had suddenly taken a serious turn for Marilyn. She discovered that she was pregnant.

Those few who knew Marilyn's secret were horrified. While friends were told that Marilyn had gone for a long weekend to Lake Tahoe, she was secretly hospitalized on July 20 in Cedars of Lebanon Hospital, and remained there for four days.

A surgical termination of pregnancy was decided upon by a doctor on the Cedars staff. The pregnancy was tubular – as was her first pregnancy with Miller – and could not have gone beyond its fifth or sixth week without the gravest complications.

CHAPTER EIGHT

Attempting to regain her strength in the Brentwood house, Marilyn began to dip into a tomorrowless world. It was nearly impossible to look back. She was pinned to each day like a moth to a panel. Who were her enemies, who were her friends?

She sought sleep, oblivion. One night in late July when the pills Dr. Engelberg had prescribed failed to work, she phoned her masseur, Ralph Roberts. It was very early morning, close to 2 A.M. when he was awakened.

"I feel terrible, Ralph. I'm about to jump out of my skin. Can you come?"

Roberts hurried over to Brentwood, arriving about fifteen minutes after her call came. He spent nearly an hour with her, giving her back and neck muscles a deep massage. She began to relax. He had to do his work in total darkness because any light would defeat his purpose – Marilyn could never sleep with the least glimmer of light in a room – but he knew the bedroom so well by now that he could reach for the rubbing alcohol and then her back and shoulders again without fumbling.

"This is a lot better than pills," she murmured, her face muffled by the pillow.

"I'm always available, Marilyn," Roberts told her.

On the weekend following her hospital stay, Paula Strasberg, nearly ill with concern over Marilyn's emotional state, flew to Los Angeles. She hurried from the airport to the Brentwood house.

Paula found the refrigerator empty and phoned her sister Bea, who lived across town. Bea sent over some choice steak fillets and other appetizing foods. A pretence of normalcy settled over the house.

It was impossible for Paula to remain away from her husband for more than a few days. Early on Monday, she made arrangements to fly back to New York, after extracting a promise from Marilyn that she would come East a week later. By mid-week Paula was relieved to learn that Marilyn had phoned the housekeeper they shared to get her New York apartment ready for her return.

Friday, August 3, was what had become a normal day for Marilyn that summer of 1962. She appeared to have made some headway, with the help of Dr. Greenson, towards resuming the business of living each day at least a step away from the abyss.

She rose late, pulled a wrapper around her, and prepared her own coffee and grapefruit. Then she went outside to the guest house to let out Maf. She was dressed in slacks by the time Mrs. Murray arrived from her apartment in Santa Monica.

Renovation of the guest house into living quarters for the people she loved, such as the Strasbergs and her ex-father-in-law Isidore Miller, was much on her mind. She had invited them on numerous occasions. She had asked Paula to explain to her husband how private his quarters would be and how much she wanted him to come after her proposed visit to New York. During her usual Sunday night phone conversation with the elder Miller, she had repeated the invitation to him.

The phone rang. It was Pat Newcomb saying she had a terrible case of bronchitis and didn't think she could spend the weekend with Marilyn as planned. "But this is just the place to get rid of it," Marilyn told her. "You can lie out by the pool for a while, and I'll get out the Desert-Aire lamp for you to use tonight. We'll bake those germs right out of you." Pat agreed to come later in the afternoon and sleep over.

After she got dressed, she put Maf back in the guest house and drove over to Beverly Hills to Dr. Engelberg's office. She asked him to give her a new sleeping pill prescription. After he was convinced that the drug she was taking – chloral hydrate – was not working, he agreed to prescribe twenty-five tablets of Nembutal.

Continuing on her medical rounds, she stopped by Dr. Greenson's office and talked awhile. She said nothing about the prescription as yet unfilled. Then she drove back along San Vicente Boulevard to a pharmacy where she had an account.

Pat was already in her bathing suit when Marilyn returned from the drug store. Marilyn did not join her. She was never known to swim in the pool, although she had a simple pride in its being there – one of her few traits in common with the newly affluent – and always urged her friends to use it. Pat came inside and the two women chatted for a while in the living-room; Marilyn sitting on the rug. Since there was nothing in the house to eat, they decided to dine at a nearby French restaurant.

Saturday had begun early for Marilyn. She had a poor night. The Nembutal pills she had promised Dr. Engelberg she would take in normal doses had not worked.

During breakfast she sat in front of Pat silent and distant.

Conversation was a strain. Marilyn would stare into space and trace patterns on the Mexican trestle table with a finger. Pat felt useless, yet had learned that her mere loyal presence was somewhat reassuring to Marilyn.

Expecting several callers, she continued taking pills to calm her jumpy nerves. Pat did not see anything unusual either in this or in the way Marilyn looked or behaved, for she had seen her in much worse states on other occasions.

Those closest to Marilyn were caught in a paradox. During that long, melancholy summer it was dangerous to leave her altogether alone, and yet she found solitude therapeutic. "I restore myself when I'm alone," she had said more than once.

When Mrs. Murray arrived, Pat must have been relieved. She was anxious to get home at least before evening. The housekeeper brought with her some articles she might need if she stayed over.

Sometime before noon, photographer Lawrence Schiller came by to see if Marilyn had signed the *Playboy* magazine contract. Marilyn shouldered up from her wave of melancholy to greet him and to report that she had not. He was to learn later, after Marilyn's death, that she had changed her mind about the front and back covers and Pat Newcomb had cancelled the special sitting by way of a personal phone call to *Playboy* publisher Hugh Hefner a day or so earlier.

"Let me show you my guest house," she told him. Marilyn with some pride showed Schiller the cottage, sandwiched between her house and the garage. "I'm doing this over for my friends," she said. "Don't mind the doggy smell." And she explained what she had in mind by way of renovation.

When Schiller left, Marilyn went to the solarium she used as a study and reviewed the batch of photographs he and William Woodfield had taken of her nude swim. Most of those she had retained were taken from behind with her buttocks in prominent view. Either to compensate *Playboy*'s loss for the front and back covers or because she had reconsidered her decision, she wrote across the back of the prints, "These should go to *Playboy*." Late on Sunday afternoon, Schiller and Woodfield found an unmarked, unstamped envelope shoved under the studio door. They knew by then, of course, that Marilyn had been found dead, and they wondered who had brought them. Had Marilyn driven over with them on Saturday afternoon? Had Pat Newcomb found them so clearly marked for their attention when she visited Marilyn's home briefly on that morning of her death? The photographers were never to know.

When Dr. Greenson drove up to the house for his session with Marilyn, the latter, on hearing the car door slam, ran towards the bedroom. "That must be Ralph," she told Pat. Since house calls were not as usual as her office visits, it is not known whether Marilyn or the housekeeper had phoned him.

Pat prepared to leave. As she moved towards the front door, Marilyn looked out from the bedroom hallway, a question mark in her glance. She seemed to be asking forgiveness for some failure on her part. Pat smiled her broad, little-girl smile that so transformed her expression and told Marilyn she would phone her in the morning.

Across the ridge of hills between Brentwood and Hollywood, Ralph Roberts was on the telephone in his studio cottage on North Palm Avenue. Roberts was talking with Rupert Allan, no longer Marilyn's press agent but still a concerned friend. An interview had just appeared in *Life* magazine based upon the series of tapes Richard Meryman had done with Marilyn earlier in the summer. Now Roberts was suggesting to Allan that Marilyn would appreciate a call from him, since Allan was as enthusiastic as he was about the interview. "I can't, Ralph," Allan told him in a nearly inaudible voice. "I have such a case of laryngitis, Marilyn is sure to rush over with aspirin or something if she hears me. You know how she is. Why don't you call her for me?"

Marilyn had been receiving calls for two days congratulating her about the interview's candour. She was delighted to know that her friends – those who really counted with her – found it a fairly accurate portrait. "I wanted it to come out as me," she said. "But I wasn't sure. . . ." The tapes made by Meryman were especially successful in mirroring Marilyn's philosophy, her attitude towards fame and success as well as failure. And perhaps most interestingly, they contained an almost pure Marilyn idiom.

Before Roberts left his cottage for a dinner engagement, he phoned Marilyn. Dr. Greenson answered, "She's not in just now." The analyst sounded tense and impatient. Roberts was puzzled, but went on to dinner.

Dr. Greenson was to say later that he found Marilyn very despondent when he arrived. This would indicate that the chemistry of the drugs was dropping her into that bottomless depression Miller had often observed. Greenson spoke with her for an hour or so and suggested that she drive over to Pacific Coast Highway. She liked to drive there, often going as far as Oxnard, north of Malibu. However, she did not heed his advice that evening.

When Dr. Greenson left, Marilyn wandered about the house. A neighbour saw her briefly outside in the yard behind her house, where she played with Maf for a few minutes in the gathering dusk. She tossed his ball and he retrieved it for a time. Finally she handed the small white poodle to Mrs. Murray and told her to put him to bed.

As she came back into the house, the phone rang. It was the lawyer's host asking if she would join them for the evening. Apparently he mentioned that they had a couple of young ladies with them (his wife was away at the time) and Marilyn was angered by it. She told an intimate friend who phoned minutes later that she had been asked to join them along with "a couple of hookers" and that she had told him "no thanks".

The invitation must have been especially upsetting for Marilyn, for it shattered the benefits of the session she had had with Dr. Greenson. But as usual, there were phone calls every half-hour or so, and one or two revived her spirits briefly. Nearly all of her life as Marilyn the phone had been an ally against loneliness for her. Friends would often get calls halfway through the night just for a chat, some words – however foolish or sleep-drugged – which from a friend were reassurance. Joe DiMaggio, Jr., telephoned sometime before eight o'clock. Their conversation lasted for some time. She finally emerged from her bedroom and told Mrs. Murray that the young man who had been her stepson had broken his engagement. But she added, "He sounded so relieved, I'm happy for him." Then she said, "Goodnight, honey," and closed her bedroom door.

In her bedroom – where there was room only for her oversized bed, a night stand, and dressing-table – Marilyn turned on her portable record-player, which was on the floor near the bed, with a stack of Sinatra records already on the spindle. Somewhat relieved, Mrs. Murray heard a record start to play.

Between ten and eleven that evening, panic must have aroused Marilyn from the stupor that always preceded an overdose. If she attempted to phone Pat Newcomb or one of her doctors, she was unsuccessful in reaching them. But she did get through to the two men who had invited her out that evening, and she told one of the men that she had just taken the last of her Nembutals and she was about to slip over the line. One of them attempted to phone Mickey Rudin, Marilyn's Hollywood attorney, but he was out for the evening. Why such indirect means of summoning help were chosen will never be known. Oddly enough, it occurred to no one who was aware of what was happening to inform the police.

As Miller had come to know too well, rescue had to be swift to prevent suffocation.

In a last conscious attempt, Marilyn dialled yet another number. Ralph Roberts's answering service reported to him that he had received a call from a woman who sounded fuzzy-voiced and troubled, but had left no name or number. In all likelihood, Marilyn's last contact with a human being was the voice of an operator informing her that Mr. Roberts was out for the evening. When Marilyn's body was found in the dark, early hours of that Sunday morning, the phone was still clutched in her hand.

The house was quiet during those critical minutes. When the house phone rang, Mrs. Murray roused herself to answer it. Dr. Greenson, in some alarm but still innocent of any knowledge of the new pills she had obtained, asked Mrs. Murray if Marilyn was all right. The housekeeper walked the few steps to Marilyn's room. A light was visible below her closed door but Mrs. Murray did not knock for fear of waking her in case she had fallen asleep. Experience had taught the woman that sleep was the most precious of all commodities in the household. Mrs. Murray reassured Greenson that Marilyn was safe in her room.

Mrs. Murray told reporters the next morning that she had awakened a little before three with an uneasy feeling, and had quickly got up and hurried to Marilyn's room. The light was still on as it had been much earlier that night. She tried the door, she said, and called Marilyn several times. Then she went outside and peered into the bedroom through the closed French windows. Marilyn, she thought at once, looked "peculiar". One arm was stretched across her bed and a hand hung limp on one of her telephones. The fact that Mrs. Murray managed to see all of this suggests that Marilyn's reflexes had already been dulled by the pills by the time she had gone to bed. She unfailingly drew her blinds upon retiring.

Mrs. Murray called Dr. Greenson, who arrived within minutes and broke a windowpane to get into Marilyn's room. He realized that Marilyn was dead, but he phoned Dr. Engelberg to confirm it. Engelberg reached the house around 3.30, confirmed Marilyn's death, and shortly after four o'clock the police were called in.

Two radio patrolmen and Sergeant Jack Clemmons were the first policemen to arrive. Within an hour, the case was taken over by Detective Sergeant R. E. Byron. Sergeant Clemmons glanced down at the dead woman and a fleeting look of bereavement crossed his face. "Is there another phone I can use?" he asked. Mrs. Murray led him back to a kitchen extension.

Sergeant Clemmons dialled a number. "Jim?" he said. "It's Clemmons. I'm over here in Brentwood, Marilyn's house." There was a pause as Jim Dougherty, for several years now a Los Angeles policeman himself, heard the news he had feared and expected for a long time. "An O.D. [overdose], it looks like," Clemmons explained. "I knew you'd want to know."

As his second wife, to whom he had been married for sixteen years, turned on the light next to their bed, Jim Dougherty sat quietly, remembering. He remembered Norma Jean when she was the girl bride he had shoved fully clothed into a shower. Even though the subject of Marilyn had been taboo in that household for years, Jim glanced at his wife and said, "Say a prayer for Norma Jean. She's dead."

Later there was some speculation about how Mrs. Murray was able to phone Dr. Greenson when the phone in Marilyn's hand was so plainly off the hook. Actually Marilyn had two privately listed phones. No more than five or six people – including Greenson, DiMaggio, and Pat Newcomb – had her private number.

Pat was awakened by a phone call at 4 a.m. It was lawyer Mickey Rudin. "Something's happened to Marilyn," he told her; then added, "She's dead." When she recovered from the initial shock, Pat got dressed and drove to the Brentwood house.

There, at the sight of Marilyn, Pat became hysterical. She blamed herself more than anyone. Probably she felt she should have stayed on, but that had not been possible when

Dr. Greenson arrived that afternoon. Even Marilyn had indicated that.

Pat returned to her apartment an hour or so later just before county detectives officially sealed Marilyn's house. Her phone was ringing as she unlocked the door. For the next eighteen hours, she was tied to that phone. There were nearly 250 calls from all over the world; journalists in Paris, Rome, Tokyo, all asking "What happened?" and *Why?*"

On Monday, Pat Newcomb left Hollywood, not to return for many months.

Rudin arrived shortly after the police car, and Inez Melson, shocked but in full command of herself, reached the house before the coroner's arrival. She asked to see Marilyn – and the bedroom.

"There were pill bottles, some empty, some full, on the night stand and dresser," Mrs. Melson recounted later. "I walked into the bathroom and saw the cabinet's shelves crowded with Marilyn's allergy pills, tranquillizers, and sleeping tablets. I had an impulse to run through these two rooms, snatching up the bottles and hiding them in my bag, but I knew that was impossible."

Mrs. Melson hadn't been close with Marilyn since her marriage to Miller. Like many other earlier friends of Marilyn she had remained on the periphery after her marriage to the playwright. None the less, she had always been deeply fond of Marilyn and now more than ever felt a keen responsibility.

A coroner's report called her death "probable suicide", after a county suicide team of medical and psychiatric experts had sifted the evidence. But aside from those who were near her that last weekend, very few of those who knew her well believed that it was an intentional act. They saw her death as a terrible accident. Even many who were familiar with her life in the months preceding her death persuaded themselves eventually that, yes, it was an accident. It had to be. There is always the possibility they were right.

CHAPTER NINE

Coroner's Case No. 81128 lay unclaimed at the Los Angeles
County Morgue on a slab in a chilled storage vault where un-
identified bodies await burial. Marilyn was dead and there
seemed to be no one to claim her. Her life had ended as it
had begun.

When Frank Taylor heard the newscasts at his Connecticut
home on that Sunday repeating over and over again that Marilyn had no family to claim her, he immediately contacted
Whitey Snyder. Taylor, knowing that Snyder had been close
to Marilyn to the end, suggested that he claim the body.
Snyder seemed embarrassed and pointed out to Taylor that
he had been only an employee of Marilyn's and that he, Taylor, as Marilyn's employer on her last finished film, had far
more justification for claiming the body.

But unknown to Taylor and Whitey Snyder, her attorneys,
Aaron Frosch of New York, executor of her estate, and
Mickey Rudin were already in touch with Berneice Miracle,
Marilyn's half-sister who was living in Gainesville, Florida,
and with Marilyn's mother's guardian, Inez Melson. Mrs.
Miracle had spoken with DiMaggio on the phone and he had
agreed to handle the funeral arrangements until she could fly
out on Monday.

Snyder received a call from Mickey Rudin during the day
on Monday. Marilyn had left word that no one but Whitey
was to touch her body. This was one of the arrangements she
had made over a year before.

In Snyder's pocket as he entered the burial place off Wilshire Boulevard was a gold-plated money clip given him by
Marilyn years earlier. It read simply: "To Whitey. While I'm
still warm. Marilyn." Costumer Margie Plecher, too, had been
asked to dress Marilyn, while Agnes Flanagan was to do her
hair. *En route* to the preparation room, Whitey felt that it
was all too much. "I just couldn't go through it sober," he said
later. He stopped at a liquor store and bought a fifth of gin.

There was an eerie sense of perverse remembered ritual
about the three members of Marilyn's staff getting her ready
for her final appearance.

CHAPTER TEN

Maggie: Quentin, what's Lazarus?
Quentin: Jesus raised him from the dead,
In the Bible. Go to sleep now.
                    After the Fall

None of Marilyn's friends, husbands, and lovers escaped a profound sense of guilt that was to supersede for a time, and in some instances for all time, the warm memory of a young woman with laughter ready at her lips, a laughter sometimes wry perhaps, but none the less there.

Yet her early death was inevitable, no matter what the immediate circumstances surrounding the act were. Nearly everyone who knew her believed that. No one could fail to notice the self-destructive pattern in her life. Marilyn was destroyed by a great many events, beginning with the circumstances of her birth. Nearly all those who crossed her path were instantly aware of her need for protection, a protection most gave, and many were still ready to give at the end.

Among those who did not attend the funeral was Arthur Miller, who had relinquished the role of saviour some twenty months earlier. But he was haunted by her more than anyone, possibly because he was aware that his commitment had been greater and his "defection" more devastating to her.

A few, who knew both Miller and Marilyn well, have said that *After the Fall*, his first play following her death, was written to exorcise Marilyn's ghost. He had remarried the same year of their divorce. His German wife, Magnum photographer Inge Morath, was equally plagued by the ghost and had urged him to put it all down, without any thought of production or publication. To put down the truth was perhaps their only chance to quiet the painful and unsettling memories and lay foundations for happiness.

But while it was all being committed to paper, Miller began seeing a universal pattern in what had been his private experience. He delved into the guilt which haunts all men and put humanity on the witness stand for the recent crimes of genocide (Auschwitz), and for character assassination (McCarthy) as companion spectres to Marilyn's. "Who can be innocent again on this mountain of skulls?" Miller was to write of Auschwitz. "I tell you what I know! My brothers died here – this place; our hearts have cut these stones! And what's the cure? ... No, not love; I loved them all, all!'"

It should be understood that Miller did not write *After the Fall* as an exploration of his own near-emasculation by Marilyn, nor as an exploitation of that relationship. A writer, as Miller himself has pointed out, cannot be expected to create out of thin air. His work must be rooted in what he knows in order for it to have any value to others.

Factual biographical details mount as the play reaches its climax: Maggie's mother attempted to smother her with a pillow "'cause I would turn out bad because of – like her sin"; Quentin tells her, "I see your suffering, Maggie; and once I saw it, all shame fell away.... You're a victory, Maggie, you're like a flag to me, a kind of proof, somehow that people can win"; and, "Everyone loves you, darling! Why are you sad?"; Maggie suggests that Quentin "Ask Ludwig Reiner (coach and teacher) what my value is!", to which Quentin replies "I married you, Maggie. I don't need Ludwig's lecture on your value"; then in despair, Quentin tells her, "Maggie, you have a great analyst, and Ludwig is a phenomenal teacher, and every stranger you meet has all the answers, but I'm putting in forty per cent of my time on your problems, not just some hot air"; and finally Quentin warns her "You can't take pills on top of whisky, dear.... You want to die, Maggie, and I really don't know how to prevent it. But it struck me that I have been playing with your life out of some idiotic hope of some kind that you'd come out of this endless spell. But there's only one hope, dear – you've got to start to look at what you're doing."

That Maggie is not Marilyn but some amalgam of Marilyn and the seamier part of her myth begins to seem irrelevant as the audience ticks off the facts they have heard before and those points in the myth that have earlier appeared in print.

When Quentin confides to the audience that Maggie was "chewed and spat out by a long line of grinning men! Her name floating in the stench of locker rooms and parlour-car cigar smoke!" and then suggests that she sleeps with men only out of a sense of charity, nearly everyone in the audience is persuaded that this confirms something they had suspected about Marilyn all along.

The resemblance was further compounded by director Elia Kazan and Miller's insistence that Maggie be seen in an ash-blonde wig not unlike the one worn by Marilyn in *The Misfits*; be sewn into skin-tight dresses; be given a whispery child-woman's voice; and move about the stage in hobbled little steps in imitation of Marilyn's walk.

In fairness to Miller, one must look beyond the parallels between Maggie and Marilyn and accept the character of Maggie as a separate, dramatic existence. Some, who have known Miller over the years, say that there is a great deal of Miller's first wife in the character of Louise as well. But, of course, few can know this.

What is difficult to defend is Miller's shoring up his portrait of Maggie with numerous weaknesses borrowed from Marilyn: "Maggie, don't use that language with me, will you?" to which Maggie replies, "Call me vulgar, that I talk like a truck driver! Well, that's where I come from. I'm from Negroes and Puerto Ricans and truck drivers!"; her mistrust of others; her need for the insulation of pills; and her will to die. His hero, Quentin, undermines much of the strength of the play through his endless self-justification. While Quentin is supposed to lead us to the truth of the guilt in us all, he slyly cops out by showing us specifically where *he* failed. The unfortunate result is that we are engaged with Maggie and are moved by her tragedy, while Quentin remains an obsessed bore.

Marilyn would not have been nearly so furious about *After the Fall* as many of her associates were. She would have recognized the elements in Maggie's character she had supplied, but she would have seen the fiction as well. Most probably she would have pointed out that there was much more of her in Roslyn of *The Misfits*, a portrait of which she was proud.

The play's production, which opened in New York, inflamed the public and stirred a theatrical controversy unlike anything before in the American theatre. While it made more money for Miller than anything he had written since *Death of a Salesman* (and probably has surpassed that success by now), he was pilloried in the press for extreme bad taste and lack of respect for the dead. In self-defence he felt compelled to state publicly that the play was no more autobiographical than any of his earlier works.

CHAPTER ELEVEN

When Dame Edith Sitwell died in early December 1964, the literary world suddenly realized that a very bright and unique light had gone out. Her obituary spread across four or five columns, a recognition usually reserved for heads of state.

Dame Edith had always puzzled people with her personality, at once imperious and clownish. Though widely read, seen, and heard during her lifetime, none the less many people became aware of her true stature only after her death. Everyone, especially in London, was to miss that original, eccentric spirit. And so it was with Marilyn. Her place in American life, her value, was made clear only after she was gone.

The parallel does not end there. Some years before her death, Dame Edith had spent a winter in Hollywood. A meeting between the poetess and Marilyn was arranged by a monthly magazine. It was thought their "opposite" personalities would throw off some journalistic sparks. No one could have foreseen that they would become immediate friends nor could anyone have known then that their deaths would be marked in an almost identical way – while their legends were growing in their lifetimes, they had been taken seriously by too few, too late.

By the time she met Dame Edith, Marilyn had come a long way. If she had not been moving in an atmosphere – much of it self-created – so removed from her beginning, they might have had nothing in common. But when the introductions were over, these new and unlikely friends were left alone and began talking of Rudolph Steiner, whose personal history, *The Course of My Life*, Marilyn was reading at the time. Dame Edith was to remark later on Marilyn's "extreme intelligence".

Marilyn laughed easily and often that day. And yet Dame Edith was to remember her as strangely tragic, "a beautiful ghost". Hindsight often lends a focus of ghostly aura to those who die prematurely, but perhaps Dame Edith was referring to the stubborn resistance which Marilyn was constantly projecting in the face of the known facts of her past.

Marilyn came to be regarded by many as uniquely American. On the set of *The Misfits* the French photographer, Henri Cartier-Bresson had noted, "She's American, and it's very clear that she is – she's very good that way – one has to be very local to be universal." Cartier-Bresson was also to say, "There's something extremely alert and vivid in her, an intelligence. It's her personality, it's a glance, it's something very tenuous, very vivid that disappears quickly, that appears again." She was more representative of the country itself than any of her Hollywood peers. She was wilful and created her own success. She was predisposed to any underdog, but often appeared to be riding herd over those closest to her. She was pre-eminently exportable, but almost never for the reasons she herself preferred.

Those newspapers which editorialized about her simply as an archetypal sex symbol badly missed the point of her appeal. Among these was the Vatican's *L'Osservatore Romano*, which said rather patronizingly: "We hope that, in the desperate solitude of this poor woman, and at the last moment, there was Someone who during life was kept away, and (we wish) that hope and peace has made the dying actress smile." *Pravda* left out any mention of God but echoed the Vatican's sentiments, and added that Marilyn Monroe was the victim of a decadent society.

Several years later, two or three properties which had been earmarked for Marilyn were done with replacements and failed. The film industry itself conceded that if her personality had been an invention, there could be no patent on it for there was simply no one else who came close to her gossamer but credible image. The mystery that surrounded her death had been countered by a resurgent interest in her films so that nearly everyone reflected more upon her life and its triumphs and defeats than upon the manner of her death. In the wake of this interest, people stopped referring to Arthur Miller's character Maggie as a definitive interior portrait of the late actress. Perhaps in the future people will come to see her not as a symbol, not as Maggie, not as Roslyn, not as Norma Jean, but will remember her as a unique human being and as the person she wished to be: Marilyn.

INDEX